AF751457

The EU as a Children's Rights Actor

University of Southampton
WITHDRAWN

Ingi Iusmen
Helen Stalford (eds.)

The EU as a Children's Rights Actor

Law, Policy and Structural Dimensions

Barbara Budrich Publishers
Opladen • Berlin • Toronto 2016

All rights reserved. No part of this publication may be reproduced, stored in or introduced into a retrieval system, or transmitted, in any form, or by any means (electronic, mechanical, photocopying, recording or otherwise) without the prior written permission of Barbara Budrich Publishers. Any person who does any unauthorized act in relation to this publication may be liable to criminal prosecution and civil claims for damages.

You must not circulate this book in any other binding or cover and you must impose this same condition on any acquirer.

A CIP catalogue record for this book is available from
Die Deutsche Bibliothek (The German Library)

© 2016 by Barbara Budrich Publishers, Opladen, Berlin & Toronto
www.barbara-budrich.net

ISBN 978-3-8474-0193-3
eISBN 978-3-8474-0412-5

Das Werk einschließlich aller seiner Teile ist urheberrechtlich geschützt. Jede Verwertung außerhalb der engen Grenzen des Urheberrechtsgesetzes ist ohne Zustimmung des Verlages unzulässig und strafbar. Das gilt insbesondere für Vervielfältigungen, Übersetzungen, Mikroverfilmungen und die Einspeicherung und Verarbeitung in elektronischen Systemen.

Die Deutsche Bibliothek – CIP-Einheitsaufnahme
Ein Titeldatensatz für die Publikation ist bei der Deutschen Bibliothek erhältlich.

Verlag Barbara Budrich Barbara Budrich Publishers
Stauffenbergstr. 7. D-51379 Leverkusen Opladen, Germany
86 Delma Drive. Toronto, ON M8W 4P6 Canada
www.barbara-budrich.net

Jacket illustration by Bettina Lehfeldt, Kleinmachnow, Germany – www.lehfeldtgraphic.de
Picture credits: Central Audiovisual Library of the European Commission/
© European Union, 2015
Editing: Alison Romer, Lancaster, UK
Typesetting: Anja Borkam, Jena, Germany
Printed in Europe on acid-free paper by paper&tinta, Warsaw, Poland

UNIVERSITY OF SOUTHAMPTON LIBRARY

00564132

Acknowledgements

We are indebted to many individuals and organisations that have supported the development of this collection. It represents a genuine attempt to engage in interdisciplinary dialogue with representatives from the legal, policy, academic, civil society and practitioner sectors. Some of the chapters were drafted in response to emerging priorities at EU level or, conversely, to shed light on more niche children's rights debates that have hitherto been overlooked. We would like to thank all of the authors who contributed to this volume in the face of many other competing demands: we are extremely grateful for the exceptional quality and originality of their analyses and for their patience with our editorial requests. We are also indebted to the publishing team at Barbara Budrich for being so patient and accommodating in the preparations of this manuscript.

We are acutely aware of the fact that children's voices do not feature as boldly or directly in this collection as we would have liked. That, perhaps, is more appropriately saved for another outlet that is more sensitively designed to ensure that such contributions are valuable and relevant to children and young people themselves. What we hope to have achieved in this collection, instead, is to bring children's rights perspectives to bear on the systemic, cultural and political factors that need to be addressed if the EU is to make a meaningful contribution to the global campaign to protect and promote children. To assist us in achieving this, we engaged children and young people in a discussion of the themes featured in the collection during the course of a two year international, interdisciplinary seminar series, *'European Responses to Global Children's Rights Issues: Building Capacity and Exchanging Knowledge'* (2013-2015). We are immensely grateful to the UK Economic and Social Research Council (ESRC) for their generous funding of this important series. We also owe a huge debt of thanks to the staff of Eurochild, particularly Jana Hainsworth, Mieke Schuurman, Mafalda Leal and Andrea Witt, who have offered such reliable and inspiring partnership in hosting the series in Brussels and contributing to this collection. Our administrative team that support the European Children's Rights Unit at the University of Liverpool, as well as the administrative staff at the University of Southampton, also played a critical role in organising the series and managing publicity and dissemination. Our heartfelt thanks go to Rachel Barrett, Wei Chen, Angie Walker, Gill Schofield and Natasha Graham in particular.

The European Commission children's rights co-ordinator, Margaret Tuite, has been a huge source of support and encouragement in our mission to bring critical perspectives to bear on the evolving EU children's rights agenda. As one of the 'true believers' in children's rights that we refer to in our concluding chapter, she has willingly contributed to the ESRC seminar series that informs this book and has been a vital cog in facilitating both formal and informal cross-disciplinary dialogue on various aspects of children's rights. Other true believers have also inspired this collection. Liam Cairns of Investing in Children, Jeff Dunn of the Liverpool Schools Parliament and Cath Larkins of the Centre for Children and Young People's Participation, University of Central Lancashire, have all facilitated the involvement of children and young people in our discussions around a range of children's rights issues, including migration, children's experiences of the justice process, child poverty and consumer protection.

Table of Contents

Introduction: The EU as a Children's Rights Actor: Law, Policy and Structural Dimensions

Ingi Iusmen and Helen Stalford

'Children have always been and remain at the heart of EU policy. Inspired by the Convention, the EU promotes children's rights through specific Guidelines as well as through the EU Agenda for the rights of the child for internal action [...] In order to prevent and respond to violence against children, which remains a harsh reality, we need to ensure that children benefit from enhanced access to justice and that, starting with birth, every child's right to his or her identity is respected [...] In promoting children's rights worldwide, the EU will continue to work closely with international organisations, UN bodies; in particular UNICEF, and relevant civil society organisations.'

(Federica Mogherini, High Representative of the Union for Foreign Affairs and Security Policy and Vice-President of the Commission, 2014)

The rise of an international child rights agenda

20 November 2014 marked 25 years since the adoption of the 1989 UN Convention on the Rights of the Child (CRC), which provided a paradigm shift in the way international law views children as both 'beings' and 'becomings' (Freeman 2011: 27). The CRC is the most ratified of all the treaties on human rights and it constitutes the first international instrument to focus on children as autonomous, rights-bearing subjects, possessing individual and inalienable human rights. Therefore, their well-being is a question of rightful entitlements (Veerman 1992; Freeman 2000; Archard 2004). The Convention provided a new *Weltanschaunng* in terms of how children should be approached in legal, policy and normative terms at the national level. For instance, the CRC included fundamental principles that should underpin all children's rights, such as the 'best interests of the child' (Article 3) and the right to have a say (Article 12) in all matters affecting them within the family, schools, local communities, public services, or judicial procedures, to name just a few. The Convention constitutes a landmark in international law by establishing children's status as legally empowered subjects of entitlement.

Over the last two decades the Convention has shaped how states and non-state actors think about children in legal, policy and normative terms at the societal level. More concretely, state parties to the CRC are legally obliged to incorporate its principles within their domestic legal and procedural infrastructure and to ensure that all national law and policy adhere to the rights and principles enshrined therein. But the CRC has also exerted a significant influence on the way in which children's human rights are considered and articulated at supra-national level, providing a universally endorsed framework within which international polities can forge greater national compliance and co-operation on children's rights issues that are either shared in common by states parties, or which straddle national boundaries. Civil society actors, NGOs, social movements and quasi-governmental bodies play a growing, crucial role both in facilitating communication between this multifarious network of children's rights interlocutors and in identifying where gaps in implementation of children's rights are evident on the ground. What the CRC has provided the backdrop to is, in effect, a genuinely global partnership whose members share remarkably clear and consistently articulated objectives for the protection and promotion of children's rights, notwithstanding the diversity of contexts within which children's rights are located across the world. Maintaining an effective and co-ordinated global partnership of this nature is all the more crucial if there is to be any hope of responding to the ever more nefarious effects of economic and political globalisation and of the rapid, almost boundless advancements in online technologies on children's lives, including a rise in child labour, child trafficking, illegal migration, sexual exploitation and violence (Timimi 2005, Aitken 2001; Pogge 2008).

But that is not to say that the CRC is uncontested; the 'partnership' of children's rights activists have far from resolved some of the tensions – culturally, ideologically, jurisdictionally and economically – that are exposed in many areas of children's rights protection, tensions which are compounded by the vague, ill-defined nature of key, ubiquitous notions such as 'best interests of the child' (Cordero Arce 2012; Van Bueren1998; Freeman 2000). Furthermore, the absence of any overarching enforcement mechanism, significant inconsistencies in the way in which the Convention has been transposed into domestic law across the signatory states, and the relatively impotent, resource-intensive nature of the Committee on the Rights of the Child's monitoring function, are critical barriers to its full and effective application (Tomás 2002; Freeman 2000; Gareth 2005, Stalford and Drywood 2011: 204).

Despite these shortcomings, the CRC retains its appeal as the *lingua franca* of children's rights advocacy at the regional, national, European and international levels. It has been highly successful in transforming declarations of 'rights' that appeared indifferent to the specific needs and interests of children's into much more sensitive, responsive tools for promoting children's rights. For instance, at the European level, the enforcement mechanisms of the European Convention on Human Rights (ECHR) are now routinely interpreted in the light of the CRC standards and principles (Kilkelly 2002). This, in turn, has given rise to 'the most extensive body of jurisprudence concerning children's civil rights of any of the regional human rights fora' (Van Bueren 2007: 15-16). A similar pattern of 'children's rights auditing' has occurred organically across other international jurisdictions such as the ICC, the Inter-American Court of Human Rights, the European Committee of Social Rights and the African Court on Human and People's Rights (Liefaard and Doek 2014), notwithstanding the inability of international polities to ratify the CRC. The jurisprudence generated by this process, in turn, acts as a powerful fortification of the children's rights obligations incumbent on domestic States.

The European Union (EU) has emerged as a more recent protagonist in this international children's rights partnership, but far from simply jumping on the bandwagon, it has carved out a distinct and potentially extremely powerful role in developing and enforcing children's rights, not just across the Member States of the EU, but in non-EU states as well.

The emergence of the EU as a children's rights actor

Since the mid-2000s, the EU has sought to extend its embrace of human rights norms to children and young people, inside and outside the European Union by drawing on the CRC as the key source of inspiration for its children's rights measures. The EU's commitment to advancing child rights measures based on the CRC principles in both its internal and external policy dimensions has been primarily steered by the European Commission (Iusmen 2013) with the European Parliament making some important (albeit rather more symbolic) rhetorical gestures in support. The promotion of children's rights-based norms, responds to the 'normative-power' image that the EU has sought to promote via its external policy (Manners 2002; Sjursen 2006).

While the EU has, for over 50 years, shown sporadic interest in areas connected with children's lives (Stalford 2012), it is only since the late 1990s, in the context of negotiations around EU Eastern enlargement and external development co-operation, that the EU's activities have been grounded in a more explicit children's rights normative framework (Iusmen 2014). The protection of child rights emerged as an issue pertaining to the Area of Freedom, Security and Justice as part of the Hague Programme 2005-2009, when the Commission adopted its first action plan on child rights included in the Communication *Towards an EU Strategy on the Rights of the Child* (2006). This action plan and accompanying statement of intent provided a set of policy measures in line with a rights-based framework (European Commission 2006: 2). Since then a wide range of policy documents and financial instruments[1] have been adopted and deployed to target child rights issues in EU external policy, particularly as part of the EU enlargement process,[2] not to mention across a growing range of internal market activities.

'Actorness'

Many studies have focused on the EU's role as an actor in world politics (Bretherton and Vogler 2006; Nuttall 2000; Ginsberg 2001; Smith 2006; Peterson and Smith 2003; Knodt and Princen 2003; Hill and Smith 2005). A number of EU 'actorness' models have been developed to capture the EU's role in and its impact on international politics. Jupille and Caporaso's (1998) model of 'actorness' focuses on four dimensions of EU international actorness: cohesion, authority, autonomy and recognition. According to Jupille and Caporaso's model, *cohesion* indicates the extent to which an actor is able to formulate internally consistent policy preferences; *autonomy* is determined by institutional distinctiveness, namely that the EU can operate independently from individual EU Member States; *authority* pertains to the legal competence of the EU to act; and *recognition* refers to acceptance of the EU by other actors. Bretherton and Vogler's (2006) model provides a process-oriented approach by focusing on the EU's behaviour in international politics. According to them 'actorness is constructed through the interplay of many factors, both internal to the Union and in the external environment of ideas and events that permit or constrain EU action' (Bretherton and Vogler 2006:2). Their model of EU 'actorness' comprises three dimensions: *opportunity,* which provides the external context; *presence*, which renders the EU's ability to have an influence beyond its borders; and finally, *capability*, which indicates the ability to exploit opportunity and capitalise on presence.

The EU's actorness with respect to international child rights includes all the dimensions captured by the two models above. It entails actions taken to address child rights violations and promote children's rights principles in both the EU's external and internal policy dimensions. More specifically, it

1 The Council adopted the *EU Guidelines for the Promotion and Protection of the Rights of the Child* (2007) and, in so far as children's rights in zones of conflict are concerned, the Council issued *EU Guidelines on Children and Armed Conflict* (2003, 2008). The Commission developed an action for EU external policies by adopting the Communication *A Special Place for Children in EU External Action* (2008). Child rights are also promoted via the EU's thematic programmes in EU development and cooperation policy, primarily via the Investing in People and the European Instrument for Democracy and Human Rights (EIDHR).

2 A new *acquis* Chapter in the Progress Reports was created in 2005 – Chapter 23 on 'Judiciary and Fundamental Rights' – and human rights, including child rights, are now monitored and assessed both under this chapter and under the political criteria (Iusmen 2014:115).

involves the EU's development and deployment of a set of clearly identified legal, policy, procedural, institutional and financial instruments, inspired by international human rights instruments (such as the CRC). Such measures have to be developed and interpreted within the confines of EU competence in policy sectors where the EU has the powers (exclusive, shared or supportive) to intervene. But it also demands some sensitive and challenging balancing of children's rights objectives with the broader, potentially competing objectives of market integration and economic growth. This is where the EU exercises the greatest potential to effect dramatic changes in the way that children's rights are perceived and disposed – above and beyond other international or national actors in fact. It is in a distinctly powerful position insofar as it wields unique legal, political and financial authority over its Member States and over the external regions that rely on its support. It has potent enforcement mechanisms, and unparalleled resources to support rigorous monitoring, data-collection and cross-national policy exchange and collaboration. It follows that if it can succeed in mainstreaming children's rights considerations into the textural spirit of all EU legal and policy making – including those areas that are of seemingly only tangential relevance to children's lives – then it is creating the context for a progressive 'normalisation' of children's rights; a context which regards respect for children's rights not just as the chance outcome of a niche set of legal or policy initiatives, but as absolutely integral to the broader success and sustainability of the EU.

Embracing the CRC

The magnitude of the EU's potential reinforces the importance of ensuring that any efforts to embed children's rights within its procedural, institutional, legal and policy architecture are firmly rooted in an ideologically persuasive framework. The explicit EU constitutional reference to the protection of children's rights as one of the core objectives of the EU (Article 3(3) TEU) and the panoply of children's rights measures included in the EU Charter of Fundamental Rights[3] carry significant credence in this regard (Lamont 2014; Stalford 2012; McGlynn 2002: 392-94; Ruxton 2005: 21-22). This is further reinforced by the increasingly explicit allusions to the CRC in the substance of binding EU legislation (Stalford and Drywood 2011; Stalford 2012). But

3 The EU Charter of Fundamental Rights (Article 24) contains explicit references to child rights provisions in the CRC, such as child participation, protection and care for children's well-being as well as the principle of the 'best interests of the child' guiding all actions relating to children. Other Charter articles are also relevant for children, for instance Article 14 – right to education; Article 21 – non-discrimination; Article 32 – prohibition of child labour and protection of young people at work or Article 33 – family and professional life.

allusions are one thing; achieving meaningful positive impacts are another thing altogether.

The EU as a 'Children's Rights Actor'

The EU's role as a child rights actor is examined in this book from two connected perspectives: first, as the development and adoption of EU-level *systems* (policies, laws, processes) aimed at the protection of children's rights; and second, as a critical assessment of the *impact* of the EU's actions on children's rights protection at the national level.

What renders this book unique in the field of EU child rights scholarship is the variety of contributions –from academics, legal experts and child rights practitioners – as well as the interdisciplinarity of the chapters, which cover international law, European politics, public policy and childhood studies. Some of the contributions draw upon qualitative evidence collected as part of empirical research or anecdotal evidence collected through years of experience of working in the NGO sector. The CRC provisions and principles, other international human rights instruments and progressive theorisations of children's rights provide primary reference points against which EU actions and performance as a child rights actor is being assessed.

The development of EU-level systems to protect child rights

The chapters included in the first section of the book scrutinise the extent to which existing EU systems facilitate the protection and promotion of children's rights. Stalford's chapter critically assesses the extent to which children can access EU-level justice remedies to hold Member States and the EU institutions themselves to account for alleged breaches of their rights. Her findings highlight the doublestandards of the EU in failing to provide children with basic access to justice at EU level, on the one hand, whilst, on the other, pursuing so vociferously the 'child friendly justice' agenda at the national level. Schuurman's chapter partially responds to some of the concerns raised in Stalford's chapter by making concrete suggestions as to how children's rights could be mainstreamed in a more comprehensive and meaningful way into all areas of EU law and policy-making. Her suggestions are informed by the findings of interviews with key EU officials and by good practice examples at the domestic level. Lind-Haldorsson and O'Donnell's chapter adds further support to a holistic, systemic approach to EU children's rights by scrutinising how the EU can add value to the development of more effective child protection systems across the Member States. Lamont's chapter, on the other hand, illustrates the important function that cross-border administrative structures, such as Central Authorities and the European Judicial Network, can and should play in reinforcing child rights principles when implementing EU family law.

The effects of EU actions (law, policy) on child rights

The second half of the book provides a critical and empirical analysis of how the current EU actions impact – directly and indirectly – on national child rights provisions and, more concretely, on children's lived experiences. Rap's chapter draws upon detailed cross-national comparative expositions of domestic juvenile justice processes to explore the extent to which they are amenable to current European initiatives pertaining to child friendly justice. Iusmen's chapter investigates the emergence of children's de-institutionalisation as an EU issue and the current EU policy on de-institutionalisation, as well as its shortcomings. How the rights of two distinct categories of children are protected and, indeed, corrupted by the operation of the EU's internal market preoccupations are examined in Drywood's and Ferreira's chapters. Drywood scrutinises the relevance of the EU's role in securing the protection of child rights in the recruitment of young foreign footballers, while Ferreira's chapter examines the extent to which the EU has achieved a satisfactory protection of child rights in the field of EU labour policy. Similarly, Savirimuthu's contribution reveals just how challenging it can be to achieve a healthy balance between protecting children and supporting the development of autonomous decision-making in an environment which is characterised by age-insensitive marketing and digital profiling. Finally, Vandenhole's chapter provides an insightful analysis of the strengths, weaknesses, opportunities and threats of deploying child rights-based approaches to EU development cooperation.

These chapters collectively provide fresh, critical insights into substantive issues that have come to characterise the EU children's rights agenda (such as child protection and child friendly justice). They also break new ground, exploring more niche, hitherto 'hidden' examples of cross-border child exploitation (such as online data protection and football recruitment). Crucially, they offer practical, methodological suggestions as to how administrative, legal and policy processes can be sensitised to children's rights so that they respond more effectively to the overarching EU children's rights agenda.

References

Aitken, S. C. (2001) Global Crises of Childhood: rights, justice and the unchildlike child, in: Area 33, 2, pp. 119-127.

Archard, D. (2004) Children: Rights and Childhood, London, Routledge.

Bretherton, C. and Vogler, J. (2006) The European Union as a Global Actor, London, Routledge.

Cordero Arce, M. (2012) Towards an Emancipatory Discourse of Children's Rights, in: The International Journal of Children's Rights 20, 3, pp. 365-421.

European Commission (2006) Communication from the Commission: Towards an EU Strategy on the Rights of the Child, COM (2006) 367 final, Brussels, 4 July.

Freeman, M. (2000) The Future of Children's Rights, in: Children and Society 14, 4, pp: 277-293.

Freeman, M. (2011) The Value and Values of Children's Rights, in: Invernizzi, A. and Williams, J. (eds) The Human Rights of Children. From Vision to Implementation, Farnham, Ashgate.

Gareth, A. (2005) Children and Development: rights, globalization and poverty, in: Progress in Development Studies 5, 4, pp. 336-342.

Ginsberg, R. (2001) The European Union in International Politics: Baptism by Fire, Lanham MD, Rowman and Littlefield.

Hill, C. and Smith, M. (2005) International Relations and the European Union, Oxford, Oxford University Press.

Iusmen, I. (2013) Policy Entrepreneurship and Eastern Enlargement: the Case of EU Children's Rights Policy, in: Comparative European Politics 11, 4, pp. 511-529.

Iusmen, I. (2014) Children's Rights, Eastern Enlargement and the EU Human Rights Regime, Manchester, Manchester University Press.

Jupille, J. and Caporaso, J.A. (1998) States, Agency and Rules: The European Union in Global Environmental Politics, in: Rhodes, C. (ed.) The European Union in the World Community, Boulder CO, Lynne Rienner, pp. 213-29.

Kilkelly, U. (2002) Effective Protection of Children's Rights in Family Cases: An International Approach, in: Transnational Law and Contemporary Problems 12, 2, pp. 336-354.

Lamont, R. (2014) Article 24 of the Charter of Fundamental Rights of the European Union, in: Peers, S., Hervey, T. and Ward, A. (eds.): The EU Charter of Fundamental Rights, Oxford, Hart.

Liefaard, T. and Doek, J. (eds) (2014) Litigating the Rights of the Child, London, Springer.

Knodt, M. and Princen, S. (eds) (2003) Understanding the European Union's External Relations, London, Routledge.

Manners, I. (2002) Normative Power Europe: A Contradiction in Terms?. in: Journal of Common Market Studies 40, 2, pp. 235-258.

McGlynn, C.M.S. (2002) Rights for Children: The Potential Impact of the European Union Charter of Fundamental Rights, in: European Public Law 8, 3, pp. 387-400.

McGlynn, C.M.S. (2006) Families and the European Union: Law, Politics and Pluralism, Cambridge, Cambridge University Press.

Mogherini, F. (2014) Joint Statement on the occasion of the Universal Children's Day and the 25th Anniversary of the Convention on the Rights of the Child, Brussels, 20 November, available from http://europa.eu/rapid/press-release_STATEMENT-14-2003_en.htm.

Nuttall, S. (2000) European Foreign Policy, Oxford, Oxford University Press.

Peterson, J. and Smith, M.E. (2003) The EU as a Global Actor, in: Bomberg, E. and Stubb, A. (eds) The European Union: How Does It Work?, Oxford, Oxford University Press.

Pogge, T. W. M. (2008) World Poverty and Human Rights, Cambridge, Polity Press.

Ruxton, S. (2005) How About Us? Children's Rights in the European Union: Next Steps, available at www.crin.org/docs/Ruxton%20Report_WhatAboutUs.pdf.
Sjursen, H. (2006) The EU as a 'Normative' Power: How Can This Be?, in: Journal of European Public Policy 13, 2, pp. 235-251.
Smith, K.E. (2006) Speaking With One Voice? European Union Co-ordination on Human Rights Issues at the United Nations, in: Journal of Common Market Studies 44, 1, pp. 113-37.
Stalford, H. and Drywood, E. (2011) The Use of the CRC in EU Law and Policy-Making, in: Invernizzi, A. and Williams, J. (eds) Children's Rights: Revisiting Visions, Assessing Progress, Rethinking Implementation, Aldershot, Ashgate.
Stalford, H. (2012) Children and the European Union: Rights, Welfare and Accountability, Oxford, Hart.
Timimi S. (2005) Effect of globalisation on children's mental health, in: Medical Journal 331, 7507.
Tomás, C. (2002) Infância como um campo de estudo multi e interdisciplinar, algumas reflexões, in: Revista Psicologia e Educação, 1 e 2, pp. 131-146.
Van Bueren, G. (1998) Children's Rights: balancing traditional values and cultural plurality, in: Douglas, G. and Sebba, L. (eds) Children's Rights and Traditional Values, Hants, Dartmouth.
Van Bueren, G. (2007) Child Rights in Europe, Strasbourg, Council of Europe.
Veerman, P.E. (1992) The Rights of the Child and the Changing Image of Childhood, Leiden, Martinus Nijhoff.

Journeys to European Justice: (How) Can the EU Enable Children to Enforce their Rights?

Helen Stalford

Introduction

This chapter examines the legitimacy and effectiveness of the EU as a children's rights actor by examining the extent to which children influence the laws and policies it develops. It interrogates what mechanisms are in place to ensure conscientious implementation of EU children's rights measures and how the EU tests and responds to the impact of those measures on the ground. In that sense the analysis departs from the common tendency to view access to justice issues through the lens of national justice processes and examines how children claim their rights in a distinctly supra-national – in this instance European Union (EU) – context. The analysis deliberately excludes any consideration of judicial enforcement of EU children's rights, either from the perspective of the national courts or from the perspective of Court of Justice[1], thereby departing from the routine conflation of 'access to justice' with 'access to the courts'. By examining more routinely available (non-judicial) justice channels through which children can actively enforce and advance their EU rights, the discussion questions whether the EU genuinely endorses practices that are compatible with a child rights-based approach.

The notion of a child-rights based approach is inherent in the notion of 'child friendly justice' (CFJ). CFJ is one of the key priorities identified by the Commission in its seminal 2011 'Agenda for the Rights of the Child' (Commission 2011: 6) and in the various legislative, policy and research funding initiatives that have ensued. CFJ has become something of a mantra in broader children's rights law and policy-making, not only at European level, but at domestic and international level too. The EU, in particular, continues to invest significant resources in research, training and knowledge exchange projects across a range of domestic children's rights contexts. This has already yielded a wealth of comparative, qualitative and quantitative data providing rich insights into children's experiences of the justice system, and into the

1 These issues are explored further by the author in Stalford 2014; and Stalford and Drywood 2011.

extent to which practitioners adapt processes to meet the needs of children.[2] These initiatives complement parallel efforts aimed at ensuring that international (supra-national) justice processes are amenable to children's rights, as well as an established and ever-expanding body of scholarship exploring the extent to which the distinct interests and needs of children are accommodated in various justice settings (see chapter 5 by Rap in this collection; Kilkelly 2001; Fortin 2006; Council of Europe 2008; Nolan 2011; Tobin 2012).This chapter adds a new perspective to this body of work by examining the extent to which the EU's *own* justice processes are amenable to claims from and on behalf of children.

The analysis focuses on the main non-judicial 'points of entry' to EU-level justice, notably the EU Ombudsman, the EU Citizens' Initiative, EU Parliamentary petitions and infringement proceedings. In focusing on these contexts, the analysis highlights the importance of securing children's access to justice at all stages of law and policy-making, whilst at the same time drawing attention to the limitations and challenges inherent in such processes. It interrogates the extent to which children can and do really access justice at EU level, and speculates on the impact of this on the way that children's rights are disposed of and developed at both EU and national level. The chapter concludes somewhat cynically that the EU, for all of its rhetorical and financial commitment to child friendly justice, is very far from practising child friendly justice within its own justice mechanisms. Indeed, it has some way to go before it evidences a meaningful commitment to children as individual and active rights holders who can readily access EU mechanisms to hold both the EU institutions and their nation states to account. This raises serious questions as to the progress the EU can really make to advance children's rights in a way that inspires other polities at the national or, indeed, the international level if the measures it enacts and the processes by which they are enforced remain impenetrable to the very individuals they are designed to protect. With this in mind, the discussion includes some thoughts on how and whether such processes can be made more accommodating of children, par-

---

2 For instance, in 2012, the EU Fundamental Rights Agency commissioned research involving over 570 interviews with justice professionals (judges, prosecutors, lawyers, guardians, people working at courts, psychologists and social workers) across 10 EU countries to gain their perspectives of how children's rights are protected within justice proceedings, particularly in courts. This was complemented by a similar number of interviews with children and young people in 2013-2014. The project findings should be released in 2015. See http://fra.europa.eu/en/project/2012/children-and-justice. Similarly, DG Justice of the European Commission funded an in-depth study of children's involvement in judicial proceedings across the 28 Member States of the EU. This was to address the significant gap in reliable, comparable and official data on the situation of children, particularly in the context of justice proceedings (Commission 2011, p. 5). See further http://www.childreninjudicialproceedings.eu/Home/Default.aspx.

ticularly given the anticipated increase in child rights-related claims arising out of EU law in the future.

To set the scene for this analysis, the initial sections define precisely what is meant by 'access to justice' and summarise the key components of 'child friendly justice' by reference to the relevant legal and policy guidance.

1. Defining Access to Justice

Access to justice governs a range of processes related to the enforcement and advancement of rights. There is a multi-layered legal framework underpinning children's access to justice in a European context, drawn both from the more generic international human rights provision as well as from dedicated children's rights law and guidance. The Universal Declaration on Human Rights, for example, asserts that "everyone has the right to an effective remedy by the competent national tribunals for acts violating the fundamental rights granted him by the constitution or by law." (UDHR 1948, Article 8). Similarly the International Covenant on Civil and Political Rights 1966 refers to an "effective remedy" (Article 2(3a)) for all the rights in the Covenant and further guarantees the right to "take proceedings before a court" (Article 9(4)), the right to a "fair and public hearing" (Article 14(1)), and the right to be tried without undue delay (Article 14(3c)). More recently, the 2006 UN Convention on the Rights of Persons with Disabilities, noted for its ratification by the EU, places an explicit obligation upon states to ensure equal access to justice to those persons with disabilities, including a requirement to provide their agents with appropriate training to accomplish this (Article 13).

In a European context (specifically the Council of Europe) the European Convention on Human Rights 1950 (ECHR) protects individuals' right to a fair trial and to an effective legal remedy (Articles 6 and 13 respectively), provisions that have been expansively interpreted to cover a range of civil, criminal and administrative proceedings. Access to justice for those seeking to uphold their economic and social rights (not traditionally the focus of ECHR proceedings) is facilitated by the European Social Charter.[3] Importantly, this instrument makes explicit reference to legal and social protection,

3 Adopted in 1961 (ETS 035) and revised in 1996 (ETS 163). All EU Member States have ratified the 1961 version of the Charter. All Member States with the exception of Croatia, Czech Republic, Denmark, Germany, Greece, Luxembourg, Poland, Spain and the UK have ratified the 1996 version of the Charter.

particularly for children in the context of criminal proceedings, family proceedings and administrative proceedings.[4]

Access to justice is equally embedded in the EU legal order. In fact, it is regarded as fundamental to the Union's constitutional claim to be grounded in the rule of law and to the EU's ongoing pursuit of good governance.[5] The Court of Justice, through an established jurisprudence dating back to the 1980s, has played a central role in articulating and reinforcing the EU and national authorities' obligations to facilitate access to justice.[6] More recent changes to the EU's constitutional architecture, particularly following the 2009 Lisbon Treaty, further reinforce (and arguably extend) the rights associated with access to justice. Notably, the Charter of Fundamental Rights which now is on the same legally-binding footing as the Treaties (Article 6(1) TEU), summarises all of the key ingredients associated with the right to an effective remedy and a fair trial (Article 47), including: the right to a fair and public hearing within a reasonable time by an independent and impartial tribunal previously established by law; the right to be advised, defended and represented; and the right to legal aid for those who lack sufficient resources in so far as such aid is necessary to ensure effective access to justice.[7] More specifically, the EU has assumed a direct correlation between achieving access to justice and ensuring cross-border recognition and enforcement of judgments, notably in the context of international family (including parental child abduction) or civil proceedings (such as cross-border child maintenance claims). Thus, a requirement has been incorporated into the Treaty on the Functioning of the European Union (TFEU) that the Union shall "facilitate access to justice, in particular through the principle of mutual recognition of judicial and extrajudicial decisions in civil matters." (Article 67(4) TFEU. See further Lamont's discussion in Chapter 3 of this collection).

Drawing on this extensive legal framework, jurisprudence and procedural guidance, access to justice is characterised by three key broad components:

---

4 See in particular Article 17 – the right of children and young persons to social, legal and economic protection.

5 The Commission has defined good governance as having five basic components: openness, participation, effectiveness, coherence and accountability (Commission, 2001).

6 The Court of Justice first recognised in the Johnson ruling of 1986 that the fundamental right to judicial process, as enshrined in Article 6 ECHR, forms part of the general principles of EU law binding upon the MS when acting within the scope of the Treaties, and thus applies for the benefit of all individuals whose Union rights are implemented through the national systems of judicial protection (Case 222/84 *Johnston* [1986] ECHR 1651). See further Dashwood et al. (2011: 289) for an overview of subsequent case law.

7 In that sense, Artice 47 Charter is more generous in scope than Articles 6 and 13 of the ECHR, insofar as it extends to a right to financing legal proceedings for those who lack the resources to pursue their rights. This is currently being used to challenge widespread cuts in legal aid that have been imposed in recent years, particularly in the context of immigration proceedings (Meyler and Woodhouse 2013).

- it is inclusive (it applies to all individuals, regardless of age, ethnicity, gender, physical or mental capacity, socio-economic, political or legal status);
- it implies access to 'an effective legal remedy', broadly construed;
- it governs justice processes at all levels, from the local, to the national, European and the international level.

Importantly, access to justice extends far beyond facilitating effective access to formal, judicial proceedings aimed at interpreting and enforcing the law; it is equally applicable to administrative processes, including the right to challenge laws and other decisions that are unfair, or to campaign for remedies that accommodate individual interests and rights more effectively. This raises questions as to how this body of guidance is brought to bear specifically on *children's* access to justice.

2. Applying Access to Justice Principles to Children

In seeking to understand how access to justice principles apply to proceedings involving children, the most comprehensive point of reference is the Council of Europe (CoE) Guidelines on Child Friendly Justice (CoE 2010, hereafter 'the Guidelines') developed as part of the CoE's comprehensive children's rights strategy.[8] They are, in legal terms, a relatively 'soft' alternative to the provisions described above. That said, they offer a detailed blueprint for child friendly justice governing all types and stages of formal proceedings affecting children and, as such, have informed a range of Council of Europe and, indeed, EU measures in the field.[9]

Consistent with our broad understanding of access to justice, the Guidelines relate to all formal investigative, judicial and administrative proceedings including the police, immigration, educational, social or health care services. Moreover, they refer to children's rights before, during and after formal pro-

8 The Council of Europe's children's rights strategy 'Building a Europe for and with children' (2012-2015), runs in parallel with the European Union children's rights strategy, the 'EU Agenda on the Rights of the Child'. There are a number of themes and priorities common to both, including child friendly justice, stimulating a degree of collaboration and resource-sharing. See further: http://www.coe.int/t/dg3/children/.

9 Directive 2012/29/EU of the European Parliament and of the Council of 25 October 2012, establishing minimum standards on the rights, support and protection of victims of crime, and replacing Council Framework Decision 2001/220/JHA, OJ L 315, 14.11.2012, p. 57-73; Proposal for a Directive of the European Parliament and of the Council on procedural safeguards for children suspected or accused in criminal proceedings, COM(2013) 822 final, see paragraph 24 of Explanatory Memorandum.

ceedings, implying a broad application to a range of democratic processes involving the enforcement and enhancement of individual rights. Specifically, 'child-friendly justice' is defined in the Guidelines as:

> ...*justice systems which guarantee the respect and the effective implementation of all children's rights at the highest attainable level* ... giving due consideration to the child's level of maturity and understanding and the circumstances of the case. It is, in particular, justice that is *accessible, age appropriate, speedy, diligent, adapted to and focused on the needs and rights of the child*, respecting the rights of the child including the rights to *due process*, to participate in and to understand the proceedings, to respect for private and family life and to integrity and dignity. (Part II.c., emphasis added)

The Guidelines identify the key mechanisms that need to be in place to achieve these guarantees, including: access to appropriate information and advice; the right to be heard; access to the court and to the judicial process; the avoidance of any undue delay in reaching and processing decisions relating to children; protection and, if necessary, anonymity, in the course of participating in proceedings; specialist training and multi-disciplinary cooperation to enable professionals to respond more effectively to children's interests and needs in the context of justice proceedings; and a clear commitment to using detention only as a measure of last resort (Part IV). As the CoE notes:

> ...the right of any person to have access to justice and to a fair trial – *in all its components* (including in particular the right to be informed, the right to be heard, the right to a legal defence, and the right to be represented) – is necessary in a democratic society and *equally applies to children,* taking ... into account their capacity to form their own views. (Para 1 preamble, emphasis added)

These standards resonate, in particular, with the UN Convention on the Rights of the Child 1989 (CRC) which is replete with references to child friendly justice. In fact, almost every substantive provision of the CRC reflects one of the child friendly justice principles, including children's right to appropriate (legal) assistance and direction;[10] to participate in the decision-making process;[11] to undue delay;[12] and to be protected before, during and

---

10 For example, Article 5 respects children's right to 'appropriate direction and guidance' in the exercise of their Convention rights; Article 8 requires that states provide children with 'appropriate assistance and protection' when they are pursuing claims relating to their identity, nationality, name and family relations; and Article 14 upholds the rights and duties of parents and, where applicable, legal guardians, to provide direction to the child in the exercise of his or her right to freedom of thought, conscience and religion, in a manner consistent with the child's evolving capacities. Article 22 requires that asylum seeking children are provided with the necessary protection, assistance and information in the context of family reunification proceedings; and Article 37 guarantees children who are deprived of their liberty the right to prompt access to legal and other appropriate assistance.

11 Article 9 provides that children should have a right to participate and make their views known in child protection proceedings.

after justice proceedings.[13] These provisions are further bolstered by the four general principles of the CRC[14] and by the recently established complaints mechanism.[15] These, together with the broader provisions referred to above, provide hefty legal and procedural armour to protect children's rights in the justice process.

Ensuring that justice processes are child friendly is as crucial at the international or inter-state level as it is at the national or regional level. International courts and complaints mechanisms offer the last resort for most justice proceedings; the ultimate opportunity to hold authorities and individuals to account for abuses where domestic processes have failed; an international platform for establishing universal moral and ethical standards and setting legal precedents on the interpretation of the expansive body of international human rights laws, whether they expressly refer to children or not. The outcome of those processes can have dramatic repercussions for millions of children. They can stimulate a gradual domino-effect of reforms in domestic child law and practice across a range of jurisdictions,[16] trigger important

---

12 Article 10 relating to family reunification resonates with the 'no delay' principle underpinning child friendly justice insofar as it requires such applications to be dealt with in a positive, humane and expeditious manner. Similarly, children are entitled to 'prompt decision' relating to whether or not they can lawfully be deprived of their liberty (Article 37).

13 Article 16 acknowledges children's right to legal protection against any interference with their right to privacy, family or correspondence; Articles 19, 20 and 21 provide similar safeguards for children in the context of child protection proceedings.

14 Article 2 (right to non-discrimination); Article 3 (best interests); Article 6 (right to life, survival and development); and Article 12 (right to participation).

15 27 January 2012. The Third Optional Protocol on a Communications Procedure entered into force on 14th April 2014 and, at the time of writing, had been ratified by 46 state parties. It allows individual children to submit complaints to the Committee on the Rights of the Child regarding specific violations of their rights under the Convention and its first two optional protocols.

16 The first ECtHR judgment to deal with children's rights was *Tyrer vs the United Kingdom* (Application No. 5856/72, judgment of 25/04/1978), in which the Court concluded that corporal punishment (in this case birching) inflicted on a young offender at the hands of the police constituted a breach of Article 3 ECHR. This decision triggered a Council of Europe-wide campaign to ban corporal punishment which has contributed, in turn, to legal reform across over half of the 47 Council of Europe states. Paradoxically, the UK remains one of the few countries in which the practice of 'reasonable punishment' by parents is still legal (s.58 Children Act 2004). See also the collective complaints submitted to the European Committee on Social Rights by civil society organisations against states regarding their corporal punishment laws: *World Organisation against Torture (OMCT) vs Greece, Collective* Complaint No. 17/2003; *World Organisation against Torture (OMCT) vs Ireland*, Collective Complaint No. 18/2003; *World Organisation against Torture (OMCT) vs Belgium*, Collective Complaint No. 21/2003; *World Organisation against Torture (OMCT) vs Portugal*, Collective Complaint No. 34/2006.

ethical and cultural debates,[17] re-define the boundaries of parental and state authority over children[18] and the interrelationship between children's welfare and autonomy.[19]

Maud de Boer-Buquicchio, former Deputy Secretary General of the Council of Europe, has explained the importance and meaning of access to international-level justice as follows:

> What do we mean by "access" to international justice for children? I believe that it means more than being able to fill in a form to lodge an application with the Court. I believe that access to international justice for children occurs when they have a real chance, be it directly or indirectly through family members, legal representatives or NGOs, to have their voices heard and interests taken care of by an international judicial or non-judicial body … For international justice to be really meaningful for children, we have to identify and act upon ways to improve children's access to information on standards, procedures and decisions; to facilitate their participation in proceedings; to incorporate children's rights in the functioning and decisions of the monitoring mechanisms; to improve the contacts between children and their representatives with the monitoring bodies; and last, to accelerate procedures and improve the scrutiny of the execution of decisions. (2008:10-11)

With this in mind, access to international justice is as much a matter of ensuring that children's rights norms, theories and empirically-verified evidence is brought to bear on decision-making as it is about ensuring that children can participate in justice proceedings, either directly or through a representative.

Maud de Boer-Buquicchio's comments reflect a growing body of case law manifesting the international courts' engagement with and application of children's rights principles and processes in interpreting international treaties.[20] References to the CRC, in particular, have become a routine feature of

17 The minimum age of criminal responsibility has been widely mooted in response to a number of key international decisions, including the conclusions of the European Committee for Social Rights (ECSR, Conclusions XV-2, Malta (2003)).

18 As evidenced, for example, in the ECtHR's interpretation of immigrant children's family rights by reference to the best interests principle: *Osman v. Denmark* (Application no. 38058/09); *Mugenzi v. France* (Application no. 52701/09, Judgment of 10 October 2014; and *Mubilanzila Mayeka and Kaniki Mitunga vs Belgium*, (Application no. 13178/03, Judgment of 12 January 2007.

19 See for instance *S.C. vs the United Kingdom*, judgment of 15 June 2004 in which the ECtHR upheld the child's right to participate in justice proceedings as central to fulfilling Article 6 ECHR right to a fair trial and required that the process be adapted accordingly. See also, *Sahin vs Germany*, (Application no. 30943/96, Judgment of 8 July 2003) confirming the child's right to full and accurate information as instrumental to the child's right to participate in custody proceedings.

20 See, for instance, the Inter-American Court of Human Rights (IACHH) ruling in *Juvenile Re-education Institute vs Paraguay* (Judgment of September 2, 2004. Series C No. 112) which referred to Article 6 and Article 27 CRC to interpret the right to life as imposing on the state an obligation to 'ensure to the maximum extent possible the survival and development of the child'. Moreover, the court referred to the Committee on the Rights of the Child's interpretation of the word 'development' in its broadest sense as a holistic concept, embracing the child's physical, mental, spiritual, moral, psychological and social develop-

all Strasbourg jurisprudence relating to children (Kilkelly 2009; Kilkelly 2011; Besson 2007; Daly 2011)[21] often to the point that the ECtHR has been accused of overstepping its function and usurping the role of the Member States in dictating the nature and scope of their children's rights obligations (*Neulinger and Shurukv. Switzerland* (Application No 41615/07) ECHR [2010]; Walker and Beaumont 2011). Other international jurisdictions, such as the inter-American Court of Human Rights (Feria-Tinta 2014), the International Criminal Court (Nyamutata 2014), and the African Commission on Human and Peoples' Rights (Seifu 2008) have followed suit in deliberately endorsing children's rights principles in their jurisprudence and in at least showing some willingness to adapt procedures to facilitate children's participation in proceedings, either directly or indirectly. The fact that more and more states parties to the CRC are ratifying Optional Protocol 3 on a communications procedure is also testament to the widespread support for the use of international non-judicial mechanisms to hold domestic authorities to account (Buck and Wabwile 2013).[22]

Save the Children make a similar observation about the importance of supra-national scrutiny of rights violations, particularly where national-level accountability is lacking, but note that "...with the exception of the Council of Europe and the Inter-American system, regional mechanisms tend to be weak or non-existent" (Save the Children 2009: 2). The next section tests this assertion in relation to different justice processes at EU level. But, as a preliminary question, it is important to understand precisely why access to justice for children holds particular significance in an EU context. In the process, it responds to a common contention that it is neither reasonable nor, indeed, feasible to expect the EU to facilitate children's access to its justice mechanisms to quite same the extent as its European or international counterparts, particularly given the former's relatively weak, or at least less mature human rights mandate.

ment. This is in spite of the US's stubborn refusal to ratify the CRC. See further Macaulay 2008. For a full review of the extent to which the IACHR draws on the CRC see Feria-Tinta 2014.

21 Children's rights-related case law is available through a dedicated database, Theseus.

22 Above note 15.

3. Children's Access to Justice at European Union Level – Why Is It Important and What Does It Involve?

There are at least two main reasons why securing children's access to justice at EU level is important. The first is strategic in nature and is about providing children and their advocates with an appropriate channel through which they can communicate with the European institutions as to the actual and desired nature, scope and impact of EU children's rights measures. It is about giving ordinary citizens a genuine say in the kind of role we want the EU to play in promoting issues that, for various reasons, be they political, financial or social, cannot be adequately dealt with at the national level. This is particularly important given the explicit constitutional undertaking by the EU to protect the rights of the child in all activities that fall within EU competence (Article 3(3) TEU; Article 24 EU Charter of Fundamental Rights of the European Union).

The legitimizing effects of enabling children and young people to have a say in how EU measures affecting them are shaped should not be underestimated. Since the adoption by the European Commission of its seminal Agenda on the Rights of the Child in 2011 (Commission 2011), there have been numerous, bold expressions by other EU institutions, attesting to their commitment to the protection and promotion of children's rights when developing EU law and policy. All of these emphasize the importance of securing children's access to justice and of involving children in decisions that affect them, including decisions at the supra-national level. For example, in November 2014, the European Parliament adopted a Resolution on the rights of the child to mark the 25th Anniversary of the UN Convention on the Rights of the Child. In doing so, the Parliament declared that "children's rights are at the heart of EU policies" and urged both the EU institutions and the Member States to "take additional measures to ensure respect for the rights of every child everywhere, especially the most vulnerable" (EU Parliament 2014: para 1). Specifically, the Resolution calls upon the Commission and the Member States "to take the necessary action to ensure that all children can effectively access justice systems that are tailored to their specific needs and rights, whether as suspects, perpetrators, victims or parties to proceedings" (Ibid.: para 12).

The EU's commitment to upholding and protecting children's rights is also evidenced in the Council of the European Union Conclusions on the Rights of the Child, adopted on 4th December 2014 (Council 2014). The Council of the European Union is the main context within which national ministers from each EU Member State meet to adopt laws and co-ordinate policies.[23] It also co-ordinates Member States' economic policies, approves the EU annual budget and co-ordinates co-operation between the courts and police forces of the Member States. As such, the Council has an important strategic and practical function in the development and actual enforcement of EU measures affecting children at both the EU and national level. It commits itself to: holding thematic debates on the promotion and protection of the rights of the child in relevant Council working groups; ensuring that all new legal and policy proposals adequately address children's rights; and engaging in regular dialogue with the other law-making institutions (namely the Parliament and the Commission) on EU measures affecting children. It invites both the Member States and the Commission to be more effective in their implementation of children's rights at the national level, particularly in relation to the right of the child to be heard, and to increase efforts to create child-friendly justice systems and child-sensitive procedures in order to facilitate children's access to justice.

These initiatives evidence a far-reaching and explicit commitment across the EU institutions to integrate children's rights considerations, as informed by children's direct and indirect participation, into all stages of the legal and policy process at EU-level, and to act in a co-ordinated, sustained way to achieve their effective implementation at the domestic level. It follows then, that the extent to which such commitments are being fulfilled should be open to scrutiny and that, in cases of default, the relevant institutions or agencies be held to account by children and their representatives.

The second reason for ensuring children's access to justice at EU level relates to effective implementation. In short, it is about ensuring that the now proliferate, binding measures contained in EU law that relate to children's rights and welfare are not only transposed in a formal sense at national level, but are conscientiously applied in practice, by agencies, professionals and the courts. Consider, for instance, the EU Victims' Directive which obliges state authorities to make protective provision available to vulnerable victims involved in different justice processes, including children (Directive 2012/29/EU of the European Parliament and of the Council of 25 October 2012 establishing minimum standards on the rights, support and protection of victims of crime, OJ L 315, 14.11.2012). Similarly, the EU trafficking directive imposes a range of obligations on States including: adopting a harmonised definition of trafficking; implementing more robust investigation and prosecution procedures; offering more tailored assistance and protection to victims of trafficking, particularly children; developing awareness-raising

23 The Council of the European Union should not be confused with the European Council where EU leaders meet to discuss the EU's political priorities. Nor should it be confused with the Council of Europe, a distinct non-EU polity, which is composed of 47 Member States and which exercises an explicit human rights mandate (as manifested most famously in the 1950 European Convention on Human Rights).

activities, as well as appropriate professional training with a view to preventing trafficking (Directive 2011/36/EU of the European Parliament and of the Council of 5 April 2011 on preventing and combating trafficking in human beings and protecting its victims, OJ L 101, 15.4.2011). Likewise, the EU Sexual Exploitation Directive imposes harmonised definitions of and procedures for tackling sexual offences committed against children. It also lays down the minimum sanctions for offenders. Included within this are provisions aimed at combating child pornography on-line and sex tourism, facilitated by rules on the sharing of criminal records information between Member States. Moreover, the directive obliges Member States to provide unconditional assistance, support and protection to victims of sexual exploitation and pornography before during and after criminal proceedings, which includes the appointment of free legal representation and counselling (Directive 2011/93/EU of the European Parliament and of the Council of 13 December 2011 on combating the sexual abuse and sexual exploitation of children and child pornography, OJ 2011 L 335/1, Articles 18-20). All of these instruments emphasise the need to provide legal assistance and support to children at all stages of the justice process, consistent with the principles and procedures laid down in the Council of Europe guidelines.

Of relevance also is the extensive social welfare provision enshrined in EU immigration and asylum law that guarantees to migrant children that their basic needs to education, health and legal assistance will be met notwithstanding their fragile immigration status;[24] and the directly effective EU Regulation governing cross-border child abduction and parental responsibility disputes. This obliges professionals in the family justice process to hear the views of the child and to adopt the best interests of the child as a primary consideration before decisions around return, custody or access are made (Regulation 2201/2003 concerning jurisdiction and the recognition and enforcement of judgments in matrimonial matters and in matters of parental responsibility, [2003] OJ L338/1: para 12 preamble, Arts 12(1)(b),12(3)(b) and 12(4), Arts 15(1), 15(5) and Art 23(a)). All of this legal entitlement is only of value if effectively implemented and legally enforceable at the national level, and if supported by sympathetic procedures and adequate financial investment, including the provision of legal aid and free, independent legal representation.

---

24 Asylum Procedures Directive 2013/32 (OJ L 180, 29.6.2013), Article 7 and 25; Child Victims Directive, 2012/29/EU (OJ L 315, 14.11.2012), Article 8; Refugee Qualification Directive, 2011/95/EU (OJ L 337, 20.12.2011), Articles 27- 29; Family Reunification Directive 2003/86/EC (OJ L 251, 3.10.2003), Article 14; Temporary Protection Directive, 2001/55/EC (OJ L 212, 7.8.2001), Article 14; Reception Conditions Directive, 2013/33/EU (OJ L 180, 29.6.2013), Article 14 and 17; Return Directive, 2008/115/EC (OJ L 348, 24.12.2008), Article 14(c). For a summary overview of EU children's rights provision in the context of immigration and asylum see FRA 2015: chapter 9.

And yet, despite these obligations, there is evidence across the Member States of inconsistent, often inadequate implementation of at least some of these obligations, leading to a widespread shortfall in the protection of children's rights. For instance, recent cross-national empirical studies of how young suspects are treated in the criminal justice process have revealed significant disparities in how young offenders are questioned, supported and informed about their rights, and widespread failure to inform child witnesses or victims of the substance and scope of their rights in a way that they can understand.[25] Similarly, a detailed, comparative evaluation of immigration laws and processes draws attention to a range of factors at the national level, both systemic (fragmentation of responsibilities across a range of agencies) and procedural (lack of communication between the various professionals working with child asylum seekers), that impede successful implementation of the extensive EU provision governing the rights and welfare of unaccompanied children (O'Donnell and Hagan 2014).

This begs the question as to who should be held accountable for inadequate implementation of such obligations and, indeed, how those responsible can be brought to account. It has already been noted that mechanisms in this regard take on a variety of forms. It does not have to involve a court-based, adversarial process or respond to a particular human rights violation. It can amount to action aimed at enhancing the legislative prominence of certain rights, amending the way that a particular right is framed within the legislation, or at encouraging more conscientious implementation of rights by the relevant domestic authorities. With this in mind, the remaining discussion is framed around three key questions:

- How do children change or propose EU laws with a view to enhancing their rights/experiences?
- How do children complain about EU actions or, indeed, omissions that adversely affect their lives or impede the exercise of their rights?
- How do children harness the EU's non-judicial authority to hold Member States to account for breaching or failing to implement their EU rights?

---

25 See notably the in-depth study, commissioned by DG Justice of the European Commission, to gather legal, procedural, statistical and qualitative data on children in judicial proceedings across the EU28, available at: http://www.childreninjudicialproceedings.eu/Home/Default.aspx. See in particular the comparative report, 'Summary of contextual overviews on children's involvement in criminal judicial proceedings in the 28 Member States of the European Union', Luxembourg, 2014, particularly chapter 4. See also the current 2 year project (2014-16), 'Protecting young suspects in interrogations', co-ordinated by Maastricht University and funded by the European Commission. This involves in-depth interviews with young suspects, lawyers and the police as well as analysis of audio samples of police interrogations across Belgium, Italy, Poland, The Netherlands and the UK. See further youngsuspects.eu.

4. How Do Children Change or Propose EU Laws with a View to Enhancing Their Rights?

The discussion has already alluded to the expanding body of EU legislation that addresses the rights of children across a range of areas that fall within EU competence.[26] The extent to which these measures positively reinforce the rights of children depends, to a degree, on when they were enacted. Those enacted post 2010 are more likely to correspond explicitly with international children's rights principles and practice. 2011 marked the launch of the EU's formal children's rights Agenda in which the Commission committed to providing "… practical internal training on the rights of the child and other fundamental rights to reinforce and further promote a culture of respect for fundamental rights", and to explaining how child rights considerations were taken into account in the drafting of legislative proposals (Commission 2011: 5). The legal elevation of the EU Charter of Fundamental Rights to the same status as EU treaties in early 2010 supported this process insofar as it made the children's rights provisions contained therein both more visible and legally binding on both the EU and the Member States in their development and implementation of EU law (Art 6(1) TEU). This, in turn, precipitated the introduction of an *ex ante* fundamental rights auditing mechanism to ensure that all new legislation proposals could be screened to ensure their compliance with the fundamental rights obligations contained in the Charter (Commission 2010). With this in mind, the Commission announced that:

> In order to reinforce its assessment of the impact of its proposals on fundamental rights, including on the rights of the child, the Commission has prepared operational guidance that will enable its departments to examine the impact of an initiative on fundamental rights, including the rights of the child, and to select the option that best takes into consideration the best interests of the child. (Commission 2011: 5)

There is every indication, from the profusion of children's rights references in more recent EU laws affecting children, that this auditing strategy has been conscientiously applied. That said, it seems to have been a largely top-down process, with limited or no input from children and young people or their advocates as to how a proposed legislative initiative responds to their lived experiences and needs. Furthermore, EU children's rights measures that predate 2011, while they might contain sporadic references to children's rights principles, tend to be significantly less considered in how they protect and promote children's rights and, in many cases, obscure or even undermine

26 For a more detailed overview, see FRA Handbook on European Children's Rights, and for a more detailed, critical look at the evolution, content and scope of EU law relating to children, see Stalford, H. (2012) *Children and the European Union: Rights, Welfare and Accountability* (Oxford, Hart).

children's rights. Take, for example, Directive 2010/13 (OJ L 95, 15.4.2010) on Audiovisual Media Services (AVMS) which contains rules limiting children's exposure to potentially harmful media content or exploitative commercial advertising. While this might be framed in terms of protecting the best interests of the child, in reality, the provisions are extremely limited, creating significant leeway for commercial operators to interpret their obligations to meet the (primary) demands of the market economy (Garde 2011 and 2013; Bartlett and Garde 2013).

In a bid to support a more inclusive, empirically-grounded approach, the Commission has conducted a number of public consultations, both to inform the development of its broader children's rights strategy,[27] and to elicit suggestions on substantive areas of legal reform.[28] These consultations are, in principle, open to any individual or organisation – including children's rights organisations – and the responses are published online. However, the extent to which such contributions are genuinely taken into account in the (re-)drafting of law and policy is rather less apparent, and there appears to be limited or no interrogation by the Commission as to the extent to which those contributions incorporate the views of children and young people.

4.1 The Citizens' Initiative

One of the arguably more transparent routes by which private individuals and their representatives can propose changes in EU law is through the Citizens' Initiative.[29] This mechanism was launched by the European Commission in April 2012 to create a 'democratic discourse'[30] on issues of concern to EU citizens by enabling them collectively to propose legislation in matters than fall within EU competence. The Citizens' Initiative can be organised and submitted by any national of an EU Member State who is old enough to vote

27 See for instance DG Justice's consultation on the European Commission's Communication (Agenda) on the Rights of the Child (2011-2014) which was open from 11 June 2010 to 20 August 2010: http://ec.europa.eu/justice/news/consulting_public/news_consulting_0009_en.htm.

28 See the Commission's Consultation on the functioning of the Brussels IIa Regulation (EC 2201/2003), the EU law governing cross-border parental responsibility and child abduction disputes, from 15 April 2014 until 18 July 2014: http://ec.europa.eu/justice/newsroom/civil/opinion/140415_en.htm.

29 Articles 11(4) TEU and 24 TFEU. The rules and procedures governing the citizens' initiative are set out in EU Regulation 211/2011 of the European Parliament and of the Council of 16 February 2011, OJ L 65/1.

30 Baldoli, R. (2013) 'Thence We Came Forth to Rebehold the Stars': A First Assessment of the European Citizens' Initiative', in: *European Journal of Risk Regulation*, Vol 4(1) 82-86, at p.82.

in the European Parliament elections (18 years old with the exception of Austria where the voting age is 16). The organiser then has 12 months in which to collect statements of support.[31] Initiatives must be signed by at least one million citizens from at least 7 Member States and there must be a minimum number of signatories from each of the Member States represented in the initiative, proportionate to the population of that Member State.[32] Designated authorities in the Member States represented in the initiative then have to verify the signatures collected, following which the final Citizens' Initiative can be submitted to the Commission. This is then published on the Commission website and the Commission has three months in which to reach a conclusion and determine its proposed action.[33]

Notwithstanding the democratic aspirations of the Citizens' Initiative, it has been heavily criticised on a number of grounds, not least for explicitly excluding children as potential petitioners (Stalford and Schuurman 2011: 389). Many of those criticisms are borne out in the exceedingly limited use of the mechanism to date by children and their advocates. This is attributable, not least, to the significant resources required to launch and manage such an initiative in terms of campaigning for and gathering the extensive cross-national support required. The not-for-profit international children's rights networks most inclined to engage in such a process already labour under significant resource constraints and are unlikely to divert valuable funds away from core advocacy or campaign agendas to pursue a protracted process that, more often than not, ends in failure. Taking these logistical obstacles into account, it is hardly surprising that, for all its democratic aspirations, there has not been a single Citizens' Initiative accepted to date that advances in any meaningful way the status of children under EU law.

4.2 Children's Rights 'Champions'

While these formal processes to support civil dialogue are largely inaccessible and, therefore, ineffective as a mechanism for advancing children's rights, there are other initiatives driven, to a large degree, by the advocacy of civil society organisations, that offer potentially better channels in this regard. For example, in 2014, in response to a concerted campaign by 14 international and European civil society organisations, over 90 members of the

31 These statements of support must be collected from other EU citizens who are old enough to vote, in accordance with the procedure set in Articles 5 and 6 of the Regulation.

32 Article 7 Regulation 211/2011. The minimum number of signatories required per Member State represented in the Citizens' Initiative is set out in Annex I of the Regulation.

33 Regulation 211/2011, Article 11.

European Parliament have become self-appointed 'children's rights champions'.[34] This, in turn, has prompted the establishment of an Intergroup on the Rights of the Child for the current parliamentary term (2014-2019). The key aims of the group are to enhance the visibility of children's rights at EU level, not least by mainstreaming the rights of the child across all areas of EU Parliamentary activity. Implicit in this role is an undertaking to engage with children and their advocates at the national level to ensure that EU measures are discharged in a way that impacts meaningfully on children's lives, and to ensure that the measures themselves are compatible with international children's rights norms and principles. While it is too early to evaluate its impact, this simple initiative has succeeded in appointing direct spokespersons for children's rights at the heart of the legal and policy-making process in a way that more formal justice mechanisms have failed (See further chapter 2 of this collection). This, in itself, illustrates the importance of strategic advocacy as a vital instrument for facilitating children's access to European-level justice. With the requisite skill and insight into how to target the right individuals in the right EU institutions with the right message at the right time, children's rights advocacy at this level can generate positive ripple effects and sustained changes in both attitude and practice.

5. How do children complain about EU actions or, indeed, omissions that impede the exercise of their rights?

A fundamental principle of access to justice is the availability of a transparent and responsive complaints mechanism, particularly in cases of alleged rights violations.[35] There are two main non-judicial routes at EU-level through which children and their representatives can hold EU institutions to account for failing to uphold their rights: complaints to the EU Ombudsman; and Petitions to the European Parliament.

34 At the time of writing 96 MEPs were registered as children's rights champions. See further http://www.childrightsmanifesto.eu/.

35 The Council of Europe Guidelines on Child Friendly Justice state that: "Children should have the right to access appropriate independent and effective complaints mechanisms." (III.E.3; IV.A.1.1.a; IV.E.75; V.e). Indeed, it is this very principle that underpins the third Optional protocol of the CRC.

5.1 Holding the EU Institutions to Account for Violations of Children's Rights: The EU Ombudsman

The office of the European Ombudsman was established in 1992 as part of a drive to engage EU citizens in the democratic life of the EU. It became fully operational in 1995 and receives complaints or requests for information and advice about alleged maladministration by the EU institutions, bodies, offices or agencies, with the exception of the Court of Justice of the EU acting in its judicial role.[36] It acts independently of any other EU institution and has the authority to launch a full investigation into allegations of maladministration that are deemed well-founded. It also has the discretion to initiate its own inquiries even when no complaint has been made. In such cases, the complaint is referred to the institution concerned which then has three months to respond and, ideally, take remedial action. If the institution in question does not take steps to resolve the issues, the Ombudsman drafts a report (which may include a series of recommendations) which is then forwarded to the European Parliament and to the EU institution or body subject to the complaint.

While the Ombudsman has been heralded as an important democratic feature of the EU, enhancing the transparency and accountability of the EU administrative process (Gregory and Giddings 2001) it is fair to say that its achievements in enhancing children's access to justice at EU level have been very modest indeed. A minute proportion of the 2,500 or so complaints it receives annually relate to children's rights. Investigations relating to children tend to be connected with relatively marginal issues, such as specific financial or educational benefits accruing to the children of EU institutional employees or the administration of niche European schools (Case: OI/3/2003/JMA), all of which fall within the remit of the Ombudsman only insofar as they are heavily subsidised by the European Commission. Even these marginal complaints have yet to really result in any decisive remedy at EU level (see further the discussion by Iusmen in chapter 6 of this collection).

There might be many reasons for the reluctance of individuals or groups to engage the intervention of the European Ombudsman: at best, it might be because the EU institutions, offices, bodies or agencies are discharging their functions in relation to children perfectly legitimately and effectively, such that no complaints have been warranted. A more likely explanation is that ordinary citizens, including those tasked with representing children, have no knowledge of the Ombudsman's existence or mandate, let alone the mechanisms by which they might submit a complaint. Moreover, such is the re-

36 Article 24(3) TFEU states that every EU citizen has the right to make a complaint to the EU Ombudsman. The duties of the Ombudsman are set out in Article 228 TFEU and in Decision 94/262 of 9 March 1994, [1994] OJ L 113/15.

moteness and bureaucratic complexity of the EU, the average citizen has no means of identifying how and where such maladministration has occurred; they merely live with the consequences of it. This highlights the sobering reality that all but the most informed of individuals regard concerns of EU-level maladministration to be beyond redress, perpetuating what might be more appropriately termed 'passive' democracy. In short, complaints mechanisms such as the Ombudsman might exist, but the majority of individuals have neither the incentive nor the capacity to proactively engage it, even if doing so might stimulate more active and conscientious enforcement of their rights at EU institutional level.

And yet the possibilities of using the Ombudsman to encourage the EU institutions and bodies to follow through on their commitments to fundamental rights – including children's rights – are noteworthy. Jacob Söderman made it abundantly clear from the very early days of taking up office as the first European Ombudsman that if an EU institution or body fails to act in accordance with fundamental rights as required by Treaties (notably Article 6 TEU), this would constitute *ipso facto* an instance of maladministration. Thus, ensuring compliance by the EU with its fundamental rights (including children's rights) obligations is an integral part of the European Ombudsman's mandate.

The potential of the Ombudsman to hold the institutions to account for their human rights compliance is rendered even more forceful as far as children are concerned since the adoption of the EU Charter of Fundamental Rights, with its express obligations to uphold children's best interests as a primary consideration, to ensure that children are heard, to protect children's relationship with their parents (Art 24), to ensure children's access to education (Art 14), and to protect children from exploitative labour or harmful working conditions (Art 32). Consider also the numerous official statements made by the European Commission and European Parliament over recent years, among other things, "to consult children and listen to them" (Commission 2011:13), to "mainstream children's rights in every policy and legislative text adopted" (European Parliament 2014: para 33) and to ensure that the best interests of the child is taken into account in all EU external actions relating to them (Commission 2008: 5). The European Ombudsman provides a transparent, 'reflective' platform for exerting some pressure on the institutions to initiate concrete action in fulfilment of these commitments, even if that only amounts to a query raised by the Ombudsman in her annual report (Vogiatzis 2014: 122). It offers a route by which one branch of the EU machinery can prompt another branch to reflect on the value and impact of its actions, to add substance to what are often ambitious but largely vacuous declarations of intent regarding children's rights, and to identify areas in which additional resources might be invested, both at EU level and at the domestic level, to give useful effect to those commitments. For instance, it is now common for the Ombudsman to scrutinise the Commission's handling of complaints under the infringement process (explained below), which may involve interviewing individual Commission officials and submitting concrete recommendations that are, in turn, made available to the European Parliament. This has proved to be a powerful political tool, as Smith notes:

> In the course of the Ombudsman's investigations into the handling of [infringement proceeding] complaints, he has uncovered some disturbing practices that range from mismanagement, administrative ineptitude, 'high handed and arrogant' treatment of the complainants, a routine lack of reasoning and the potential for corruption due to a lack of administrative controls. These practices have been inured into infringement handling over decades of unregulated activity; without the intervention of the Ombudsman they would no doubt have continued unabated. (Smith 2008: 787)

But the European Ombudsman also plays another important role in terms of liaising with national ombudsmen, particularly in areas where the children's rights issue would be better addressed at the national, as opposed to the European level. National ombudsmen representing children across the EU Member States maintain strong links with the European Ombudsman and, indeed with the other institutions, facilitated through the European Network of Ombudspersons for Children (ENOC). This relationship lends itself to fluid communication between national stakeholders and those at European level, to identify the most appropriate level at which to campaign for effective enforcement of existing children's rights obligations or for the development of new children's rights measures. It is just unfortunate that evidence so far suggests that ENOC is focused less on opening up children's access to and influence over European-level decision-making processes, and more as an opportunity for national ombudsmen to gain (financial and political) support for their localised activities (Thomas, Gran and Hanson 2011).

5.2 Alleged breaches of EU children's rights by EU or domestic level authorities: European Parliament Petitions

Another way of holding those in authority to account in relation to children's rights is by petitioning the European Parliament. The petitions process enables individuals or organisations to bring alleged violations or incorrect applications of EU law by a Member State, local authorities or other institutions, to the attention of the European Parliament (Articles 24 and 227 TFEU). Petitions can be submitted either individually or collectively by EU citizens or those who are resident in a Member State, as well as by legal persons (businesses, associations, civil society organisations) who have their registered office in an EU member state. It can take the form of a request, a complaint or an observation concerning the application of EU law. Alternatively, it can involve a direct appeal to the European Parliament to adopt a position on a specific issue of public or private interest.

Parliament petitions are a particularly alluring mechanism for pursuing children's rights claims because of their simplicity and transparency. Unlike the Citizens Initiative, there are no complicated criteria for collecting signatures, the process is not limited to those of EU nationality, it is not confined to those over the age of 18, and it is a relatively quick process. In fact, there are only two conditions for admissibility: the petitioner must be directly affected by the matter raised (a condition that has been interpreted broadly); and the issue must fall within the scope of EU activity. Importantly, as far as access to justice is concerned, petitioners have the opportunity to observe (online) and even participate in committee debates concerning their petition. The Parliament has a range of remedies at its disposal if a petition is deemed admissible and there are sufficient grounds for further action. For instance, it can make representations to the offending national authorities requesting that they address the concern raised; it may initiate action at EU level in the form of a resolution, or even legislation; or it may request that the Commission issue infringement proceedings against an offending Member State for failure to properly implement their EU legal obligations (considered below).

This accessible and potentially far-reaching mechanism corresponds with the Parliament's long-standing support for children's rights. Of the 1,500 or so petitions heard each year, a relatively small but significant number relate to children. These include: complaints against the Romanian ban on international adoption (Petition 1154/2013); a call for a ban on smoking in public places or other areas in which young children have access (again in Romania, Petition 0951/2013); complaints about cuts to spending on children's services in Italy, Greece and France; complaints against several national courts' rulings on custody, access and parental child abduction proceedings; and several complaints against local authorities in the UK for forcibly removing children from their parents and restricting contact thereafter (Petition 1707/2013 and Petition 2468/2013). The wide-ranging nature of these petitions demonstrate how the EU justice process can be used, not just to challenge remote, top-down laws and policies enacted or omitted by Governments, but to bring authorities to account for alleged breaches of children's rights that are happening on a very localised, everyday basis. What is also interesting about the petitions process is its potential to reinforce domestic processes such as judicial review, with a view to maximising European-wide exposure of and support for issues of individual concern, even if they have only the most tenuous connection with EU law and policy-making competence.

For all of its accessibility, however, the petitions process is not particularly child-rights sensitive. Even if some submissions might be couched in the cosy language of children's rights, in reality they are more concerned with the enforcement of parents 'proprietorial' rights' over their children, making it difficult to extricate from the submissions made (by adults) the specific interests and needs of the children. There is no transparent or routine consideration of the best interests of the child as a mediating principle; no explicit requirement or mechanism by which children's views on the matter can be heard, either directly or through an independent representative; and no discernible attempt to present the findings of such petitions in a way that can be understood by children, regardless of the impact such findings might have on them. The absence of these staple components of child friendly justice significantly undermines the petitions process as a legitimate mechanism for upholding children's rights.

6. How can children harness the EU's authority to hold *Member States* to account for breaching or failing to implement their EU rights?

It has already been noted that access to European-level justice serves a dual function: it holds the EU institutions to account for the children's rights obligations by which they are bound and it activates the EU institutions' authority to ensure implementation of EU children's rights at Member State level. The main non-judicial mechanism for achieving the latter is the European Commission's infringement proceedings.

6.1 Challenging Member States' failure to implement EU law relating to children: Infringement Proceedings

It is somewhat pedestrian to note that explicit integration of children's rights provision within EU law only takes us half way towards protection of such rights; they have to be accompanied by an accessible and effective mechanism of enforcement, and there have to be sanctions for non-compliance. The European Commission plays a key role in this regard. Where a Member State fails to comply with its obligations under EU law, either by failing to implement EU law properly, or by implementing it in a manner that is inconsistent with the law, the Commission can commence infringement proceedings (Article 258 TFEU). Described as "… a unique space of interaction for a multitude of actors" and "… a valuable opportunity for the perceived unaccountable EU institutions to deliver valuable inter-institutional accountability" (Smith 2008: 781) these proceedings are perhaps the most common and accessible justice mechanism at EU level. They are administrative in nature and complaints submitted by individuals are pursued at the discretion of the Commission. They precede (and aim to prevent) court-based-litigation by providing Member States (including any national body controlled by the State) with an opportunity to comply voluntarily with their EU legal obligations.

In the average year, the Commission investigates around 2,500 allegations of Member State non-compliance with EU law per year. There are essentially four stages to the infringement procedure, although most complaints will be dealt with in the first three (largely administrative) stages (Commission 2012). The first stage is *submission of the complaint*. In principle, anyone, including a child, can lodge a complaint free of charge against a Member State for any specific measure (law, regulation or administrative action), or, indeed, the absence of a measure or practice by a Member State which they consider incompatible with EU law. An individual does not have to demonstrate a formal interest in bringing proceedings. Neither does the individual have to prove that they are principally and directly concerned by the alleged infringement. The only condition regarding admissibility is that a complaint has to relate to an infringement of EU law by a Member State. On receiving the complaint, the Commission exercises discretion whether or not to take further action. The second stage is the *investigation*. The Commission examines the complaint further in co-operation with the Member State concerned within one year of the complaint being registered. Within this time, the Commission determines if there are grounds to issue formal infringement proceedings against the Member State or, conversely, whether no further action should be taken. The third stage involves the Commission issuing a letter of *formal notice* to the Member State concerned, defining the subject-matter of the complaint and setting out a period in which the alleged failure must be corrected. If, after the expiry of this period, the Member State is still in breach of its obligations, the Commission may issue a reasoned opinion setting out the legal arguments supporting compliance, the action that needs to be taken to achieve compliance, and fixing a new time limit within which the remedial action must be taken. If the Member State persists in its non-compliance, the Commission may proceed to the fourth, *judicial stage* and issue proceedings before the Court of Justice which may ultimately lead to the imposition by the Court of pecuniary sanctions (Article 260 TFEU).[37] This can include an order for damages in favour of any individual affected by non-implementation of EU law (Cases C-6/90 and C-9/90 *Francovich and Bonifaciv Italy* [1991] ECR I-5375).

---

37 Less than 10% of alleged infractions proceed to this stage (Smith 2008: 782).

Infringement proceedings have already been used to enforce Member States' compliance with their children's rights obligations under EU law. Specifically, since the passing of the deadline for implementation of the EU Trafficking Directive (6 April 2013), the Commission has issued reasoned opinions to 12 Member States[38] requesting compliance. Similarly, the deadline for domestic transposition of the EU Sexual Exploitation Directive was 18 December 2013. Since then, formal notices have been issued against 11 Member States[39] requesting that they fully comply with the requirements set out in the Directive.

While proceedings in relation to these two particular directives are still ongoing, there is some evidence that the very threat of further action by the Court of Justice acts as an effective deterrent.[40] It is a popular option as far as justice proceedings go, insofar as it offers an early-warning mechanism enabling the Commission to admonish Member States for failing to comply with their obligations under EU law, whilst providing them with an opportunity to present their defence. Once the Commission has investigated the matter fully, determined that the breach is still ongoing and issued proceedings before the Court of Justice, it is extremely difficult for Member States to justify their non-compliance. Infringement proceedings thus offer a potentially effective means of achieving compliance with very explicit children's rights obligations, particularly those contained in the raft of EU law relating to criminal law and child protection. As an online form that anyone can submit it is much more accessible and cost effective for children's rights advocates or private individuals than other justice routes.

The difficulty, of course, lies in knowing what is in the law in the first place to be able to identify gaps in implementation. It requires significant, up-to-date knowledge of the transposition dates, content and scope of the obligations imposed by EU measures, and an in-depth understanding of progress made at domestic level to respond to those obligations. In most cases it would not even occur to children and their advocates that binding obligations pertaining to, for example, children's best interests, their right to be heard, the right to legal representation, to expedient decision-making or to non-detention emanate from EU legislation. To be effective, such actions generally require the support of civil society organisations with a specialised and pro-active legal department who can distinguish the EU children's rights entitlement that can be directly claimed from that which requires more crea-

---

38 Cyprus, Belgium, Greece, Hungary, Italy, Malta, Netherlands, Portugal, Romania, Slovakia, Spain and the UK.

39 Cyprus, Greece, France, Germany, Ireland, Italy, Luxembourg, Malta, Netherlands, Portugal, Slovakia and Spain.

40 In the UK, for instance, the recent Modern Slavery Bill represents the UK's attempt to comply with the obligations set out in the EU Trafficking Directive and, indeed with its obligations under international human rights law.

tive advocacy at the national level. For example, the EU Directive on combating child sexual abuse, sexual exploitation and pornography reinforces child victims' protection and support by imposing an obligation on Member States to provide the child with access to free legal counselling and representation without delay, in premises designed or adapted for child victims, by professionals trained to work with children (Art 20). These are qualified rights, however, insofar as they need only be provided in accordance with national procedures; there is no legal requirement that national procedures are themselves compatible with the principles of child friendly justice. It follows, then, that Member States can still comply with the requirements imposed by the Directive by simply providing child victims of sexual exploitation with access to available provision in these areas, even if their established procedures and settings for providing legal assistance to children are lengthy, ill-adapted to children's specific needs, and administered by professionals with no specific child-related training. Evidently, the more effective route for children's rights advocates in this context is to campaign at national level to integrate more explicit, child friendly requirements into national law and process, whilst also building capacity among practitioners on the ground (for example through training programmes) as to how they might adapt practice and processes to meet the aspirations set out in the Directive.

Even where EU children's rights obligations are unequivocal and non-negotiable and specialist legal support is available to initiate a submission to the Commission, it can take several months, years even for such proceedings to result in effective implementation, by which point the child or children originally affected are unlikely to benefit. This point highlights the intrinsically altruistic nature of most EU-level justice proceedings involving children; virtually none provide a quick fix response to the interests of children currently affected by alleged breaches of their EU rights. The best most complainants can hope for is a modest legal or attitudinal shift that may benefit children in the future.

Conclusion: The future of children's access to justice at EU level?

If the EU's role as children's rights adherent is to be persuasive and of international standing, there have to be discernible, accessible mechanisms by which children can influence the way in which laws and policies affecting them are framed. Only then can the EU ensure that its laws are based on the reality of children's lives, experiences and needs. Beyond this, to be truly effective and legitimate in advancing and protecting children's rights, there has to be some way that children can actively enforce the rights that emanate from the EU legal order. Such enforcement mechanisms need to be visible not just at the Member State level, but at EU level too.

This chapter has deliberately extended the analysis of 'access to justice' beyond the adversarial, court-based processes that are routinely associated with the concept to embrace a broader range of democratic mechanisms that facilitate participation in all stages of the legal and policy-making process. In doing so, it has sought to capture the majority of children and their advocates whose claims never get to court, and to explore alternative (non-judicial) opportunities for democratic dialogue with those that wield the decision-making authority at EU level. In doing so, the discussion has sought to highlight and critically evaluate the channels through which children and their representatives can not only react to violations of their rights but, more positively, to actively shape how those rights are expressed in EU law and policy in the first place. Closer scrutiny of existing non-judicial mechanisms in place at EU level reveals that their bureaucratic, skills-, knowledge-, financial-, age- and nationality-based requirements render them distinctly arcane when it comes to pursuing children's claims on a routine basis.

But the process of developing, implementing and monitoring children's rights is not just a question of the EU acting alone; it implies a joint responsibility of a range of actors. At the most basic level the EU can initiate and enact laws but it is for the Member States to actually discharge them and for civil society organisations, parents and others in authority to empower children to claim those rights or to suggest new contexts in which they need to be articulated. Peter Newell, a long-standing advocate of children's rights, provides a fitting reflection on the two-way direction (top-down and bottom-up) in which reform needs to take place to make European level children's rights a meaningful endeavour:

> Fault doesn't just lie at the feet of the EU … one wonders whether children's access to European justice would be any more apparent/effective if all of the mechanisms were refined and adapted to conform with the Child Friendly Justice Guidelines. To be truly effective, this has to be complemented with more investment in awareness-raising and training among those who represent children …; complaining to the Commission about inadequate implementation of EU children's rights obligations by various national actors; or by calling on the European Ombudsman to investigate complaints against European authorities in their administration of the various children's rights duties which they have endorsed …
>
> Let's be clear that children themselves are not going to flood these mechanisms with their own complaints, however child-friendly they become. It is going to remain largely an adult responsibility and obligation to pursue breaches of children's rights: our obligation because of our adult success in breaching them. (Newell 2008: 131)

Significant legal, policy and procedural advancements have been made at EU level to stimulate access to justice and democratic participation in decision-making, but these have occurred largely in isolation from developments in the field of EU children's rights. Consequently, no matter how well-intentioned and persuasively articulated EU children's rights provisions are, they will remain largely decorative until EU-level justice processes are adapted to accommodate children's specific capacities, vulnerabilities and interests.

References

Bartlett, Oliver and Garde, Amandine (2013) Time to Seize the (Red) Bull by the Horns: The EU's Failure to Protect Children from Alcohol and Unhealthy Food Marketing, in: European Law Review 38, 4, pp. 498-520.

Besson, Samantha (2007) Enforcing the child's right to know her origins: contrasting approaches under the Convention on the Rights of the Child and the European Convention on Human Rights, in: International Journal of Law, Policy and the Family 21, 2, pp. 137-159.

Buck, T. and Wabwile, M. (2013) The Potential and Promise of Communications Procedures under the Third Protocol to the Convention on the Rights of the Child, in: International Human Rights Law Review 2, 2, pp. 205-239.

de Boer-Buquicchio, Maud (2008) Preface to International Justice for Children, Strasbourg, Council of Europe.

Communication from the Commission to the Council and the European Parliament updating the handling of relations with the complainant in respect of the application of Union law, COM (2012) 154, final.

Communication from the Commission of 25 July 2001 European governance - A white paper, COM(2001) 428, final - Official Journal C 287 of 12.10.2001.

European Commission Strategy for the effective implementation of the Charter of Fundamental Rights by the European Union COM (2010) 573, final, 19 October 2010

Communication from the Commission to the European Parliament, the Council, the European Economic and Social Committee and the Committee of the Regions, An EU Agenda for the Rights of the Child, COM(2011) 60, final.

Communication from the Commission to the Council, the European Parliament, the European Economic and Social Committee and the Committee of the Regions: A special place for children in EU external action {SEC(2008) 135} {SEC(2008) 136}, COM (2008) 0055, final.

Council of Europe (2008) International Justice for Children, Strasbourg, Council of Europe.

Council of the European Union (2014) Draft Council Conclusions on the promotion and protection of the rights of the child Brussels, 18 November 2014, 15559/14.

European Parliament (2014) Resolution on the 25th anniversary of the UN Convention on the Rights of the Child, 2014/2919(RSP).

EU Fundamental Rights Agency (2015) Handbook of European Law on the Rights of the Child, Vienna, FRA.

Guidelines of the Committee of Ministers of the Council of Europe on child friendly justice, adopted by the Committee of Ministers on 17 November 2010 at the 1098th meeting of the Ministers' Deputies, 2010.

Daly, Aoife (2011) The right of children to be heard in civil proceedings and the emerging law of the European Court of Human Rights, in: The International Journal of Human Rights 15, 3, pp.441-461.

Dashwood, Alan et al. (2011) Wyatt and Dashwood's European Union Law, Oxford, Hart.

Fortin, Jane (2006) Accommodating Children's Rights in a Post Human Rights Act Era, in: Modern Law Review, 69(3), pp. 299-326.

Feria-Tinta, Monica (2014) The CRC as a Litigation Tool Before the Inter-American System of Protection of Human Rights, in: Liefaard, Ton and Doek, Jaap (eds) Litigating the Rights of the Child, London, Springer.

Garde, Amandine (2011) Advertising Regulation and the Protection of Children-Consumers in the European Union: In the Best Interests of … Commercial Operators?, in: International Journal of Children's Rights 19, pp.149-171

Garde, Amandine (2013) Food Marketing and Childhood Obesity: Is there a Link?, in: Sociology Review 23, pp. 10-12.

Gregory, Roy and Giddings, Philip (2001) Citizenship, Rights and the EU Ombudsman, in: Bellamy, Richard and Warleigh, Alex (eds) Citizenship and Governance in the European Union, London, Continuum.

Kilkelly, Ursula (2001) The Best of Both Worlds for Children's Rights? Interpreting the European Convention on Human Rights in the light of the UN Convention on the Rights of the Child, in: Human Rights Quarterly, 23(2), pp. 308-326.

Kilkelly, Ursula (2009) Child Law and the ECHR: issues of Family Life, Adoption and Contact. In Kilkelly. Ursula (ed.) ECHR and Irish Law 2nd Ed, Bristol, Jordans.

Kilkelly, Ursula (2011) Protecting Children's Rights under the ECHR: The Role of Positive Obligations, in Northern Ireland Legal Quarterly 61, 3, pp 245-261.

Liefaard, Ton and Doek, Jaap (eds.) Litigating the Rights of the Child, London, Springer.

Macaulay, Margarette May (2008) Access of children to the Inter-American Court of Human Rights, in: Council of Europe, International Justice for Children, Strasbourg, Council of Europe.

Meyler, Frances and Woodhouse, Sarah (2013) Changing the Immigration Rules and Withdrawing the 'Currency' of Legal Aid: The Impact of LASPO 2012 on Migrants and their Families, in Journal of Social Welfare and Family Law 35, pp. 55-78.

Newell, Peter (2008) The principles of child-friendly justice at international level, in: Council of Europe, International Justice for Children, Strasbourg, Council of Europe.

Nolan, Aoife (2011) Children's Socio-Economic Rights, Democracy and the Courts, Oxford, Hart.

Nyamutata, Conrad (2014) From Heroes to Victims: An Analysis of the Mutation of the Social Meaning of Child Soldiering, in: International Criminal Law Review 14, 3, pp. 619 - 640.

O'Donnell, R. and Hagan, M. (2014) Connect: Identifying good practices in, and improving the connections between actors involved in reception, protection and integration of unaccompanied children in Europe, Project Report, accessible at: www.connectproject.eu.

Save the Children (2009) Improving Accountability for Child Rights: The Need for a New International Mechanism, Policy Brief, London, Save the Children.

Seifu, Helen (2008) Access of children to the African human rights protection system, in: Council of Europe, International Justice for Children, Strasbourg, Council of Europe.

Smith, Melanie (2008) Enforcement, monitoring, verification, outsourcing: the decline and decline of the infringement process, in: European Law Review 33, 6, pp. 777-802.

Smith, Melanie(2015) The evolution of infringement and sanction procedures: of pilots, diversions, collisions and circling, in: Arnull, Anthony and Chalmers, Damian (eds.) The Oxford Handbook of EU Law, Oxford, Oxford University Press.

Stalford, Helen (2014) Using the Convention on the Rights of the Child in litigation under EU law, in: Liefaard, Ton and Doek, Jaap (eds) Litigating the Rights of the Child, London, Springer.

Stalford, Helen and Drywood, Eleanor (2011) The Use of the CRC in EU Law and Policy-Making, in: Invernizzi, Antonella and Williams, Jane (eds) The Human Rights of Children: From Visions to Implementation, Aldershot, Ashgate.

Stalford, Helen and Schurmann, Mieke (2011) Are we there yet?: The Impact of the Lisbon Treaty on the EU Children's Rights Agenda, in: International Journal of Children's Rights 19, 3, pp. 381-403.

Thomas, Nigel, Gran, Brian and Hanson, Karl. (2011) An independent voice for children's rights in Europe? The role of independent children's rights institutions in the EU, in: International Journal of Children's Rights 19, 3, pp. 429-449.

Tobin, John (2012) Courts and the construction of childhood: A new way of thinking, in: Freeman, Michael (ed.) Law and Childhood Studies: Current Legal Issues. Oxford, Oxford University Press.

Vogiatzis, N. (2014) Communicating the European Ombudsman's Mandate: An Overview of the Annual Reports, in: Journal of Contemporary European Research, 10, 1, p. 122.

Walker, Lara and Beaumont, Paul (2011) Shifting the Balance Achieved by the Abduction Convention: The Contrasting Approaches of the European Court of Human Rights and the European Court of Justice, in: Journal of Private International Law 7, 2, pp. 231-249.

Developing a Model for Mainstreaming Children's Rights into EU Law and Policy-making

Mieke Schuurman[1]

1. Introduction

It is widely acknowledged that the EU needs a more comprehensive approach to the promotion and protection of children's rights now that the first official EU children's rights Agenda (European Commission 2011a) has come to an end and legal and policy measures relating to children have proliferated. Mainstreaming children's rights allows for a comprehensive approach to any key priorities insofar as it enables children's rights to be firmly embedded in all EU-level processes. This, in turn, achieves sustainability and rigor in the EU's future children's rights activities. With the Council of the European Union (Council of the European Union 2014) and the European Parliament (European Parliament 2014) stressing the importance of mainstreaming children's rights, the question remains as to how this can be achieved in practice. In seeking to respond to this question some valuable lessons can be drawn from other mainstreaming models, both nationally and internationally.

This chapter reports on the findings of a year-long study carried out by the author on behalf of Eurochild (Eurochild 2014), a network NGO promoting the rights and well-being of children in Europe. The study was aimed at developing a child-mainstreaming model to guide EU processes and activities relating to EU legislation, policies, budgetary decisions and judicial decision-making. The primary focus of Eurochild is EU internal policy with a view to promoting the rights and well-being of children across the Member States. Nonetheless the study recognises the importance of ensuring coherence with the EU's external policy, including enlargement, neighbourhood, development cooperation, trade and external action. There have already been some attempts to mainstream children's rights into EU external activities. The EU-UNICEF Child Rights Toolkit on Integrating Child Rights in Development

---

1 External child rights consultant and policy advisor to Eurochild. This chapter is based on a study led by the author and funded by Eurochild. Thanks go to the members of Eurochild's *'Expert group on the impact of the Lisbon Treaty on Children's Rights'* and to Mafalda Leal (Senior Policy Coordinator) and Jana Hainsworth (Secretary General), all of whom provided valuable feedback on the design, implementation and reporting of the study.

Cooperation (UNICEF 2014), in particular, can usefully inform the development of a more robust internal mainstreaming mechanism.

This chapter should be seen as complementary to the strategic report *Realising the rights of every child, everywhere: Moving forward with the EU* (Eurochild/UNICEF 2014). Mainstreaming children's rights in EU processes should be one of the two key pillars, next to a pillar with concrete actions, in a new EU Framework on Children's Rights, which should succeed the EU Agenda on Children's Rights.

Background to the study

The study on which this discussion is based involved interviews with a range of EU officials (European Commission, Council of the European Union and input from the European Parliament) (European Parliament 2012). Fourteen officials from the European Commission and three officials from the European Council Secretariat were interviewed about how children's rights are mainstreamed into their current work, including preparing current and recent legislative proposals and policy proposals. This included questions on their knowledge of the UNCRC and EU legal mechanisms to guarantee children's rights. Suggestions for improving the mainstreaming of children's rights were also taken on board. Officials were asked about their cooperation with civil society and their expertise on children's rights and whether they had consulted with children directly.

The Commission officials interviewed included nine desk officers, three heads of unit, a Commissioner's Cabinet member and the children's rights co-ordinator and included Directorate Generals Justice, Home Affairs, Education, Culture, Multilingualism and Youth, Employment, Social Affairs and Inclusion, TRADE, Health and Consumers, Communications Networks, Content and Technology, and Enterprise and Industry.

In general, all of the officials were aware of the content of the UNCRC, though some had more knowledge than others because of previous work experience, training and education. All of the persons interviewed were aware of the inclusion of children's rights in the objectives of the Lisbon Treaty and the Charter of Fundamental Rights, though, according to some officials, this is not always reflected in the legislative process.

In addition, a literature review was carried out, analysing academic articles on mainstreaming of children's rights. The study identified best practices at EU level, as well as a range of best practice examples of mainstreaming children's rights at the national level. The Directive 2012/29/EU of the European Parliament and of the Council establishing minimum standards on the rights, support and protection of victims of crime (the Victims Directive) was explored in more detail as an example of children's rights having been effectively mainstreamed.

2. Child Rights Mainstreaming: A review of current practice

Mainstreaming is a familiar concept at EU level. It is supported by specific provisions of the Treaty on the Functioning of the European Union[2] and has been firmly embedded in EU policy and legislative processes for a host of cross-cutting issues, including: gender equality, fundamental rights, disability, health care[3], environmental protection, consumer protection and culture.

The most prominent area in which mainstreaming has been developed and applied is in the gender equality arena,[4] The gender mainstreaming process is based on a gender mainstreaming strategy, 'Strategy for equality between women and men 2010-2015' (COM (2010) 491, final), which refers to girls and clearly works on the equality of men and women. Girls are referred to in relation to violence and stereotypes. Key features underpinning the success of the EU's gender mainstreaming model are its legal base in the Treaty (Art 8 TFEU). Key to the success of the gender mainstreaming, according to the European Women's Lobby (EWL), has been the institutional framework, which is in place to drive the process. According to the EWL an institutional framework is needed to drive the process, which includes: political will, bringing several actors on board, data, impact assessment, financial means, human resources, training and the participation of the people concerned at the different stages of the process (Eurochild/Euronet 2007)

Institutionally and politically, support comes from the Inter-service group representing most DGs which meets every half year with the Gender Equality Unit to look at progress on the EU's strategy on gender mainstreaming based on a list of actions adopted by the Member States every three years. These components are complemented by a focus on capacity building: training programmes are offered by the Gender Equality Unit, including the discussion of case studies and a programme with concrete actions.

---

2 See Article 8 on gender mainstreaming; Article 152 on public health; Article 153 on consumer protection; Article 151 on culture and Article 174 on the environment.

3 'Health in all policies' is one of the key principles of the EU Health Strategy. Implementation of the health strategy is supported by a Council working party on public health meeting at senior level and an inter-service group on public health, in which more than 20 departments are represented, including sub-groups on dynamic health systems, global health, health and the environment(evidence obtained from project respondent).

4 The definition of gender mainstreaming is "... the (re)organisation, improvement, development and evaluation of policy processes, so that a gender equality perspective is incorporated in all policies at all levels and at all stage, by the actors normally involved in policy making" (Council of Europe, 1998).

2.1 How does the EU mainstream children's rights?

So to what extent can mainstreaming models applied in areas of EU law and policy, including gender mainstreaming, inform the development of a children's rights mainstreaming strategy? An initial, constitutional obstacle to simply transposing mainstreaming into a children's rights context is the fact that, unlike in other areas such as gender, there is a less explicit Treaty obligation to mainstream children's rights across the Union's areas of activity (Drywood 2011: 405-428). That said, there is a reference to children in the objectives of the Treaty (Art 3 TEU). (Drywood 2011: 405-428) Moreover the EU institutions have to ensure that their actions are in line with the EU Charter of Fundamental Rights provisions, including the dedicated child rights provisions in Article 24, and the equality commitment contained in Article 20 (Bell 2004: 252).[5] These commitments are even more persuasive since with the entry into force of the Treaty of Lisbon, by which the Charter became legally binding on the EU institutions and on national governments to the same extent as a the EU Treaties (Art 6(1) TEU).

In policy terms, mainstreaming is identified by the Commission as a central plank of the EU's developing children's rights agenda:

> The EU's commitment to the rights of the child requires a coherent approach across all relevant EU actions. This objective can be reached by using the Treaties, the Charter of Fundamental Rights of the European Union and the UN Convention on the Rights of the Child (UNCRC) as a common basis for all EU action which is relevant to children. The 'child rights perspective' must be taken into account in all EU measures affecting children (European Commission 2011a)

In the same vein, a study commissioned by the European Parliament Committee on Civil Liberties, Justice and Home Affairs, in its Note *EU Framework of Law for Children's Rights* (European Parliament, 2012) includes specific recommendations regarding the development of a more comprehensive mainstreaming strategy. Recommendation 6 of the Note states:

> The European Parliament should call on the Commission to develop a plan for the *mainstreaming of children's rights* in all areas of EU competence, informed by the principles of the UNCRC. The elements of such a plan might include, for example: 1) taking further into consideration children's rights and needs within the EU institutions such as varying childhood and adolescence situations including disadvantage and exclusion; 2) further enhancing children's rights expertise within the EU institutions; 3) coordination within EU institutions aimed specifically at addressing children's rights; 4) on-going monitoring to evaluate the impact of the mainstreaming process.

---

5 E. Drywood has used Bell's definition, who stated that mainstreaming should be regarded as an equality issue and defined it as the "integration of equality considerations into all aspects of policy formulation, implementation".

2.2 Shortcomings in EU children's rights mainstreaming

The main shortcomings of the EU's current approach to mainstreaming children's rights have been revealed by several academics who have criticised, in particular, the inadequate attention paid to children's rights in the legislative process.

Eleanor Drywood has looked, for example, at the EU's asylum and immigration law (Drywood 2011: 404-428). Children can experience these procedures differently from adults even if these regulations are supposed to be age-neutral. Drywood refers to the inconsistent attention to children's rights across the EU asylum and immigration directives; some directives make explicit reference to the importance of upholding the best interests of the child (Asylum procedures Directive 2003/9/EC, Article 18 (1)), whilst others do not include a single reference to children's rights principles (Long-term residents Directive 2003/109/EC). Another criticism is that even where reference is made to a children's rights principle, on the whole a fairly low level of children's rights protection is endorsed. For example the apparent endorsement of detention centres to house child asylum-seekers (particularly those over the age of 16) have been heavily criticised by children's rights NGOs (Save the Children 2012).

Similarly, Amandine Garde (Garde 2011: 523-545) challenges the inadequacy of mainstreaming of children's rights within the EU's internal market and consumer policies, and illustrates this by reference to two instruments: Directive 2005/29 on Unfair Commercial Practices (UCP Directive) and the Audio-visual Media Services Directive (AVMS) (OJ 2010 L 95/1). The UCP Directive explicitly recognises that children constitute a group of particularly vulnerable consumers deserving special protection, and age is referred to as a relevant criterion for determining the impact of a commercial practice on consumers (UCP Directive 2005/29, Article 5(3) and Point 28 Annex I). However, according to Garde, the wording of the UCP Directive is too restrictive to support the argument that it upholds the best interests of the child. She refers to the *travaux preparatoires* which do not contain any evidence that the question of whether advertising to children is inherently unfair has been at all discussed. Moreover, she identifies, on the basis of an analysis of the wording of Article 5(3) UCP Directive 2005/29, several gaps in the protection the Directive offers to children. In particular, she points out that the Directive allows "the common and legitimate advertising practice of making exaggerated statements or statements which are not meant to be taken literally" – even though children are the very consumers most likely to take exaggerated statements literally (Garde 2011: 528).

In the same token, the AVMS Directive includes provisions to protect children from advertising and harmful contents, but while the AVMS Directive provides that "audio-visual commercial communications shall not cause moral or physical detriment to minors" by directly targeting minors, the use of the word 'directly' restricts the scope significantly (Ibid.: 533). Garde also argues that the AVMS Directive does not sufficiently protect children from the harmful effects of alcohol and HFSS[6] food … and recommends that the protection of children's health should be strengthened within this Directive in light of existing evidence on the impact of alcohol and food marketing on children's consumption patterns and purchase requests (Bartlett and Garde 2013: 498).

Regarding the EU's work-family reconciliation framework, consideration of children's needs have been missing according to Grace James (James 2012: 363-379). Reconciliation measures have traditionally been developed, promoted and critiqued as a means of promoting gender equality and economic growth within the EU and is an area that is not routinely considered from a children's rights perspective. For example the Pregnant Worker's Directive (Council Directive 92/85/EEC), which entitles women to a minimum of 14 weeks leave, has underestimated the plurality of pregnancy and birth experiences and their impact on children's needs (James 2012: 363-379)

Studies such as these reveal the shortcomings of wider areas of EU legislative provision for children and further reinforce the importance of developing a more comprehensive EU-level mainstreaming strategy. A range of criteria for mainstreaming children's rights have been suggested as a result of this body of research. These, coupled with the outcomes of the interviews with EU officials and best practice models identified at national level, have informed the development of a 'seven steps' approach to effective child rights mainstreaming (discussed below).

2.3 Better outcomes for children when mainstreaming children's rights

The most important reason for effective mainstreaming of children's rights in EU policies and legislation is that this would lead to better compliance with the CRC. Integration of the principles of the CRC would act as a 'child-proofing tool' and ensure that the EU abides by the Convention. According to the UN Committee on the Rights of the Child, a continuous process of child impact assessment (predicting the impact of any proposed law, policy or budgetary allocation which affects children and the enjoyment of their rights) and child impact evaluation (evaluating the impact of the implementation)

6 Foods and beverages high in fat, trans-fatty acids, salt/sodium or sugars, whose excessive intake is not recommended as part of a balanced diet are so-called HFSS food.

has to take place at all levels of government and as early as possible in the development of policy (UN Committee on the Rights of the Child 2005: General Comment No. 5). Both of these processes are implicit in a child mainstreaming strategy.

All stakeholders have to bear in mind that no policy is child neutral (De Vylder 2004: 431). This means that any policy can have unintended consequences for children, as the examples detailed below illustrate. Therefore a process to legislate or develop policies and budgets needs to anticipate its impact on children with a view to mitigating their negative and maximising their positive consequences.

3. Child Rights Mainstreaming: *Lessons from Practice*

It is recommended that the EU follows seven steps to ensure thatchildren's rights will be at the heart of all that the EU does and that the process is transparent and authentic. The steps are as follows:

- Step 1 requires political will and leadership.
- Step 2 requires awareness, capacity and resources within the services responsible.
- Step 3 requires a commitment to apply the CRC.
- Step 4 requires the application of mainstreaming tools to legislation, policy and funding throughout the policy cycle.
- Step 5 entails the systematic use of impact assessments in policy formulation and implementation.
- Step 6 ensures the consultation and involvement of stakeholders in decision-making.
- Step 7 ensures that the views and experiences of children and young people are elicited and taken seriously.

To illustrate how these steps can be applied, good practices examples from across the EU Member States have been collected. These examples illustrate where children's rights mainstreaming has led to a real improvement for children and/or their rights. It should be noted, however, that the selected good practices examples are not presented as 'perfect' cases of mainstreaming that meet all seven criteria. Rather, the selection aims to highlight how particular aspects of our mainstreaming model can be achieved effectively.

3.1 Step 1: The need for political will and leadership

Without leadership and political will children's rights will not be mainstreamed consistently in the EU's legislation, policies and budgets. It was political will (particularly within the European Parliament and EU governments) that led to the inclusion of children's rights within the Treaty on European Union and which has supported the development of a number of child-focused measures within the EU's *acquis*.

It follows, then, that the most persuasive expression of political will to mainstream children's rights is where it is embedded as an explicit constitutional obligation. For example, The Rights of Children and Young Persons (Wales) Measure 2011 requires Welsh Ministers to "have due regard" to children's rights when working on or developing proposed new legislation, proposed new policies and any review of, or change to, an existing policy (Welsh Government, Children's Rights Scheme 2012). Under the Welsh process, government staff will need to follow six steps, starting with identifying which piece of work is being reviewed and applying the due regard duty by reference to the relevant CRC rights. They then check that the proposed policy or legislation does not breach any of those rights and identify what action the Welsh Minister could take next. The Minister will then respond to this advice through appropriate action.

3.2 The impact of political will and leadership on the EU's role as children's rights actor

Leadership and political will to implement children's rights is relevant to all decision making levels, including local, regional, national and the EU. At EU level political will and leadership has already led to several positive impacts for children's rights, such as the 2013 European Commission Recommendation 'Investing in children: breaking the cycle of disadvantage' (OJ L 59, 2.3.2013: 5-16). This Recommendation stresses the importance of early intervention and preventative approaches to reduce the risk of child poverty and social exclusion among children. The Belgium EU Presidency contributed a lot to this Recommendation, whilst the Spanish Presidency in the same year adopted gender and children's rights, in particular unaccompanied minors, as its key priorities (Kehoe 2010).

Regarding the leadership within the European Commission it is recommended that this is not only left to a single fundamental rights and children's rights unit within DG JUST. In this respect the divide between internal and external dimensions should be bridged by using the EEAS Child Rights

Guidelines (EU Guidelines for the Promotion and Protection of the Child 2007), which serve as a framework to observe as a matter of priority the promotion and protection of all children's rights in the EUs external human rights policy via all available tools, and the EU-UNICEF Child Rights Toolkit on integrating child rights in development cooperation (UNICEF 2014).

The European Parliament as co-legislator and budgetary authority needs to be encouraged to take leadership for promoting children's rights and should be championing children's rights through their inclusion in all European Parliament political documents and processes. The Parliamentary Committee on Civil Liberties, Justice and Home Affairs (LIBE) in principle is tasked with leading on children's rights, but in reality children's rights constitutes a relatively limited part of its work. In an informal exchange with Eurochild in 2012, the LIBE Committee secretariat declared that mainstreaming children's rights currently remains the only realistic possibility to advance the children's agenda. This was formally reinforced by the newly elected European Parliament in its Resolution on the 25th anniversary of the UN Convention on the Rights of the Child, adopted in November 2014 (European Parliament Resolution 2014). In this Resolution, the European Parliament:

> ...calls on the Commission to ensure increased coordination within its different services with a view to effectively mainstreaming children's rights in all EU legislative proposals, policies and financial decisions and monitoring their full compliance with the EU acquis on children and with obligations under the UN Convention on the Rights of the Child. It also calls on the Commission to ensure that the mandate and resources of the children's rights coordinator adequately reflect the EU's commitment to systematically and effectively mainstreaming children's rights. (European Parliament Resolution 2014, para. 7)

Positive changes have already occurred within the Parliament, which indicate that these aspirations might well be achieved. Notably, following a campaign of a group of 14 international and European children's organisations around the European Parliament elections, over a hundred newly-elected members of the European Parliament have signed up to a Children's Rights Manifesto (http://childrightsmanifesto.eu/), which amongst others called for the creation of a permanent mechanism in the European Parliament with explicit responsibility for protecting and promoting children's rights across all policy sectors in internal and external affairs. This call was brought into practice by a decision of the European Parliament to create a parliamentary Intergroup on children's rights in December 2014. This is an important step forward in having a permanent child rights governance system in place at a political and decision-making level in the EU. Though a parliamentary intergroup has no formal decision-making power, it can play an important role in contributing to the mainstreaming of children's rights in EU policies and legislation, both in the context of internal and external action. To achieve this, the Intergroup should ensure the representation of its members as 'focal points' in the different

Committees of the European Parliament, with at least one MEP focal point in each Committee. The co-chair of the Intergroup, Annamaria Corazza-Bildt, has already committed to have a focal point on children's rights and well-being in each parliamentary committee who is also a member of the Intergroup. They can then alert the Intergroup on files that would have an impact on children in the respective committees.

With regard to the Council of Ministers, the extent to which they mainstream children's rights depends on their willingness and knowledge. This is something of a challenge given that the Council needs to deal with 28 different Member States, with different cultures on children's rights and the rotating Presidencies, all of which have different priorities. However, the EU Presidencies can be a driver for children's rights, as was seen in the example given above of the Belgium Presidency contributing to the development of the Commission Recommendation, 'Investing in Children'. The Council of the European Union in its Conclusions on the promotion and protection of the rights of the child in November 2014 (Council of the EU 2014) invites both Member States and the European Commission to give full recognition to children as rights holders. It also calls on Member States, the High Representative and the Commission to ensure that the rights-based approach endorsed by the Council in its earlier Conclusions of May 2014 pays due regard to children's rights and to their mainstreaming in all EU policies and actions.

According to Drywood there is a need for a willingness among the key actors to drive forward a children's agenda and one has to overcome the myriad competing agendas that exist in any area of legal and policy activity (Drywood 2011: 425). Adding to this is that the political climate can change and, with this, the political will to mainstream children's rights lose momentum. It is therefore important to have a mainstreaming process in place, which will function regardless of the political climate. The recent initiatives outlined above mark an important step in creating a more sustainable commitment in this regard. With political will to mainstream children's rights demonstrated by all three main EU institutions – the European Commission, the European Parliament and the Council of the European Union – the next step is to adopt a robust successor to the Agenda on the Rights of the Child, including a resource effective mainstreaming of children's rights in all EU processes.

3.3 Step 2: Awareness, capacity and resources in the services responsible

Political will alone does not guarantee that mainstreaming is successful. Officials and politicians developing policies and legislation need to be informed and trained on children's rights.

Further investment in training and awareness-raising among key personnel within the EU is important to develop the appropriate level of capacity to mainstream children's rights. Within the European Commission Inter-service Group on Children's Rights (ISG), members have been calling for more training, including on mainstreaming of children's rights and the content and scope of the CRC. From interviews with officials in different DGs it turned out that officials would like to have more targeted training in the area of their work and within their DG. It was also raised that training should not only focus on the usual 'suspects in the ISG', but also extend to those working outside this group.

Next to training and awareness-raising among officials and politicians, changing public opinions and mobilising individuals to act is equally important. Both adults and children must be informed and convinced about children's rights and understand this in practice. This step is rooted in General Comment No. 5 (Art 42 CRC), which states that States have to make the CRC known to adults and children so that they can actively claim and enforce their rights. Various Eurobarometer surveys reveal that knowledge and understanding of the CRC among children and young people is generally low (Eurobarometer reports 2010, 2009 and 2008), but children in vulnerable situations, including Roma children, children in alternative care, children in juvenile justice institutions, disabled children, etc. is known to be even lower (Eurochild 2012).

3.4 Step 3: Commitment to use the CRC as the starting point

The CRC is the most comprehensive statement of children's rights, applying to all aspects of their life, with broad international consensus. If the EU assesses its policies against the CRC it will promote positive outcomes for children and reinforce existing international efforts to comply with the obligations set out therein.

Experience shows that placing the CRC at the centre of primary law (e.g. the national constitution) facilitates inclusion of a children's rights perspective within secondary legislation and budgetary instruments. This is highlighted by two national examples in particular.

The CRC was ratified by Austria in 1992, but was initially given a low legal standing. Its constitutional status was denied, and Parliament also prevented its direct application by the Austrian authorities. The Convention could not be relied on in courts, or provide a legal basis for initiating child rights impact assessments of draft legislation nor for checking compliance of existing laws with CRC standards. Consequently, it had little meaningful legal impact in practice. Once this gap was identified, the Austrian National Coalition for the Implementation of the CRC engaged in a lengthy lobbying action to raise the legal status of the Convention. The main objectives of the action were to clearly and comprehensively establish children as holders of constitutional rights, to end the questioning of their capacity to hold and to claim rights, and to establish a binding legal basis for mainstreaming of children's rights into legislation, policy and practice. The 'Federal Constitutional Act on Children's Rights' (*Bundesverfassungsgesetzüber die Rechte von Kindern*) was eventually adopted and entered into force in 2011. Although not as comprehensive as was advocated by civil society it contains seven substantial Articles on key principles and rights, some of them taken almost literally from the CRC, and a final Article on the responsibility of the entire government for its implementation. Furthermore, legislation effective as of 2013 imposes a mandatory impact assessment of draft legislation on children, and its accompanying guidance documents make explicit reference to the CRC and the Children's Rights Act (The Federal Constitutional Law on the Rights of the Child (Federal Gazette I No. 4/2011). Although the formal assessment of the impact of the Children's Rights Act is yet to be undertaken, the constitutional guarantees such as the ones introduced in Austria provide an important foundation on which more child-friendly, CRC-compliant law and policy can be enacted.

In 2006, the then Taoiseach Bertie Ahern, TD, in Ireland committed to hold a children's rights referendum and following a general election in 2007, a Joint Parliamentary Committee on the Constitutional Amendment on Children was established to examine how to "elevate the rights of all children in the Constitution" and to propose wording for the amendment. In 2010, an all-party consensus was reached on the wording and this was published in 2011. The Government committed in its 2011 *Programme for Government* (Government of Ireland 2011) to hold a referendum to amend the Constitution to strengthen children's rights. On 19 September 2012, the Government published the Thirty-first Amendment to the Constitution Bill, which contained the revised text of a proposed constitutional amendment. On 10 November 2012 the referendum was held and the People of Ireland voted 58% to 42% in favour of the Thirty-first Amendment. While the amendment does not incorporate the UN Convention on the Rights of the Child (CRC) into the Irish Constitution, it does, however, reflect certain aspects of the Convention, namely the best interests of the child and hearing the views of the child in certain circumstances. Once the amendment is signed into law it will require further legislation to implement the principles contained within it and this will provide a further opportunity to ensure that significant legislation, which will impact on children, will be underpinned by children's rights.

Why is using the CRC as a starting point relevant to the EU?

The EU has a constitutional obligation to adhere to the principles and provisions set out in international human rights law, including the CRC, in relation to those matters that fall within the scope of EU competence. Child Rights mainstreaming is a crucial mechanism for ensuring that EU activities are fully compatible with the CRC. The Children's Rights Unit (DG Justice) is responsible for mainstreaming children's rights in all Commission proposals, including all future legislation as well as funding regulations. They make use of the fundamental rights check list[7], CRC country reports[8], alternative reports submitted to the UN Committee on the rights of the child by civil society organisations, a wide range of studies and the UNICEF Implementation Handbook on CRC (Hodgkin and Newell 1998). DG EMPL makes use of some of these resources, but not other DGs. There is no support for developing a child rights checklist within the Commission hierarchy, but there is support for the development of a more comprehensive guide on children's rights mainstreaming, which would achieve a greater level of consistency and quality and assist Commission services for whom children's rights mainstreaming is not yet an obvious task.

Adopting the CRC as the starting point for all EU-level decisions affecting children does not mean that a simple reference to the CRC is sufficient. Nor doesit mean that the dominant focus should be on protecting children's welfare. Rather, the impact of legislation needs to be assessed by reference to all of the rights contained within the CRC that are relevant to the legislation. In that sense, the UNCRC should be regarded not simply as a starting point, but rather as a referral framework within which all EU legislation, policies and budgets has to be developed.

An example of good practice where the EU has taken the CRC into account is the EU Victim's Rights Directive (2012/29/EU), which makes specific provision for child victims.It is a horizontal directive meaning that it is focusing on victims' rights throughout criminal proceedings and includes several provisions to protect and promote the rights of children.[9]

7 To facilitate the fundamental rights impact assessment, the Commission in 2011 provided in its 'Staff Working Paper: Operational guidance on taking account of Fundamental Rights in Commission Impact Assessments'. This Commission working paper provides guidance, accompanied by a range of legislative examples and taking the fundamental rights check list as a basis. Communication from the Commission 'Strategy for the effective implementation of the Charter of Fundamental Rights by the European Union', COM (2010) 573, final, 19.10. 2010.

8 Periodic Country Reports submitted by State parties to the UN Committee on the Rights of the Child can be found on the UN Committee's website.

9 The Directive has to be transposed by the EU Members States into national laws, regulations and administrative proceedings by 16 November 2015. The United Kingdom and Ireland

The Commission's proposal for the EU Victim'sRights Directive was published following an impact assessment, external study and consultations with interested parties and stakeholders, including children's rights advocates. The Justice and Home Affairs Council suggested several amendments to the Commission proposal and the most significant improvements for children were that information provided to victims had to be provided in a "simple and accessible language" (2012/29/EU: Art.3.2) and "for the purposes of this Directive children shall be presumed to have specific protection needs due to their vulnerability ..." and therefore need specific protection (2012/29/EU: Art 22.4). Similarly, the European Parliament report on the Commission's proposal for a victims' directive proposed many amendments to strengthen the protection of child victims in line with the CRC (European Parliament Report 2012).

Many of the European Parliament's amendments were supported by the Commission, which proposed to deal with them as a 'package' in the negotiations between the European Parliament and the Council – which proved successful. Together these two institutions convinced the Member States, led by the Danish Presidency, to adopt the European Parliament's child specific amendments resulting ina much higher level of protection of child victims and guaranteed a child rights approach. In particular the reference to the specific needs of child victims in the objectives of the Directive (Article 1) ensured a general mainstreaming of children's rights across the Directive. But also specific CRC provisions regarding non-discrimination (2012/29/EU: Art 3.2), the right to participate (2012/29/EU: Art 10), guaranteeing the best interests of child victims (2012/29/EU: Art 1), information provision (2012/29/EU: Art 3) privacy and appropriate treatment for recovery (2012/29/EU: Art 21) have been explicitly incorporated into the directive.

3.5 Step 4: Mainstreaming applies equally to legislation, policy and funding and throughout the policy cycle

A mainstreaming process needs to be comprehensive. This means remembering a children's perspective not only in legislative processes but also in soft law and policy measures, funding and programming and judicial proceedings. In federal states, like Austria, Germany and the UK, this means that national processes will have no impact at all if these are not mainstreamed and linked to the regional level of government, where in many cases the resources relevant for children are located. In practice, it appears that these other policy

have decided to opt-in in the adoption of the directive and Denmark is not taking part and will therefore not be bound by it.

areas are often forgotten or mistakenly deemed to have little impact on children's rights.

In general, state budgets are not very clear in reflecting what proportion is to be spent on children, and need to become more comprehensive and accountable as to the extent to which they take children's perspectives and interests into account.

Why is mainstreaming equally important in all EU processes?

At the EU level in particular, there are many issues affecting children, which are not covered by 'hard' legislation, but by soft law measures and/or specific funding programmes. For example Europe 2020 (European Commission 2010), specifically addresses the issue of combating child poverty and social exclusion. It sets concrete targets for children and youth with a focus on education and training. Such targets include the reduction of early school leavers to less than 10% and giving all children access to early childhood education and care (European Commission 2011 b). The Europe 2020 Strategy additionally established a flagship initiative, 'Youth on the Move', that aims to improve education and training systems at all levels (Youth on the Move 2012). Another example is the Commission Recommendation 'Investing in Children: breaking the cycle of disadvantage' (European Commission Recommendation 2013), which provides a wide range of angles from which to address child well-being: it talks about social investment towards children, adequate income, quality services and child participation.

Notwithstanding their relatively weak (non-binding) legal status, soft law measures are an invaluable means of developing children's rights in areas that fall outside the strict legal competence of the EU. It follows, therefore, that they should be equally subject to a child rights impact assessment.

3.6 Step 5: Impact assessments are applied systematically

An *ex ante* child impact assessment is needed at an early stage of the process to reflect what possible impact legislation and policies can have on children, and to take this into account when drafting proposals. However, mainstreaming of children's rights in policies and legislation does not stop with the adoption of a legislative act or a policy but continues throughout the implementation process. Next to the *ex ante* impact analysis, there is a need for a continuous monitoring of the impact of adopted legislation and policies, in other words an *ex post* impact analysis is needed. The implementation of laws and policies can result in an impact on children and young people which had not been foreseen during drafting; monitoring of implementation is therefore necessary to ensure that the children's perspective has not been lost. This includes scrutiny of how the Court of Justice or the European Ombudsman deals with child-related cases.

The UN Committee on the Rights of the Child in its General Comment No 14 on the right of the child to have his or her best interests taken as a primary consideration (UN Committee on CRC General Comment 14 (2013): Art 3, para 1) and in General Comment No 5 on general measures of implementation of the CRC (UN Committee on CRC General Comment 5 (2003): para 45) refers to the need for States and Governments to carry out a continuous process of child rights impact assessment (CRIA) to predict the impact of any proposed law, policy or budgetary allocation on children and the enjoyment of their rights. According to General Comment No 14, CRIA needs to be built into Government processes at all levels and as early as possible in the development of policy and other general measures in order to ensure good governance for children's rights (para 99).

Garde calls for an integrated child impact assessment for all EU initiatives with a potential economic, social and/or environmental impact, which should apply to most legislation, White Papers, action plans, expenditure programmes and negotiated guidelines for international agreements (Garde 2012). Similarly, Drywood calls for a systematic child impact assessment of legislative proposals before these are adopted (Drywood 2011) and refers to the set of child rights indicators, which have been developed on behalf of the EU's Fundamental Rights Agency, as a potential model for achieving this (Fundamental Rights Agency Report 2009).

Why are systematic impact assessments relevant to the EU?

Impact assessments of child-rights-related legislation have been shown to have a discernible impact on the substance of the EU legislation. As the example of the EU Victim's Directive revealed (2012/29/EU), a child impact assessment had not been carried out prior to drafting the legislative proposal. This resulted in a number of important omissions on the specific situation of child victims of crime. The European Parliament later corrected this thanks to the involvement of interested parties and external experts.

A good practice example at domestic level of an *ex ante* impact analysis is found in Flanders in Belgium, where a child impact report is required by law. In 1997, the Flemish Government in Belgium introduced a child impact report, abbreviated KER, which was developed into 'child and youth' impact report, abbreviated JoKER, by the *Decree* of 18 July 2008. JoKER *is an ex ante impact assessment which* uses the rights-based approach rooted in the CRC. The aim of the JoKER is to enable policy makers to reflect on how the proposed regulations will impact on children and young people. Every legislative proposal submitted by the Flemish government that has a direct impact on the interests of persons under the age of 25 has to be accompanied by a JoKER.

The JoKER has to include a description of the impact of the proposed decision on the situation of the child or young person. It must contain what the impact on their situation would be without the proposed decision as well as the alternatives, including a description of measures that must be taken to avoid, limit or remedy important negative consequences of the future legislation on the child or the young person. Such a process can be a powerful instrument for protecting children's rights. That said, the JoKER model has revealed that in order to have impact and to be able to influence the decisions and proposed legislation, the assessment should be undertaken for every legislative initiative and launched as early as possible in the elaboration of new legislation.

Next to the *ex ante* impact analysis, the European Commission has a particular duty to monitor the implementation of EU legislation, meaning that they need to assess whether EU laws are implemented in the right way and are producing the desired outcomes. With regard to fundamental rights, a check-list has been developed to assess the compatibility of EU legislation with fundamental rights as enumerated in the EU Charter of Fundamental Rights (European Commission 2005). According to Commission officials interviewed, these guidelines are taken very seriously; fundamental rights are taken into account from the start of the legislative process throughout the process, including during negotiations with the Member States. The fundamental rights and rights of the child unit in DG JUST uses this checklist to monitor the implementation of legislation and produces progress reports for internal use.

Commission officials throughout different Directorate Generals have provided a wide range of examples where they have included children's rights in their legislative and policy work. The majority of those interviewed indicated that the main competence for this is allocated to the fundamental rights and children's rights unit in DG JUST. It is not surprising, therefore, that with the exception of DG JUST, there is no comprehensive approach to undertaking children's rights impact assessments across other Commission departments. Moreover, Commission officials had differing views on the importance of mainstreaming children's rights: in relation to legislative proposals they considered it to be of higher priority, almost an obligation to do so, while for policy and other proposals, it was not considered necessary.

A good example of a sustained approach to monitoring and assessing the impact of particular measures on children is found in Bulgaria. The implementation of their National Strategy, 'Vision for Deinstitutionalisation of Children in the Republic of Bulgaria' evidences a long-term commitment to mainstreaming children's rights through the comprehensive mobilization of all national resources, interest groups and the general public. Adopted in

2010 and rooted in the CRC, the Strategy commits to abolishing the existing specialised institutions for children within a 15-year period. To respect the commitments of the Strategy, a pragmatic Action Plan was adopted, specifying the activities, tasks, responsibilities and resources for implementing the Strategy. The Action Plan set up an institutional framework for its implementation that included NGO representatives, experts and public authorities.

The practical implementation of the Action Plan was assessed by the Bulgarian Council of Ministers in October 2011 and a report produced. The Bulgarian commitment to deinstitutionalization was also included in its 2012 National Social Report submitted to the European Commission as part of the Europe 2020 monitoring process. The final element of the comprehensive approach to deinstitutionalisation in Bulgaria was the decision to underpin the implementation of the National Strategy using the EU Structural Funds to create a lasting change for Bulgarian children.

3.7 Step 6: Stakeholders are consulted and involved in decision-making

To ensure that a proposal takes into account the multitude of issues required for comprehensive and effective mainstreaming, all interested parties must be involved in the process of agreeing on a law or a policy. The process of consultation must be continuous and transparent. This means that the parties should be able to find out what policies and laws are subject to impact assessment, what the process of assessment looks like and what information and evidence is being taken into account. They need to be provided with necessary information, facilities and time to provide their input, and the results of the consultation and any changes that were made as a result need to be communicated to them. This enables them to challenge or improve the process, and hold the decision-makers to account for ensuring a meaningful and rigorous process.

The CRC Committee in its General Comment No. 14 states that impact assessments of proposed legislation and policies "could be based on input from children, civil society and experts, as well as from government departments, academic research ..." (Art 99), and in General Comment No. 5 it sets out that State Parties need to engage with all sectors of society (Art 56), these include professionals, families, communities, NGOs and the private sector.

Note has to be made of a possible conflict of interest between the different stakeholders, where private actors, for example industry representatives, which are powerful in the EU, may impact negatively on the public interest and on children's rights and interests (as seen, for instance, in the context of consumer protection law – see further Garde, 2011). A transparent and inclusive process for involving expert stakeholders needs therefore to be in place. Civil society and organisations advocating for children's rights are as responsible as the EU institutions themselves for achieving this; they have a responsibility to engage proactively with the EU institutions, to represent children's interests and voices in all relevant legal and policy developments (see further Stalford, Chapter 1 and the conclusion of this collection).

An example of involving civil society organisations in social and economic policies of the government can be found in the social partnership agreement in Ireland. The current social partnership agreement – *Towards 2016: Ten-Year Framework Social Partnership Agreement 2006-2015* (Taoiseach website) – uses a social policy approach based on the lifecycle of the citizen which focuses on specific groups including children, people of working age, older people and people with disabilities.

The Community and Voluntary Pillar is one of the five pillars of the social partnership alongside the Employers Pillar, the Trade Union Pillar, the Farmers Pillar and the Environmental Pillar. The Community and Voluntary Pillar consists of seventeen organisations invited by the Government to provide voice and representation for vulnerable people and communities in developing Ireland's social and economic policies. The Children's Rights Alliance is an active member of the Community and Voluntary Pillar, and has been a designated Social Partner since 2003, advocating on behalf of children and feeding directly into elements of the policy-making process. As part of this agreement, the Irish Government has "committed to involving the Social Partners in the development of policy, to ensure meaningful input by the Partners into the shaping of appropriate individual policy issues, on the design of implementation arrangements, and to provide the Partners with sufficient notice, information and appropriate process for engagement" (Taoiseach website). The Alliance participates in a number of bilateral meetings with officials from different government departments throughout the year including the Departments of Finance and Public Expenditure, Education, Social Protection and Health.

Each year the Alliance makes a Pre-Budget submission to the different government departments and attends the Pre-Budget forum hosted by the Department of Social Protection. In 2013, the Department of Social Protection carried out a Social Impact Assessment of Budget 2013 and found that families with children were most impacted by cuts in that budget (Department of Social Protection 2013). Civil society organisations are also invited to present to parliamentary committees on their Pre-Budget submissions to brief members on relevant issues.

In addition to the Irish example, in France, in 2005, the Act Reforming Child Protection Provisions was drafted with the continuous involvement of all interested parties, including NGOs representing children, children's services providers, parents, and social workers, in every stage of the process. 15

working groups comprising experts from public agencies, districts, NGOs and universities were constituted by the Minister for Health and Solidarity. It was his personal commitment which ensured these consultations took place. From the beginning of the process, the CRC served as a basis for the development of the Act. Once it was adopted, the Ministry was put in charge of its enforcement in line with the CRC philosophy. The resulting French Child Protection Act has greatly contributed to mainstreaming children's rights in France and demonstrated the added value of early and continuous involvement of a broad range of interested parties to the quality of legislation on child rights.

Why is it relevant for the EU to consult and involve stakeholders in its decision-making process?

The European Commission now more readily consults with the public about the issues it plans to address. In addition, it often conducts targeted consultations with the parties that are directly concerned by a specific proposal (critically discussed by Stalford in Chapter 1 of this collection). Making this consultation open and accessible to civil society organisations, service providers, children and young people themselves, parents and academics potentially strengthens the process, improving the quality of the final product. European Commission officials consulted during our study indicated that most of them consult to some degree with civil society, though these are not necessarily children's rights NGOs. Additionally, the Fundamental Rights and Rights of the Child Unit of the Commission are routinely consulted in the inter-service consultation of the Commission, ensuring that there is at least some opportunity to consider the children's rights implications of a proposed measure.

Drywood, observing the crucial role played by the European Women's Lobby in developing an accountable and comprehensive gender mainstreaming strategy, calls for more routine, detailed input from children's civil society in the Commission's decision-making. She also observed from the gender mainstreaming process that the representation of women in decision-making bodies stimulated this process (Drywood 2011: 417). Though this could not be exactly replicated for children, there are numerous examples of children participating in EU youth events, and there is scope to think more creatively about how national children's rights advocates (such as ombudspersons) might be deployed at a higher level to represent children's perspectives in EU law and policy making processes. (Ibid.: 420-421).

Services working on internal market initiatives rarely consult with children's rights NGOs. For example, the lack of meaningful consultation with children's rights experts during the drafting of the Audio-visual Media Directive (OJ 2010 L 95/1) resulted in the virtual absence of children's perspectives in the Directive (Garde 2011: 523, see further Stalford, Chapter 1 of this collection). According to a Commission official interviewed for the study, the NGOs they consult only give subjective views and not what is scientifically proven to be harmful to children. This shows the need to encourage EU officials to be selective in their consultation with NGOs to ensure that their input is both truly reflective of the community they purport to represent and grounded in verifiable evidence. More generally, Garde calls for a stronger involvement of children's rights advocates in the legislative process in all areas of EU intervention, including areas which have traditionally been perceived as affecting children only indirectly or tangentially (Garde 2011; Garde 2012).

Within the Council Secretariat there is very little contact with civil society organisations and experts on children's rights. They noted that they would like to receive more information from civil society and other external experts on how the EU's legislation is working in practice.

As already noted, the responsibility for engaging in civil dialogue does not lie solely at the feet of the EU; there is a need for civil society to engage more effectively in EU-level legislative and policy making processes. But to stimulate more routine engagement of this nature requires some capacity building and transparency at EU level and national level, to build clearer channels of communication between EU decision-makers and those working with children at grassroots level.

3.8 Step 7: The views and experiences of children and young people are sought and taken seriously

Children's representation by civil society organisations and the direct participation of children is a requirement laid down by the CRC. Article 12, in particular, states that "States Parties shall assure to the child who is capable of forming her or his views the right to express those views freely in all matters affecting the child, the views of the child being given due weight in accordance with the age and maturity of the child". This is reinforced by the Council of Europe Recommendation on 'Participation of children and young people under the age of 18' (Recommendation CM/Rec (2012) 2), which states that it needs to be ensured that "participation is mainstreamed in decision- and policy-making structures" (Section II: Principles).

Decades of research shows that meaningful involvement of children and young people in the decision-making process not only makes it more legitimate in the eyes of society and of children, but also facilitates implementation of the resulting measures and strengthens their sustainability and impact (Austin 2010: 245-253; Tisdall 2010.: 318-329; Theis 2010: 343-355). Children are best placed to define what problems they have and what solutions work for them. Central to this endeavour is the participation of children from different backgrounds, including children living on the margins of society (socially, economically, legally, politically, culturally, physically and mentally), to ensure appropriate representation.

Why is it relevant to the EU to seek the views of children and young people?

At the European, as well as the national level, children's opinions contribute to good outcomes. Of course, the logistics of achieving direct participation and representation of the EU's 100 million children are more challenging at supra-national level. However, there are numerous national mechanisms by which children can voice their opinions, which can be communicated to the EU representatives through nominated delegates. Within the European Commission most officials indicated that they never consult with children and young people for different reasons such as 'no time' and 'not appropriate due to the subsidiarity principle'. There are, however, positive exceptions, such as DG EAC, which routinely consults with young people and DG SANCO, which involved young people in its Youth Health Initiative (European Commission DG SANCO (2009). DG EMPL which has tried to build on the outcomes of research projects involving children directly and to explore ways to strengthen their participation, for example by involving them in the Cypriot EU Presidency meeting (October 2012). However, these initiatives mainly involve young people aged 15 years and older; engaging with younger age groups and children in vulnerable situations remains a challenge.

Again, civil society plays a key role in representing children's views and experiences at EU level, in facilitating children's direct involvement in EU level consultations, and in raising awareness of EU-derived entitlement among children and their advocates. Eurochild, for instance, has enabled children to contribute to discussions around a number of EU policies, such as the Belgium EU Presidency conference on child poverty in September 2011, which contributed to the eventual adoption of a Commission Recommendation on child poverty and child welfare (Belgium EU Presidency 2011).

There are many national examples which stress the immense value of child participation and which have led to positive outcomes for children. For example in Lithuania, the 'Stop Bullying' campaign led by Child Line Lithuania has sought to draw children and teenagers' attention to bullying and to stimulate the development of bullying prevention measures. The campaign is driven by children and since 2010 they organise annual anti-bullying weeks. The campaign has contributed to a discernible decline in bullying across Lithuania (abbreviated 'Health Behaviour in School Aged Children Study' Currie et al. 2012).

In the Netherlands the city of The Hague routinely involves children and young people in public life through mechanisms such as The Hague Youth

Ambassadors. They advise the municipality of The Hague and meet with local decision and policy makers on a regular basis to make the needs of the youth known to them.

Conclusions

The commitments of the European Commission in its Agenda for Children's Rights, the European Parliament in its Resolution on the 25th anniversary of the CRC, and the Council Conclusions on the promotion and protection of the rights of the child all indicate a clear political will across the EU institutions to take a lead in mainstreaming children's rights. This should serve to embed international children's rights standards more firmly in the development and implementation of EU measures.

Mainstreaming of children's rights in policies, legislation, budgeting, programming and judicial proceedings needs to be a transparent process. This does not stop with the adoption of a legislative act, a policy, programme or budget, but continues throughout the implementation process. The seven step process outlined above suggests a model that would ensure that children's rights, as laid down in the CRC, are at the heart of EU policy and legislation processes: political will and leadership; awareness, capacity and resources within the services responsible; commitment to use the CRC as the starting point; application of mainstreaming tools to legislation, policy and funding throughout the policy cycle; systematic use of impact assessments in policy formulation and implementation; consultation and involvement of stakeholders in decision-making and the seeking of the views and experience of children themselves.

To achieve these steps a range of actions need to be initiated. Firstly the European Commission has to propose a comprehensive and robust successor to the Agenda on the Rights of the Child. Such a framework would include two pillars. One pillar should focus on specific time-bound and well-resourced actions in substantive areas where the EU can have the greatest added value, and be accompanied by an action plan, with ambitious and measurable objectives. The second pillar would focus more on the procedures by which these actions were achieved, central to which should be a comprehensive mainstreaming strategy, covering the EU's internal and external policies, and accompanied by the requisite financial and institutional resources. It is also recommended that the European Commission's coordinator on children's rights is accorded the necessary power, autonomy and resources to be able to effectively coordinate the interventions across different DGs. In this way, she could act as a more formal focal point for scrutinising children's rights compliance within the European Commission.

The European Commission is also encouraged to further develop its idea of an internal manual or tool (inspired by EU-UNICEF Tool 2014) on children's rights mainstreaming, and invest sufficient resources in developing capacity building-initiatives (training) and consultations to support the inclusion of children's perspective in the work of all its services. Such training should support more interdisciplinary and inter-sectorial working within the European Commission. At the same time the EU acquis and policy documents on the rights of the child (European Commission 2013) need to be critically audited to identify the potential for further strengthening them to protect children's rights.

With regard to the European Parliament, the newly established Intergroup on children's rights will have to take a lead in ensuring that the Parliament adheres to the CRC when adopting measures. To contribute to this it is crucial that members of the Intergroup are appointed as Focal Points in each of the different Committees of the European Parliament.

The Council of Ministers has to take leadership and be a driver for the implementation of children's rights across the Member States, and indeed across the other EU institutions. This could involve establishing within the Council Secretariat a child rights focal point. This would play a vital coordinating role with the other EU institutions and bridge the gap between the internal and external dimension of the EU when promoting children's rights.

Last but not least, civil society plays a critical role in the innovation, empowerment and engagement of children and young people, particularly through their campaign and advocacy activities. Strengthening their capacity and involvement in decision-making processes can contribute to the recognition of children as active agents and bearers of rights. In this respect the European Union would benefit from greater collaboration with the UN Committee on Children's Rights.

If the EU were to implement the seven mainstreaming steps in combination with the recommendations described above it could make significant strides in advancing children's rights, not just within Europe but across the world.

References

Austin, S. (2010) Children's participation in citizenship and governance, in: Thomas, N. and Percy-Smith, B. (eds) A Handbook of Children and Young People's Participation: Perspectives from theory and practice, Oxon, Routledge.

Bartlett, O. and Garde, A. (2013) Time to Seize the (Red) Bull by the Horns: The EU's Failure to Protect Children from Alcohol and Unhealthy Food Marketing, in: European Law Review 38 (4) p. 498.

Belgian Presidency of the Council of the European Union (2011) Conference: 'Who Cares? Roadmap for a recommendation to fight child poverty', http://www.mi-is.be/sites/default/files/doc/EN-Report%20child%20poverty_BAT.pdf, last accessed August 2015.

Council of the European Union (2014) Draft Council conclusions on the promotion and protection of the rights of the child: From Presidency To Permanent Representatives Committee (Part 2)/Council, 15559/14, Brussels, 18 November 2014.

Council of Europe (2012) Recommendation of the Committee of Ministers to Member States on the participation of children and young people under the age of 18, CM/Rec (2012) 2.

Currie C. et al. (eds) (2012) Social determinants of health and well-being among young people: Health Behaviour in School-aged Children (HBSC) study: international report from the 2009/2010 survey, Copenhagen, WHO Regional Office for Europe (Health Policy for Children and Adolescents, No. 6).

Department of Social Protection Ireland (2013) Social impact assessment of the main welfare and direct tax measures in Budget 2013, available at: http://www.welfare.ie/en/downloads/2013-03_SIABudget2013_Final.pdf. Last accessed August 2015.

De Vylder, S. (2004) Macroeconomic issues and the rights of the child, in: Weyts, A (ed) Understanding Children's Rights: Collected Papers presented at the Seventh International Disciplinary Course on Children's Rights, Ghent, Children's Rights Centre, University of Ghent.

Drywood, E. (2011) Child-proofing' EU law and policy: interrogating the law-making processes behind European asylum and immigration provision, in: International Journal of Children's Rights 19(3), pp. 405-428.

Eurobarometer reports (2010, 2009 and 2008) available at: (www.tinyurl.com/eurobarometer-2008, www.tinyurl.com/eurobarometer-2009, www.tinyurl.com/eurobarometer-2010).

Eurochild and UNICEF (2014) Realising the rights of every child, everywhere: Moving forward with the EU, available at: http://issuu.com/eurochild_org/docs/eurochild_unicef_realising-children. Last accessed August 2015.

Eurochild (2014) Mainstreaming Children's Rights in EU Legislation, Policy and Budget, Lessons from Practice, Discussion Paper, Unpublished.

Eurochild, Euronet Report (2007) Mainstreaming children's rights in EU policy, Event at European Parliament, Brussels, Unpublished.

Schuurman, M. (ed.) (2012) Speak Up! Giving a voice to European children in vulnerable situations, Project Report, Eurochild.

European Commission (2005) Compliance with the Charter of Fundamental Rights in Commission legislative proposals – Methodology for systematic and rigorous monitoring, Communication from the Commission, COM (2005) 172, final.

European Commission (2010) EUROPE 2020: A strategy for smart, sustainable and inclusive growth, Communication from the Commission, COM (2010) 2020.

European Commission (2010) Strategy for equality between women and men 2010-2015 COM (2010) 491, final.

European Commission (2011a) An EU Agenda for the Rights of the Child, Communication from the Commission, COM (2011) 60, final.

European Commission (2011b) Tackling early school leaving: A key contribution to the Europe 2020 Agenda, Communication from the Commission to the European Parliament, the Council, the European Economic and Social Committee and the Committee of the Regions COM (2011)18.

European Commission (2013) EU acquis and policy documents on the rights of the child, Version 1.1, JUST.C1/MT.

European Commission, DG Health and Food Safety (2009) Youth Health Initiative, available at: http://ec.europa.eu/health/population_groups/children_young_people/index_en.htm.

European Commission Recommendation (2013) Investing in children: breaking the cycle of disadvantage, OJ L 59, 2.3.2013, pp. 5-16.

European Parliament (2012) EU Framework of Law for Children's Rights, Note, DG for Internal Policies, Policy Department C, Citizens' Rights and Constitutional Affairs, PE 462.445.

European Parliament (2012) Report on the proposal for a directive of the European Parliament and of the Council establishing minimum standards on the rights, support and protection of victims of crime (COM (2011) 0275 – C7-0127/2011 – 2011/0129 (COD)), Committee on Civil Liberties, Justice and Home Affairs, Committee on Women's Rights and Gender Equality, A7-0244/2012, 18 July 2012.

European Parliament (2014) Motion for a Resolution to wind up the debate on the statement by the Vice-President of the Commission/High Representative of the Union for Foreign Affairs and Security Policy on the 25th anniversary of the UN Convention on the Rights of the Child (2014/2919(RSP)), B8-0285/2014, 24.11.2014.

European Union Fundamental Rights Agency (2009) Developing indicators for the protection, respect and promotion of the rights of the child in the EU, Summary Report, accessible at: http://fra.europa.eu/sites/default/files/fra_uploads/358-RightsofChild_summary-report_en.pdf Last accessed August 2015.

EU Guidelines for the Promotion and Protection of the Rights of the Child (2007), available at: http://eeas.europa.eu/human_rights/guidelines/child/docs/16031_07_en.pdf. Last accessed in August 2015.

EU-UNICEF (2014): Child Rights Toolkit: Integrating Child Rights in Development Cooperation, UNICEF.

Garde, A. (2011) Advertising Regulation and the Protection of Children-Consumers in the European Union: In the best interests of … Commercial Operators?, in: International Journal of Children's Rights 19(3), pp. 523-545.

Garde, A (2012) The Best Interest of the Child and EU Consumer Policy: A Major Gap between Theory and Practice?, in Devenney, J. and Kenny, M.(eds) The Theory and Practice of EU Consumer Law and Policy, Cambridge, Cambridge University Press.

Government of Ireland (2011) Programme for Government 2011, Dublin, Stationary Office.

Hodgkin, R. and Newell, P. (1998) Implementation Handbook for the Convention on the Rights of the Child, UNICEF.

James, G. (2012) Forgotten children: work-family reconciliation in the EU, in: Journal of Social Welfare and Family Law, 34, 3, pp. 363-379.

Tisdall, E. (2010) Governance and participation, in: Thomas, N. and Percy-Smith, B. (eds) A Handbook of Children and Young People's Participation: Perspectives from theory and practice, Oxon, Routledge.

Kehoe, K. (2010) The Spanish Presidency Priorities – the same game but different rules, in: The Institute of International and European Affairs, Blog, http://www.iiea.com/blogosphere/the-spanish-presidency----the-same-game-but-different-rules.

Save the Children (2012) Save the Children's position on the Asylum and Migration Fund 2014-2020 available at: https://www.savethechildren.net/sites/default/files/libraries/SC_position_Asylum_and_Migration_Fund_horizontal_regulation_2014_2020.pdf.

Taoiseach (Irish government)(2006) Towards 2016: Ten-Year Framework Social Partnership Agreement 2006-2015, Social partnership agreement, available at: http://www.taoiseach.gov.ie/attached_files/Pdf%20files/Towards2016PartnershipAgreement.pdf.

Theis, J. (2010) Children as active citizens: an agenda for children's civil rights and civic engagement, in: Thomas, N. and Percy-Smith, B. (eds) A Handbook of Children and Young People's Participation: Perspectives from theory and practice, Oxon, Routledge.

UN Committee on the Rights of the Child (2013) General comment No. 14 on the right of the child to have his or her best interests taken as a primary consideration, CRC/C/GC/14, 29.
UN Committee on the Rights of the Child (2003) General comment No. 5 on general measures of implementation of the Convention on the Rights of the Child, CRC/GC/2005/5.
Welsh Government (2014) The Children's Rights Scheme: Arrangements for having due regard to the UN CRC when Welsh Ministers exercise any of their functions, available at: http://www.assembly.wales/Laid%20Documents/GEN-LD9732%20-%20Children's%20Rights%20Scheme%202014-22042014-255569/gen-ld9732-e-English.pdf. Last accessed August 2015.

Central Authorities and the European Judicial Network: Mainstreaming Children's Rights into Cross-border Cooperation in EU Family Law

Ruth Lamont

Introduction

The EU's Agenda for the Rights of the Child states that: "... it is now the time to move up a gear on the rights of the child and to transform policy objectives into action" (European Commission 2011a: 3). The Union is charged with protecting the rights of the child under Article 3(3) TEU, but putting the rights expressed in the UN Convention on Children's Rights 1989 (CRC) and Article 24 of the Charter of Fundamental Rights of the European Union (Charter)[1] into practice for the individual citizen child across the scope of EU law remains problematic. This contribution will examine the process of mainstreaming children's rights throughout the legal process in the context of EU cross-border family law. It will assess the value of mainstreaming and its challenges as a strategy for children's rights protection by considering the role of two national bodies specifically engaged in implementing European family law: Central Authorities and the European Judicial Network (the Network).

Mainstreaming children's rights into the development of law and policy is one of the strategies advocated as transforming the protection and promotion of children's rights in Europe (Drywood 2011: 412; Schuurman, this volume). In the context of European family law, the inclusion of children's rights in legislation has been relatively successful. However, securing these rights in proceedings is the responsibility of national bodies and courts. For mainstreaming to be effective as a strategy, actors at all levels, supranational and national, must be engaged. Bodies outside the core of the EU's institutional framework cannot be overlooked and should be utilised in developing effective protection of children's rights. The nature of Central Authorities and the Network, existing in the Member State but working with other national bodies across Europe, means that they provide an opportunity to develop the protection of children's rights in European family law by reference to both the CRC and Art 24 of the Charter. Both in their practice of implement-

1 [2010] OJ C 83/02.

ing EU family law, and through their cross-border information sharing processes, both Central Authorities and the Network have the capacity to raise awareness of children's rights and embed rights protection in EU family law both at a strategic, supranational level and in domestic proceedings involving children. This contribution will examine this opportunity, and the current limitations and challenges for mainstreaming children's rights throughout the European legal framework.

Part one discusses mainstreaming in European family law and the opportunities and limitations provided by this strategy. Part two identifies the role of Central Authorities and the Network and their responsibility to secure and promote children's rights in their work. Part three examines the potential for Central Authorities and the Network to build capacity in understanding and developing children's rights protection in cross-border family law, across the Member States.

1. Mainstreaming children's rights in EU family law through Art 24 of the Charter

The EU Agenda on the Rights of the Child emphasises the importance of protecting children's rights in a variety of policy contexts, including EU family law, immigration policy and cross-border criminal justice. The Commission has shown increasing awareness of the broad impact of its activities on children, stating that:

In the future, EU policies that directly or indirectly affect children should be designed, implemented and monitored taking into account the principle of the best interests of the child enshrined in the EU Charter of Fundamental Rights and in the UNCRC. (European Commission 2011a: 3).

Mainstreaming can be defined as the process of accounting for a right or an interest at all stages of policy-making and implementation (Lamont 2011: 368). In the context of gender mainstreaming, Daly has described the process as embedding gender-sensitive practices and norms in the structures and environment of public policy (Daly 2005: 435). Mainstreaming children's rights requires sensitivity and awareness of the needs and rights of children by actors in the policy and legal framework. Incorporating children's rights into policy, even if the policy is not obviously related to children, should mean that issues that affect children differently or require special consideration are addressed before the policy comes into operation, and are taken into account in its implementation. In this way, mainstreaming is intended to embed children's rights into EU law and policy, having a generalised impact on the protection of children's rights across the full range of policy contexts.

Mainstreaming has been welcomed as a strategy for change focusing on organisational processes, structure and culture, having the effect of challenging embedded assumptions across a range of policy frameworks (Ibid.: 440). A recent report by Eurochild has defined child rights mainstreaming as:

…the mechanism of ensuring that all actors involved in EU legislative and policy processes as well as programme design and implementation comply with children's rights, including those that do not explicitly work on children's rights. (2014: 2) (see further: Schuurman, this volume)

A legal basis for mainstreaming children's rights can be identified in the EU treaties: Art 3(3) TEU states that the Union shall "… promote … protection of the rights of the child" as one of its core objectives (see Drywood 2011: 412). This is supported by the European Commission's Agenda which makes explicit reference to a mainstreaming strategy in its own activities (European Commission 2011a: 3). In its Agenda, the Commission makes reference to Art 24 of the Charter on the rights of the child. Art 24 of the Charter contains three rights of direct application to children involved in family law disputes: the right of the child to express their views freely and have their views taken into account in decisions affecting them; in all actions relating to children, the child's best interests must be the primary consideration; and the child has the right to contact with both parents, unless contrary to the child's best interests. The Explanations relating to the Charter of Fundamental Rights[2] identify the basis of the rights expressed in Art 24 of the Charter in the CRC (see Lamont 2014). The Commission supports this approach, suggesting that the standards and principles of the CRC should guide EU policy and action (European Commission 2011a: 3).

All EU Member States are signatories to the CRC and are obligated to secure the rights expressed in the CRC in their territory. EU activity may provide a further motivator to action these rights in the national environment. In addition, under Art 51 of the Charter, when implementing EU law, the Member States are required to respect the rights expressed in the Charter, including the rights of the child under Art 24. The authority for the implementation of children's rights in practice at the national level can be based upon a combination of EU law, Art 51 of the Charter, and Member States' obligations to comply with the CRC.

International family law is an apposite context in which to explore the processes of mainstreaming children's rights. The importance of securing children's rights in family law proceedings has been prioritised by the EU Agenda on the Rights of the Child as an aspect of 'child-friendly justice' (European Commission 2011a: 6). The Agenda focuses on the importance of Art 24(3) of the Charter and the maintenance of contact between the child and both parents, and securing the well-being of the child in family proceed-

---

2 OJ [2007] C303/17.

ings. EU private international family law is one area of European law where children's rights have been most clearly articulated and identified as an aspect of the legal framework. The rights expressed in Art 24 are explicit in the text of the Regulation 2201/2003 (hereafter Brussels II Revised), regulating jurisdiction in parental responsibility disputes, and international child abduction in the EU.[3] Indeed, Brussels II Revised offers "… one of the most prolific sources of children's rights at EU level" (Stalford 2012: 116). Referring to Art 24 of the Charter, Recital 33 of Brussels II Revised states that the legislation should be interpreted in accordance with children's rights. The legislation contains specific guarantees, for example requiring decisions over transfers of jurisdiction to be taken in the child's best interests (Art 15) and requiring a child of appropriate age and maturity to be heard in abduction return proceedings (Art 11(2)). The explicit inclusion of children's rights in the text is evidence of the consideration of children's interests in the development of family law legislation by the EU.

Beyond Brussels II Revised, children's rights are less clearly embedded in the legislative framework. The Maintenance Regulation,[4] which manages cross-border applications and enforcement of decisions on child maintenance, and the Regulation on the cross-border taking of evidence[5] in civil proceedings do not contain direct reference to the Charter or to children's rights. Despite omission from the text, compliance with Art 24 is implicit in their implementation. Actions taken under these Regulations will be implementing European law and as such will fall under the scope of the Charter (Art 51) and must respect the rights expressed in Art 24.

2. Making child rights mainstreaming effective in European family law

Mainstreaming was originally adopted by the EU as a tool in policy-making in relation to gender, where it has a much longer history (European Commission 1996; Schuurman, this collection). Gender mainstreaming is now based on Art 8 TFEU which states that the EU shall aim to eliminate inequalities, and promote equality between men and women. Although gender main-

---

3 Regulation 2201/2003 concerning jurisdiction and the recognition and enforcement of judgments in matrimonial matters and the matters of parental responsibility, repealing Regulation 1347/2000 [2003] OJ L 338/1.

4 Regulation 4/2009 on jurisdiction, applicable law and enforcement of decisions and cooperation in matters relating to maintenance obligations [2009] OJ L 7/1.

5 Regulation 1206/2001 on cooperation between courts of the Member States in the taking of evidence in civil or commercial matters [2001] OJ L174/1.

streaming is clearly established, experience has demonstrated that there are difficulties in effectively operationalising mainstreaming in practice (Lamont 2011: 371-373). First, the conception of the rights pursued as the basis of mainstreaming is important for the outcome in the policy created. Secondly, for mainstreaming to be effective in practice requires commitment and support to provide training of all actors in the policy-making and implementation process. Isolated pockets of expertise are not sufficient to raise awareness of rights across all spheres of policy-making and implementation activity. Mainstreaming often requires engagement with external bodies of expertise, but unless awareness of rights is strong enough to highlight that there may be a concern to be addressed, mainstreaming loses its effectiveness. Thirdly, Pollack and Hafner-Burton have identified that as the EU is a multi-level polity, mainstreaming not only requires implementation by all the EU institutions, including the Commission, the European Parliament and the Council of Ministers, but also within the different national legal and policy orders (2000: 442). The challenges identified by Pollack and Hafner-Burton are also relevant to mainstreaming children's rights into EU law and policy.

2.1 The conception of rights underpinning mainstreaming

The weight to be placed on the different rights expressed in Art 24, and their implementation in practical situations remains contested and not clearly defined (Lamont 2014: 678). This reflects the underlying tensions in the CRC that Art 24 draws upon. Commenting on the rights expressed in Art 24, McGlynn states that: "Article 24(1) is a curious mix of what might loosely be termed children's 'protection' and 'empowerment' rights, which are often found to be in conflict" (2002: 397). This comment on Art 24 highlights the apparent tension between the right of the child to be heard and to have their opinion taken into account expressed in Art 24(1), and the right of the child to have decisions taken with their best interests as the primary consideration under Art 24(2).

A paternalistic approach to the child's best interests may emphasise the child's need for protection, potentially undermining the importance of their participation and opinion in decision-making affecting their interests (Fortin 2009: 19). Realisation of the child's developing interest in choice and their own autonomy may pose a direct challenge to the protection of the child's *best interests*, as perceived by an external decision-maker (Ibid.: 23). The processes designed to protect these rights must take account of this tension and identify how decision-makers are to hear a child and reconcile and incorporate his/her opinion with his/her best interests. Stalford has highlighted that, thus far, in its policies related to children's rights the EU has focused on the protective conception of children's rights, calling it the 'hegemony of child protection' (Stalford 2012: 224).

The Court of Justice has not closely debated the tensions within Art 24 in the context of family law, but has favoured a paternalistic approach over engaging with the child's opinion and its effect on the decision of the court (Lamont 2014: 685). This was evident in Case C-403/09 PPU *Deticek* [2009] E.C.R. I-12193 where the Court did not address the weight to be placed on a child's opinion, but instead focused on Art 24(3) and the right of the child to have contact with both parents as being in the child's best interests. The Court's approach to children's rights is important because it sets the tone for implementation of Art 24 across the EU. However, as Stalford had identified, most of the decisions taken in relation to children will be taken at the national level, by national bodies and judges. There remains significant scope for difference and national interpretations of the rights expressed in Art 24 (Stalford 2012: 113-115). This has two elements, first, in defining the content and meaning of the 'child's best interests', including the relationship between the child's opinion (if elicited and/or expressed) and their best interests. Secondly, the procedures for securing a child's rights, particularly the processes for hearing the child during proceedings vary widely (Parkes 2013: 48).

The indeterminacy of Art 24 means that the rights expressed are open to cultural difference and interpretation, impacting on the realisation of Art 24 in the particular national context informed by national traditions of rights protection under the CRC. All EU Member States have ratified the CRC, but face the same questions in terms of interpreting the rights in practice. The conception of children's rights adopted at the national level may differ between the Member States and even between bodies within the Member States. The first difficulty with mainstreaming, the conception of the underpinning rights, is evident here as each national interpretation may be legitimate. There is space for negotiation over scope and meaning of rights in the EU context.

The extent to which Art 24 rights are realised and protected is dependent on those interpreting and applying the law in practice (Stalford 2012: 117). The conception of children's rights adopted by any actor in a mainstreaming process will affect how the policy is both formed and implemented. The choices that are made by individual policy actors can effectively enable child participation in decision-making, but if the 'hegemony of child protection' is adopted, the emphasis will be on notions of the child's best interests with the child's opinions playing less of a role in decision-making. Either approach may be regarded as politically legitimate, but it must be acknowledged that these choices will underpin mainstreaming, and affect the outcomes of the process as it is applied to different policy contexts.

2.2 Resourcing and training for child rights mainstreaming

To accurately identify concerns affecting children's rights during policy-making and what it means to respect and promote children's rights in implementation, understanding of children's rights must be developed across a range of actors. This training should provide guidance on the nature of children's rights, the balancing of children's rights against one another and against other rights, and the methods and processes for the effective protection of children's rights. The scope and purpose of the training however, may depend on the nature of the actor engaged with children's rights. The number of bodies engaged in implementing EU law and policy is broad and providing effective training and resources across these bodies, at both supranational and national level, for mainstreaming is challenging.

In exploring the potential for mainstreaming children's rights within the EU, Eurochild recommends the development of a tool on child rights mainstreaming to help build capacity and experience (Schuurman, this collection). This is an extensive and ongoing commitment across the institutions and the Member States. The Commission's Agenda states that it will draw on the expertise of the European Forum of the Rights of the Child, which advises and assists the Commission and other EU institutions on children's rights (European Forum on the Rights of the Child), along with insight from external NGOs and specialists to provide resources, training and support for effective mainstreaming (Commission 2011a: 14). For mainstreaming to operate fully, awareness of children's rights must be inculcated in all those individuals within organisations responsible for creating and implementing policy for mainstreaming at national, as well as supranational, level where policy is normally implemented in practice.

2.3 Implementation at all levels of the polity

To embed children's rights in the EU framework, both the institutions of the Union and national bodies implementing law and policy must all be capable of responding to the obligation to protect children's rights. The focus of the research in the EU context has been on the potential for securing mainstreaming in the institutions (Eurochild 2014: 8). In the context of Brussels II Revised, this focus is reflected in the actual text of the Regulation in expressly protecting children's rights. However, bodies operating at the national level normally secure the interpretation and implementation of law and policy created by the EU. Even if children's rights have been mainstreamed into the legal framework by the EU institutions, if they are not respected at the national level where the law is implemented, they are not secured in practice.

The experience of mainstreaming children's rights thus far by European institutions has been described as mainly rhetorical, remaining undefined and failing to gain traction for children's rights against other policy interests (Drywood 2011: 371). Mainstreaming of children's rights has focused on the policy-formation processes and the EU institutions, rather than the protection of children's rights in circumstances where children are actually experiencing the implementation of European law and policy in practice. The following discussion will use the example of cross-border family law to explore the potential for securing children's rights as part of the processes of implementing EU law, including building capacity and co-operation across the Member States. By considering two organisations specifically charged by the EU with cooperating to secure positive outcomes for cross-border disputes over children at the national level, the importance of mainstreaming children's rights at all levels will be demonstrated, and the scope for future development in the protection of children's rights explored.

3. Central Authorities and the European Judicial Network: Cross-border cooperation over family law disputes

Central Authorities and the European Judicial Network are both organisations aimed at encouraging cross-border cooperation and practice sharing in family proceedings in the EU. These organisations have developed from previous practice by the Hague Conference on Private International Law. The Hague Conference, of which the EU is now a member,[6] is an international organisation consisting of State parties working for the unification of private international law rules through international treaty. The Conference is not specifically a human rights organisation, but it has developed a number of Conventions to promote inter-State co-operation over cross-border family proceedings. The EU has built on and developed existing concepts, structures and legal frameworks, including Central Authorities and networks of national judicial contacts, created by previous Hague Conference measures. In this section the role of both Central Authorities and the European Judicial Network in cross-border family law and the responsibility of these bodies to protect children's rights in their activities will be briefly discussed.

---

6 Council Decision 2006/719 on the accession of the Community to the Hague Conference on Private International Law [2006] OJ L 297.

3.1 Central Authorities

Central Authorities originated in several treaties promulgated by the Hague Conference and are bodies established to provide a point of contact between States to help resolve private international legal proceedings. Central Authorities assist individuals involved in international family law disputes and are vital to the operation of the Hague Convention on the Civil Aspects of International Child Abduction 1980 (Hague Convention 1980). Art 7 requires each signatory State to establish a Central Authority charged with cooperating with other Central Authorities, and with authorities in their home State, to ensure the rapid return of abducted children to their home State. The Central Authority is a point of communication between two countries and it has a protective role, ensuring the effective operation of the Convention (de Chiodi 2012: 65). Where a child has been unlawfully removed or retained in a Convention country a parent can call on their own Central Authority, or the foreign Central Authority, for assistance in locating the child and issuing legal proceedings. This has proved a valuable and important part of practice under the Hague Convention 1980, leading Bruch to describe the Central Authority as "quite literally, a friend in deed" (Bruch 1994: 52).

Under Art 7, Hague Convention 1980, the Central Authority is charged with a range of responsibilities including protection of the child, seeking voluntary return or issuing proceedings for the return of the child, exchange of information and the more general responsibility to eliminate any obstacle to the Convention's effective application. In practice, the Central Authority has become the focus of the practical functioning of the Convention as two-way bodies, both initiating and receiving requests in relation to abducted children to facilitate their return (Lowe et al. 2004: 226). However, they have also adopted a wider role educating the public about international child abduction and the Hague Convention 1980, meeting to share good practice and develop relationships between Central Authorities, and participating in discussions about the reform and development of the Convention (Bruch 1994: 50).

Building on the Hague Convention 1980, the role of Central Authorities was extended by Arts 29-38 of the Hague Convention on Jurisdiction, Applicable Law, Recognition, Enforcement and Cooperation in Respect of Parental Responsibility and Measures for the Protection of Children 1996. The 1996 Convention is wide in scope, covering cross-border disputes over custody and access, and child protection. The obligations on Central Authorities include encouraging mediation to reach decisions in relation to a child, facilitating the exchange of information in relation to a child, and requesting assistance to ensure implementation of measures in relation to the child. The Hague Convention on the Protection of Children and Cooperation in Respect of Inter-country Adoption 1993 also contains specific obligations on Central Authorities under Arts 6-13 in cross-border adoptions. The role of the Central Authority has been further extended by the EU's international family law measures. Under Arts 54-58 of Brussels II Revised, each Member State must establish and resource a Central Authority. Central Authorities are obligated to collect and exchange information about the child and decisions taken in relation to the child, facilitate communication between national courts, and between holders of parental responsibility to help them reach agreement through mediation. Central Authority services are to be provided free of charge. The Central Authority therefore has a role across a range of cross-border proceedings having an impact, directly or indirectly, on children's welfare. The role of the Central Authority may vary in each context, but child welfare should be central to their operations.

The developing role of the Central Authority has been re-emphasised by the consultation paper on the revision of Brussels II Revised, which states that their "… cooperation is essential for the effective application of the Regulation." (European Commission 2014: 11). The importance of Central Authorities to the scheme of Brussels II Revised is demonstrated by Case C-523/07 *A* [2009] ECR I-02805. In this case, the children had been moved from Sweden to Finland by their parents. In Finland the children were not in attendance at school and were living a peripatetic lifestyle. Consequently, for the protection of their welfare, all three children had been taken in to emergency foster care by the Finnish social services under Art 20, Brussels II Revised. The emergency measures taken in Finland were temporary in nature, and the procedure for seising the court with substantive jurisdiction over the long-term welfare of the children, Finland or Sweden, was not clear. There is no provision for the direct transfer of jurisdiction to another court in the Regulation (para 56), creating problems if the Swedish court in fact held substantive jurisdiction over the children's welfare. In these circumstances, the information exchange obligation on Central Authorities was employed to ensure that, if the best interests of the child required it, and the Swedish court held substantive jurisdiction, the Central Authority would inform the Swedish authorities of any provisional protective measures taken by the Finnish authorities, and the circumstances surrounding the emergency care order (para 65). Protection of the children's long-term welfare could depend on the intermediary information-sharing role of the Central Authority. To protect the children's interests effectively, the welfare and rights of the child must be at the centre of their practice, and the focus of effective co-operation between Authorities.

EU Regulation 4/2009 on the recovery and enforcement of cross-border maintenance obligations has significantly extended the role of the Central Authority to locating maintenance debtors and information about their financial circumstances, including their assets (Art 51). Central Authorities are charged with cooperating with one another and with the competent maintenance authorities in the Member State, and seeking possible solutions to any problems arising through the application of the Regulation (Art 50). These provisions are directed at securing maintenance where relationships have broken down, for the financial welfare of children where family members are in different Member States. They can also be called upon to facilitate the cross-border taking of evidence.[7] The obligations on Central Authorities are wide-ranging obligations representing an evolution in private international law, accepting that individuals involved in international family proceedings need significant assistance in instituting and resolving complex legal proceedings. Central Authorities sit between the State and the individual, providing a point of contact and exchange between States and a significant element of trust and stability in cross-border proceedings (Bruch 1994: 48).

There is little information available on the resourcing and staffing or training of Central Authorities across the Member States. Each Member State takes responsibility for establishing and resourcing their Central Authority. The makeup of the Central Authority in terms of staffing and position in the legal system will depend in part on the number of applications dealt with by the Central Authority and the nature of the requests they receive. Lowe et al. identified that Central Authorities respond to the amount of litigation traffic they experience but they must be adequately staffed to carry out their role (2004: 228). Where the Central Authority has only a minimal role in the national legal system, essentially transferring inquiries to legal professionals, the impact of children's rights on their practice may in fact be limited.

From the obligations placed upon them, Central Authorities are closely concerned with the practical resolution of cross-border family law disputes over children. Their role in safeguarding children involved in cross-border litigation and in managing legal proceedings for parents and children means that they could be a prominent actor in securing children's rights protection in the national context across the EU. The EU did not create the concept of the Central Authority and they are not EU institutions, but in the process of implementing EU law they are required to comply with Art 24 of the Charter. By operating at the national level, they are also subject to the CRC, and the national procedures and interpretation of rights created by the legal framework of each Member State. However, the process of mainstreaming children's rights into their practice has not been identified as relevant to Central Authorities, despite the importance of these bodies in promoting and securing the welfare of children in cross-border family proceedings. The extent to which individual Central Authorities have explicitly engaged with the protection of children's rights is unclear because the work of Central Authorities is significantly under-researched. There is no current research evidence on

7 Art 17(1), Regulation 1206/2001 on cooperation between courts of the Member States in the taking of evidence in civil or commercial matters [2001] OJ L174/1.

levels awareness in national Central Authorities of the requirements of effective rights protection, or of the current practices, or standards of good practice, in relation to children's rights in cross-border proceedings. The potential for such practice will be explored further in part 4.

3.2 European Judicial Network

The European Judicial Network in civil and commercial matters was established by Decision in 2001 with the aim of improving, simplifying and expediting effective judicial cooperation across the EU.[8] The civil and commercial Network covers cross-border family law proceedings and forms one part of a wider framework, including a European Judicial Network for criminal law,[9] and a European Judicial Training Network (Commission 2011b). The Network is responsible for facilitating judicial cooperation between the Member States, even where there is no existing EU or international law instrument governing a cross-border situation, and for the provision of information to members of the Network, and the public (Art 3).

The Network has three objectives: improving and facilitating judicial cooperation in civil and commercial matters; improving the effective and practical application of EU instruments; and promoting effective access to justice for the public (European Commission 2006: 5). Claes and de Visser suggest that the European legislature has set up judicial networks to improve the functioning of the European judicial system and to increase mutual trust (2012: 108). The Network applies to civil and commercial matters generally and is not specific to family law. However, in outlining the obligations on Central Authorities in the EU, both Brussels II Revised (Art 58), and the Maintenance Regulation (Art 50(2)) encourage close cooperation between Central Authorities and the Network such that they both play a direct role in developing practice in relation to cross-border family disputes in the EU.

The Network is part of a wider phenomenon of closer contact between national judges and legal bodies in a variety of different international contexts, including treaty law and human rights obligations (Kirby 2008: 171). The International Hague Network of Judges was created in 1998 to designate a member of the national judiciary to act as channel for communication and liaison with Central Authorities in Hague Abduction Convention 1980 cases, and has subsequently extended to cover cross-border proceedings affecting children more generally. The Hague Network is regarded as successful in

8 Recital 4, Decision 2001/470 establishing a European Judicial Network in civil and commercial matters [2001] OJ L174/25.

9 Decision 2008/976 on the European Judicial Network [2008] OJ L348/130.

promoting contact between judges and Central Authorities and cross-border judicial communication (Diamond 2013). The European Judicial Network adopts the Hague Network's approach of encouraging contact between Central Authorities and the members of the Network, exchange of information and discussion of difficulties in applying the law in cross-border family cases.

Within the Network, each Member State nominates a contact point (Art 5) to facilitate cross-border contact between judges. The nature of the contact point is not clearly defined (Storskrubb 2008: 236) and more than one contact point can be nominated. In 2005, the Network had 424 members consisting of: 93 contact points, 159 Central Authority members, 13 liaison magistrates and 159 judicial authorities responsible for judicial cooperation (European Commission 2006: 2). The Network therefore has much wider membership than just judicial members. The contact points have periodic meetings, (Arts 9-10 of the Decision), organised by the European Commission, to discuss practical problems in the application of the EU's measures on judicial cooperation, build relationships between contact points and identify best practice. The Network also has a website providing information on national law in the Member States on the issues covered by the Network, including the law on divorce and parental responsibility (European Judicial Network).

The Network has been called upon to create contact between national judges in family law cases, to provide insight into the processes and protection available in the foreign Member State. In *Re S (care: jurisdiction)* ([2008] EWHC 2013 (Fam)), the child had been trafficked from Romania to the UK and was in the care of an English local authority. The child's return to Romania had been sought under the Hague Abduction Convention 1980 by her mother. The English judge hearing the return application used the Network to contact the Romanian judge to try and establish what protective measures could be put in place on the child's return to Romania to prevent any risk of the child being re-trafficked. This contact can be particularly valuable in family law cases where it promotes decision-making which takes account of the full range of circumstances affecting the child, but is limited by the requirements of fairness to both parties and the inability of the foreign judge to make a decision before their courts have jurisdiction over the substantive issues. In *Re S*, whilst the Romanian judge could advise the English judge of the broad question of the orders and protective measures available to the Romanian court, no advice could be given on likely courses of action as the court was not seised of the case and had not heard from the parties. To give further advice could prejudice any subsequent Romanian proceedings.

The success of the Network in encouraging closer cooperation and developing closer links between legal systems is difficult to assess, in part because there has been little investigation into the role and effect of the Network in practice by either the EU or external researchers. It has been criticised for being relatively closed to the input of external stakeholders from outside the EU institutional framework (Storskrubb 2008: 243). This is inevitable in a Network focused on improving links between nominated contact points, but there is potential for greater input by external bodies, including NGOs and other actors on children's rights to promote awareness of children's rights concerns in family proceedings across the Network. There is no evidence of this process in the current framework.

The Commission has identified a lack of resource available to contact points within the Network as a limit on their capacity, but the nature of this lack of resource, whether attached to funding, training or administrative support, is not clear. The Commission has also criticised the use of Central Authorities as the central contact point, rather than a judge, as a particular problem in the operation of the Network (European Commission 2006: 9) because of the duplication of roles. These limitations on the contact points means that the engagement with children's rights concerns are likely to be constrained in the current operation of the Network.

Despite these difficulties, the Network is envisaged as an essential aspect of judicial cooperation, providing an additional resource for the resolution of cross-border disputes and as a facilitator and information exchange route between the national and the EU levels. It is distant from individual children and ongoing family law disputes, but is intended to play an important role in developing consistent cross-national responses to family law disputes. The extent to which high standards of rights protection, including children's rights, could become a more explicit part of that role is discussed in the following section.

4. Enhancing Children's Rights Mainstreaming in Central Authorities and the Network

Having explored the nature and purpose of Central Authorities and the Network, in this section the potential scope for mainstreaming children's rights throughout their practice will be further explored. The Network and Central Authorities are both bodies operating at the national level, but subject to the obligations of EU law. As actors in international family law, their work engages with children involved in these proceedings. Both bodies should therefore have a role in protecting and promoting children's rights in the national context (see 2.3 above).

Central Authorities and the Network exist as part of the national legal system, but operate specifically in intra-State disputes, under European and international legal obligations. The Network and Central Authorities retain a close relationship with one another. In terms of implementing children's rights in their practice, the different roles played by these bodies mean that their potential role will also differ. They occupy an unusual space within the legal system, operating in their national legal environment, but closely connected to, and concerned with, foreign legal systems and proceedings. The national/international nature of these bodies makes them a potentially important space in which both the interpretation and implementation of children's rights in Europe can be debated and promoted across all Member States.

4.1 Raising awareness of children's rights

An effective mainstreaming strategy requires a raised awareness of children's rights by actors in international family law disputes. This process has two elements, first in implementing children's rights in the practice of national bodies, and secondly in highlighting the role of children's rights in cross-border family law disputes.

To embed understanding of children's rights within practice, training of individuals involved in cross-border family law will be necessary. The need for training within Central Authorities to help them understand and manage their obligations under EU law and its complexities has been recognised (Trimmings 2013: 145). The explicit protection of children's rights within the legal framework is an additional obligation of which Central Authorities must be aware, and be able to implement in practice. The Commission has accepted the need for judicial training on fundamental rights obligations in the EU legal landscape (European Commission 2011b: 5), and this training should include employees of Central Authorities (Trimmings 2013: 140). This recognition must be translated into funding and development of specific training projects, which are accessible by Central Authorities across the Member States and could form part of the work carried out by the European Judicial Training Network. Training must be sensitive to the national context, and should be based on the rights expressed in the CRC. Training permits individuals to discuss and build understanding of rights obligations through learning experience and can be tied to understanding of the changing EU legal framework and the new obligations arising under that framework. This forms an important aspect of changing cultural attitudes to children's rights, enabling implementation in practice.

Beyond internal training processes, the Network has specific obligations in relation to awareness-raising of legal entitlements within Europe. As well as providing internal cooperation between national legal systems, the Network is also an outward facing body, responsible for providing information to the public. The Commission has stated that:

To ensure better and more effective information for children about their rights and about relevant EU policies will require consolidation and modernisation of existing information tools. (European Commission 2011a: 14).

The provision of information, accessible to both parents and children, is emphasised as important in family law proceedings to allow the parties to defend their rights. The necessity of child-friendly procedures and information in legal proceedings affecting children has been highlighted by the Council of Europe's Guidelines on Child-friendly Justice (see Council of Europe 2011). The Network could make a significant contribution to the Commission's goal of providing information of an appropriate nature to children and parents involved in international family law disputes (European Commission 2011a: 6) by engaging with the Council of Europe's Guidelines. Thus far, the information provided by the Network is only appropriate for adults, and perhaps only adults with legal training (see European Judicial Network). The Guidelines provide a detailed framework on how information should be more effectively conveyed to children and could provide the basis of future information packs provided by the Network for children in the EU involved in cross-border family law proceedings. The Network can distribute this information throughout the EU online, through Central Authorities, and through third parties such as relevant charitable organisations and NGOs, reinforcing the work done in this field by the Council of Europe and potentially further raising awareness of children's rights in cross-border legal proceedings.

4.2 Debating children's rights protection through EU family law

One of the concerns about children's rights in the EU is over their interpretation and operation in practice (see 2.1 above). Mainstreaming children's rights requires consideration of children by all bodies involved with actions affecting children, and building understanding of how best to protect and promote these rights. The cooperation between Central Authorities and the Network provides space for deliberation and debate over the interpretation and implementation of children's rights in cross-border family law disputes in Europe. The nature of this process will draw on different national traditions and interpretations of the CRC, and enable comparison of practice and the development of common understanding of rights protection. For example, discussion of the conception of the best interests of the child involved in a cross-border dispute governed by Brussels II Revised, or effective ways of facilitating the hearing of a child who is in another country, could be usefully explored. This process cannot produce a definitive interpretation of Art 24, (which remains the responsibility of the Court of Justice), or of the CRC, but it could contribute to the realisation of the rights in practice, and to debates over conception and interpretation of rights.

If the bodies implementing EU family law are involved in articulating and debating the content of children's rights and operationalising them in a meaningful way, their practice has the potential to develop children's rights protection in family law across Europe. This form of cross-border debate has the benefit of furthering understanding between Member States over their processes for children's rights protection in family law proceedings. Central Authorities hold frequent meetings between themselves to share practice and build relationships between national bodies. These meetings have played an important part in developing Central Authority practice and building strong relationships between Central Authorities to help with the resolution of disputes. Cooperation develops through regular communication at an operational level of individual cases, and periodic discussion of specific problems where expertise can also be shared (Lowe et al 2004: 233). These discussions include concerns over how best to protect child welfare in cross-border proceedings (Diamond 2013), encouraging the faster resolution of disputes and developing examples of good practice in different forms of cross-border family proceedings, such as mediation.

The Network does not deal as closely with individual cases, but has a mandate for sharing information and developing cooperation across the EU. It has been suggested that: "… policy coordination through the Network has potential as a tool for Europeanizing or converging policy rather than fostering diversity." (Storskrubb 2008: 239). The Network provides an opportunity to share good practice in relation to children's rights at a specifically European level but engaging national actors, permitting debate over the conception of rights and their protection in family law. The meetings of the Network are convened and chaired by the European Commission under Art 12(1) of the Network Decision. Although the agenda for meetings is created in consultation with the members, the Commission has a certain level of control over the agenda of Network meetings and could use this role to include explicit discussion of children's rights by the Network and the Central Authorities who are members of the Network. This provides an opportunity to discuss both practical and theoretical differences in approach and realisation of children's rights in family law across the EU.

Discussion of children's rights in a cross-border family context may expose differences as much as agreement. Dialogue may in fact encourage advocacy of a particular national approach, rather than reasoning about national procedures and values (Claes and de Visser 2012: 112). There may be strong divisions in national approaches, for example in the approach taken to determining when a child should be heard (Stalford 2012: 114). National procedural differences are expressly permitted by EU legislation, which is not intended to modify national procedures for hearing the child (Recital 19, Brussels II Revised). Whilst national approaches may be compared and discussed in a cross-border context, maintaining national procedures is entirely legitimate. However, articulating difference is important to understanding the value of national practices encouraging the trust between States necessary for the operation of cross-border family law. Discussion may also help convergence on particular standards and encourage engagement with both the CRC and Art 24 of the Charter.

4.3 Capacity for children's rights in the implementation of EU law

The process of mainstreaming should increase the capacity for protection and promotion of children's rights across all levels of activity in Europe, developing awareness of children's rights and equivalent levels of protection across the Member States. Central Authorities implement EU cross-border family law and form the basis of international cooperation in family law disputes. They are bodies on the ground in the Member State and can be active in legal proceedings involving children. As such they could play a valuable role in securing children's rights during proceedings in the national legal system. As a public authority, they are obliged to take decisions and actions in relation to children with the child's best interests as their primary consideration under Art 24(2) of the Charter. Since Central Authorities' decision-making processes often involve children, this is an important obligation running throughout Central Authority practice.

The Central Authority should be knowledgeable about the legislative framework, the obligations on the court and the factors taken into decision-making in international family law (Trimmings 2013: 144). If there is sufficient awareness by the members of the Central Authority of Art 24 rights, and in particular the right of a child of appropriate age and maturity to be heard, this could help in ensuring that the child's views are solicited and heard in proceedings. For example, in cases where effective protection of a child's right to be heard requires cross-border cooperation as the child is in a different State to the court taking a decision over their welfare, good understanding of another Member States' court processes, and strong communication between Central Authorities facilitates the cross-border taking of evidence. The importance of this cooperation for effective handling of family cases and the protection of a child's right to be heard in cross-border proceedings under Art 24(1) of the Charter has been highlighted by the Court of

Justice (Case C-491/10 *Aguirre Zarraga* [2010] E.C.R. I-14247, paras 64-66).

Without strong co-operation, the child's right to be heard can be lost in cross-border proceedings amidst procedural concerns. In *Aguirre Zarraga,* the mother had unlawfully retained her daughter, aged ten, in Germany. Her father sought her return to Spain under Brussels II Revised but the German courts refused on the ground that that child objected to returning (Art 11(4), Brussels II Revised, Art 13b, Hague Convention 1980). The father subsequently seised the Spanish courts of a full custody hearing to decide the welfare and future living arrangements of the child (Art 11(6)-(8), Brussels II Revised). The child was given the opportunity to be heard, but she refused to travel to Spain and her views were not expressed to the Spanish court. The Spanish court subsequently ordered the return of the child to Spain, effectively overriding the child's initial objection to returning previously accepted by the German court. The CJEU ruled that the right of the child to be heard in Art 24(3) of the Charter had been respected as the child had had an opportunity to be heard in the Spanish proceedings (para 52). It is therefore essential for national authorities to secure the actual exercise of the child's right to be heard through the child's participation in national proceedings. Central Authorities can play a key role in exploring different processes for hearing the child in proceedings to ensure their opportunity is not lost. The failure of the Spanish court to actually hear the child, although legitimate, led to a fundamental breakdown in the processes for the protection of the child's welfare and a conflict between the German and Spanish courts. *Aguirre Zarraga* demonstrates the importance of securing the practical exercise of children's rights at all levels of implementation of EU family law, particularly in the national context, to secure their effective protection.

This process of cooperation to enable the child's views to be effectively expressed should not be limited to judicial proceedings where national court processes should already be in place. Not all cross-border disputes are resolved in court. Central Authorities are also required to assist in processes of mediation between holders of parental responsibility (Art 55(e), Brussels II Revised). Meaningful engagement of children in mediation outcomes requires that their views be solicited and heard within the process (Stalford 2010: 159). Open discussion with children, as well as the adults, involved in international family proceedings is important for a child's understanding of the processes and potential outcomes, and reducing future conflict (Stalford 2012: 108). The Central Authority can play a key role in facilitating mediation in international disputes (de Chiodi 2012: 68). Involving children in the processes of decision-making through Central Authorities would contribute to the Commission's goal of achieving child-friendly justice in cross-border family law proceedings of all types (European Commission 2011a: 6).

Despite these opportunities, Central Authorities are individualistic organisations within the State framework and, although they will carry out the same broad range of obligations under EU law, they may do so in significantly different ways. Their idiosyncratic nature means that how they are set up, resourced and identifying the personnel appropriate for training will vary depending on the Member State. Central Authorities will have different awareness of children's rights and openness to changing and developing their practice. National procedures are also linked to legal cultures forming a system, so exchanging experience and best practice requires understanding of foreign processes to be genuinely useful (Storskrubb 2008: 241). What works for one Central Authority will not necessarily translate into another national context. Guidance and training provided to Central Authorities should highlight the CRC and Charter obligations, but this translation is an inherent element of mainstreaming children's rights into very different national contexts.

By contrast with Central Authorities, the Network has a more distant relationship with the individuals involved in international family disputes, but where cross-border assistance is sought between Network contact points, securing the child's best interests in proceedings should be the focus of discussions. Within the Network, confusion exists over the role of Central Authorities, particularly whether Central Authorities should act as Network contact points (European Commission 2006: 9). Embedding children's rights within a confused framework will not be a linear or consistent process. The Commission's report on the Network identified time and resource as problems for the designated contact points in the Member States. The contact points need greater financial and training resources, and contact points should be a designated role that is not mixed with other responsibilities (European Commission 2006: 9).

If the Network engaged with children's rights, it could play a valuable role in provoking and improving dialogue on children's rights between the European and national level because the contact points are national, but co-operating across the Member States. Greater dialogue can provoke more consistent approaches across the Member States, as standards of rights protection converge through processes of transposition and contamination of practices for the effective protection of children's rights in cross-border family law proceedings (Örücü 2007: 31-33). As legal systems come into contact and inter-relate with one another, practices and concepts can be explicitly transposed between systems, or ideas and processes can be horizontally transferred through contamination of ideas. The Network is an intended as an environment in which such legal exchanges are identified and encouraged and, if children's rights could form part of this debate, it provides a site of significant possibility for debate over the development of effective rights protection in EU family law.

Both Central Authorities and the Network have potential as agents of children's rights mainstreaming in the EU, but this first requires further engagement both by the EU, external actors and the Member States to improve their capacity as actors and advocates of children's rights in the EU. If mainstreaming could be secured throughout these bodies, then capacity for children's rights protection across the EU will be significantly expanded.

Conclusions

This contribution has considered the previously unexplored scope for mainstreaming the rights expressed in the CRC and Art 24 of the EU Charter of Fundamental Rights throughout the European framework on international family law. Effective mainstreaming must secure children's rights protection at all levels, not just in the EU institutions, but also in the national bodies implementing EU obligations. Central Authorities and the Network exist at the national level, but are charged with the protection of children's rights in international family law, both by the CRC at national level, and by the Charter at the EU level. The relationships between Central Authorities and within the Network provide fertile and, as yet, largely untapped opportunities for sharing practice, and for discussion of the practical protection of CRC rights within the context of European obligations in international family law.

Both Central Authorities and the Network have significant potential to expand capacity in promoting and protecting children's rights in family law across the Member States. However, consideration of the role of both Central Authorities and the Network demonstrates the problem of translating European children's rights into national level action. Effective training in understanding and implementing children's rights in practice is needed across different national contexts. Improving awareness of CRC rights and Art 24 should promote standards of rights protection across the Member States but will also highlight differences in procedure and interpretation. These differences are inevitable, but this process provokes both debate between national bodies over good practice in international family law, and convergence on key concerns.

The EU can facilitate national promotion of children's rights; it cannot secure children's rights through its activities alone. Engagement by the EU, NGOs and academics with the actors at national level remains imperative to secure the protection of children's rights arising from EU law and the CRC in each Member State.

References

Bruch, Carol (1994) The Central Authority's Role under the Hague Abduction Convention: A Friend Indeed, in: Family Law Quarterly 28, 1, pp. 35-53.

de Chiodi, Maria del Carmen Seoane (2012) New trends in Networks and cooperation among Central Authorities: mediation as an alternative means for the solutions of controversies and the role of the Central Authority in its application in international return and access procedures, in: International Family Law, March, pp. 65-69.

Claes, Monica and deVisser, Maartje (2012) Are you Networked yet? On dialogues in European Judicial Networks, in: Utrecht Law Review, 8, 2, pp. 100-114.

Council of Europe (2011) Guidelines of the Committee of Ministers on the Council of Europe on child-friendly justice and their explanatory memorandum: http://www.coe.int/t/dghl/standard setting/childjustice/Guidelines%20on%20child-friendly%20justice%20and%20their%20expl anatory%20memorandum%20_4_.pdf (25-08-13).

Daly, Mary (2005) Gender Mainstreaming in Theory and Practice, in: Social Politics 12, 3, pp. 433-450.

Drywood, Eleanor (2011) Child-proofing EU Law and Policy: Interrogating the law-making processes behind European asylum and immigration provision, in: International Journal of Children's Rights 19, 3, pp. 405-428.

Eurochild (2014) Mainstreaming Children's Rights in EU Legislation, Policy and Budget: Lessons from Practice: http://bit.ly/Mainstreaming_CR_in_EU (08-04-14).

European Commission (1996) Incorporating Equal Opportunities for Women and Men into all Community Policies and Activities, COM (1996) 67, final.

European Commission (2006) Report from the Commission on the application of Council Decision 2001/470 establishing a European Judicial Network in Civil and Commercial Matters, COM (2006) 203, final.

European Commission (2011a): An EU Agenda for the Rights of the Child, Communication from the Commission, COM (2011) 60, final.

European Commission (2011b) Communication from the Commission Building Trust in EU-wide Justice A New Dimension to European Judicial Training COM (2011) 551, final.

European Commission (2014) Report from the European Commission to the European Parliament, the Council and the European Economic and Social Committee on the application of Council Regulation 2201/2003 concerning jurisdiction and recognition and enforcement of judgments in matrimonial matters and the matters of parental responsibility COM (2014) 225, final.

European Forum on the Rights of the Child: http://ec.europa.eu/justice/fundamental-rights/rights-child/european-forum/index_en.htm (08-02-15).

European Judicial Network: http://ec.europa.eu/civiljustice/index_en.htm (22-08-13).

Fortin, Jane (2009) Children's Rights and the Developing Law, 3rd edition, Cambridge, Cambridge University Press.

Kirby, Michael (2008) Transnational judicial dialogue, internationalisation of the law and Australian judges, in: Melbourne Journal of International Law, 9, 1, pp. 171-189.

Lamont, Ruth (2014) Article 24: The Rights of the Child, in: Peers, Steven et al. (eds) The EU Charter of Fundamental Rights: A Commentary, Oxford, Hart.

Lamont, Ruth (2011) Mainstreaming Gender into European Family Law?: The Case of Child Abduction and Brussels II Revised, in: European Law Journal, 17, 3, pp. 366-384.

Lowe, Nigel et al. (2004) The International Movement of Children: Law, Practice and Procedure, Bristol, Jordan Publishing.

McGlynn, Clare (2002) Rights for Children?: The Potential Impact of the European Union Charter of Fundamental Rights, in: European Public Law, 8, 3,pp. 387-400.
Moglove Diamond, Robyn (2013) International judicial initiatives dealing with cross-border child protection, Conference paper delivered at 6th World Congress on Family Law and Children's Rights, March 2013 (unpublished).
Örücü, Esin (2007) Convergence and Divergence: Theoretical Issues, in: Antokolskaia, Masha (ed.) Convergence and Divergence of Family Law in Europe, Antwerp, Intersentia.
Parkes, Aisling (2013) Children and International Human Rights Law: The Right of the Child to be Heard, Abingdon, Routledge.
Pollock, Mark and Hafner-Burton, Emilie (2000) Mainstreaming Gender in the European Union, in: Journal of European Public Policy, 7, 3, pp. 432-456.
Stalford, Helen (2012) Children and the European Union: Rights, Welfare and Accountability, Oxford, Hart.
Stalford, Helen (2010) Crossing boundaries: reconciling law, culture and values in international family mediation, in: Journal of Social Welfare and Family Law, 32, 2, pp. 155-168.
Storskrubb, Eva (2008) Civil Procedure and EU Law: A Policy Area Uncovered, Oxford, Oxford University Press.
Trimmings, Katarina (2013) Child Abduction within the European Union, Oxford, Hart.

The EU and Child Protection Systems: The Role and the Impact of the EU in Advancing Children's Protection Rights

Olivia Lind-Haldorsson and Rebecca O'Donnell

Introduction

In recent years and, in particular, since the entry into force of the Lisbon Treaty, there has been a proliferation of EU activities that have an impact on protecting children from violence, abuse, neglect and exploitation, within and outside Europe. Outside of Europe, the EU has increasingly taken action in its role as a promoter of human rights and donor to reinforce and advance the international framework for child protection. Indeed, the EU has begun to move away from addressing specific protection issues such as child trafficking or children associated with armed forces or armed groups, towards a more comprehensive, systematic approach to child protection. As regards EU internal affairs, EU child protection measures have arisen mainly in the young and rapidly evolving environment of justice and home affairs. Key legal instruments addressing specific issues such as sexual abuse and trafficking have recently been adopted; other strategic policy initiatives, such as guidance on integrated child protection systems, are underway and recently established EU agencies are becoming involved in providing practical and operational measures.

At this stage in EU law and policymaking, it is timely to gauge the overall potential which EU action and resources have to help secure the protection of children from violence throughout the world. Looking back at how some key measures came into existence, we can also begin to decipher the extent to which international processes contribute to EU policy and, conversely, how EU policy may influence international processes.

Our review demands an exploration of the following issues:

i. the international law and policy framework with regard to child protection;
ii. the general role of the EU in protecting children;
iii. the growing recognition internationally and within Europe of the need for a more comprehensive approach to child protection and the implications this may have for future EU action.

In examining this subject, we offer a practitioners' viewpoint. Our perspectives and analysis derive from day-to-day experience as EU policy and advocacy advisers in the field, and in particular, from our work following and contributing to the development of EU actions on child protection in the context of emergencies and conflict, sexual abuse of children, trafficking of children and those which address the precarious circumstances of children seeking asylum or in situations of irregular migration. From the coalface of regional policy-making, we will hone in on key features of current EU policy and reflect on some of the practical opportunities and challenges that may lie ahead for the EU institutions.

In considering the actors involved in EU policy-making and implementation, it is important to look at both the EU institutions and the Member States themselves and beyond. A whole spectrum of actors involved in the situation of children, including NGOS, IGOs, national authorities and specialized national agencies contribute and respond to EU measures. In the coming years, the perspectives of these actors on the opportunities (and limitations) for child protection generated by new EU measures will be a vital contribution to the ongoing policy debates.

But what is already apparent is the fact that EU measures indeed form important building blocks of more comprehensive national child protection systems. The EU is increasingly alert to the need to support such systems, and indeed is clearly drawing from, and contributing to, the international processes that inspire and encourage such systems.

1. Child protection – The international legal framework

Background

A large number of international, regional and national instruments stipulate children's civil, political, economic, social, health and cultural rights. The main international instrument on children's rights is the UN Convention on the Rights of the Child 1989 (CRC) and its two Optional Protocols on the Sale of Children, Child Prostitution, and Child Pornography and the Optional Protocol to the Convention on the Rights of the Child on the Involvement of Children in Armed Conflict.[1]

1 Examples of other international instruments include the International Covenant on Economic, Social and Cultural Rights (1966), the International Covenant on Civil and Political Rights (1966), the International Labour Convention No 138 (1973) and No 182 (1999). Regional instruments include, for example, The African Charter on the Rights and Welfare of the Child (African Union 1990), as well as issue-specific Conventions such as the Council of

1.1 Definition of child protection

There is no universally accepted definition of 'child protection rights' per se; the scope of what to protect children from, and how, can differ. In this chapter, we adopt a definition that captures the core elements of Article 19 CRC as 'measures and structures to prevent and respond to violence, abuse, exploitation and neglect affecting children'.

Article 19 CRC offers an important foundation for the conceptualisation of child protection, in that it defines different forms of violence and affirms children's right to protection from all forms of violence in all settings (CRC Article 19):

1. States Parties shall take all appropriate legislative, administrative, social and educational measures to protect the child from all forms of physical or mental violence, injury or abuse, neglect or negligent treatment, maltreatment or exploitation, including sexual abuse, while in the care of parent(s), legal guardian(s) or any other person who has the care of the child.
2. Such protective measures should, as appropriate, include effective procedures for the establishment of social programmes to provide necessary support for the child and for those who have the care of the child, as well as for other forms of prevention and for identification, reporting, referral, investigation, treatment and follow-up of instances of child maltreatment described heretofore, and, as appropriate, for judicial involvement.

Article 19 CRC thus requires State parties to take a wide variety of measures to prevent and address violence, to identify, protect and assist victims, to report, refer and investigate violence and to ensure action to redress violations against children's protection rights.

The UN Committee on the Rights of the Child identifies Article 19 as the core provision for child protection. Children's rights to protection, however, are reflected in many other articles of the CRC. Key child protection articles are Articles 3 (States Parties' obligations), 9 (family separation), 10 (family reunification across borders), 11 (illicit transfer of children), 16 (right to privacy, honour and reputation), 19 (protection from violence, injury, abuse, neglect, maltreatment or exploitation), 20 (alternative care), 21 (adoption), 22 (refugee children), 23 (disabled children), 24 (harmful practices), 25 (periodic review of alternative care), 32 (economic exploitation), 34 (sexual abuse

Europe Convention on Protection of Children against Sexual Exploitation and Sexual Abuse (2007), the Inter-American Convention on Conflict of Laws Concerning the Adoption of Minors (1984) and the Hague Convention on the Protection of Children in Intercountry Adoption (1993).

and exploitation), 35 (abduction, sale or trafficking of children), 36 (other forms of exploitation), 37 (juvenile justice and protection from torture or other cruel, inhuman or degrading treatment or punishment), 38 (protection in armed conflict), 39 (recovery and reintegration) and 40 (children in conflict with the law).There are also other Articles in the CRC that are important to securing children's protection rights. These include Articles 5 (support for the parent, extended family and community); 7 (birth registration and protection of identity), 18 (parental responsibility), 26 (social security), 27 (adequate standard of living and social protection), 28 and 29 (education), and 31 (play and leisure).

The four general principles of the CRC underpin and guide any work on child protection: Article 2 (non-discrimination); Article 3 (the best interests of the child); Article 6 (survival and development); and Article 12 (children's right to be heard).

1.2 UN Study on Violence Against Children

Clearly the almost universal ratification of the CRC presents a great opportunity to move towards eliminating violence against children, through underlining State obligations to prevent and address violence against children. This was recognized in the UN Secretary-General's Study on Violence against Children which was undertaken by Paulo Sérgio Pinheiro in 2006, with the involvement of a wide range of stakeholders including children themselves. Violence, for the purposes of this study, is defined according to CRC Article 19: "all forms of physical or mental violence, injury and abuse, neglect or negligent treatment, maltreatment or exploitation, including sexual abuse". The study also draws on the definition in the World Report on Violence and Health (2002): "the intentional use of physical force or power, threatened or actual, against a child, by an individual or group, that either results in or has a high likelihood of resulting in actual or potential harm to the child's health, survival, development or dignity" (A/61/299: 6).

The study concludes that, in every part of the world, violence against children remains widespread and indeed some forms are, to a large extent, legally and socially accepted. Beyond the more extreme forms of violence, such as sexual exploitation and trafficking, female genital mutilation (FGM), the worst forms of child labour and the impact of armed conflict, the study reveals that children routinely experience physical, sexual and psychological violence in many different settings (A/61/299: 8-9).

However, in his accompanying report "World Report on Violence Against Children", Pinheiro also confirms that the knowledge and capacity to address violence exists at international, regional and national level and that creative approaches to preventing and responding to violence can make a real difference if supported with adequate investment and commitment (Pinheiro 2006: 5, 353). Positive developments include a growing body of international and regional instruments, opportunities for children to speak out on violence and have their voices heard, as well as expansion of research to reveal the impact of violence on children in the neurobiological, behavioural and social sciences (Pinheiro Ibid.: 5). Pinheiro also welcomes the emerging recognition that prevention of violence against children requires cooperation and collaboration among many partners (Ibid.).

1.3 General Comment No. 13 (2011): The right of the child to freedom from all forms of violence

Within Europe and indeed globally, approaches to addressing child protection concerns have traditionally focused on particular issues or specific groups of vulnerable children, such as trafficking, sexual abuse, alternative care, children affected by armed conflict. This has generated a wealth of issue-based initiatives, which have contributed to addressing specific child protection concerns and developing knowledge about how these concerns should be addressed.

However, in recent years, there has been an increasing recognition that issue-based approaches to child protection are not the only solutions, and indeed may suffer from severe limitations if they are isolated interventions to address often complex and multi-faceted protection problems. The reality is that many children face multiple protection problems and inter-linked violations against their rights, which require a holistic response, involving different sectors. Moreover, issue-based approaches do not necessarily contribute to advancing long-term, sustainable and coordinated action[2].

In 2011, the UN Committee on the Rights of the Child presented its General Comment No.13 (2011) on the right of the child to freedom from all forms of violence (GC 13) to support a strong and expansive application of the measures laid down in the CRC to address violence. GC 13 provides an authoritative interpretation of the CRC's provisions relating to child protection, with the purpose of assisting and encouraging State Parties, and other important actors, to take appropriate action towards implementing them. It provides an analysis of the CRC's obligations in relation to child protection

2 See for example UNICEF et al. (2010): *Adapting a Systems Approach to Child Protection: Key Concepts and Considerations* and UNICEF, UNHCR, Save the Children and World Vision (2013): *A Better Way to Protect ALL Children: The Theory and Practice of Child Protection Systems*, Conference Report.

and proposes a broad set of appropriate legal, administrative, social and educational measures. GC 13 is not legally binding on the State Parties to the CRC; however, national courts may refer to it and base judgments on it as part of treaty jurisprudence.

GC 13 calls for administrative measures to include the establishment of policies, programmes, monitoring and oversight systems which are required to ensure that children are protected from violence. This can include the establishment of a coordinating focal point, inter-agency steering committees and transparent budgeting in order to make the best use of resources for child protection. Administrative measures can also put in place processes to monitor quality, accountability and equitable distribution of child protection services, provide guidance and protocols for practitioners and secure data collection and impact analysis (GC 13: 15f). Social measures are highlighted in GC 13 to secure the basic and targeted services to reduce risk and prevent violence against children and to support individual children and their families or other care-givers. These include, but are not limited to, poverty reduction strategies, access to health, social welfare and justice services, childcare and therapeutic programmes (GC 13: 16f).

GC 13 notes that national legislation, including the national budget, must conform to Article 19 and establish an absolute prohibition of violence against children. Such measures must ensure adequate protection of children in all settings, as well as in relation to media and Information and Communication Technology (ICT). Legal measures must also provide for effective and appropriate sanctions against perpetrators, whilst also emphasising that the law and judicial procedures must be child-friendly (GC 13: 14ff). Finally, GC 13 emphasises that educational measures should address attitudes, traditions, customs and behavioural practices which condone and promote violence against children. Such measures should encourage discussion about violence, including the engagement of media and civil society. It can include public information programmes, education on positive parenting, risks, and how to listen to children and take their views seriously, training for professionals and non-professionals working with, and for, children and promoting research on child caregiving and protection (GC 13: 17).

While emphasising the obligations of State Parties and the primary responsibility of Governments in ensuring that adequate measures are in place, both the Committee and Pinheiro draw attention to the fact that societies as a whole share the responsibility of condemning, preventing and responding to violence against children. Children themselves are recognised as important actors for change. The international community, regional actors, State parties and societies also have a shared responsibility to reinforce the international child protection framework by promoting children's rights to protection and condemning violence.

1.4 Child Protection Systems

As we have seen above, the UN Violence Study and GC 13 place substantial emphasis on an integrated and holistic approach, drawing together structures, functions and capacities, which together form a child protection system.[3] GC 13 and the Violence Study identify the following components as crucial to a well-functioning system:

- Solid *coordination mechanisms* and *national child protections strategies, policies or plans,* enabling multiple actors from different sectors to work together to ensure effective and quality prevention, response and monitoring, and services (CRC/C/GC/13: 25ff; A/61/299: para 96; Pinheiro 2006: 18);
- A legal and policy framework, which ensures that laws, policies, plans and programmes comply with international human rights and prohibits all forms of violence against children in all settings, including in the home (CRC Art 19:1; CRC/C/GC/13: 14f; A/61/299: para 97 and 98; Pinheiro 2006: 18);
- Local preventive and responsive services and delivery mechanisms (CRC Art 19:2; CRC/C/GC/13: 15ff; A/61/299: para 99, 102; Pinheiro 2006: 20) and child friendly justice (CRC Art 19:2; CRC/C/GC/13: 15, 19ff, A/61/299: para 105, 112; Pinheiro 2006: 21). Services and responses to violence should be effectively regulated through standards, regulations, monitoring and oversight (CRC/C/GC/13: 16, 17; A/61/299: para 101; Pinheiro 2006: 21f).
- A trained and committed workforce (CRC/C/GC/13: 17; A/61/299: para 101; Pinheiro 2006: 20), alongside an aware and supportive public, actively involved in efforts to prevent and respond to violence (CRC/C/GC/13: 17ff; A/61/299: para 100; Pinheiro 2006: 19). Children's right to participation is a central component of child protection systems (CRC Art 12; CRC/C/GC/13: 16ff, 28; A/61/299: para 103; Pinheiro 2006: 20) and special efforts should therefore made to actively involve children.
- Data collection systems, which provide regular information on both the prevalence and knowledge of children protection issues and good practice, informing law, policy and action (CRC/C/GC/13: 15; A/61/299: para 107; Pinheiro 2006: 22f)
- Adequate resources for child protection from national and local budgets. States and local authorities must ensure systematic and

3 Also see UNICEF, UNHCR, Save the Children and World Vision (2013): *A Better Way to Protect ALL Children: The Theory and Practice of Child Protection Systems*, Conference Report, p. 1.

transparent budgeting processes, so that allocated resources are spent efficiently (CRC/C/GC/13: 15). Resource constraints cannot provide a justification for a State party's failure to take any, or enough, measures to secure child protection (CRC/C/GC/13: 28).

2. The general role of the EU in protecting children from violence

Against this international backdrop, let us review the actual and potential value brought by the EU to this field, at home and throughout the world. Section 2 will consider the general character and role of EU measures and their interaction with national measures, before looking at the actions of the EU in protecting children from violence, from first steps to recent more specialised measures. Section 3 will then survey the ways in which EU measures can and already do contribute to child protection systems as set out by the UN Committee on the Rights of the Child and the UN Violence Study in Europe and around the world. This shows how the EU holds the potential, and the promise, to make a more concerted effort, whilst pointing to the challenges that lie ahead.

2.1 The general character and role of EU measures

As has been examined in chapters 2 and 6 of this volume, EU powers are clearly defined and delimited by the EU Treaties, in some areas throwing up a distinct border between EU and Member State responsibilities, whilst in others creating areas of overlapping competences. In its external affairs activities with third countries, whether through political dialogue, development cooperation, human rights demarches or humanitarian assistance, EU action has the possibility broadly to promote the fulfilment of children's rights in third countries. Protecting children from violence is a frequent focus of its activities. In the internal affairs setting, the picture is more complex. It is clear that the EU has no general responsibility or powers as regards protecting children in Europe from violence. Member States bear the primary responsibility to establish comprehensive child protection systems. However, in the specific policy areas where the EU has competence to act, such as combatting child sexual abuse and exploitation and trafficking, certain EU measures manifestly and directly relate to protecting children from violence in specific settings and may establish mandatory standards. In other fields, such as social inclusion and social protection, the EU usually acts to foster consensus and cooperative engagement between the State actors within the region, with typical activities including exchange of national experience and good practices.[4] Consequently, the nature and extent of EU intervention within Europe takes different forms depending on the policy area involved and largely depends on the interactions between EU and national competences.

Before scrutinising key recent EU measures, it is useful to identify some features of EU action which help us calibrate the potential scope and impact of EU action. As a preliminary point, at EU level, child protection issues typically arise in the context of other policy concerns such as migration or crime control. It is legitimate to be cautious about how human rights, including child protection concerns, will fare when they are embedded in what traditionally have been primarily considered as economic or security concerns. For example, what risks exist that EU measures concerning trafficking or sexual abuse focus more on the definition of criminal offences, prosecutorial responses or immigration concerns than adequately addressing the needs of children? Second, there is dynamic interaction between EU laws and their implementation at national level which means that the full effect of EU legislation can best be judged only after a number of years, once national implementation has taken shape. This arises because EU directives (the most common form of legislative expression of EU child protection measures) typically contain general obligations which are then transposed into the national legal framework, leaving Member States' discretion to identify the appropriate means for their implementation. Moreover, whilst the EU and Member States must strive for a harmonized implementation of directives across countries, it is a clear challenge to achieve common and coherent understandings between actors at each level, as the baton is passed from the EU institutions to national actors in twenty-eight countries. In sum, the journey from the adoption of common EU provisions through to national implementation can be difficult to navigate, particularly in the sensitive field of child protection.

Notwithstanding these features of EU law-making, it is also clear that there is a real opportunity for the EU to contribute to a safer environment for children at risk of violence. Although crime control and immigration control have been a starting point for key legislation addressing the situation of children in vulnerable situations, recent legislative progress – explored in 2.2.1 below – suggests that there is a growing knowledge of, and commitment to, children's rights by the EU and this is gradually permeating the EU Justice and Home Affairs Agenda. This means that, increasingly, EU legislation

4 In this context, the EU can act under the so-called Open Method of Coordination, which involves, inter alia, the setting of broad policy goals, and guidelines on how to achieve them and benchmark results.

contains more explicit and focused safeguards. Equally, the EU provides unique opportunities to take particular kinds of measures, or to generate a broad reach for certain actions. As one example, the EU frequently represents the best means to establish enforceable transnational child protection mechanisms through cooperation between national border, police and child protection actors across borders. There is an increasing awareness of this role, and improvements in the engagement between national actors on cross-border issues, including, for example, an augmented role for a child's representative in cases exploring family reunification across EU countries of unaccompanied asylum seeking children (Commission Implementing Regulation (EU) No 18/2014 of 30 January 2014, amending Regulation (EC) No 1560/2003 laying down detailed rules for the application of Council Regulation (EC) No 343/2003 establishing the criteria and mechanisms for determining the Member State responsible for examining an asylum application lodged in one of the Member States by a third-country national, Article 1 (7) OJ 8.2.2104).

Furthermore, in Case C 540/03, *European Parliament vs Council of the European Union*, the European Court of Justice has held that:

> It should be remembered that, in accordance with settled case-law, the requirements flowing from the protection of general principles recognised in the Community legal order, which include fundamental rights, are also binding on Member States when they implement Community rules, and that consequently they are bound, as far as possible, to apply the rules in accordance with those requirements.

Thus, although the Member States exercise some discretion, they are clearly bound to act in compliance with fundamental rights and are subject to scrutiny by both their own courts, and the European Court as the final arbiter on the interpretation of EU law. This situation has been reinforced in recent times, given that the EU Charter of Fundamental Rights has become legally binding following the adoption of the Lisbon Treaty. Indeed, in some circumstances, EU law may enhance respect for fundamental rights in a particular sector at national level, as might be the case where a specific reservation to the application of the CRC was made by a Member State.[5]

Finally, it is also evident that, precisely through the adoption of a common EU framework in particular areas such as asylum law, there are ways to leverage experience, tools and funding throughout the region. For example, given the existence of common standards, regional EU guidance can be provided on issues that prove a common challenge to Member States, including training on interviewing asylum seeking children as is provided by the European Asylum Support Agency, or best practice models for guardianship of trafficked children as prepared by the EU Fundamental Rights Agency.

5 For example, in the past, some countries, including the UK, entered reservations against the application of the UN CRC to migrant children.

2.2 Illustrations of EU Action – Achievements to date

Within this intricate framework of different competences and instruments, our analysis below will show that, in their early forays into areas which impact on the protection of children, EU actions were certainly somewhat tentative and less ambitious than they might have been. This includes some of the first steps by the EU in the field of asylum, where EU measures tended simply to make rather general references to the need to protect children, as they are particularly vulnerable. In the first round of EU asylum instruments, safeguards for children tended to be expressed in rather general allusions to the need to respect children's rights. For example, Council Directive 2003/9/EC of 27 January 2003 laying down minimum standards for the reception of asylum seekers contained only limited and general provisions concerning the situation of children. As an example, it noted that "the best interests of the child shall be a primary consideration for Member States when implementing the provisions of this Directive that involve minors". This contrasts significantly with the 2013 recast of the Reception Directive (Directive 2013/33/EU of the European Parliament and of the Council of 26 June 2013 laying down standards for the reception of applicants for international protection (recast)) which contains a provision which specifies a range of factors to be taken into account when assessing the best interests of the child.

Indeed, a number of recent instruments have articulated more specific child protection measures. This was encouraged by the extension of the EU's powers following the Lisbon Treaty (OJ C 306 17.12.2007) in the areas relevant to combatting trafficking and sexual abuse and exploitation, and strengthened the EU's role in this area. We will examine a recent directive to illustrate this development. It is also evident in the activities of the EU in the field of Justice, including, for example, the proposal addressing children suspected or accused in criminal proceedings (European Commission (2013): Commission proposal of 27 November 2013 (COM (2013) 822 final) for a directive of the European Parliament and of the Council on procedural safeguards for children suspected or accused in criminal proceedings).

And whilst these EU measures relating to the protection of children have emerged in a fragmented fashion from disparate policy areas, recent policy discussions have also begun to consider the need and means for a more integrated approach to child protection in EU action. We will consider the Action Plan on Unaccompanied Minors in this regard.

2.2.1 *Directive of 13 December 2011 on combating the sexual abuse and sexual exploitation of children and child pornography*

The UN Violence Study shows that sexual abuse of girls and boys takes place in all settings – in the home, at school, in the community, in institutions and in work places. It is estimated that between 10 to 20 % of children in Europe experience sexual abuse or exploitation during their childhood[6]. Child abuse material (child pornography) has rapidly increased in prevalence on the Internet, and the severity of the abuse shown in the images is worsening[7].The EU responded to this issue with the adoption of a Framework Decision on combating the sexual exploitation of children and child pornography (Council Framework Decision 2004/68 of 22 December 2003, OJ L 13/44, 21.01.2004) in December 2003 under its (former) third pillar on 'Police and Judicial Cooperation in Criminal Matters'. As noted above, the Framework Decision mainly addressed criminalisation of offences and sanctions, touching only lightly on assistance to victims (Article 9).

In 2011, following the entry into force of the Lisbon Treaty, the Framework Decision was replaced by a Directive, introducing a binding legal instrument subject to judicial scrutiny, which Member States had to transpose into their national laws by early December 2013 (Directive 2011/92/EU of 13 December 2011 on combating the sexual abuse and sexual exploitation of children and child pornography, OJ L 335/1, 17.12.2011[8]). The Directive harmonises around twenty criminal offences against children and introduces a comprehensive approach to preventing and addressing child sexual abuse, exploitation and child abuse images. The Directive significantly enhances provisions to support child victims of sexual abuse and exploitation, obliging Member States to provide assistance, support and protection, taking into account the best interest of the child (Article 18). Measures must be taken to ensure that professionals can, and know how to, report suspicion that a child is a victim of child sexual abuse or exploitation. Assistance and support must be provided as soon as competent authorities have indication that abuse or exploitation has taken place, and should be extended to parents or guardians if appropriate (Articles 18-20).

The Directive moreover includes specific emphasis on preventative measures, ranging from reducing demand, to disqualification, to supporting offenders and preventing recidivism (Articles 10, 22, 23, 24). This includes,

---

6 See for example Lalor, and McElvaney, (2010) Overview of the nature and extent of child sexual abuse in Europe, at http://www.coe.int/t/dg3/children/1in5/Source/PublicationSexual Violence/Lalor-McElvaney.pdf and http://ec.europa.eu/dgs/home-affairs/what-we-do/poli cies/organized-crime-and-human-trafficking/child-sexual-abuse/index_en.htm.

7 See for example UNICEF Innocenti Research Centre (2011): Child Safety Online: Global Challenges and Strategies (p. 1).

8 An amendment of the reference number was published in OJ L18/7 of 21.1.2012.

for example, education and training targeting a public audience through information and awareness-campaigns, research and education programmes on a child rights based approach (Article 23(2)). Regular training for officials shall be provided in order to better enable professionals to identify and address cases of child sexual abuse and exploitation (Article 23(3)) and information services providing information on how to recognise 'signs' of sexual abuse and exploitation (Paragraph 45, Preamble) should be set up. Member States are also encouraged to create mechanisms for data collection or focal points which, together with civil society, should observe and evaluate both prevalence and action to combat child sexual abuse and exploitation (Paragraph 44, Preamble). A role is envisaged for the EU to contribute to developing methodologies and data collection to secure comparable data across the EU. Other mechanisms of a transnational character include exchange of information from criminal records between Member States and collaboration across borders to combat child abuse images ('child pornography') as well as 'sex tourism' (Articles 10(3) and 21).

The Directive also includes a broad set of provisions to ensure child friendly justice. Member States must ensure that children have free and easy access to legal remedies. This includes, for example, free legal counselling and representation. A special representative must be appointed in special circumstances, for example, if there is a conflict of interest between the child and the holders of parental responsibility or if the child is separated or unaccompanied (Article 20)). Other provisions aim to prevent children's participation in criminal investigations proceedings causing additional trauma, for example as a result of interviews or visual contact with offenders. Member States must also take necessary measures to ensure non-prosecution or non-application of penalties to victims (Article 20(3), (4) and (5)).Children's right to be heard is also addressed in the context of establishing appropriate action to assist and support victims. Measures should be taken in the best interest of the child on the basis of an adequate assessment of the individual case, taking due account of the child's views, needs and concerns (Articles 18 (1) and 19 (3) CRC).

In formulating the proposal for the Directive, the Commission also sought to ensure that it offered a regional response to current trends and 'new' realities that children face. The legislators aimed at, and in many ways succeeded in, addressing challenges presented by the increasing use of IT technology by introducing provisions on the dissemination of child abuse images and grooming by use of the Internet (2011/92/EU article 5, 6 and 25). This has, in the case of grooming, for instance, generated a regional response, which was limited to five Member States before the Directive.[9]

9 Denmark, Latvia, Poland, Sweden and the UK (Survey and Workshop Reviewing the Transposition of Directive 2011/93/2011 in 11 EU Member States: Overview of national legisla-

The provisions of the Directive are to a large extent inspired by the Council of Europe Convention on the Protection of Children against Sexual Exploitation and Sexual Abuse (Lanzarote Convention). They are also, while less detailed and more limited in scope, in line with the Council of Europe Guidelines on Child-Friendly Justice (Committee of Ministers of the Council of Europe (2010): Guidelines on child-friendly justice, 17 November 2010).[10] Furthermore, the Directive also echoes the approach and content of GC 13 and covers a number of elements that contribute towards building child protection systems, beyond providing a legal framework for prohibiting and addressing sexual abuse and exploitation. As such, it provides for a new, more comprehensive approach, which places children at the centre of legislation and action to protect children.

Therefore, it is clear that the Directive has made a significant contribution towards bringing EU legislation in this area closer to the CRC and the Optional Protocol on the sale of children, child prostitution and child pornography. This includes clear definitions of terms such as 'child' as "any person below the age of 18 years" (Article 2 (a)) and 'child pornography' (Article 2 (c) and 5). The Directive also sets out provisions for the application of the CRC guiding principles, for example "best interest of the child" (Paragraph 2, 6 and 30 Preamble, and Article 18.1). Other important elements include the provisions on, for example, attempt (Article 7.2), confiscation of proceeds (Paragraph 23, Preamble and Article 11) and assistance and protection of victims (Paragraph 31, Preamble, Articles 18 and 19).

Ultimately, the impact of the Directive will, to a large extent, depend on how Member States implement, and integrate, the different provisions. As noted above, Member States may choose the form and methods to transpose the provisions into their national legal system[11], and will most certainly attach different levels of political priority and resources to addressing its various elements. The Directive will also be implemented in different national legal and cultural contexts. For example, the age of legal consent varies across the Member States, ranging from, for example, 13 years in Spain, 15 years in Denmark and 18 years in Malta. This means that while the definition of child sexual abuse is harmonized through the Directive, the legal context in the different Member States will determine how it is implemented.

---

tion transposing Directive 2011/93/EU on combating the sexual abuse and sexual exploitation and child pornography).

10 This includes, for example, the Fundamental Principles set out in Chapter III of the guidelines, including child participation and best interest (Articles A and B.1, Chapter III); the General Elements of Child Friendly Justice (chapter IV), for example Legal Counsel and Representation (Articles Section 2, Article 37, Chapter IV.D), and organization of criminal court proceedings (Section 5, Chapter IV.D).

11 Article 288 of the Treaty on the Functioning of the European Union (TFEU, OJ C 115 of 9 May 2008).

As a legally binding instrument, however, the Directive stands a fair chance at advancing compliance in EU Member States with the international and regional instruments it draws on. The Directive sets out minimum rules, allowing Member States that wish to offer a 'higher level' of protection to do so.[12] As such, it makes an important contribution towards reinforcing the regional and international framework to protect children against sexual abuse and exploitation.

2.2.2 The Action Plan on Unaccompanied Minors

At the same time as the adoption of the Directive on combatting child sexual abuse and exploitation, the EU was negotiating and adopting legislation which provided assistance to trafficked persons, including children, as well as making progress in improving the child protection provisions in the recast of the EU asylum legislation. All of these instruments, as well as the EU Return Directive of 2009 (Directive 2008/115/EC of the European Parliament and of the Council on common standards and procedures in Member States for returning illegally staying third-country nationals, OJ L 348/98, 24.12.2008), contained specific provisions relating to unaccompanied children.

Unaccompanied and separated children in the EU may find themselves in a number of different situations. Some children are in transit, passing through one EU country en route to a final destination. Some unaccompanied and separated children are seeking asylum or protection because of a fear of persecution or because of human rights violations, armed conflict or disturbance in their own country. Other unaccompanied and separated children are the victims of trafficking for sexual or other exploitation. Others have travelled to Europe to escape conditions of serious deprivation or to look for new opportunities or a better life. Some unaccompanied and separated children arrive in Europe seeking family reunification with family members already present. And children may move from 'category' to 'category' over time, or belong to several categories, i.e. they may be looking for family reunification and they may also have been trafficked.

Regardless of their nationality or immigration status, or the category into which they fall, these children have common rights under the UN Convention Rights of the Child to special protection and assistance. However it is clear that there are considerable differences in Member States' laws and practices relating to these children, with divergent practices sometimes also apparent within different regions of the same country. For example, in some countries, the unaccompanied or separated child normally has access to accommodation, health and education services; in other countries, the children may es-

---

12 Article 83 (1) of the Treaty on the Functioning of the European Union (TFEU, OJ C 115 of 9 May 2008)

sentially have to survive on the streets. Detention may be used in some Member States, in particular in cases where the child's age is disputed; in other countries unaccompanied children essentially have a right to remain until they are 18. And although the emerging EU laws sought to harmonise the national standards for reception and applicable procedures in certain settings, this effort was fractured and inconsistent, with different basic provisions within the different laws that apply to children where they seek asylum, are trafficked or become subject to deportation procedures.[13] This lack of a more integrated approach gave rise to clear gaps in protection for these children. The challenge was to find a means for the EU to take a more coherent approach and to seek to draw together, in a coordinated way, actions across the different policy areas involved.

The negotiation and adoption of the Stockholm Programme 2010-2014 (which was to set out a new five year agenda for the EU in the field of justice and home affairs) afforded an opportunity to call for a political prioritization of the issue of unaccompanied children, with significant and proactive discussion and recommendations from civil society and INGOs on the issue; in particular, Save the Children, the Separated Children in Europe Programme, Human Rights Watch, UNICEF and UNHCR. It was a considerable step forward when the Programme indicated that the European Council welcomes the Commission's initiative to "develop an action plan, to be adopted by the Council, on unaccompanied minors which underpins and supplements the relevant legislative and financial instruments and combines measures directed at prevention, protection and assisted return."

The subsequent Commission Communication on the Action Plan on Unaccompanied Minors (2010-2014) had some important and welcome features, including the fact that it expressly puts the best interests of the child and the UN Convention on the Rights of the Child at the heart of all actions. The Action Plan also took a horizontal approach across the policy areas, recognizing the common needs and rights to special protection and assistance of these children, regardless of their reasons for being on the move. A so-called 'global' approach to the situation of unaccompanied children was also promoted in the Action Plan, covering prevention of unsafe migration from countries of origin where possible, ensuring proper conditions of reception in Europe and addressing the need to identify durable solutions in relation to these children. In relation to actions in third countries, the strengthening of child protection systems was explicitly identified.

In September 2012, a mid-term Report on the implementation of the Action Plan was adopted which catalogued actions by the EU, its agencies and Member States in the field. The mid-term report noted that: "The EU Action

13 For a full list of the provisions relating to unaccompanied children in EU asylum and migration legislation, see the Reference Document on Unaccompanied Children: a compilation of EU law and policy, www.connectproject.eu.

Plan on Unaccompanied Minors and the Council conclusions have been important steps in shaping a common, rights-based EU approach to this group of migrant children". It emphasised that an important benefit of this common EU approach was that it "enabled more effective cross-cutting policy reflections on how to address the situation of children, regardless of their migratory status, and has facilitated discussions among EU institutions, national authorities, inter-governmental and nongovernmental organisations in different policy arenas, allowing enhanced exchange of knowledge and practices concerning unaccompanied minors." The Report also referred to the fact that "greater prominence was given to funding measures to address the situation of those children". From a substantive perspective, the Action Plan emphasized that "the explicit recognition of the best interests of the child as the guiding principle has contributed to provisions that ensure increasing protection in the new EU legislative instruments for this particularly vulnerable group of migrants."

The Report provides an indication of the immediate virtues of a more coordinated approach, including those which are important but often somewhat intangible, such as cross-cutting policy reflection. In and of itself, the Action Plan has served as a framework within which to bring together a range of relevant activities, and a means to forge links between them. It is the case that EU measures have made progress in relation to respecting children's rights. However, it is also clear that more can be done; for example, EU provisions continue to permit detention of asylum seeking children, albeit only under certain conditions (Directive 2013/33/EU of the European Parliament and of the Council of 26 June 2013 laying down standards for the reception of applicants for international protection (recast), Article 11). This stance is not in line with the stark recommendation to prohibit such detention by the UN Committee on the Rights of the Child in its Report following a General Day of Discussion on Children in International Migration (Committee on the Rights of the Child, Report on the 2012 Day of General Discussion, the Rights of all Children in International Migration).

And whilst some specific EU practical measures have been taken, such as the development of reference material on age assessment by the European Asylum Support Office, it is also clear that the Action Plan had the potential to inspire further practical improvements regionally, and it is important that the Commission continue to dedicate resources and energy to this end. The own-initiative resolution on the situation of unaccompanied children by the French MEP Natalie Griesbeck, which was adopted by European Parliament in August 2013, importantly noted that "the comprehensive protection of unaccompanied minors requires further measures" (REPORT on the situation of unaccompanied minors in the EU (2012/2263(INI) Committee on Civil Liberties, Justice and Home Affairs).

2.3 Conclusion

This experience of developing law and policy in these fields at EU level has generated, and should continue to generate, a more confident and sophisticated approach to addressing these issues from the perspective of child rights, and, in particular, a child's right to protection. Indeed, there is clearly a growing recognition by the EU of the role of child protection systems in protecting children from violence, as witnessed by the theme of the Annual European Fora on the Rights of the Child hosted by the European Commission in November 2012 and December 2013, namely: 'Supporting child protection systems through the implementation of the EU Agenda for the rights of the child'. Indeed, at the meetings in 2012 and 2013, the Annual EU Child Rights Forum has considered how national child protection systems can reach out to children in migration ("children on the move"). The Parliament's political views, and ongoing policy discussions, should add momentum to taking further steps in this field. Moreover, as provided by the EU Strategy towards the Eradication of Trafficking in Human Beings, the EU is currently engaging in the development of guidance on child protection systems. To contribute to this process, the Fundamental Rights Agency engaged in a mapping of Member States' child protection systems. The mapping examines the scope and key components of national child protection systems across the EU. It focuses on the systems' laws, structures, actors and how the systems function, as well as human and financial resources and the existing accountability mechanisms. The Commission also held an on-line public consultation on the issue.[14] In June 2014, the 9th European Forum was on "Coordination and cooperation in integrated child protection systems.[15] The Forum was accompanied by a Reflection Paper from the Commission which is intended, inter alia, to "enhance understanding of where and how the EU can act to reinforce national child protection systems and forge the necessary links between them to address cross-border protection needs".[16] It contains ten overarching principles of integrated child protection systems.

Section 3 will examine what this means for future opportunities for the EU, Member States and stakeholders to work together to strengthen child protection systems within Europe more closely. .

14 S. http://ec.europa.eu/justice/newsroom/fundamental-rights/opinion/140402_en.htm. The results of the consultation can be found here: https://ec.europa.eu/eusurvey/publication/EU-guidance-on-integrated-Child-Protection-Systems.

15 S. http://ec.europa.eu/justice/fundamental-rights/rights-child/european-forum/ninth-meeting/index_en.htm.

16 S. http://ec.europa.eu/justice/fundamental-rights/files/2015_forum_roc_background_en.pdf.

3. Future directions – How can the EU effectively contribute to national child protection systems

At this juncture, the central question is how can the EU best respond to the commonly acknowledged need to build and reinforce child protection systems within and outside Europe. In Section 2 above, we examined the EU's general role and reviewed some landmark efforts to date. Below we look at a few examples of how the EU contributes to the *components* of a child protection system. This will demonstrate that, through a wide range of the legal and non-legal tools in its arsenal, the EU can support and resource child protection systems.

The potential impact of the EU deriving from such measures is undeniable, both within the EU and outside. However, it is also evident that coordination is vital to fulfil the full potential of the EU role. A necessary immediate step is ensuring a more comprehensive and shared understanding of how EU measures can be designed and applied to reinforce the national systems, and how the EU's partners benefit from and support their development. Guidance from the Commission, broadly sustained and used consistently in EU actions, would help achieve this, and we will also touch upon other challenges that lie ahead in this regard.

3.1 EU support to national and regional coordination mechanisms

The EU Agenda on the Rights of the Child commits the EU to promoting the exchange of best practice, cooperation and communication with and between Member State national authorities to protect children's rights (European Commission 2011: 5). In the field of child protection, the EU has contributed to strengthening national and regional coordination in specific areas. As an example, the EU has adopted legislation to secure cooperation between Member States to protect and implement rights of victims (Directive 2012/29/EU establishing minimum standards on the rights, support and protection of victims of crime: Article 29). As we have seen above, the EU can also develop regional strategies concerning the protection of children, such as the Action Plan on Unaccompanied Minors (European Commission Communication *Action Plan on Unaccompanied Minors 2010-2014*, COM(2010)213 final).

EU agencies can also play a specific role in coordinating regional responses to specific child protection issues. As an example, Europol (CIRCAMP) has acted to coordinate transnational investigations on child abuse images. Funding is another means by which the EU supports coordination. For instance, the programme on Prevention of and Fight against Crime (ISEC), has allocated funds towards co-operation between experts and law enforcement authorities to gain common understanding and combat cybercrimes (European Commission 2012: 9)[17].

In the context of EU external affairs, the EU Guidelines on the Rights of the Child (European Council 2007) commit to giving children's rights more weight on the international agenda by systematically including children's rights in meetings and discussion with international and regional organizations. The Guidelines also promote partnership and coordination with international stakeholders including the UN, regional organisations, such as the CoE, OSCE and ENOC as well as civil society, research institutions and international financial institutions.

3.2 Legal and policy frameworks

As examined above, EU legislation addressing child protection concerns can establish important safeguards. As we have seen, recent EU legislation, such as the *Directive to combat child sexual abuse, child sexual exploitation and child pornography*, has contributed to bringing EU legislation closer to the CRC and the CoE Conventions[18]. This is a crucial development, since EU Directives are binding on Member States, and therefore can make an important contribution towards enforcing international agreements.

In the past ten years, we have seen an increased recognition of the role of the EU in strengthening the legal and policy framework for child protection in third countries. In July 2015, the EU adopted a new EU Action Plan on Human Rights and Democracy, which includes action to: "Support partner countries' efforts to promote, protect and fulfil children's rights with a particular focus on strengthening child protection systems to protect children from violence, exploitation, abuse and neglect".[19]

Children's rights are systematically raised in the context of third country dialogue. In 2012, for example, the EU discussed children's rights in political dialogue with a range of countries including Russia, Israel/Palestine, the

17 Implementing Decision of 19.9.2012 on adopting the annual work programme for 2013 for the specific programme on the 'Prevention of and Fight against Crime' as part of the General Programme *Security and Safeguarding Liberties*, C(2012) 6402 final.

18 See 2.5 for detailed discussion of the Directive on combating child sexual, abuse child sexual exploitation and child pornography.

19 Council of the European Union (2015): *Council Conclusions on the Action Plan on Human Rights and Democracy 2015 -2019*, 10897/15, Brussels July 2015.

Republic of Moldova and Brazil, and included children's rights as a specific topic of concern in more than 60 of its human rights strategies (Council of the EU 2013: 82-83).[20]

The EU actively promotes universal ratification and implementation of the CRC and its Optional Protocols as well as other international and regional human rights instruments relevant to the protection of children against all forms of violence. In 2012, the EU implemented a global campaign to promote ratification of the two Optional Protocols to the UN Convention on the Rights of the Child and ILO Convention 182 on the worst forms of child labour (EU/EEAS 2013: 20, 81).[21] According to the EU, this had a positive impact on ratification of these instruments by EU partner countries ((EU/EEAS 2013: 20). Political dialogue with third countries also presents opportunities to encourage governments to review and reform their legal and regulatory framework. In the area of trade, the Generalised Scheme of Preferences (GSP+) link trade preferences with ratification and implementation of human rights instruments, including the UN Convention on the Rights of the Child (European Parliament and Council 2012)[22].

The EU Guidelines on children's rights promote action to raise particular violations or shortcomings through political statements, declarations or so-called démarches which remind third countries of their obligations to adopt effective measures to protect children against harm. Child protection is one of the topics that are prioritized in this context (EU/EEAS 2012: 20)[23]. Examples of such action include a statement on the issue of child marriage in Yemen (EEAS 2013)[24], and EU concerns raised on the death penalty on minors in Ethiopia in 2012 (Council of the EU 2013: 103)[25]. In 2012, the EU also called for the protection of vulnerable groups, including children, in Syria, through Council conclusions in October and December (EU 2013: 84).[26] Demarches can also serve as a tool to encourage governments to take into account concluding observations of the Committee on the Rights of the Child and of other relevant treaty bodies, using information from UN agen-

20 Council of the European Union (2013): *EU Annual Report on Human Rights and Democracy in the World in 2012* (Thematic Reports), Brussels, May 2013.

21 European Union (2013): *EU Annual Report on Human Rights and Democracy in the World in 2012* (Thematic Reports).

22 Regulation No 978/2012 applying a scheme of generalised tariff preferences OJC L 303/60, Chapter III, article 9 and Annex VIII.

23 European Union (2012): *Human Rights and Democracy in the world: Report on EU Action in 2011*, Brussels 2012.

24 European Union External Action Service (2013): Statement by EU High Representative Catherine Ashton on child marriage in Yemen/130913/01.

25 Council of the European Union (2013): *EU Annual Report on Human Rights and Democracy in the World in 2012* (Country Reports), Brussels, October 2013.

26 Council of the European Union (2013): *EU Annual Report on Human Rights and Democracy in the World in 2012* (Thematic Reports).

cies, regional organizations, national independent institutions and civil society organizations (European Council 2007: 8).

The EU accession process is an example of how regional processes can provide opportunities to raise child protection concerns and contribute to legal reform. For example, children's rights, including child protection, feature heavily in the questions from the Commission to pre-accession countries[27].A concrete example of change includes the alteration of the criminal code in relation to child sexual abuse in Serbia (European Commission 2013)[28]. Research carried out in Romania also shows that the accession process contributed towards bringing Romania closer to the international framework for child protection.[29]

It is worth highlighting that the EU also contributes towards the development and adoption of new instruments that reinforce international agreements. The EU annually sponsors a UN resolution on the Rights of the Child, together with Latin American States (European Council 2007: 2). In 2007, the EU took the lead in drafting a resolution on the elimination of violence against children (UN General Assembly (2006): Article 13-19)[30]. The resolution encouraged all stakeholders to disseminate the UN Study on Violence against children and called on actors to explore its role in taking the recommendations forward. The resolution also establishes a mandate for a UN Special Representative on Violence against children. The EU has actively supported the establishment and renewal of the mandate and has enjoyed support for the implementation and review of the EU Guidelines on Children's Rights from the Representative.[31]

3.3 Services and justice for children

EU law presents an important opportunity to secure adequate services and child friendly justice. The Directive on combating child sexual abuse, child

---

27 See for example the Commission's Questionnaire to Serbia at http://www.seio.gov.rs/home.50.html: Answers to the European Commission's questionnaire.

28 Staff Working Document: *Serbia 2013 Progress Report SWD* (2013) 412 final, p. 40).

29 Manole, M. (2011) *Governance Fit for Children: To what extent have the general measures of implementation of the UNCRC been realised in Romania?* Save the Children Romania. See also Iusmen, I. (2014) *Children's Rights, Eastern Enlargement and the EU Human Rights Regime*, Manchester, Manchester University Press.

30 United Nations General Assembly (2006): Resolution A/RES/61/146 Rights of the Child of December 2006

31 See for instance http://srsg.violenceagainstchildren.org/category/regions/europe and Statement delivered by Mr Pit Koehler, Delegation of the EU to the UN, at General Assembly Third Committee on Item 65: Right of the Child, New York October 2013

sexual exploitation and child pornography, the Directive on preventing and combating trafficking in human beings and protecting its victims and the Directive establishing minimum standards on the rights, support and protection of victims of crime all establish obligations on assistance, reporting and referral, as well as provisions to protect children before, during and after criminal proceedings.[32] The EU has moreover established legal obligations in relation to guardians, legal representatives and special procedures in trafficking proceedings concerning international protection status and returns to third countries (Directive 2011/36/EU: Articles 11 and 12). Other possible measures include funding for projects to support prevention and assistance, such as the 116 000 hotlines, which are designed to report missing children and provide social support services for children and families when a child goes missing.[33]

In the context of EU external affairs, the EU offers practical support for the establishment and maintenance of adequate child protection systems in third countries, for example by providing technical assistance and financial support for the provision of services as well as establishment and enforcement of minimum standards and monitoring mechanisms. In 2012, the EU provided over 40 million under the 'Investing in People' programme, targeted towards the eradication of violence against children (European Commission (2012)[34].

Collection and sharing of regional and national data on child protection issues within the EU and in third countries is also a priority for the EU. In Europe, the Commission has, for instance, supported mapping and data collection on missing children (European Union 2013)[35]. The European Commission has also proposed new legislation, which encourages Member States to collect data recorded by judicial authorities and healthcare and social welfare services so that progress in terms of implementing the legal provisions can be monitored and evaluated (European Commission 2013)[36].

32 Directive on combating child sexual abuse, child sexual exploitation and child pornography, Article 20, Directive 2012/29/EU establishing minimum standards on the rights, support and protection of victims of crime OJ L 315/57 14.11.2012; in particular Article 24 and Directive 2011/36/EU on preventing and combating trafficking in human beings and protecting its victims, OJ L 01/1 15.4.2011 Articles 12 and 15.

33 S. http://ec.europa.eu/justice/fundamental-rights/rights-child/hotline/index_en.htm.

34 European Commission (2012): Investing in People, Actions for child protection – Violence against children Restricted call for Proposals, Guidelines for grant applicants EuropeAid/ 133527/C/ACT/Multi.

35 Missing Children in the European Union: Mapping, data collection and statistics.

36 Commission proposal of 27 November 2013 (COM(2013)822 final for a directive of the European Parliament and of the Council on procedural safeguards for children suspected or accused in criminal proceedings, Preamble para 44, p. 16.

3.4 Child participation

Various EU instruments, including both law and policy, recognize child participation as a fundamental right to all children.[37] For instance, the Directive establishing minimum standards for victims of crime includes provisions to ensure children's rights to information and to understand, to be heard and to be understood (Directive 2012/29/EU: Articles 3, 4, 6 and 10).

The importance and impact of child participation has also gained increased emphasis and support in EU development policy and funding. Promoting the involvement of civil society, including children, is now recognized as an important aspect of EU development cooperation including, for instance, the Cotonou Agreement Article 26[38] and 'A Special Place for Children in EU External Affairs' (p. 7), which gives the EU a role in supporting children to play an active role in matters that affect them[39]. In 2009, the Commission launched a call for proposals on child participation, with the specific purpose of contributing to the Commission's commitment to enable children's involvement in development and in the realisation of their rights (European Commission 2009). The call became extremely popular, and the Commission eventually funded a broad range of child participation projects across the globe including, for example, children's participation in decision-making in the context of return and resettlement (Azerbajan), Awareness Raising and Empowerment for Bedouin Girls (Israel), empowering children with disabilities in Russia to actively participate and express their concerns, and children's participation in news and Media (South Africa and Zambia)[40].

3.5 Training for professionals

EU law imposes service provision, and training and monitoring obligations for professionals in contact with children. For instance, EU asylum legisla-

37 "Children shall have the right to such protection and care as is necessary to their well-being. They may express their views freely. Such views shall be taken into consideration on matters which concern them in accordance with their age and maturity" (Charter of Fundamental Rights of the EU: Article 24(1)). See also for instance the EU Agenda on the Rights of the Child COM (2011) 60 final 15.2.2011, Chapter 3, p. 13ff.

38 European Union (2000): *Partnership agreement between the Members of the African, Caribbean, and Pacific Group of States and the European Community and its Member States*, Cotonou, June 2000.

39 A special place-

40 For a complete list of projects see https://webgate.ec.europa.eu/europeaid/online-services/index.cfm?ADSSChck=1256571293611&do=publi.detPUB&searchtype=AS&Pgm=7573845&debpub=&orderby=upd&orderbyad=Desc&nbPubliList=15&page=1&aoref=129133.

tion requires the involvement of actors who are periodically trained (Directive 2011/95/EU of the European Parliament and the Council on standards for the qualification of third country nationals or stateless persons as beneficiaries of international protection, for uniform status for refugees or for persons eligible for subsidiary protection, and for the content of the protection granted, OJ L 337/9, 20/12/2011, Article 31). The Directive establishing minimum standards for victims of crime and the Directive on combating child sexual abuse, child sexual exploitation and child pornography also contain provisions to ensure training of professionals who come into contact with victims (Directive 2012/29/EU: Article 25, Directive 2011/92/EU: Article 23(3)).

EU financial support is also available for the training of professionals; as an example, the Commission launched a call under the Fundamental Rights and Citizenship Programme on training of practitioners who work with children in detention or residential care and on child friendly justice for legal and other professionals who come in contact with children (European Commission (2013): JUST/2013/FRC/AG – Fundamental Rights and Citizenship).

Funding for the training of professionals has also been channelled to third countries through the EU's development cooperation. This was, for instance, done in the call under Investing in People, on Action on Child Protection, which included a specific priority on "training and education programmes for professionals and non-professionals who work with or for children (teachers, coaches, policemen, etc.), with formulation and implementation of codes of conduct, ethics and standards of practices, incorporating children's rights" (Investing in People, Actions for child protection – Violence against children, Restricted call for Proposals, Guidelines for grant applicants, UuropeAid/133527/C/ACT/Multi), p. 6).

3.6 Adequate resources

The EU budget is an important instrument in resourcing initiatives which aim to address specific protection concerns, as well as different components of national child protection systems. Above, we have seen examples of funding allocated from the Fundamental Rights and Citizenship programme. The Daphne programme (European Parliament and of the Council 2007)[41], which aims to contribute to the protection of children, young people and women against all forms of violence, has funded a number of projects over the years

41 Decision No 779/2007/EC of the establishing for the period 2007-2013 a specific programme to prevent and combat violence against children, young people and women and to protect victims and groups at risk.

with impact on child protection, including on trafficking, domestic violence, sexual abuse and bullying.[42] There are also other programmes including, for example, Prevention of and Fight against Crime (ISEC) and the European Refugee Fund, which address national and cross-border child protection concerns. For example, in 2013, ISEC allocated 5 million € to targeted calls for proposals on a broad set of activities to combat child sexual exploitation (European Commission 2012).[43]

The EU is a major donor to third countries, and has allocated funding towards implementation of children's protection rights. As noted above, the EU has provided funding for child protection under the Investing in People Programme. The European Instrument for Democracy and Human Rights (EIDHR) has also specifically prioritized children in pre-accession countries[44], and children affected by armed conflict (European Parliament and Council 2006: Article 2:1b). Moreover, the EU can impose legal obligations or enter into agreements with third countries, which have implications on how national child protection systems are resourced. Development cooperation can, in combination with political dialogue, provide opportunities to encourage, and in some cases require, an approach which centres on child protection.

3.7 Future Challenges

The direct impact of the EU deriving from the measures described above is undeniable, both within the EU and outside.

However, as we have seen above, of its nature, and particularly in the field of strengthening child protection systems, the EU must work closely and on an ongoing basis with Member States and stakeholders. And whilst international guidance such as GC 13 provides a clear overview of what elements need to be in place for systems to thrive, there remain challenging questions on how to work collectively in this field in practice. Unless the EU and its Member States can make effective and strategic use of collective strengths and resources across policy areas, the EU may simply end up largely paying lip-service to the goal of reinforcing and linking national child protection systems. In contrast, by committing politically to the issue and investing in

---

42 For a list of illustrative projects visit: http://ec.europa.eu/justice_home/daphnetoolkit/html/illustrative_projects/dpt_illustrative_projects_en.html.

43 Implementing Decision of 19.9.2012 on adopting the annual work programme for 2013 for the specific programme on the 'Prevention of and Fight against Crime' as part of the General Programme *Security and Safeguarding Liberties*, C(2012) 6402 final, p. 9.

44 See for instance http://www.europa.rs/en/srbija-i-evropska-unija/eu_assistance_to_serbia/EIDHR.html.

efforts to reinforce national systems and coordinate efforts, we should see the emergence of concrete practices having a real impact throughout Europe.

All stakeholders (including civil society, international organisations and agencies) have a palpable role to play in charting the best course for EU action to take. This will raise some difficult questions; solutions will not always be easy. But clearly this process will involve consolidating existing EU measures and it will require that child protection concerns are put at the heart of new initiatives. It will be helped by fostering the exchange of practice and information between child protection actors regionally. It may demand the development of further transnational mechanisms involving child protection actors, alongside existing transnational mechanisms involving crime control and border officials. And, crucially, it should take on the challenge of prevention in a more robust and effective way.

4. General conclusions – The EU as a global actor

Drawing back from the specific activities of the EU, what conclusions can we reach as to the impact of the EU as a global actor in the field? It is clear that, day-to-day, the EU has a direct impact on the extent to which rights are realized in practice (or not), in the EU and beyond, in its various guises as a legislator, policy maker, donor, development cooperation partner, to name a few. As we have seen, the diversity of its activities provides it with an opportunity to support comprehensive approaches to child protection, in conjunction with national systems.

Globally, the EU can and does use its political and economic/financial leverage to drive national and international child protection agendas forward. As an entity that is conscious of the combined force it represents on the world stage, the EU has been able to promote and generate international response to specific child protection issues, e.g. atrocities against children in a specific conflict. A key challenge remains to ensure policy coherence and systematic consideration of children's rights in the context of, for example, security, defence and trade.

Within the EU, the EU law effectively acts as an 'agent' of international law, in that the international rights which EU law embodies essentially become directly enforceable at national level when applying EU instruments, with the machinery of the Member States' national courts obliged immediately to ensure its application. The Court of Justice of the European Union (CJEU) also plays an important role in securing judicial scrutiny. In the future, post the accession of the EU to the European Convention on Human

Rights as foreseen in the Lisbon Treaty, the added scrutiny of EU action by the European Court of Human Rights will also be important.

Of course, in its law and policy making, the EU grapples with political and practical realities within the Member States and sometimes struggles to translate the often general provisions of international law obligations into practical contexts. It is undeniable that, within the EU legislative and policy process, respect for rights may also suffer, as in any political process, when confronted by powerful competing concerns, such as security issues. We see this in the provisions which continue to permit detention of asylum seeking children.

However, as we have also seen, in translating general rights into concrete and actual contexts, EU laws may sometimes go beyond what is required by international law, for example, in relation to online grooming. Moreover the EU can be a valuable contributor of precedent on the practical implementation of child rights in specific contexts, globally. For example, the Action Plan on Unaccompanied Minors is a striking attempt to coordinate concrete actions and efforts in an area that is legally complex and politically sensitive.

In conclusion, it is both interesting and challenging to be on the brink of a deepening EU response to issues of child protection. With the development of guidance on integrated child protection systems, the EU is faced with a unique opportunity to achieve more effective outcomes in terms of both preventing and responding to violence against children. However, it is also clear that synchronizing the many disparate activities of the EU to this end will take significant effort. Beyond the major step of achieving a common understanding of the issues, it will require both political commitments and dedicated processes across EU policy areas, across EU institutions and in a variety of different national, regional and international settings. Transparency and stakeholder engagement, both regionally and nationally, will be of vital importance. The EU should continue to seek actively and visibly to draw on, and contribute to, international law and policy processes on the issues. Clearly the challenges faced are long term, but equally clear is the critical importance of the goal pursued – preventing and responding to violence against children. And the current steps within the EU to take these challenges on, including continued political commitment to address violence against children in the context of EU external affairs, stronger legislative safeguards within the EU, the engagement of the EU Annual Child Rights Forum on these issues and the development of EU guidance, hold the promise of better outcomes.

References

Committee of Ministers of the Council of Europe (2010) Guidelines on child-friendly justice, 17 November 2010.
Council of Europe (2010) Convention on the Protection of Children against Sexual Exploitation and Sexual Abuse, CETS No. 201, Lanzarote 25.10.2007.
Council of the European Union (2003) Directive 2003/9/EC of 27 January 2003 laying down minimum standards for the reception of asylum seekers, OJ L 31/18, 6.2.2003.
Council of the European Union (2013) EU Annual Report on Human Rights and Democracy in the World in 2012 (Country Reports), 15144/13, Brussels October 2013.
Council of the European Union (2013) EU Annual Report on Human Rights and Democracy in the World in 2012 (Thematic Reports), 9431/13, Brussels May 2013.
Council of the European Union (2015): Council Conclusions on the Action Plan on Human Rights and Democracy 2015 -2019, 10897/15, Brussels July 2015.
Council of the European Union (2003) Framework Decision on combating the sexual exploitation of children and child pornography, 2004/68 of 22 December 2003, OJ L 13/44, 21.01.2004.
Cox, T., Lind-Haldorsson, O. and O'Donnell, R. (2012) Keys to creating a safe place for children: The role of the EU in strengthening national child protection systems, Brussels, Save the Children.
Delegation of the EU to the UN (2013): Statement delivered by Mr Pit Koehler at General Assembly Third Committee on Item 65: Right of the Child, New York, October 2013.
European Commission (2013) SAFER INTERNET: A multi-annual programme on protecting children using the Internet and other communication technologies, Work Programme 2013 C (2013) 1954 Brussels, 11 April 2013.
European Commission (2013) CALL FOR PROPOSALS FOR ACTION GRANTS JUST/2013/FRC/AG SUPPORT TO TRANSNATIONAL PROJECTS - Fundamental Rights and Citizenship.
European Commission (2010) Communication Action Plan on Unaccompanied Minors 2010-2014,COM(2010) 213, final.
European Commission (2011) Communication EU Agenda on the Rights of the Child, COM (2011) 60, final.
European Commission (2012) Implementing Decision of 19.9.2012 on adopting the annual work programme for 2013 for the specific programme on the 'Prevention of and Fight against Crime' as part of the General Programme Security and Safeguarding Liberties, C(2012) 6402, final.
European Commission (2009) Investing in Children, Children's Participation, EuropeAid/ 129133/C/ACT/Multi.
European Commission (2012) Investing in People, Actions for child protection — Violence against children, EuropeAid/133527/C/ACT/Multi.
European Commission (2012) Communication The EU Strategy towards the Eradication of Trafficking in Human Beings 2012-2016, COM(2012) 286, final.
European Commission (2012) Report from the Commission to the Council and the European Parliament, Mid-term report on the implementation of the Action Plan on Unaccompanied MinorsCOM (2012) 554, final.
European Commission (2013) http://ec.europa.eu/justice/fundamental-rights/rights-child/hotline/ index_en.htm.

European Commission (2012) Background Paper, Forum on the Rights of the Child: 'Supporting child protection systems through the implementation of the EU Agenda for the rights of the child', Brussels, November 2012.
European Commission (2013) Commission proposal of 27 November 2013 for a directive of the European Parliament and of the Council on procedural safeguards for children suspected or accused in criminal proceedings COM(2013) 822, final.
European Commission (2013) Staff Working Document: Serbia 2013 Progress Report SWD(2013) 412, final.
European Council (2007) EU Guidelines on the Rights of the Child.
European Council (2010) The Stockholm Programme – An open and secure Europe serving and protecting citizens, OJ C115/1, 4.5.2010.
European External Action Service (2013) Statement by EU High Representative Catherine Ashton on child marriage in Yemen/130913/01, Brussels. September 2013.
European Parliament (2013) Resolution of 12 September 2013 on the situation of unaccompanied minors in the EU, P7_TA-PROV (2013)0387, Strasbourg.
European Parliament and Council (2007) Decision No 779/2007/EC of the establishing for the period 2007-2013 a specific programme to prevent and combat violence against children, young people and women and to protect victims and groups at risk.
European Parliament and Council (2012) Directive 2012/29/EU establishing minimum standards on the rights, support and protection of victims of crime OJ L 315/57 14.11.2012.
European Parliament and Council (2013) Directive 2013/33/EU laying down standards for the reception of applicants for international protection (recast) OJ L 180/96, 29.6.2013.
European Parliament and Council (2011) Directive 2011/92/EU on combating the sexual abuse and sexual exploitation of children and child pornography, OJ L 335/1, 17.12.2011.
European Parliament and Council (2011) Directive 2011/36/EU on preventing and combating trafficking in human beings and protecting its victims, OJ L 01/1 15.4.2011.
European Parliament and Council (2006) Regulation (EC) No 1889/2006 on establishing a financing instrument for the promotion of democracy and human rights worldwide, December 2006 OJ L 386/1.
European Union (2000) Charter of Fundamental Rights of the European Union, OJ C 364/01, 18.12.2000.
European Union (2015): EU Action Plan on Human Rights and Democracy (2015-2019).
European Union (2012) Human Rights and Democracy in the world: Report on EU Action in 2011, Brussels.
European Union (2007) Lisbon Treaty OJ C 306 17.12.2007.
European Union (2013) Missing children in the European Union: Mapping, data collection and statistics, Belgium.
European Union (2000) Partnership agreement between the Members of the African, Caribbean, and Pacific Group of States and the European Community and its Member States, Cotonou, June.
European Union (2008) Treaty on the Functioning of the European Union, OJ C 115 of 9.5.2008.
Iusmen, I. (2014) Children's Rights, Eastern Enlargement and the EU Human Rights Regime, Manchester, Manchester University Press.
Lalor, K and McElvaney, R.(2010) Overview of the nature and extent of child sexual abuse in Europe, in: Council of Europe (2010) Protecting children from sexual violence – A comprehensive approach, Strasbourg, Council of Europe.
Lind-Haldorsson, O. (2011) Governance Fit For Children: To what extent have the general measures of implementation of the UNCRC been realized by the EU?, Stockholm, Save the Children Sweden.

Manole, M. (2011) Governance Fit for Children: To what extent have the general measures of implementation of the UNCRC been realised in Romania?, Bucharest, Save the Children Romania.

Missing Children (2012) Survey and Workshop Reviewing the Transposition of Directive 2011/93/2011 in 11 EU Member States: Overview of national legislation transposing Directive 2011/93/EU on combating sexual abuse, sexual exploitation and child pornography, Brussels, Missing Children.

Pinheiro, P. S. (2006) World Report on Violence against children, Geneva, New York, United Nations Secretary-General's Study on Violence against Children.

Save the Children (2009) Background Paper to Conference Addressing the Protection gap for unaccompanied and separated children in the EU: Role of the Stockholm Programme, Brussels 15 September 2009.

Schuurman, M. and Stalford, H. (2011) Are We There Yet?: the Impact of the Lisbon Treaty on the EU Children's Rights Agenda, in: International Journal of Children's Rights 19 pp. 381-403.

UNICEF, UNHCR, Save the Children and World Vision (2013) A Better Way to Protect ALL Children: The Theory and Practice of Child Protection Systems, Conference Report.

United Nations Children's Fund (2011) Child Safety Online: Global Challenges and Strategies, UNICEF, Innocenti Research Centre.

United Nations Committee on the Rights of the Child (2011) General Comment No. 13, The right of the child to freedom from all forms of violence.

United Nations General Assembly (1989) Convention on the Rights of the Child, General Assembly resolution 44/25 of 20 November 1989.

United Nations General Assembly (2000) Optional protocol on the involvement of children in armed conflict to the Convention on the Rights of the Child, General Assembly resolution A/RES/54/263 of 25 May 2000.

United Nations General Assembly (2000) Optional Protocol on the Sale of Children, Child Prostitution and Child Pornography to the Convention on the Rights of the Child, General Assembly resolution A/RES/54/263 of 25 May 2000.

United Nations General Assembly (2006) Report of the Independent expert for the United Nations study on violence against children A/61/299.

United Nations General Assembly (2006) Resolution A/RES/61/146 Rights of the Child of December 2006.

The Implementation of the Right to be Heard in Juvenile Justice Proceedings in Europe

Stephanie Rap

1. Introduction

The adoption of the Convention on the Rights of the Child [CRC] by the United Nations [UN] and its subsequent ratification by nearly all countries around the world marked a turning point in the way that the rights of children are perceived. Since then children have been increasingly recognised as rights holders and social actors who are attributed autonomy and agency (Article 12 CRC; Doek 2007; Fitzgerald et al. 2009; Freeman 1992, 2007; Hanson 2012; Sinclair 2004). Having specific rights means that one can exercise agency and, according to Freeman (2007), being recognised as an agent means that children can participate in decisions that affect their life.

However, claiming the right to participate is not yet possible for many children across various different settings (Fitzgerald et al. 2009). This is especially true for participation in juvenile justice procedures. Although children are criminally responsible from a certain age,[1] the acknowledgement that children have certain rights in this context is not always a matter of course (Freeman 1992). Recently, in Europe several developments have taken place to increase child-friendly justice practices. The 2011 EU Agenda for the Rights of the Child identified making the justice system in Europe more child-friendly as a key priority of the European Commission (Commission, 2011:6).[2] Moreover, the European Commission (2011: 8) states that the use of the Council of Europe Guidelines on child-friendly justice (2010)[3] should

1 The UN Committee on the Rights of the Child (2007) recommends that 12 years should be the absolute minimum age of criminal responsibility (MACR) (para. 32). Some of the European countries involved in this study have a MACR that is below the age of 12. Greece and Scotland have the lowest age level, set at 8 years. In England and Wales, France and Switzerland the MACR is set at 10 years, and in Ireland and the Netherlands the MACR is 12 years. In Germany, Italy and Spain the MACR is higher, namely 14 years.

2 Communication from the Commission to the European Parliament, the Council, the European Economic and Social Committee and the Committee of the Regions, *An EU Agenda for the Rights of the Child,* COM(2011) 60 final.

3 *Guidelines of the Committee of Ministers of the Council of Europe on Child-Friendly Justice* (adopted by the Committee of Ministers on 17 November 2010 at the 1098th meeting of the Ministers' Deputies).

be promoted and taken into account in future legal instruments (see further Stalford, this collection).

The participation of juvenile defendants in the youth court is the central theme of this chapter. The analysis is informed by a cross-national comparative study of the practical implication of Article 12 CRC in juvenile justice procedures across 11 European countries. This involved a detailed study of juvenile law and policy documents across different jurisdictions, as well as systematic observations of more than 3,000 youth court hearings.[4] To set the scene, the children's rights framework with regard to the right to be heard will be outlined. Special attention will be given to the implementation of this right in an EU context.

2. Child-friendly justice in Europe

The concept of participation in juvenile justice procedures emerged for the first time in the 1985 UN Standard Minimum Rules on the Administration of Juvenile Justice (commonly known as the Beijing Rules).[5] Rule 14.2 provides that juvenile justice proceedings should take place in "an atmosphere of understanding, which shall allow the juvenile to participate therein and to express herself or himself freely". The Beijing Rules can be seen as a framework and model for national juvenile justice systems (Van Bueren 1992) and are seen as "the first child-specific instrument setting standards for the administration of juvenile justice" (Liefaard 2008: 110). Moreover, it influenced the drafting of Art 40 CRC, which contains provisions related to juvenile justice (Liefaard 2008; Sloth-Nielsen 2001). Although the Beijing Rules are not legally binding the UN Committee on the Rights of the Child (CRC Committee 2007) has recommended applying the rules to all children who are in conflict with the law (para. 4). The right to participate in juvenile justice proceedings as laid down in rule 14.2 can be seen as having served as an example for Art 12 CRC.

---

4 For the purpose of uniformity the term *youth court* will be used when referring to different types of courts and administrative bodies that are competent to deal with juvenile defendants.

5 The rules are named after the city, Beijing, where the conference was held and where much of the drafting of the document took place. The Beijing Rules were prepared as a response to a call made by the Sixth United Nations Congress on the Prevention of Crime and the Treatment of Offenders in 1980 (UN Doc. Res. 4, Sixth United Nations Congress on the Prevention of Crime and the Treatment of Offenders, No. E.8.IV.4.) to develop minimum rules regulating the administration of juvenile justice.

2.1 The right to be heard – Art 12 CRC

The CRC is the first international children's rights instrument in which participatory rights for children are introduced explicitly (Cantwell 1992). Moreover, the participatory rights of children are the most significant feature of the CRC because they acknowledge the growing autonomy of children and grant children the opportunity to participate in the decisions that affect their lives (Van Bueren 1995).

Art 12 forms one of the general principles of the CRC (CRC Committee 1991: para. 13). The right to be heard encompasses "the right to express those views freely in all matters affecting the child, the views of the child being given due weight in accordance with the age and maturity of the child" (Art 12 (1) CRC). Art 12 places a duty upon the states parties to the CRC to involve children in all matters that affect them (Van Bueren 1995). According to Abramson (2006), one of the most valuable developments stemming from the CRC is that its provisions promote the participation of children at all levels of society. As a consequence, the right to be heard and, more broadly, the right to participate[6] has important implications for the treatment of juvenile defendants in the youth court. Art 12 (2) CRC provides that the child should be given "the opportunity to be heard in any judicial and administrative proceedings". This means that special procedures and guidelines should be created by the states parties for the judicial and administrative bodies (such as youth courts) that have to ensure the participation of children in matters that affect them directly (see also CRC Committee, 1996: paras. 43-44). The accused child's procedural capacity to be heard in juvenile justice proceedings (either directly, or through a representative) is provided by this provision. Art 12 (2) CRC implies that juvenile defendants should always be heard in criminal cases against them and authorities should not obstruct the juvenile in exercising this right, on the basis of his age or maturity (Van Bueren 1995).

According to Lücker-Babel (1995) the right of the child to be heard implies that the child can no longer be seen as a passive and silent being and individual children should be heard in all cases affecting them concretely and directly. Listening to the views of the child and giving those views due weight seems to be a simple message, but it has to be fulfilled effectively and with respect for the child (Krappmann 2010). In general the UN Committee on the Rights of the Child has asserted that giving due weight to children's views is challenging and requires change. The Committee (2003) continues that "Listening to children should not be seen as an end in itself, but rather as a means by which States make their interactions with children and their actions on behalf of children ever more sensitive to the implementation of chil-

6 The term *participation*, however, is not explicitly used in Art 12 CRC.

dren's rights" (para. 12). In General Comment No.12 the CRC Committee gives further guidelines on how to implement Art 12 CRC, with special provisions concerning the right to be heard in judicial proceedings. The goal of the recommendations is among others to "propose basic requirements for appropriate ways to give due weight to children's views in all matters that affect them" (CRC Committee, 2009: para. 8).

However, in the CRC no further guidelines are given concerning the implementation of this right to be heard in justice procedures. States are implicitly encouraged to make the decision-making process with regard to matters affecting the child accessible to the child because states must "assure to the child … the right to express those views freely" (Art 12 (1) CRC). This may mean that the decision-making process, or at least a part thereof, has to be adapted to the age and level of maturity of the child (Van Bueren 1995). Lundy (2007) notes that the word 'assure' indicates that proactive steps should be taken to obtain children's views and that adults should not wait until children give their own views by themselves. Opportunities should therefore be created for children, within a safe space, to be involved in a certain procedure or decision-making process.

The CRC follows a holistic approach towards children's rights (Sloth-Nielsen 1995). Hammarberg (1995) notes that all the rights in the CRC are interdependent and interrelated. This means that every right adopted in the CRC must be acknowledged when dealing with children in specific situations, such as when the child is suspected of having committed an offence. For example, the right to be heard is instrumental to the application of the best interest of the child principle as laid down in Art 3 CRC, and vice versa; to fully implement Art 3 the right to be heard should be taken into consideration, because the best interest of the child cannot be adequately determined without hearing the views of the child (Krappmann 2010; Lücker-Babel 1995). The best interest of the child can only be adhered to when keeping a balance between, on the one hand, the decision-making executed by adults and, on the other, the growing autonomy and capacity of the child to give his or her opinion on matters that closely affect him or her. Cipriani (2009) states that a delicate balance exists between Arts 3 and 12. Adults should determine and protect the best interest of children, but the right to express views cannot be denied on the basis that adults in the life of the child know what is best for him (Lundy 2007). Art 12 guarantees children the possibility to express their views in all matters affecting them, and therefore "imposes obligations on how adults interpret and implement the best interest of the child" (Cipriani 2009: 27). However, when hearing the views of the child authorities must determine how much weight to attach to them in determining what is in the best interest of the child, taking into account the age and level of maturity of the child.

In this regard, Art 12 should also be read in light of Art 5 CRC, which stipulates the 'evolving capacities' of the child to exercise his rights. Both Art 5 and 12 relate to the development of the child and both have implications that change over time as the child develops into maturity (Lücker-Babel 1995). The concept of evolving capacities means that the child's 'competence to exercise his rights autonomously may be subject to limitations and fall under the responsibility of others, such as parents' (Beijer and Liefaard 2011: 74). Therefore, the child's level of maturity should be taken into account when he or she is heard; only children who are capable of forming their own views have the right to be heard; moreover, the views of the child should be weighed in accordance with his age and level of maturity. Art 5 gives guidelines on how to interpret the term *maturity* in Art 12. Maturity increases when the child grows older, and as a consequence, the weight to be given to the child's views becomes heavier. In some instances, it may be in the best interest of the child not to adhere to his or her views or wishes entirely in the decision-making process. Although the views of the child must be seriously considered, the final responsibility for making the decision about the child lies with the adult (Krappmann 2010).

The concept of evolving capacities implies that a balance must be maintained between regarding children as active agents in their own lives who can exercise their own rights and providing them with protection, because of their immaturity and development (Lansdown 2005). Art 12 (1) CRC can be considered to be of a dynamic nature, because of the implications that the age and maturity of the child have on his or her (level of) participation (Beijer and Liefaard 2011). Individual assessments of the level of maturity have to be made in every case involving a child, because the weight given to the views of the child depends on his or her level of maturity. Therefore, it is rather difficult to establish fixed age limits with regard to the right to be heard because children's developmental trajectories vary so much. As a consequence, individual differences in the capacity to express views should be taken into account when assessing the weight to be attached to them (Lansdown 2005; Saywitz et al. 2010; Stalford 2012).

The UN Committee on the Rights of the Child has further specified the notion that child-centred procedures should be employed in a specialised youth court, in its General Comment No. 10 and No. 12 (CRC Committee 2007; 2009).[7] The CRC Committee states explicitly in General Comment No. 10

7 The UN Committee on the Rights of the Child has been established to monitor the implementation of the CRC. It compromises of 18 elected members drawn from the states parties that act independently of their country. The Committee reviews the obligatory reports that states submit to the CRC Committee every five years. Furthermore, it issues general comments, providing states parties with guidelines on how to apply the provisions of the CRC in practice. General Comment No. 10, titled *Children's rights in juvenile justice*, serves the purpose of providing guidelines on the implementation of articles 37 (on deprivation of lib-

that "the right to be heard is fundamental for a fair trial" (para. 44). The Committee assumes that if a juvenile can be held accountable for having committed an alleged offence (and therefore can be prosecuted), he or she should also be capable of participating in criminal proceedings. Subsequently, the Committee argues that this may also require that courtroom procedures and practices should be modified, depending on the age and maturity of the child (para. 46).

The call for modified procedures in court for juvenile defendants is substantiated by the CRC Committee by giving more concrete guidelines on what these procedures should entail. The child has the right to be informed of the charges brought against him as soon as possible in a language he or she understands (para. 47). Information should be communicated to the young person directly and the provision of information to parents or legal guardians should therefore not be seen as an alternative to communicating information to the young person (para. 48). The responsibility of professionals to ensure that the juvenile defendant understands the charges that are brought against him or her requires a certain amount of specialisation in communicating with young people. This is underpinned by the fact that the CRC Committee notes that to treat children in accordance with their age and to promote their reintegration, all professionals involved in the administration of juvenile justice must have knowledge of child development, the continuing growth of children and what is considered to be appropriate to their well-being (para. 13; see also CRC Committee 1996: para. 46).

In General Comment No. 12, the CRC Committee recommends that every judicial procedure concerning minors should be both "accessible and child-appropriate" (para. 34). The meaning of this notion is further specified by indicating that attention needs to be paid to, for instance, the provision and delivery of child-friendly information, appropriately trained staff, design of courtrooms, clothing of judges and lawyers, sight screens and separate waiting rooms (para. 34). The views of juvenile defendants should be heard in any proceeding – throughout the entire juvenile justice process (paras. 35; 58) – and it should take place by means of a talk or dialogue, rather than a "one-sided examination" (para. 43). The dialogue can best be held in an environment in which the child feels safe and respected and the states parties are responsible for creating such a child-appropriate court environment (paras. 26; 60). The CRC Committee (2009) states that "simply listening to the child is insufficient; the views of the child have to be seriously considered ..." (para. 28). The context in which the child is heard should be enabling and encouraging, and the child should favourably be heard in closed court ses-

---

erty) and 40 CRC (on the administration of juvenile justice). General Comment No. 12, titled *The right of the child to be heard*, gives further guidelines on how to implement article 12 CRC, in different legal procedures such as civil judicial proceedings, divorce proceedings and juvenile justice proceedings.

sions (paras. 43, 61). So, a judge should make room for the child to give his views on the matter, should be willing to listen to the child and should seriously consider the child's story in his decision-making (para. 42). Furthermore, the Committee makes a connection between expressing views freely and conducting the hearing behind closed doors. Hearings held through video-link to facilitate the child's participation and protection should be the rule and exceptions should be very limited (para. 61; see also CRC Committee, 2007: para. 65). Moreover, the juvenile defendant should be properly informed about the outcome of the hearing and about the extent to which his views have played a role in the decision-making of the judge. The Committee states that "the feedback is a guarantee that the views of the child are not only heard as a formality, but are taken seriously" (para. 45). Furthermore, adults need to be trained in communicating with children, because they require "preparation, skills and support to facilitate children's participation effectively ..." (para. 134 (g)).

2.2 Impact of the CRC at EU level

In recent years, the CRC has had considerable impact on standard setting and the implementation of children's right across Europe, including in the European Court of Human Rights (Kilkelly 2011). Other chapters in this collection have also highlighted that, alongside the CRC, the Charter of Fundamental Rights of the European Union[8] is considered to be of considerable value to the European Commission in moulding their children's rights programme. In Art 24 of the Charter two general principles of the CRC (the best interests of the child and the right to be heard) are incorporated. It is stated that children "may express their views freely. Such views shall be taken into consideration on matters which concern them in accordance with their age and maturity" (Art 24(1)). Moreover, the child's best interests must be a primary consideration in all actions relating to children (Art 24 (2)). These provisions are clearly inspired by the CRC and the ECHR (Stalford 2012).

Of importance is the fact that the Charter has gained considerable legal force. The Charter's rights must be respected and its application should be promoted by EU institutions and Member States (see Stalford 2012). The Commission aims to make sure that its legislative proposals are in full compliance with the fundamental rights guaranteed in the Charter (the so-called fundamental rights check). The rights of the child, as guaranteed by Art 24 of the Charter, are included in the fundamental rights check, which the Com-

8 Solemn Proclamation of the European Parliament, the Commission and the Council at Nice on 7 December 2000, OJ 2000 C346/1, amended in 2007, [2010] OJ C 83/02, 389.

mission applies to relevant draft EU legislation (European Commission, 2011).

As already noted, the European Commission makes clear in its EU Agenda for the Rights of the Child that making justice systems in Europe more child-friendly is an important priority. With regard to juvenile justice procedures child-friendly justice is linked to the right to a fair trial. This implies "the protection of privacy, the right to be informed about the charges and the proceedings in a way which is adapted to the child's age and maturity,[9] legal assistance and legal representation" (European Commission 2011: 7; see also Stalford, this collection).

Responding to the priorities set by the EU Agenda several measures have been put in place to strengthen the procedural position of children involved in criminal proceedings. First, in 2012 the EU issued a directive with regard to minimum standards on the rights of crime victims.[10] The purpose of the directive is to ensure that crime victims receive appropriate information, support and protection and are able to participate in criminal proceedings. Special provisions apply to the protection of child victims in criminal procedures (Art 24) and children are granted the right to be heard, whilst taking into account their age and maturity (Art 10). Second, in 2013 a directive has been issued regarding the right of access to a lawyer in criminal proceedings.[11] This directive inter alia ensures that child suspects have access to a lawyer and are provided with adequate information to understand the consequences of waiving the right to be legally represented (Art 3). Third, the Commission has proposed a directive on procedural safeguards for children suspected or accused in criminal proceedings.[12] Most important to this study is Art 16 in which the right of children to appear in person at the trial is assured (see para. 2.4).

9 For example, in 2010 the EU adopted rules on interpretation and translation that ensure that all persons, including children, receive information about their rights in the proceedings in a manner that they can understand (Directive 2010/64/EU of the European Parliament and the Council of 20 October 2010 on the right to interpretation and translation in criminal proceedings).

10 Directive 2012/29/EU of the European Parliament and the Council of 25 October 2012 establishing minimum standards on the rights, support and protection of victims of crime, and replacing Council Framework Decision 2001/220/JHA.

11 Directive 2013/48/EU of the European Parliament and the Council of 22 October 2013 on the right of access to a lawyer in criminal proceedings and in European arrest warrant proceedings, and on the right to have a third party informed upon deprivation of liberty and to communicate with third persons and with consular authorities while deprived of liberty.

12 Proposal for a Directive of the European Parliament and the Council on procedural safeguards for children suspected or accused in criminal proceedings, 22 May 2014, 2013/0408 (COD).

Before turning to a more detailed analysis of how child-friendly juvenile justice processes are in reality, the next paragraph elaborates more generally on the right to a fair trial in light of the ECHR and case law of the ECtHR.

2.3 The right to a fair trial – Art 6 ECHR

The CRC is not directly enforceable on states parties and no sanctions can be imposed on States who fail to comply with the provisions laid down in the Convention (Stalford 2012). Stalford (2012) argues that while provisions of the CRC are embedded in EU legislation, the EU is limited in the extent to which it can actually bring about changes in child-related issues if they fall solely or largely within domestic (as opposed to EU law-making) competence.

That said, the right to a fair trial has been laid down in Art 47 of the Charter of Fundamental Rights of the European Union. This states that "Everyone is entitled to a fair and public hearing within a reasonable time by an independent and impartial tribunal previously established by law. Everyone shall have the possibility of being advised, defended and represented". In this context 'everyone' includes minor suspects. As such, even though domestic juvenile justice issues do not traditionally fall within EU competence, the expanding reach of EU fundamental rights protection at least ensure that children's rights in justice proceedings are protected in areas where the EU is competent to legislate.

The ECHR is also an important supra-national reference point in ensuring that domestic juvenile justice procedures conform to the CRC. Importantly, the ECtHR has produced some critical jurisprudence which has interpreted the right to a fair trial (Art 6 ECHR) in the light of children's rights principles, often referring explicitly to the CRC (Cipriani 2009; Kilkelly 2008b). It helps, of course, that Art 6 (1) of the ECHR specifically mentions children: it is specified that the press and public can be excluded from the court hearing when it is deemed to be in the interest of the juvenile. Notable examples include *Stanford v. UK* (Application no. 16757/90, Judgment 23 February 1994) in which the ECtHR stated that Art 6 ECHR "guarantees the right of an accused to participate effectively in a criminal trial" and that "...this includes, inter alia, not only his right to be present, but also to hear and follow the proceedings" (para. 26). Significant also is the ECtHR's reasoning in the 1999 notorious cases of *T. and V. v.. UK* (Application no. 24724/94, Judgment 16 December 1999; Application no. 24888/94, Judgment of 16 December 1999). This involved two 10-year-old boys who had kidnapped and beat to death a two-year old, James Bulger. The two minors (at the time of trial they were 11 years old) were prosecuted on indictment in the Crown Court.

Their trial took place in public before a judge and 12 jurors and both defendants were found guilty by the trial jury. Subsequently, both defendants complained before the ECtHR that a number of their fundamental rights had been violated during the trial and sentencing. Both argued that they had not been given a fair trial because they were not able to fully participate (Beijer and Liefaard 2011; Cipriani 2009; Dohrn 2006). Notably, in the judgment the Court refers to provisions of the Beijing Rules (rules 4 (age of criminal responsibility), 8 (protection of privacy) and 17 (adjudication and disposition)), the CRC (Arts 3 (best interests of the child), 37 (deprivation of liberty) and 40 (administration of juvenile justice)), a Council of Europe recommendation on social reactions to juvenile delinquency[13] and the concluding observation made by the CRC Committee on the United Kingdom in 1995.

In its judgment, the ECtHR ruled that '…it is essential that a child charged with an offence is dealt with in a manner which takes full account of his age, level of maturity and intellectual and emotional capacities, and that steps are taken to promote his ability to understand and participate in the proceedings' (paras 84-86). Moreover, the Court maintained the view that '…the formality and ritual of the Crown Court must at times have seemed incomprehensible and intimidating for a child of eleven' (paras 86-88) and that the defendant(s) had been 'unable to participate effectively in the criminal proceedings against him and was, in consequence, denied a fair hearing …'. As a result, the ECtHR concluded that the juvenile defendants were denied a fair trial by prosecuting them in an adult criminal court and in public (paras 85-91).

The approach of the ECtHR to youth justice issues is an important source of inspiration for the EU in the development of its own measures in the field of criminal justice. The proposed EU directive on procedural safeguards for children suspected or accused in criminal proceedings[14] introduces measures that are consistent with the reasoning in *T. and V.* The Commission states that from Art 6 ECHR follows that an accused person has the right to appear in person at the trial (Art 16). Therefore Member States should take appropriate measures to promote that children are present at their trial and they should lay down practical arrangements regarding the presence of the child at the trial. Moreover, it is acknowledged that children should be "treated in a manner appropriate to their age, their special needs, their maturity and level of understanding, and bearing in mind any communication difficulties they may have".[15] Trials against children should be organised away from the glare of public attention (Art 14 (1)) and children should have the right to be accompanied by an adult (Art 15 (1)), because they "are vulnerable and are not able

13 Recommendation No. R (87) 20 of the Committee of Ministers to member states on Social Reactions to Juvenile Delinquency, 17 September 1987.

14 Above note 12.

15 Above note 12.

to fully understand and follow criminal proceedings".[16] Moreover, they should not be able to waive their right of access to a lawyer (Art 6).

ECtHR case law also offers guidance on how court procedures should be adapted to respond to the developmental stage of the juvenile defendant. In the 2004 case of *S.C. v. UK* (Application no. 60958/00, Judgement of 15 June 2004), an 11-year-old was charged with the attempted robbery of an 87-year-old woman and was indicted to the Crown Court. The hearing in the Crown Court was adjusted to the child's age: the defendant was accompanied by a social worker, he was not required to sit in the dock, the judge did not wear a wig and gown and frequent breaks were taken (Dohrn 2006). Despite the special arrangements that were made, the Court concluded that S.C. *'was unable fully to comprehend or participate in the trial process'* (para. 26). The Court explained that the juvenile defendant needs to understand the charges and the possible consequences and outcomes of the trial in order to be able to effectively participate in his trial (para. 29). However, Art 6 ECHR does not imply that a juvenile defendant should understand every legal detail during the criminal trial: *'Given the sophistication of modern legal systems, many adults of normal intelligence are unable fully to comprehend all the intricacies and all the exchanges which take place in the courtroom'* (para. 29). The purpose of legal representation is therefore to inform and guide the defendant through the trial. Furthermore, the Court decided that the defendant should have been tried in a specialised court, with adapted procedures, which would have had regard for his young age and low level of intellectual maturity (para. 35). Interestingly, in this judgment no direct references are made to the CRC or other children's rights standards.

A fourth ECtHR case to offer concrete guidance on how to interpret children's rights in the context of justice proceedings is that of *Güveç v. Turkey* (Application no. 70337/01, Judgement of 20 April 2009). This involved a 15-year-old Turkish boy who complained that he had been deprived of a fair trial because he was not able to participate effectively. Again, in the judgment several provisions of the CRC, parts of the concluding observations made by the CRC Committee with regard to Turkey and the recommendation of the Council of Europe on social reactions to juvenile delinquency (Recommendation no. R (87)20) are considered to be relevant international texts. The Court concluded that a *'...lack of legal assistance for most of the proceedings exacerbated the consequences of the applicant's inability to participate effectively in his trial and infringed his right to due process'* (para 132). The importance of the presence of a lawyer at a court hearing was stressed because a lawyer could have contributed to more effective participation.

16 Above note 12.

2.4 The Council of Europe Guidelines on Child-Friendly Justice

The discussion has already alluded to the (legally non-binding) Guidelines of the Committee of Ministers of the Council of Europe on child-friendly justice (2010, hereafter referred to as the guidelines). In its EU Agenda on the Rights of the Child the European Commission (2011) committed to promoting the use of the guidelines and to taking these into account in future legal instruments. Although the guidelines are of a non-legally binding nature, they provide the most extensive account of how child-friendly justice should be defined and substantiated in national juvenile justice systems, offering a detailed supplement to the guidance provided by the CRC[17] (Kilkelly 2011).

In the guidelines it is stated that child-friendly justice is:

"...in particular, justice that is accessible, age appropriate, speedy, diligent, adapted to and focused on the needs and rights of the child, respecting the rights of the child including the rights to due process, to participate in and to understand the proceedings, to respect for private and family life and to integrity and dignity (para. II, c)".

The guidelines contain what are called general elements of child-friendly justice. One of these elements is to be informed and given advice from the first involvement with the juvenile justice system and throughout the justice process. Children should, for example, be informed of their rights, the juvenile justice system and its different procedural steps that have to be taken, the charges and the court dates. Parents should be informed when charges are brought before the court as well, but giving information to parents should not be an alternative to providing the child with information (para. IV, art. 3; see also CRC Committee 2007: para. 48).

Concerning the right to be heard it is stated that it is of importance to explain the judgment or outcome of the court case to the child and it is stressed that this is of particular importance when the views of the child are not followed in the decision-making (para. IV, art. 49). Whether this is the responsibility of the judge or another professional is left open. However, it is stated that the lawyer (or legal guardian or legal representative) "should explain the given decision or judgment to the child in a language adapted to the child's level of understanding" (para. IV, art. 75). The lawyer, therefore, has an important role in assisting the juvenile defendant not just before and during, but *after* the court hearing has taken place, not least in advising on whether to take further steps in the procedure (e.g. an appeal or complaint).

With regard to the organisation of the proceedings it is recommended that children should be dealt with 'in non-intimidating and child-sensitive set-

17 The general comments of the CRC Committee have a broader reach: the CRC has 194 states parties, compared to 47 Member States of the Council of Europe.

tings' (para. IV, art. 54), although no further specification of these terms is given. Furthermore, children should be given an explanation of the layout of the court and the roles of the professionals before the youth court hearing starts (para. IV, art. 55). The child's lawyer can play an important role in preparing his client before the hearing. Judges can play an important role in providing information to the juvenile defendant during the hearing, on the roles of the different parties and on the procedures that will be followed. Furthermore, it is recommended that language should be used that children understand (para. IV, art. 56); that professionals should treat children "with respect and sensitivity" (para. IV, art. 57); that children should be able to be accompanied by their parents (para. IV, art. 58); and that court sessions are adapted to the "child's pace and attention span" (para. IV, art. 61). It is recommended that hearings should not last too long, that regular breaks should be scheduled and that during the hearing distractions should be avoided (para. IV, art. 61). It seems that these recommendations refer mainly to the youth court hearings in adversarial procedural systems, where trials can last for a long time as a result of the oral presentation of evidence and where it is more common especially for lawyers to walk in and out of the courtroom during hearings (see for example Kilkelly 2008a). Arguably the optimum means of ensuring compliance with the guidelines on child-friendly justice is to put in place specialised youth courts which are staffed by appropriately trained professionals.

2.5 EU law and child-friendly justice

There is already some evidence of the European Union embracing the guidelines in its own legal and policy measures. Several of the guidelines have been incorporated in the proposed Directive on procedural safeguards for children suspected or accused in criminal proceedings.[18] Next to more general provisions, such as the right to information (Art 4), the right to legal representation (Art 6) and the right to privacy in criminal proceedings (Art 14), more child-specific provisions are laid down in this directive. First, the right of children to be accompanied by a parent or carer during the court hearing is acknowledged (Art 15). It is explained that a holder of parental responsibility should be informed about the procedural rights of the child, because "children are vulnerable and are not always able to fully understand and follow criminal proceedings".[19] Second, children have the right to be present at their court hearing (Art 16). In an earlier version of the proposed

18 Above note 12.
19 Above note 12.

directive this right was framed as a right to a procedure in which the child can participate. In the explanatory memorandum it was explained that special measures should be taken to ensure that vulnerable suspects, such as children, can effectively participate in criminal justice proceedings in compliance with their right to a fair trial.[20] Unfortunately, in the most recent draft only the *presence* of the child is laid down and not his or her *participation* in the procedure (Art 16(1)). Therewith, the role of the juvenile defendant in the criminal procedure falls short of upholding the child's right to be actively involved in the procedure.

Third, providing adequate training to professionals is acknowledged in the directive. Art 19(1) states that professionals "who deal with cases involving children receive adequate training to a level appropriate to their contact with children with regard to children's legal rights, appropriate interviewing techniques, child psychology, communication in a language adapted to the child and pedagogical skills". The directive does not go as far as to state that children should be tried in specialised youth courts, but strong demands are made on the Member States to provide training to judges and prosecutors involved in criminal proceedings and to lawyers, in order to raise awareness of the needs of children (Art 19(1a)-(2)).When and if the directive is eventually adopted, insofar as Member States will be obliged to achieve the objectives set out therein, it will add significant *legal* force to Member States' existing political and moral obligation to incorporate more fully the components of child-friendly justice as expressed in the CRC and the Council of Europe guidelines.

3. Methodological considerations: Juvenile law in action

The international children's rights law and standards described above demonstrate that there is an unequivocal obligation to provide juvenile defendants with the opportunity to participate in youth court procedures. This demands some scrutiny, then, of how these international standards are actually substantiated in national juvenile justice systems. Substantial room for discretion is left for states to determine how specialised laws, procedures, authorities and institutions should be implemented. Some countries have a separate juvenile justice system, with youth courts (resembling the adult criminal court to a greater or lesser extent) in which juvenile defendants are tried, whereas

20 Proposal for a Directive of the European Parliament and the Council on procedural safeguards for children suspected or accused in criminal proceedings, 27 November 2013, COM(2013) 822 final.

other countries have a welfare or family law system in which both delinquent and endangered children are steered towards protection and intervention (Sloth-Nielsen 2001). To answer this question it is necessary to study juvenile law 'in action' in addition to studying 'law in books'.[21] This is confirmed by Doob and Tonry (2004) who state that the understanding of a youth justice system can be greatly enhanced by not only studying the law as it is written but also the law as it is administered in practice.

The findings discussed below compare and contrast the role and experiences of juvenile defendants in youth justice proceedings in a number of European jurisdictions. Goldson and Muncie (2006: 95) state that "examining contemporary youth justice systems through a comparative lens informs rethinking by providing a number of both general and specific insights". The insights presented below focus on a specific part of youth justice systems: youth court hearings.

It is of importance to study the participation of juvenile defendants in practice to identify and perhaps even achieve an EU-wide converging approach to child participation in youth justice proceedings. A first step towards successfully implementing optimum child-friendly justice standards is to gain knowledge on current practices. Goldson and Kilkelly (2013) state that considerable dissonance exists between international human rights standards and the reality of youth justice interventions and the everyday experiences of children involved in youth justice proceedings. The dissonance between rhetoric and reality is considered to be "a wider global phenomenon" (Goldson and Kilkelly 2013: 367). Moreover, an important shortcoming of most international children's rights law is the fact that states still exercise a large degree of discretion in the implementation of these provisions and few control systems are in place. Several scholars have therefore argued that the enforcement mechanisms (of the CRC, for example) are too weak to ensure the child's right to be heard (Freeman 2007; Goldson and Muncie 2012).

In recognition of the disparate approaches to youth justice, and in a bid to address the lack of systematic reliable data on which to develop evidence-based policies (EU Agenda, p. 5), the European Commission has funded far-reaching research on children's involvement in criminal, civil and administrative judicial proceedings. The first part of this study consists of the collection of statistical data and the examination of the legal and policy situation in the 28 Member States of the EU with regard to children's involvement in judicial proceedings (European Commission 2014). To supplement this, the European Union Agency for Fundamental Rights (FRA) has completed a qualitative study examining the treatment of children in criminal and civil proceedings.

21 The distinction between 'law in books' and 'law in action' was first made by Pound (1910). These terms refer to the activities of lawmakers and law enforcers. Law in the books refers to rules and norms and what those say about what is supposed to happen. Law in action refers to the application of the law in practice (in Nelken 2010).

This study focuses specifically on the theme of children's participation across a selection of 10 EU Member States, and is primarily informed by interviews with professionals and children involved in criminal and civil judicial proceedings. This study shows that child participation practices vary widely across and within the 10 Member States. Moreover, these practices do not always qualify as child-friendly. FRA concludes that training and multidisciplinary cooperation of professionals involved in proceedings are key to ensuring child-friendly justice (FRA 2015). These two research initiatives show that the EU is investing in data gathering and knowledge exchange across its Member States. The data collected by the author and presented below supplements EU-funded work, providing a fuller picture of how the participation of juvenile defendants is manifested in court (see also Rap 2013).

3.1 An overview of the study

Between 2005 and 2012, a total of 3,019 juvenile defendants were observed in youth courts and other competent administrative bodies in the youth justice systems in 11 European countries. The countries involved were: Belgium, England and Wales, France, Germany, Greece, Ireland, Italy, the Netherlands, Scotland,[22] Spain and Switzerland. The countries are selected on the basis of purposive sampling (and not with the aim of reaching a statistically-representative sample) (Boeije 2010). The aim was to select a wide variety of juvenile justice systems in Europe, representing the Anglo-Saxon legal tradition as well as the continental legal tradition. However, the selection of countries also depended on practical constraints, such as limitations in language skills and gaining access to court hearings. The cases that were observed per court were not pre-selected, but merely coincided with the period in which the observations were scheduled to take place. In each country contact was sought with courts, through contact persons (e.g. fellow academics and professionals working in criminal courts). Moreover, in each country attempts were made to gain access to a court in an urban area (in many cases the country's capital) and a court in a smaller town or rural area, to be able to study regional differences as well.[23] The observations in the different countries were conducted by several researchers, who worked under the supervision of the author of the current chapter. Every researcher mastered the language of

22 It should be noted that England and Wales and Scotland are part of the same nation state, the United Kingdom. They do, however, represent separate jurisdictions.

23 Only in Greece and in Scotland (the children's hearings system) this aim was not achieved and cases have been observed in only one site. To overcome this limitation, previous studies have been used to complement the findings of this study. Moreover, in Greece a larger number of cases have been observed in the one site involved in this study.

the respective country. Gaining access to youth court hearings before starting the study was of special importance, because in most countries these hearings are closed to the public (except for Belgium and the Scottish youth court). In every country, permission to observe youth court hearings was granted by the president of the respective court or head of the juvenile section of the court, as well as from the judge hearing the case. Moreover, consent was obtained from the juvenile defendant and his or her parent(s) before the start of every hearing. In cases where a parent or legal guardian was not present, the legal representative of the young person was asked to give consent. Juveniles, parents and lawyers were able to object to the presence of a researcher by indicating so to the judge, in which case the researcher left the courtroom. Only in a small number of cases the young person or the judge decided that the researcher could not observe the hearing.

4. Hearing the views of juvenile defendants

The participation of juvenile defendants in the juvenile justice system – and more specifically in the youth court and other competent administrative bodies dealing with juvenile criminal cases – poses a major challenge for youth court professionals. In this section the extent to and manner in which the views of juvenile defendants are heard in Europe will be presented. First, though, the setting in which hearings take place will be described.

4.1 The physical setting

On the basis of the observations of hearings a distinction can be made between the types of youth court settings. First, it must be made clear that different types of hearings have been observed. Youth court hearings range from the first and subsequent pre-trial (detention) hearings, hearings in which the case is settled before one judge in chambers or in court, trials before one judge or a panel of judges (a full court), sentencing and sentence review hearings. It is worth noting that in some countries different types of hearings are dealt with in chambers. For example in France and Germany minor cases are handled by the judge in chambers, whereas in the Netherlands only pre-trial detention hearings are held in chambers. Moreover, in the Anglo-Saxon countries every type of hearing takes place in court. Accordingly, a distinction is not made between (judicial) types of hearings, but between types of settings in which the hearings take place.

First, the Scottish children's hearing can be seen as an example of a hearing taking place outside a court.[24] A children's hearing takes place before a children's panel, which consists of lay members of the community. The hearings are conducted at the office of the *Scottish's Children's Reporter Administration* and not in a court building. The hearings take place in a room, resembling an office space, around an oval-shaped table in the middle of the room. The setting in which the children's hearing takes place is relatively informal. On one side of the table the three panel members are seated next to each other, with the chair occupying the position in the middle. In front of the panel members the child and his or her parent(s) and other relevant persons (such as a social worker, a lawyer,[25] a safeguarder,[26] or other representative) have a seat. On the far side of the table, the reporter has a seat with a small table next to him or her on which a computer rests. The room is generally rather small, sparsely decorated and the windows have the blinds drawn. Because the hearings are not open to the public (s.78 (2) Children's Hearings (Scotland) Act 2011), no space has to be reserved for members of the public. Moreover, the chairman has the duty to keep the number of people present at the hearing to a minimum (s.78 (4) Children's Hearings (Scotland) Act 2011). The informality of the setting is emphasised by the fact that the lay panel members wear normal clothes (as opposed to a judicial gown) at the hearing and speak in laymen's terms. Moreover, they come from the same community as the child and his family and are often familiar with the neighbourhood and the community where the family lives. The relatively small, informal and closed setting of a children's hearing facilitates active participation of children and parents, as will be shown in the following sections.

The setting in which the children's hearing in Scotland takes place resembles the Swiss practice. In the German-speaking part of Switzerland the large majority of cases are handled by the prosecutor *(Jugendanwalt)*. The meeting with the prosecutor takes place at the office of the *Jugendanwaltschaft*, which is usually located in a separate building from the general prosecution service

24 In Scotland, children between 8 and 16 years of age who display delinquent behaviour can in principle not be found guilty of a crime. In the case of delinquent behaviour a child can be sent to a children's hearing, where a welfare measure might be imposed. However, the minimum age of criminal prosecution is set at 12, which means that children from 12 years of age and on can be transferred to the adult court (i.e. the Sheriff court or the High court) in case of a serious offence (s. 41A Criminal Procedure (Scotland) Act, 1995; s. 52 Criminal Justice and Licensing (Scotland) Act, 2010). Moreover, from the age of 16 children are in principle prosecuted in the adult criminal court (s. 42 Criminal Procedure (Scotland) Act 1995).

25 No lawyers were observed at the hearings, in contrast with social workers who were present at every hearing.

26 A safeguarder is an independent person appointed by a children's hearing (or by a sheriff) to safeguard the interests of the child in the proceedings. A safeguarder is not a representative or advocate of the child (Comben et al. 2003).

(*Staatsanwaltschaft*). The hearing has a distinct informal character: the prosecutor does not wear a gown; the young person is generally seated at the same table as the prosecutor; and parents or other representatives are either seated behind the or next to the young person at the same table. It is noteworthy that, when a lawyer is present,[27] he or she does not sit next to the juvenile defendant, but at another table behind or next to the young person.

In France it is common practice to conduct hearings in the office of the youth court judge (*enchambre*) which is often located in a general court building. The judge hears in principle every young person in chambers (except when the young person is taken into pre-trial detention). Mouhanna and Bastard (2011) call the interaction between the judge and young people and their families the core of the work of the judge. In chambers the atmosphere can be characterised as informal. In contrast with the youth hearings in court, the judge in chambers wears no gown and the prosecutor is usually not present. A lawyer for the young person and a clerk are always present.

Besides the hearings in chambers, in every country involved in this study youth hearings were observed in a proper courtroom. The largest contrast with the hearings in chambers can be found with the court settings in the Anglo-Saxon countries, where an adversarial court tradition is prevalent (in this study the countries that fall under this tradition are England and Wales, Ireland and Scotland). The youth courts in England, and Wales and Scotland[28], and the children's court in Ireland are generally larger than the courtrooms described above. Moreover, the atmosphere in court can be considered as more formal. For example, judges generally wear gowns and wigs.[29] Courtrooms in these countries are generally divided into two sections: the professionals working in and for the court occupy the front part of the room; the public seating area is located at the rear, where defendants have to wait until their case is called and where family members can have a seat. Between

27 A lawyer was present for 5 of the 22 juveniles (23%) appearing in the prosecutor's office. And only 6 of the 66 juveniles (9%) appearing before a single judge youth court were accompanied by a lawyer. It has to be noted, however, that at the time of data collection the 2011 federal juvenile criminal procedural code (*Jugendstrafprozessordnung*) was not yet in force. As a consequence, the cantons were responsible for the appointment of lawyers and criteria were less strict compared to today.

28 See note 24 on the MACR in Scotland. From the age of 16 children are in principle prosecuted in the adult court and they do not fall under the jurisdiction of the children's hearings anymore. During the time of this study the court hearings of 16 and 17-year-old defendants were observed in specially arranged youth courts, which existed as pilot projects in two Sheriff courts in the Glasgow area.

29 Exceptions are observed in England and Wales, where in some youth courts only the usher wears a gown. The formal attire of the usher can, however, cause confusion among juveniles and parents regarding his role in the youth court, whereas his task is to be the first point of contact for the defendants and their parents (see also HMI Probation, HMI Courts Administration, HM Crown Prosecution Service Inspectorate 2011;Plotnikoff and Woolfson 2002).

these two sections is a defendant's dock where the young person is seated during the hearing. The Centre for Social Justice (2012) reports that in England and Wales it is common for juvenile defendants who are being detained to sit in a secure dock surrounded by a glass screen. It is argued that the involvement of the defendants is inhibited by the screen because they have difficulty in hearing what is being discussed in court and they are physically detached from the other participants. The judge sits on a raised bench, which makes it possible for the judge to oversee the whole courtroom and to look straight at the defendant. The English *Youth Court Bench Book* (Judicial Studies Board 2010) encourages magistrates to sit at the same level as the other participants in court. However, the present study shows that this is not always the case. The juvenile defendant has to stand up when he or she is spoken to by the English judge or magistrate.

Some districts in England and Wales have separately housed youth courts. In other districts the youth court is located within the magistrates' court and has a separate entrance from the adult court (see also Arthur 2010). In Ireland and Scotland youth court cases are usually handled in courtrooms that are used to deal with adult cases as well.[30] In Ireland the children's court hearings mostly take place at a different time or on a different day from the adult court hearings. Mostly, there is no specially assigned place for the juvenile defendant to take a seat. As a consequence, defendants can sit anywhere in the courtroom, mostly near the door or in the middle or to the rear of the courtroom. The large courtrooms enhances the physical distance between the judge and the young person which can even be more pronounced when prosecutor(s) and lawyers are seated in the space between the judge's bench and the defendant's dock. Moreover, the acoustics in most of the larger courtrooms is fairly poor, which makes communicating with the young person especially difficult (see also Kilkelly 2008a; Piacentini and Walters 2006).

On the European continent an example of a courtroom with more adversarial characteristics can be found in the Spanish youth court (*juzgado de menores*). The youth court is generally located within a general court building. The prosecutor and the lawyer are seated opposite each other, each on one side of the judge. The juvenile defendant faces the judge right in from of him or her and, for example, in the large courtroom in Madrid he or she has to speak through a microphone. In principle, Spanish youth court judges are obliged to wear a gown. However, judges have the possibility to decide not to and practices seem to differ between courts.

---

30 Except for the Dublin children court which sits in a different building from the district court, which has a specially designed courtroom (Kilkelly 2005).

4.2 Juvenile defendants' views

Legislation across all EU Member States guarantees juvenile defendants "an express right to be heard in one form or another during the course of criminal judicial proceedings" (European Commission 2014: 32). The European Commission (2014) acknowledges that the scope of this right varies between Member States and can be limited in some states.

In the current study countries are grouped into three categories with regard to hearing the views of juvenile defendants; 1) countries in which the views and personal circumstances of the young person lie at the heart of the hearing; 2) countries in which a dialogue between the juvenile defendant and the judge takes place, but are mainly directed by the contribution and questions of the judge and; 3) countries in which the views of juvenile defendants are hardly heard at all.

Hearings in which the views of the young person are heard to a large extent take place in, for example, the Scottish children's hearings system, the Swiss and the French juvenile justice system. The story of the young person and his or her personal circumstances are at the centre of the hearing and the judge leaves a great deal of room to allow the young person to speak. For example at the French youth court hearing a dialogue between the judge and the young person often emerges. In contrast with the hearings held in chambers, at the hearings in the youth court the judge(s), prosecutor and lawyers wear gowns and have fixed places, and certain rituals and rules are in place. However, the young person is given the opportunity to tell their side of what has happened, resulting in his appearance in court. In this setting the judge spends much time reviewing the offence and the personal circumstances of the young person (see also Blatier 1999). Moreover, when a social worker is present they are given the opportunity to give their views on the life of the young person.

The Greek youth court practice presents an example of how the views of the young person are heard to some extent. The young person is, however, not invited to present his or her own views on what has happened. He or she is only invited to answer the specific questions posed by the judge. The judge does not appreciate an independent contribution by the young person to the hearing. Moreover, the average duration of the observed hearings is strikingly short (only 5 minutes on average). In Italy the same type of practice is observed: the judge only hears juvenile defendants to a limited extent and sometimes only their lawyer speaks to the judge on their behalf (European Commission 2014). The duration of the hearings is, however, longer than in Greece (on average 31 minutes).

In the adversarial legal tradition of the Anglo-Saxon countries (England and Wales, Ireland and Scotland), the practice of hearing juvenile defendants in the youth court is very distinct from the practices described above. In the adversarial tradition the debate between the prosecutor and the defence lawyer lies at the heart of the hearing. During a trial the views of the juvenile defendant hardly play a role. The defendant is only given the opportunity to speak when he or she is summoned as a witness in the case (Brants 2011). As a consequence, the young person can only answer the questions posed by his lawyer and by the prosecutor in the cross-examination. Generally the young person is asked closed-ended questions, to which he or she can only respond to with a 'yes' or 'no'. Moreover, in other parts of the proceedings the judge only addresses the young person when he requires information from him or her. But even then, this request for information is mainly directed towards the lawyer representing the young person. Virtually without exception, every juvenile defendant who tries to say something during the trial or other kind of hearing is cut off by the judge (see also Kilkelly 2005).

In several countries a genuine reaction to the views of juvenile defendants was observed. A genuine reaction means that the judge shows interest in the offence and everything the young person would like to share about it, and that he shows interest in the young person's personal background (Rap and Weijers 2014). In this way the judge shows respect for the young person's story and can show that he is a benevolent listener (Tyler 2006). Moreover, this is of importance in light of Art 12(1) CRC, because it ensures that the young person's views are considered seriously in determining what should be decided and that the young person's contribution carries weight in the decision-making process (see also para. 5.2 of this chapter).

Most notably at the Scottish children's hearing, and in Switzerland, France, Germany and the Netherlands juvenile defendants are encouraged to give their own views and they are actively questioned about their personal circumstances. The possibility to impose welfare measures in criminal cases influences the role of the decision maker and the topics that are discussed during the hearing. In these hearings the judge, the prosecutor or, in the Scottish case, the panel members, decide among other things about whether a measure is necessary to prevent the young person from slipping further into recidivism. A welfare approach is prevalent in these jurisdictions and the purpose of the hearing is to assess whether an educational or therapeutic measure is necessary to deal with the problems the young person experiences (instead of or alongside a penal sanction). In general terms, there is much to suggest that serious consideration is afforded to the views of the young person and to his or her personal circumstances which, in turn, informs the judge's decision as to whether the young person is in need of care or protection.

In the youth courts in England and Wales, Ireland, Scotland and Spain serious consideration of the views of the young person was far less frequently observed, largely because their views were only heard to a limited extent in the first place. A distinct feature of the Anglo-Saxon youth courts – as opposed to the Scottish children's hearings, which form an exception in this regard – is the distant attitude of the judge, which is amplified by the formal proceedings and attire of the participants. Only in the rare case were judges observed taking a genuine interest in the views and personal circumstances of the young person. Moreover, welfare measures targeting the threatened development of the young person because of abuse, neglect or other personal problems cannot be imposed by these youth courts. The dispositions available focus on the delinquent behaviour of the minor, although, for example, probationary measures can target other problems in the life of the young person as well.

5. Juvenile defendants' understanding

In the proposed EU Directive on procedural safeguards for children involved in criminal proceedings[31] it is acknowledged that children are vulnerable and not always fully able to understand and follow criminal proceedings, although that is considered to be essential for receiving a fair trial.[32] Therefore, parents of the child should be notified of the rights of the child, children have the right to be accompanied by a parent during court hearings and they have the right to access a lawyer. Moreover, it is stated that children may have communication difficulties, which should be taken into account in their treatment in criminal proceedings.[33]

In this study it is argued that understanding what is discussed during the hearing, and what the consequences are of what is decided, is essential for the young person to give their (informed) views but that national justice processes are far from achieving that in practice. In this section, first, the results with regard to giving explanations and the use of legal terminology will be presented. Second, the extent to which the judgment and sentence are clarified to the young person will be discussed.

31 Discussed above note 12 and 20.

32 Above note 12.

33 Above note 12.

5.1 Explanation and legal terminology

A fundamental part of the capacity for the juvenile defendant to understand can be improved by preparing him or her properly before the youth court hearing. The lawyer can best provide this preparation. However, these preparatory activities cannot be taken for granted. It cannot be assumed that the young person is always prepared and/or that he or she has remembered everything correctly. Therefore, judges also have an important task in explaining the youth court proceedings to the juvenile defendant, in order for him or her to effectively participate at the hearing.

With regard to the explanation of procedures and participants' roles in the youth court a clear divide exists between countries in which the youth court procedures are influenced by the adversarial legal tradition (England and Wales, Ireland, Scotland and Spain) and countries in which the inquisitorial legal tradition (or a welfare model) prevails (e.g. Belgium, the Scottish children's hearings and Switzerland). It can be concluded from the findings of this study that the Scottish children's hearings system and the Swiss hearings are best suited to facilitate young people's understanding of the procedures. In these countries substantial attention is paid to giving explanations to the young person during the hearing.

Moreover, the results of this study show that at hearings in chambers, as opposed to hearings in large courtrooms, more attention is paid to providing the young person with explanations. This might be interpreted as an unexpected result, because hearings in chambers in several countries (e.g. Germany, France and Switzerland) revolve around less serious cases and it might be expected that in more serious cases handled in court young people need more explanations to be able to participate effectively. In reality the contrary has been found: in the youth court fewer explanations are given to juvenile defendants and in chambers more explanations are given. It was apparent from the observations that in a more intimate setting the juvenile defendants feel more at ease with asking questions or with indicating that they do not understand certain matters.

In principle, lawyers can contribute to giving explanations to young people. In practice, in some countries, in the majority of cases observed during the study, a lawyer was not present. That said, the young people concerned were provided with substantial explanations as appropriate and required, so in that regard the presence of a lawyer was not strictly necessary. In fact, no notable difference was observed in the amount of explanations provided at the Swiss hearing when a lawyer was present compared to when a lawyer was absent. On the other hand, social workers do play an important role at the hearings, because they, next to the judge, engage in giving explanations about possible sanctions or measures, as well as ongoing support that can be made available. In sum, it can be concluded that the informal atmosphere, the slight physical distances and the lower number of people present in chambers all contribute to giving explanations, irrespective of the seriousness of the case and the presence of a lawyer.

At the other extreme, at the hearings observed in Ireland, Scotland and Spain the judge did not provide any explanation to the young people as to the procedural or substantive aspects of the case. It was observed that if a young person was not properly prepared *before* the hearing, this led to confusion and distraction *during* the hearing. This confirms the important role of the lawyer in preparing the young person before the hearing and explaining what has been decided afterwards. At the hearings observed in these countries, a lawyer was always present. However, it does not become clear from this study to what extent lawyers engage in providing the young person with information before and after the hearing.

In the countries that fall between these two extremes – France, Germany and the Netherlands – explanations are given to a limited extent by lawyers before, during and after formal proceedings. Again, social workers also play an important role in conveying information to the young person and his or her parents. The young person is even better equipped to understand what is happening in court when the explanations provided by the lawyer and social worker are supplemented by the judge. In reality, it was observed that judges only gave explanations to a limited extent in these jurisdictions.

Of course, information has to be conveyed to young defendants in a language and format that they can understand which implies the avoidance of the use of legal jargon. England and Wales, by virtue of their lay magistrates, score better on his point, while in the Netherlands judicial jargon is used more often compared to its neighbouring countries on the European continent. It can be concluded from the observations that within the inquisitorial tradition and especially at hearings in chambers (such as in Belgium, France, Germany, the Scottish children's hearing and Switzerland) the use of jargon is less apparent. In Ireland, Scotland, the Netherlands and Spain, the greater tendency to use legal jargon correlated with a more profound lack of understanding of the process among the young people involved.

5.2 Clarifying the judgment and sentence

According to Art 12(1) CRC the right to be heard means that the views of the child must be given due weight in accordance with their age and maturity. This implies that the decision maker in question has to inform the young person of the outcome of the process and to explain how the views of the child are considered in the decision-making process. The CRC Committee

(2009) argues that giving feedback to the child is a guarantee that the views of the child are not only heard as a formality, but are actually taken seriously in the decision-making process (para. 45). Explaining the judgment and the choice for a specific sentence can be seen as a requirement that follows from the right to be heard. Moreover, explaining the sentence helps the young person to better understand the process and its outcome.

Regarding the clarification of the judgment and sentence from the results of this study it can be concluded that the judgment is not necessarily better explained in youth courts that show characteristics of the inquisitorial tradition. Especially in Ireland and the Southern European countries (i.e. France, Greece, Italy, Spain) at the observed hearings no special attention was paid to explaining the judgment and sentence orally at the end of the hearing. In larger courts in France the judgment is pronounced publicly at the end of the day in relation to every juvenile defendant who has appeared in court on that particular day (art. 14 Ordonnance n° 45-174 du 2 février 1945 relative à l'enfance delinquente, 02.02.1945 [Juvenile court instruction]). Every defendant, together with his lawyer, parents (and/or other family members) and social worker, waits in the same courtroom until the judge delivers his judgment. Generally, the judgements are read out very speedily by the judge and, as a consequence, defendants find it hard to keep up. Therefore, young people depend on their lawyer for further information and explanations. What is lacking in these countries in general is an explanation to the young person about the extent to which his views have played a role in the decision-making and consequently the type of decision that has been taken. A lack of time seems to be the most important reason for the judge to omit further explanations and reasons for the judgment and sentence.

A difference between hearings in chambers and hearings in court was observed. In chambers, the content of and reasons for judgment tends to be clarified at least to some extent. Switzerland and Scotland (i.e. the children's hearings system) are again good examples of making use of this element of the hearing. In the more formal court hearing in Germany, the judgment and sentence tend to be very well clarified and explained to the young person as well. Indeed, in the hearings observed in Germany, after the judge has issued the judgment formally, everyone was invited to sit down and the sentence was explained to the young person in more accessible terms. Moreover, this technique is clearly used to give the young person a message to take home with regard to avoiding future delinquent behaviour.

6. Conclusion

Acknowledging children's autonomy and agency as rights holders implies that children should be able to participate in decisions that affect their lives. Art 12 CRC requires states parties to provide juvenile defendants with the opportunity to participate in youth court procedures. Juvenile defendants should be encouraged to give their personal views on the criminal case and the professionals in court should consider these views seriously. Moreover, the European Court of Human Rights has put forward the notion that (juvenile) defendants should be able to participate *effectively* in a court hearing which, among other things, means that the young person understands in general the proceedings he or she is involved in. This implies that the young person is assisted by a lawyer and that he or she is provided with adequate information in a language and format that the young person understands. In recent years the notion of child-friendly justice has gained considerable traction at EU level, with the European Commission explicitly endorsing the Council of Europe Guidelines on Child-Friendly Justice. These EU initiatives to strengthen child-friendly justice practices are manifested in binding legislation that reinforces Member States' obligations to uphold children's rights in justice proceedings, but it also puts effort into identifying best practice and facilitating knowledge exchange between Member States. However, to complete the process of full and effective implementation of European child-friendly justice measures, more knowledge is needed as to how Member States currently organise the hearing of children in criminal proceedings.

The findings reported in this chapter aim to contribute to our understanding of the domestic youth justice landscape. From this comparative study involving 11 European countries it can be concluded that national practices regarding children's participation in proceedings are largely influenced by the legal tradition in which a justice system is situated. Hearing juvenile defendants' views takes place to the largest extent in the Scottish children's hearings system and in the juvenile justice system in Switzerland. In these countries hearing juveniles and giving serious consideration to their views is commonplace. Procedures, participants and their roles are generally explained, legal terminology is used to a limited extent, and the judgment and sentence are clarified to the young person.

On the other side of the coin, in the youth courts in England and Wales, Ireland, Spain and Scotland (i.e. hearings of 16 and 17-year-olds in the adult criminal justice system) hearing juveniles and giving serious consideration to their views occurs to a more limited extent. It can be concluded that a more intimate and informal setting facilitates the hearing of young people and renders it more meaningful. As a result, an informal setting proves to be best geared towards implementing the right to be heard in practice; in a more intimate setting the juvenile defendant is more inclined to ask questions and for further explanations, when he or she does not understand a certain matter.

In this chapter is has been shown that a dissonance between rhetoric and reality is apparent with regard to child participation in juvenile justice proceedings. Several international and regional children's rights standards give guidance as to how participation should take place. In reality, though, children are not always given the opportunity to give their views on the matter at hand. Because states exercise a considerable degree of discretion with regard to how international standards are put into practice, it is even more important to gain knowledge on current practices. With this study, professionals working in youth courts and other competent administrative bodies and policy-makers in the field of juvenile justice can be made aware of the gaps that exist in their system with regard to the fulfilment of the right to be heard, as part of states' obligation to implement this fundamental right of juvenile defendants. However, the evidence strongly suggests that the fulfilment of this right is only being achieved to a limited extent in the adversarial youth courts in Europe. Before child-friendly justice becomes a reality in these jurisdictions, significant work has yet to be done to ensure that youth court practices are adapted and improved to enable juvenile defendants to exercise their right to be heard, irrespective of the legal tradition in which the youth court operates.

References

Abramson, B. (2006) Juvenile justice: The 'unwanted child'. Why the potential of the Convention on the Rights of the Child is not being realised, and what we can do about it, in: Jensen, E.L. and Jepsen, J (eds) Juvenile law violators, human rights, and the development of new juvenile justice systems, Oxford, Hart.

Arthur, R. (2010) Young offenders and the law: How the law responds to youth offending, Oxon, Routledge.

Beijer, A. and Liefaard, T. (2011) A Bermuda Triangle? Balancing protection, participation and proof in criminal proceedings affecting child victims and witnesses, in: Utrecht Law Review 7, 3, pp. 70-106.

Blatier, C. (1999) Juvenile justice in France. The evolution of sentencing for children and minor delinquents, in: British Journal of Criminology 39, 2, pp. 240-252.

Boeije, H. (2010) Analysis in qualitative research, London, Sage.

Brants, C. (2011) Comparing criminal process as part of legal culture, in: Nelken, D.(ed.) Comparative Criminal justice and Globalization, Farnham, Ashgate.

Bueren, van G. (1995) The International Law on the Rights of the Child, Dordrecht, Martinus Nijhoff Publishers.

Bueren, van G. (1992) Child-oriented justice – An international challenge for Europe, in: International Journal of Law and the Family 6, pp. 381-399.

Cantwell, N. (1992) The origins, development and significance of the United Nations.

Convention on the Rights of the Child, in Detrick, S. (ed.) The United Nations Convention on the Rights of the Child. A guide to the "Travauxpréparatoires", Dordrecht, Martinus Nijhoff Publishers.

Centre for Social Justice (2012) Rules of Engagement: Changing the heart of youth justice, London, Centre for Social Justice.

Cipriani, D. (2009) Children's rights and the minimum age of criminal responsibility – a global perspective, Farnham, Ashgate.

Comben, C. et al. (2003) The Children's Hearings System in Scotland -Training resource manual, Edinburgh, Scottish Executive.

Council of Europe (2010) Guidelines of the Committee of Ministers of the Council of Europe on Child-Friendly Justice (adopted by the Committee of Ministers on 17 November 2010 at the 1098th meeting of the Ministers' Deputies), Strasbourg, Council of Europe.

Doek, J.E. (2007) The eighteenth birthday of the Convention on the Rights of the Child: Achievements and challenges, in: University of Michigan Journal of Law Reform 41, 1, pp. 61-75.

Dohrn, B. (2006) Something's happening here: children and human rights jurisprudence in two international courts, in: Nevada Law Journal 6, 3, pp. 749-773.

Dohrn, B. (2005) Last resort, dignity and re-integration: Infusing 'best interests of the child' with substantive and procedural rights in juvenile justice, in: Bruning, M. and Ruitenberg, G. (eds) Rechten van het kind in (inter)nationaalperspectief, Amsterdam, Uitgeverij SWP.

Doob, A.N. and Tonry, M. (2004) Varieties of youth justice, in: Tonry, M. and Doob, A.N. (eds) Youth Crime and Youth Justice: Comparative and cross-national perspectives, Chicago, The University of Chicago Press.

European Commission (2014) Summary of contextual overviews on children's involvement in criminal judicial proceedings in the 28 Member States of the European Union, Luxemburg, European Commission – Directorate-General for Justice.

European Commission (2011) Communication from the Commission to the European Parliament, the Council, the European Economic and Social Committee and the Committee of the Regions, An EU Agenda for the Rights of the Child, COM (2011) 60, final.

FRA – European Union Agency for Fundamental Rights (2015) Child-friendly justice. Perspectives and experiences of professionals on children's participation in civil and criminal judicial proceedings in 10 EU Member States, Luxembourg, Publications Office of the European Union.

Fitzgerald, R. et al. (2009) Children's participation as a struggle over recognition, in: Percy-Smith, B. and Thomas, N (eds) A handbook of children and young people's participation: Perspectives from theory and practice, Hoboken, Routledge.

Freeman, M. (2007) Why it remains important to take children's rights seriously, in: International Journal of Children's Rights 15, 1, pp. 5-23.

Freeman, M. (1992) Taking children's rights more seriously, in: International Journal of Law and the Family 6, 1, pp. 52-71.

Goldson, B. and Kilkelly, U. (2013) International human rights standards and child imprisonment: Potentialities and limitations, in: International Journal of Children's Rights 21, 2, pp. 345-371.

Goldson, B. and Muncie, J. (2012) Towards a global 'child friendly' juvenile justice?, in:International Journal of Law, Crime and Justice 40, 1, pp. 47-64.

Goldson, B. and Muncie, J. (2006) Rethinking youth justice: Comparative analysis, international human rights and research evidence, in: Youth Justice 6, pp. 91-106.

Hammarberg, T. (2001) Children, in: Eide, A., Krause, C. and Rosas, A. (eds) Economic, Social and Cultural Rights. A textbook (2nded.) Dordrecht, Martinus Nijhoff Publishers.

Hanson, K. (2012) Schools of thought in children's rights, in: Liebel, M. (ed.) Children's Rights From Below: Cross-cultural perspectives, Hampshire, Palgrave Macmillan.

HMI Probation, HMI Courts Administration, HM Crown Prosecution Service Inspectorate (2011) Not making enough difference: A joint inspection of youth offending court work and reports. Retrieved from http://www.scie-socialcareonline.org.uk/ profile.asp? guid=f3a5f365-8a44-4067-85e6-4b881638e049.

Judicial Studies Board (2010) Youth Court Bench Book, London, Judicial Studies Board.

Kilkelly, U. (2011) The CRC at 21: assessing the legal impact, in: Northern Ireland Legal Quarterly 62, 2, pp. 143-152.

Kilkelly, U. (2008a) Youth Courts and Children's Rights: The Irish Experience, in: Youth Justice 8, 1, pp. 39-56.

Kilkelly, U. (2008b) Youth justice and children's rights: Measuring compliance with international standards, in: Youth Justice, 8, 3, pp. 187-192.

Kilkelly, U. (2005) The Children's Court: A children's rights audit, Cork, University College Cork.

Kilkelly, U. (2001) The best of both worlds for children's rights? Interpreting the European Convention on Human Rights in the light of the UN Convention on the Rights of the Child, in: Human Rights Quarterly 23, 2, pp. 308-326.

Krappmann, L. (2010) The weight of the child's view (Article 12 of the Convention on the Rights of the Child), in: International Journal of Children's Rights 18, 4, pp. 501-513.

Lansdown, G. (2005) The evolving capacities of the child, Florence, UNICEF Innocenti Research Centre.

Liefaard, T. (2008) Deprivation of liberty of children in light of international human rights law and standards, Antwerp, Intersentia.

Lücker-Babel, M.F. (1995) The right of the child to express views and to be heard: An attempt to interpret Article 12 of the UN Convention on the Rights of the Child, in: International Journal of Children's Rights 3, 3-4, pp. 391-404.

Lundy, L. (2007) 'Voice' is not enough: Conceptualising Article 12 of the United Nations Convention on the Rights of the Child, in: British Educational Research Journal 33, 6, pp. 927-942.

Mouhanna, C. and Bastard, B. (2011) Deux justices au banc d'essai. Comparer les mondes judiciaires pour analyser l'évolution des modèles de justice, in: Déviance et Société, 35(2), pp. 239-260.

Nelken, D. (2010) Comparative Criminal Justice: Making sense of difference, London, Sage.

Piacentini, L. and Walters, R. (2006) The politicization of youth crime in Scotland and the rise of the 'Burberry Court', in: Youth Justice 6, 1, pp. 43-59.

Plotnikoff, J. and Woolfson, R. (2002) Young Defendants' Pack: Scoping study for the Youth Justice Board, London, Youth Justice Board.

Rap, S.E. (2013) The participation of juvenile defendants in the youth court. A comparative study of juvenile justice procedures in Europe, Amsterdam, Pallas Publications (doctoral dissertation).

Rap, S.E. and Weijers, I. (2014) The Effective Youth Court. Juvenile Justice Procedures in Europe, The Hague, Eleven International Publishing.

Saywitz, K., Camparo, L. B. and Romanoff, A. (2010) Interviewing children in custody cases: Implications of research and policy for practice, in: Behavioral Sciences and the Law 28, 4, pp. 542-562.

Sinclair, R. (2004) Participation in practice: Making it meaningful, effective and sustainable, in: Children & Society, 18(2), pp. 106-118.

Sloth-Nielsen, J. (2001) The role of international law in juvenile justice reform in South Africa (Unpublished doctoral dissertation), University of the Western Cape, Bellville.

Sloth-Nielsen, J. (1995) Ratification of the Convention on the Rights of the Child: Some implications for South African Law, in: South African Journal of Human Rights 11, 3, pp. 401-420.

Stalford, H. (2012) Children and the European Union: Rights, Welfare and Accountability, Oxford, Hart.

UN Committee on the Rights of the Child (2009) The right of the child to be heard, General Comment no. 12, CRC/C/GC/12.

UN Committee on the Rights of the Child (2007) Children's rights in juvenile justice, General Comment no. 10, CRC/C/GC/10.

UN Committee on the Rights of the Child (2003) General measures of implementation of the Convention on the Rights of the Child (arts. 4, 42 and 44, para. 6), General Comment no. 5, CRC/GC/2003/5.

UN Committee on the Rights of the Child (1996) General guidelines for periodic reports, CRC/C/58.

UN Committee on the Rights of the Child (1991) General guidelines regarding the form and content of initial reports to be submitted by States Parties under Article 44, paragraph 1(a), of the Convention, CRC/C/5.

UN Committee on the Rights of the Child (2007) Children's rights in juvenile justice, General Comment no. 10, CRC/C/GC/10.

UN Committee on the Rights of the Child (2003) General measures of implementation of the Convention on the Rights of the Child (arts. 4, 42 and 44, para. 6), General Comment no. 5, CRC/GC/2003/5.

The EU and the De-Institutionalisation of Children

Ingi Iusmen

Introduction

In recent years the European Union (EU) has embraced as a policy objective the removal of children from large scale residential institutions (de-institutionalisation) both within the context of EU child rights policy as well as part of the EU Disability Strategy (European Commission 2003, 2010) and Mental Health Pact (2008). The promotion of children's de-institutionalisation as a policy objective, both inside the EU and in relation to third countries, underscores the EU's broader role as a normative (Manners 2002; Padoa-Schioppa 2001) and ethical power (Manners and Diez 2007; Lucarelli and Manners 2006; Whitman 2011) in world politics. More recently, it constitutes one of the key objectives of the EU's child rights policy within the context of vulnerable groups. By endorsing the advancement of children's de-institutionalisation interlinked with the creation of alternative child care services, the EU has committed to align its actions with the main international instruments and provisions in the area of children's rights and alternative care (e.g. UN Convention on the Rights of Persons with Disabilities and UN Guidelines on the Alternative Care of Children). To this end, the EU has developed and applied a set of legal, financial and policy instruments aimed at supporting the transition from residential care to family[1] or community-based alternative care[2]. However, the effective implementation of de-institutionalisation is a complex process and the EU's success in advancing de-institutionalisation – both as a norm and as a policy objective – depends

1 This has been defined as a 'form of alternative care that involves a child living with a family other than his/her birth parents. This includes kinship care, foster care, adoption, kafala (an Islamic form of adoption) and supported child-headed households' (Save the Children 2009: vi).

2 Alternative care has been described as a 'formal or informal arrangement whereby a child is looked after at least overnight outside the parental home, either by decision of a judicial or administrative authority or duly accredited body, or at the initiative of the child, his/her parent(s) or primary caregivers, or spontaneously by a care provider in the absence of parents. This includes informal fostering by family or non-relatives, formal foster care placements, other forms of family-based or family-like care placements, places of safety for emergency child care, transit centres in emergency situations, other short and long term residential care facilities including group homes and supervised independent living arrangements for children' (Save the Children UK 2007).

on overcoming a set of challenges rooted both in the EU's legal mandate in this area and the multi-faceted nature of the de-institutionalisation process itself.

By examining the role played by the EU in advancing the de-institutionalisation of children, this chapter addresses broader questions regarding the EU's embrace and interpretation of global child rights norms and instruments. How do EU actions promote children's de-institutionalisation at the national level? How effective are the EU's instruments in sustaining the transition from institutional care to community-based care? Finally, what are the main challenges and obstacles encountered by the EU in advocating primarily family-based alternatives of child care? EU actions conducive to de-institutionalisation span across a number of policy sectors; nonetheless, the EU's role in relation to this issue has come to be decisive in ensuring that the Member States take action to reform their child protection systems in line with the main international standards applicable in this area.

1. Children's rights and de-institutionalisation

The main international and European child rights instruments include direct or indirect provisions relevant for the regulation of children's de-institutionalisation at the national level. At the same time, specific international guidelines have been adopted that target the key aspects of the process of de-institutionalisation and its effects on national child protection systems. All international instruments and provisions in this area highlight the negative and damaging effects of institutional care on child development and well-being (Burson-Marsteller 2005) and particularly, show how the employment of residential care, rather than community-based alternative care, in fact constitutes a violation of children's rights, as enshrined in the UN Convention on the Rights of the Child (CRC – see further below). There are various meanings attached to what constitutes an 'institution'or 'institutional care'[3] depending on national factors and legal traditions. Generally, however, institutions are equated with large-scale residential facilities, often branded as 'orphanages', hosting between tens and hundreds of children. For instance, an institution has been defined as 'a residential, health or social care facility of elven or more children regardless of age' (Browne et al. 2005:25). Indeed, size is an important feature of an 'institution', yet the type and quality of

3 Institutional care amounts to 'care provided in any non-family-based group setting. This includes orphanages, small group homes, transit/interim care centres, children's homes, children's villages/cottages complexes, and boarding schools used primarily for care purposes and as an alternative to a children's home' (Save the Children 2009:vi).

care, along with children's well-being constitute the central factors that differentiate institutional care from other forms of child care. In the same vein, UNICEF defines institutions in terms of 'whether children have regular contact and enjoy the protection of their parents or of their family or primary caregivers, and whether the majority of children in such facilities are likely to remain there for an indefinite period of time' (UNICEF 2010: 12-13). Furthermore, institutional care can be described by a number of key characteristics, such as depersonalisation, block treatment, rigidity of routine and social distance (European Commission 2009). The harm caused by institutionalisation to children's development has been widely documented (Hodges and Tizard 1989a, 1989b). According to European experts (European Commission 2009: 9) institutional care is detrimental to child development and well-being due to three factors: children's isolation from the broader community; their lack of sufficient control over their lives and decisions affecting them, and finally, the prioritisation of the institution's requirements over children's individualised needs. In a nutshell, 'institutional care' indicates the care provided in segregating residential institutions (European Commission 2009), and therefore there is a strong link between the quality of child care and child development and well-being.

The key international instruments upholding children's rights include provisions and principles that specify the role and scope of institutional care in relation to child protection and children's rights. The CRC, as the main international instrument for the protection of children's rights, outlines a catalogue of rights that, taken together, illustrate that most children should be cared for and live with their birth families (Articles 7 and 9), that they have the right to be protected from harm and abuse (Article 19), along with the right to adequate healthcare (Article 24) and to education (Article 28). The CRC ascribes responsibility to the state for supporting the parents to raise their children (Article 18). Moreover, the Convention includes specific provisions regarding the situation of children deprived of a family environment, which have to be interpreted in conjunction with the 'best of interests of the child' (Article 3) principle[4]. For instance, Article 20 CRC stipulates that a child deprived of a family has the right to special care by the state and when child care solutions are considered, those that focus on family-like environments, as well as the preservation of the child's cultural identity, should be prioritised. Additionally, Article 21 CRC states that children have a right to care and protection if they are adopted or in foster care, and that any child care solution adopted by relevant authorities should pay heed to the 'best interests of the child' (Article 3 CRC).

The UN Convention on the Rights of Persons with Disabilities (CRPD) includes a catalogue of rights that are relevant for the provision of care solu-

---

4 According to Article 3 CRC, the best interests of children must be a primary consideration in making decisions that may affect them.

tions for disabled children. For instance, Article 19 sets out the right of people with disabilities, including children, to 'live in the community with choices equal to others', while Article 7 specifically provides for the access of children with disabilities to all human rights and fundamental freedoms 'on an equal basis with other children'. These provisions are particularly relevant for the situation of institutionalised children as in some countries the vast majority of these children have disabilities. In essence, the CRPD recognises the equal right of children with disabilities to live independently in the community, with choices equal to other children. At the European level, Article 8 of the European Convention on Human Rights (ECHR) guarantees the right to respect for private and family life, therefore restraining any interference with this right by a public authority unless in accordance with the law. With respect to children, Article 8 ECHR forbids the arbitrary separation of children from their family or a placement that interferes with the child's ability to maintain contact with their family unless it is in the child's best interests.

The UN has adopted a set of specific recommendations – *Guidelines on the Alternative Care of Children* (2009) – targeting the situation of children in child protection systems, specifically those lacking a family environment. For instance, the Guidelines single out material and financial poverty as the key factors conducive to child's removal from parental care, therefore emphasising the need for appropriate support to be provided for the family to prevent them from abandoning the child (Article 15). Moreover, the Guidelines oppose, in line with the predominant expert opinion in this area, the institutionalisation of children under the age of three years, advocating, instead, for the provision of care in family-based settings (Article 22). Echoing the stipulations of CRC and CRPD, the UN Guidelines recommend children's de-institutionalisation, which should be accompanied by the establishment of alternative care solutions, in line with international child rights principles and standards.

In light of the above international provisions, the process of de-institutionalisation amounts to more than the mere removal of children from institutions and the closure of institutions. 'De-institutionalisation' has come to refer to a strategy or strategic approach involving a set of interlinked processes and courses of action occurring in parallel. According to UNICEF (2010:52) de-institutionalisation is a lengthy process that includes planning, transformation, downsizing and closure of institutions, while the development of alternative child care services, underpinned by rights-based standards, unfolds simultaneously. In essence, the de-institutionalisation process encompasses measures aimed at preventing a child's separation from his/her biological parents in the first place, while secondly, for those children deprived of a family environment, community-based services have to be created as alternative care solutions to institutions. The key principle underlying de-institutionalisation is that when alternative care solutions are considered for unparented children, family-type care – such as extended family, domestic adoption or foster care – has to be prioritised over institutional care. Residential care is an option only in exceptional cases, namely for the provision of short-term care for vulnerable children who are in need of specialist services or who are waiting for a suitable longer-term alternative (Save the Children 2009:1). Institutional care is envisaged as a last resort measure (Save the Children 2014). In short, de-institutionalisation is a complex and multi-faceted process which does not amount merely to the closure of residential institutions.

The promotion of de-institutionalisation as a key objective of national systems of child protection is rooted in convincing scientific evidence which demonstrates that institutional care is detrimental to the development of children (Browne et al. 2006). A significant number of studies have demonstrated the damaging physical and psychological – cognitive, emotional, behavioural – long-term effects of institutional care on children's development (McLean 2003; Mulheir and Browne 2007; Browne 2009). Furthermore, it has been shown that the institutionalisation of children under the age of three is particularly harmful to child development in the longer term (Save the Children UK 2007, Nelson et al. 2009). The type of care provided in institutions – characterised by the provision of a typically non-stimulating, clinical environment with limited social interaction – along with the young age of children institutionalised are some of the key factors accounting for these negative effects. It has been shown that the impact of institutional care on child development is more damaging – socially, intellectually and emotionally – the younger the age of the child, as young children – particularly those under the age of three – are more exposed to physical underdevelopment, deterioration in brain growth, developmental delay and emotional attachment delays (Browne 2009: 1). No wonder, therefore, that the institutionalisation of children in general, and young children (between 0 to 3 years) in particular, has been opposed as a childcare solution. International instruments and child rights principles provide guidance as to how and why the institutionalisation of children ought to be a temporary and seldom deployed measure of child care. Therefore, the development and provision of alternative childcare solutions has to be targeted both by national and supranational actors.

2. The EU and the de-institutionalisation of children: The EU enlargement process

2.1 Romania

The European Union advanced for the first time the de-institutionalisation of children as part of the Eastern enlargement process (1998-2004/2007). More specifically, EU accession conditionality applied in relation to the former communist states included requirements targeting the closure of big, old-style institutions along with the creation of alternative care services. Given the breadth and ambiguity contained in the Copenhagen accession criteria[5] (1993) – which candidate countries need to meet before they join the Union – the European Commission skilfully crafted and applied a human rights conditionality in candidate countries, such as Romania, which prioritised the reform of child protection by means of, amongst other measures, the closure of old-style institutions. The former communist states had a large number of children in institutional care primarily due to the fact that residential care, as provided by the state, was the predominant childcare solution. For instance, in the late 1960s the Ceausescu regime adopted a pro-natalist policy aimed at increasing the size of the population by banning abortions and contraception. The effects of this policy were a rise in unwanted babies, whom parents were unable to support. Parents were encouraged to place their children in residential care institutions, and thus, the state took responsibility for raising these abandoned children, and a popular saying during communism claimed that 'the state wanted children, let the state look after them'. In particular, due to the international media coverage of Romanian children in orphanages and the politicisation of international adoptions from Romania (Iusmen 2013b), the reform of child protection and children's de-institutionalisation constituted some of the main objectives pursued by the EU in Romania before it joined the Union in 2007. The moratorium imposed by the EU on international adoptions from Romania in the early 2000s generated a political rift between the Romanian government and some of the Western countries, such as the US, which adopted children from Romania.

All former communist countries had child protection systems that violated children's rights from legal, social, economic and political perspectives. Before 1989, the vast majority of Central and Eastern European countries primarily employed residential care in large-scale facilities as the main solution of care provided for children in the child protection system. The approach to

5 According to the Copenhagen political conditionality, the applicant country has to have 'achieved stability of institutions guaranteeing democracy, the rule of law, human rights and respect for and protection of minorities' (European Council 1993).

care was rooted in the Bolsheviks' belief that social care was far superior to parental care (Burson-Marsteller 2005: 10), while parents' right to care for their children was considered a delegated right, decided by the state (Alt and Alt 1959). During the Eastern enlargement process, the child protection in Romania was singled out due to international media coverage (Iusmen 2013a, 2014) and subsequently, became a high-profile accession condition as part of Romania's accession agenda. The EU's role, and more specifically the European Commission's, with respect to the issue of children's rights in Romania amounted to its intervention in a policy sector where the EU institutions lacked the necessary expertise and policy experience (Iusmen 2013a), and where the Union had virtually no *acquis communautaire* of its own since child protection is a national matter (Lataianu 2001). This meant that the Commission's policy of conditionality (Schimmelfennig and Sedelemeier 2004) – namely the set of reforms that candidates need to undertake in order to meet the Copenhagen accession conditions – in relation to the child protection in Romania developed incrementally by following a 'learning by doing' approach to the situation on the ground. Lacking the necessary expertise and experience in addressing the issue of institutionalised children, the Commission's intervention in the Romanian children's case entailed the acquisition of the necessary know-how by responding to the developments in this sector during the accession negotiations.

The post-1990 child protection system in Romania, as in other ex-communist states, prioritised institutional care at the expense of other child care solutions, and given the vast number of institutionalised children, deemed to be adoptable by the system, the key issue concerning Romanian children became the practice of inter-country-adoption (ICA), which was poorly regulated and violated the key international provisions in this area (Iusmen 2013a, 2013b). For instance, although Romania was a state party to both the CRC and the Hague Convention on Protection of Children and Co-operation in Respect of Inter-Country Adoption, the principles and provisions in the two conventions were not reflected in the Romanian legislation and child protection system. Moreover, the post-1990 Romanian legislation generated a child protection system that facilitated the proliferation of ICA as a solution by finding families for children in institutional care (Iusmen 2013b: 7). For instance, in the Romanian case there was a positive correlation between the number of children institutionalised and the extent of ICA (Iusmen 2014:88), which was regarded as a quick solution intended to provide families for the children in the system. Additionally, national policy and practice in Romania violated Article 8 ECHR – which focuses on respect for private and family life – as the state had the responsibility to support families at risk of abandoning their children. On the contrary, due to poverty-related reasons, Romanian families would abandon children in institutions: in fact, most of these children were not orphans, yet their families lacked the financial means to look after them. Above all, the legislation and child protection system failed to reflect the principles contained in the CRC, particularly 'the best interest of the child'.

The European Commission's key objective was to overhaul the child protection system and ICA legislation in Romania in line with the CRC principles (European Commission 2001; Jacoby et al. 2009). Despite lacking specific know-how or competence in these areas during the accession negotiations with Romania, the Commission found three 'workarounds' (Jacoby et al. 2009: 111) to generate change in child protection in Romania: first, by asserting legislative targets it did not possesses itself; second, by inventing new policy tools and finally, by drawing inspiration from international instruments such as the ECHR and the CRC. The reform of child protection in Romania occurred as a result of targeted EU instruments and mechanisms, which were employed specifically in relation to this area only in the Romanian case (Iusmen 2014). For instance, the EU deployed the financial instrument PHARE (Poland and Hungary: Assistance for Restructuring their Economies) – which consists of financial assistance to help candidate countries adopt structural reforms to meet the accession criteria – for the development of modern alternative childcare services and for the radical reform of the system (European Commission 2002: 14).

The EU financial instrument PHARE targeted, amongst others, the 'root-and-branch' reform of the child protection system. The EU's key objective was, on the one hand, to support the closure of old-style institutions and the de-institutionalisation of children living in residential care, and the prevention of institutionalisation and child abandonment via the provision of modern alternative care services, on the other (Iusmen 2014:65; National Authority for Child Protection and Adoption 2004: 2). The de-institutionalisation process unfolded in parallel with the development of alternative care services, such as family type modules, day care centres, maternal centres, recuperation centres or foster care networks. These alternative care solutions were meant to support institutionalised children to find new homes or return to their biological families. For instance, by the end of 2005 over 170 large institutions had closed down across Romania, while a range of new services had been set up (National Authority for the Protection of Child's Rights 2006: 11). Consequently, the number of children in institutions dropped from 57,060 (in 2001) to 27,188 (in 2006) (National Authority for the Protection of Child's Rights 2006: 13).The European Commission unequivocally advanced institutional care as a child protection measure to be employed only in relation to disabled children or in order to provide special residential care for children with severe disabilities (European Commission 2005), while ensuring that the Romanian government provided a wide range of services targeting families at risk of abandoning their children. The development and implementation of family-based alternative care solutions, such as fostering or guardianship, was the key objective of the reform process of child protection in Romania as supported by the EU before 2007 (Iusmen 2014: 75).

Apart from the financial[6] support channelled towards the radical overhaul of the system, the EU had to ascertain that the legislative framework in place upheld the rights of the child. Lacking expertise in the protection of children's rights (Iusmen 2013a), the Commission appealed to the technical know-how and experience of child rights experts from the EU Member States who advised[7] the Romanian government on the adoption of new legislation based on the CRC and other child rights instruments. The EU's central aim was to support the Romanian authorities to enforce new legislation that placed children's rights and the best interests of the child at the heart of the child protection system, in line with the CRC. The new Romanian legislation on children's rights and adoptions (272/2004 and 273/2004), which was inspired by the CRC, the ECHR and the latest Council of Europe conventions (Iusmen 2013a, 2014), such as the Convention on Contact concerning Children if the parents are separated or divorced, came into force in 2005, namely after the reform process had been unfolding for a significant amount of time, i.e. since 1998. The new legislation drew on the key CRC principles, such as the 'best interests of the child', and prioritised the provision of community-based care solutions. The EU accession financial instruments, along with the international instruments on child rights, were deployed by the EU in order to reform child protection system in Romania. In short, the Romanian case constitutes the first time when the EU had advanced de-institutionalisation as an EU policy objective, and the EU's actions to achieve this aim had been guided by the key international instruments and provisions in this area.

2.2 Bulgaria

The plight of institutionalised children in Bulgaria was similar to the one in Romania, before Bulgaria joined the Union in January 2007. However, the child protection system in Bulgaria had not been reformed at the time of Bulgaria's accession to the EU. For instance, when Bulgaria became an EU Member State, there was limited provision of alternative care services, such

6 For instance, between 1990 and 2000 the EU provided more than 100 million Euros as humanitarian aid to the childcare system (Jacoby et al. 2009: 120). After the adoption of the moratorium on ICA, the EU financial aid was channeled towards the reform of the system rather than humanitarian aid (Post 2007).

7 From 2003 to 2005 an Independent Panel of Experts on Family Law, consisting of child rights experts from the EU Member States, provided their expertise and know-how on the drafting of the new Romanian legislation on children's rights.

as foster care, and a significant number of children in institutions were still sent for international adoption (European Parliament 2009).

The reform of the child protection system was on Bulgaria's accession agenda during the accession negotiations with the Union (European Commission 1997). However, the protection of child rights failed to gain a high-profile before 2007, unlike in Romania (Iusmen 2014), and thus, the EU exerted limited leverage over the transformation of this human rights area before Bulgaria became an EU Member State. One reason for this disparity between Romania and Bulgaria related to the way in which local authorities in the latter would manipulate the figures of institutionalised children by shifting the definition of what an institutionalised child was (Ivanova and Bogdanov 2013: 204) and hence, there was a lack of objective, official data on the actual number of children in residential care. Despite some piecemeal initiatives to overhaul the system and align Bulgarian legislation with international child rights provisions, Bulgarian authorities lacked the political will and necessary EU pressure to forge a 'root-and-branch' reform of child protection in Bulgaria.

The plight of institutionalised children in Bulgaria caused international outcry after the airing of a BBC documentary (*Bulgaria's Abandoned Children*) in 2007 about an institution for children with disabilities in the village of Mogilino. The movie about the Mogilino care home showed the living conditions of 65 severely disabled children who received no rehabilitation, healthcare or education and were malnourished (Ivanova and Bogdanov 2013: 206). The film brought international attention to the damaging effects that institutionalisation had on children's development and the material conditions in residential institutions in a country that had recently joined the Union. The Mogilino case bore a striking resemblance to the situation of institutionalised children in Romania covered by Western media in the early 1990s. Given that Bulgaria was already an EU Member State when the issue of institutionalised children came under the international spotlight, the EU had limited instruments and legal competence to intervene in this area in a country that was already a Member State. Indeed, while the EU had more leverage and instruments to forge change in the candidate countries (Iusmen 2013a, 2014), as the Romanian case demonstrates, inside the Union it is the Member States that have the primary responsibility for steering the process of de-institutionalisation. Yet the Commission reacted swiftly by setting up a group of European child rights experts – the Ad Hoc Expert Group on the Transition from Institutional to Community-based Care, later known as the De-Institutionalisation Expert Group – to provide guidance and recommendations on the de-institutionalisation process that would be applicable across Europe. To this end, the Ad Hoc Expert Group produced a report –*Report of Ad Hoc Expert Group on the Transition from Institutional to Community-based Care* (2009) – which includes a set of Common Basic Principles and recommendations that should guide the de-institutionalisation process at the national level. The Report outlines the benefits of community-based care for users and their families, and highlights, at the same time, the challenges faced by child protection systems during the transition period from institutional care to community-based care, as will be shown below.

Not only did the issue of institutionalised children gain momentum at the EU level due to the Mogilino case in Bulgaria, but it also brought onto the European political agenda the question of the role that the EU can and ought to play in addressing this issue in the Member States. Inside the Union, the main instruments available to the EU to support national efforts in implementing children's de-institutionalisation are the Structural Funds, which constitute the key financial instruments of EU regional policy and their scope is to narrow the development disparities among regions and Member States. More specifically, the Structural Funds available to support de-institutionalisation are the European Social Fund (ESF) and the European Regional Development Fund (ERDF). The two financial instruments, as applied in the Bulgarian case, can be deployed jointly for the build-up of community care centres and the facilitation of the de-institutionalisation process (ERDF) and for running activities such as training or staff recruitment (ESF). It has been argued that this sort of crosswise funding in relation to the Bulgarian case can act as a model (Ivanova and Bogdanov 2013: 210) or reform template to address institutionalisation in other European countries. As will be shown in the next section, the Bulgarian case generated a radical shift regarding how the EU Structural Funds are deployed to support child protection services and de-institutionalisation at the national level.

Prior to the Mogilino case Structural Funds were excessively employed to finance and prolong institutional care instead of being invested in the creation of community-based services. Indeed, even in relation to Eastern candidates, such as Bulgaria and the Czech Republic, the funding provided as part of ERDF was primarily employed to refurbish residential institutions (Eurochild 2011), which radically contradicted the international provisions regarding childcare and children's rights and actually enhanced the attraction of the institutions for families unable to care for their children. Therefore, the Mogilino case brought to European attention how EU funds should be channelled towards promoting the de-institutionalisation process rather than perpetuating the use of institutional care. After the Mogilino case, the Bulgarian government adopted a new national strategy – *Vision for De-Institutionalisation of Children in the Republic of Bulgaria* (2010) – aimed at reforming the child protection system with the use of EU financial support. For instance, between 2010-2014 the ESF has been funding the project *Childhood for All*[8], which underscores the main efforts taken by the government to promote transition from residential to community-based services for children with disabilities. The ESF project aims 'to change the philosophy of care for children with disabilities' (EEG 2014:69) by focusing on prevention services, such as support to families, and provision of a family-based care environment for children placed in specialised institutions for children with disabilities (EEG 2014). Civil society organizations played a key role in campaigning for reform in this area and launching projects intended to support the de-institutionalisation process (Ivanova and Bogdanov 2013: 209). The Bulgarian national strategy aims to close all residential institutions for children by 2025, while community-based services and family-type homes are being developed in parallel. Therefore, the Mogilino case constituted a turning point for child protection in Bulgaria, even if the reform itself is expected to be a complex and long-term process. All governmental and non-governmental efforts were channelled towards advancing the closure of institutions and reforming the system in line with child rights principles and instruments, such as the CRC and CRPD. Hence, EU funds bolstered indirectly Bulgaria's compliance with its international legal commitments, such as respect for the CRC and the CRPD.

The role played by the EU in Romania and Bulgaria in relation to the de-institutionalisation process varied significantly, even if the EU's intervention was guided by the same principles and model of reform. The EU's accession leverage, along with the PHARE instrument, was successful in forging the de-institutionalisation process in Romania before 2007, while the international and political attention attracted by Romanian children in orphanages meant that a fair amount of political pressure was exerted on Romanian authorities to conduct the reform process before Romania joined the Union. The situation of institutionalised children in Bulgaria resurfaced on the EU's agenda after 2007, when the EU lacked the necessary leverage to pressure the Bulgarian government to address this issue. The reform model pursued by the Union in these two countries consists of the closure of institutions and, in parallel, the creation of community-based services via projects run by local authorities in partnership with NGOs. Particularly in the Romanian case, the policy template applied by the EU outlined the need to financially support local authorities via project-funding (via PHARE), given that it is their responsibility to provide social services to children and families, even if they could run services with the support of civil society organisations. The EU pursued de-institutionalisation processes in these countries by working in a really supportive, constructive manner with national stakeholders, providing financial backing both to transform child protection systems – that still bore

8 The project consists of two components: one focusing on the 'Planning of measures for de-institutionalisation' (2,5 million Euros) and another targeting the 'Provision of community-based social services' (16.5 million Euros) (EEG 2014: 69).

the communist legacy of childcare provision – whilst also supporting awareness raising at grassroots level to achieve wholesale attitudinal and paradigm shifts by individuals and communities as to the damaging effects of institutionalised childcare.

The de-institutionalisation of children is one of the policy objectives pursed by the Commission in relation to current candidates and potential candidates. By using the CRC and CRDP as the main international instruments to foster change in the candidate countries, the EU advocates the closure of large institutions and the development of community-based care solutions by using EU accession instruments, such as the Instrument for Pre-Accession Assistance (IPA) to achieve these goals. The cases of Romania and Bulgaria, therefore, prompted the Union to adopt a comprehensive and creative de-institutionalisation policy that not only targeted countries wishing to join the EU, but that now actively addresses the institutionalisation of children within the Member States (see section below).

3. The EU's de-institutionalisation policy

The de-institutionalisation of children as an EU internal policy issue emerged on the EU's agenda after the Mogilino case. Given the unprecedented awareness raised at the European level by the Bulgarian children's case, the EU had to respond and to provide its own position and role in relation to the situation of institutionalised children across Europe. EU actions and measures taken regarding the issue of institutionalisation gradually led to the emergence of a more comprehensive EU stance and scope on the de-institutionalisation of children in the Member States. However, the EU's policy on de-institutionalisation had to accommodate the diversity of child protection systems[9], particularly the variety of types of residential care employed in Europe, and above all, the lack of official cross-national statistical data regarding the numbers of children in residential care. Equally, national child protection systems are highly distinctive and diverse across Europe, and furthermore, child protection is a national matter. Some have argued that the data and availability of historical and empirical facts on residential care varies considerably from country to country (Courtney and Iwaniec 2009), although it has been estimated that there are 819,000 children in residential

9 At the time of writing, the EU's Fundamental Rights Agency is conducting research to map the national child protection systems of the EU Member States by focusing on the systems' laws, structures, actors and how the systems function, as well as human and financial resources and the existing accountability mechanisms (http://fra.europa.eu/en/project/2014/mapping-child-protection-systems-eu).

institutions in Central and Eastern Europe, along with the Commonwealth of Independent States (UNICEF 2007) and 23,099 children aged under three in care institutions across 33 European countries (Browne 2009). A European Commission study conducted in 2007 found that more than one million people with disabilities, including children, lived in residential settings across Europe (Mansell et al. 2007). Despite the lack of more up-to-date data, a survey run by Eurochild (2010) estimated that around 1% of children are taken into public care across the EU – approximately 1 million children[10]. This figure includes all children in care across Europe. Apart from the lack of disaggregated data on the number of children in residential settings in Europe[11], another hurdle constitutes the diversity of both residential care and the population that employs it across the EU Member States, which renders cross-country comparisons extremely difficult. At the same time, some countries prioritise certain forms of care at the expense of others: for instance, in Norway and the UK most children are placed in foster care, while Central and Eastern European countries employ residential care for special categories of children, such as children with disabilities.

When the Mogilino case grabbed the attention of the international media, the then Commissioner for Employment, Social Affairs and Equal Opportunities, Vladimir Spidla, set up the Ad Hoc Group of Experts on the Transition from Institutional to Community-Based Care (EEG)[12] in February 2009 in order to address the issues of institutional care reform in the Union. The immediate EU response to the Bulgarian case was the commissioning of a study – *Deinstitutionalisation and Community Living – Outcomes and Costs* (Mansell et al. 2007) – on the provisions of institutional care for disabled people across Europe. The study outlined the poor quality of institutional care provisions across Europe and concluded that community or family-based care solutions can deliver better outcomes in terms of quality of life, and can enable disabled people to live as full citizens.

The EEG played a pivotal role in establishing the principles and guidelines that should accompany EU action in supporting Member States' efforts to implement de-institutionalisation. The EEG produced the *Report of the Ad Hoc Expert Group on the Transition from Institutional to Community-based Care* (2009), which provided significant evidence in support of the positive results that the transition from institutional care to community-based care has

10 The survey conducted by Eurochild included 30 European countries, including the four nations of the UK and Moldova (Eurochild 2010).

11 According to COFACE (Confederation of Family Organizations in the European Union) there are more than 1 million children and adults who live in institutions across Europe (COFACE 2012).

12 The EEG is a coalition consisting of stakeholders representing people with care or support needs, including children, people with disabilities and mental health problems, families, as well as service providers, public authorities and intergovernmental organisations.

on users and their families. Furthermore, the EEG Report outlined a set of Common Basic Principles to assist European countries in steering the process of de-institutionalisation; these principles highlight the need to respect users' rights and also involve them in the decision-making process, while national authorities are expected to have in place a holistic system of preventing institutionalisation in the first place, to name just a few (European Commission 2009: 19-20). The Report signals out the distinctive features of 'institutional culture' – block treatment, depersonalisation, rigidity of routine, social distance, paternalism (European Commission 2009: 6) – which are often preserved due to national governments' decisions to fund improvements in the physical conditions of existing institutions, rather than close them.

In order to further assist EU Member States in their efforts to reform their child protection systems and advance de-institutionalisation, the EEG produced the *Common European Guidelines on De-Institutionalisation* (2012) and the *Toolkit* (2012, revised in 2014), on using the Structural Funds to support the process of de-institutionalisation. The Toolkit is intended to provide concrete guidelines on how EU funds can be deployed to assist national, regional and local authorities in designing and implementing reforms aimed at developing community-based alternatives to institutional care. The Toolkit outlines measures and actions that should be taken in the management of Structural Funds in relation to all stages, namely programming, implementation, monitoring and evaluation (EEG 2014), in support of de-institutionalisation reforms. The Toolkit has legal and policy significance for two reasons. First, it ensures that the employment of EU funding will be consistent with EU legal obligations, such as those arising from the CRPD, which the EU has ratified and which has committed the EU to ensuring that all its actions, including its funding, shall respect the rights of persons with disabilities (particularly Article 19). In other words, the EU has to ascertain that its financial tools are consistent with and supportive of its human rights obligations. Second, the recommendations in the Toolkit are explicitly connected to broader EU policy objectives, such as social inclusion and education included in Europe 2020, the Union's ten-year growth and jobs strategy that was launched in 2010. Indeed, the Structural Funds and the Toolkit are intended to support, among others, the EU's social policy objectives, including some central priorities such as tackling child poverty and social inclusion, and promoting child well-being, particularly the transition from institutional to community-based care services (European Commission 2013). In the same vein, the Common European Guidelines on De-Institutionalisation provide concrete advice about how to support a sustained transition from institutional to family – and community-based care alternatives that can be used by policy-makers at both national and EU levels.

The latest legal provisions regarding the use of Structural Funds for 2014-2020 include *ex-ante* conditionalities that specifically target the process of de-institutionalisation at the national level. More specifically, the employment of EU funds is made conditional on targeting certain policy sectors, such as the issue of de-institutionalisation, at the national level. The Common Provisions Regulation[13] lists transition from institutional to community-based care as part of the thematic objectives of the Structural Funds. More specifically, the Regulation stipulates that the ERDF and the ESF should be employed to assist the process of de-institutionalisation in the Member States, and to this end, specific *ex ante* conditions have to be met at the national level in order for the thematic objectives of the ERDF and ESF, namely promotion of social inclusion, combating of poverty and discrimination, to be achieved. The thematic *ex ante* conditionalities outline that Member States have to provide evidence that a national strategy or policy is in place before EU funding can become available for projects addressing de-institutionalisation (European Commission 2014b). The *ex ante* condition specifically mentions that in order for an EU Member State to receive EU funding, a national or regional plan for the shift from institutional to community-based care must be in place (European Commission 2014b), along with other national strategies targeting poverty reduction objectives. Put tersely, there is a clear link between the national provisions that have to be in place and access to EU funds.

The EU's de-institutionalisation policy pursued inside the Union is now a constitutive part of the EU's broader children's rights policy, as well as the EU's evolving competences vis-à-vis children since the late 2000s. When the EU intervened to address the issue of institutionalised children in Romania as part of the enlargement process, the Union lacked a comprehensive and broader strategy for children's rights, hence the Commission had to deploy the accession conditionality creatively. However, now the EU has a children's rights policy targeting specific child rights issues and policy sectors. For instance, the protection of children with disabilities and those at risk of poverty and social exclusion are included in the category of vulnerable children that the Commission aims to address as part of the EU Agenda for the Rights of the Child (2011). Furthermore, after the entry into force of the Lisbon Treaty in December 2009, there is a comprehensive legal and constitutional framework to support EU actions to address various child rights issues, in line with its legal mandate. For instance, the Lisbon Treaty includes

13 Regulation (EU) No 1303/2013 of the European Parliament and of the Council, laying down common provisions on the European Regional Development Fund, the European Social Fund, the Cohesion Fund, the European Agricultural Fund for Rural Development and the European Maritime and Fisheries Fund; laying down general provisions on the European Regional Development Fund, the European Social Fund, the Cohesion Fund and the European Maritime and Fisheries Fund; and repealing Council Regulation (EC) No 1083/2006, available from http://eur-lex.europa.eu/LexUriServ/LexUriServ.do?uri=OJ:L:2013:347:0320:0469:EN:PDF.

clear legal obligations for the EU institutions to ensure that EU actions do not violate the rights of the child, including those of vulnerable children. Indeed, Article 24 of the EU Charter on Fundamental Rights explicitly focuses on the rights of the child in line with the CRC principles, such as the 'best interests of the child'. Yet, since the Lisbon Treaty has entered into force, the EU has to ensure that its actions do not breach the provisions in the Charter. Another policy sector where the issue of de-institutionalisation is addressed is the Union's disability policy. In line with the CRPD provisions, the Commission made commitments to support the de-institutionalisation process at the national level within the context of the *European Disability Strategy 2010-2020* (European Commission 2010). The Strategy pledges for the employment of EU Structural Funds to assist community-based services and particularly, for the need to raise awareness of the situation of children with disabilities living in residential institutions (European Commission 2010:6). Indeed, there is wider scope now, both legally, constitutionally and financially, for the EU to support the rights of vulnerable children, such as institutionalised children, across Europe by assisting national efforts to close institutions and provide community-based services.

4. The EU and de-institutionalisation: key challenges

The EU's effective promotion of children's de-institutionalisation in the Member States faces a number of challenges linked both to the EU's actions in relation to this issue, and the complexity of the de-institutionalisation process itself. The obstacles faced by the EU in advancing the transition from institutional care to community-based care impacts on its capacity to align its actions with the key international instruments in this area, and to a certain extent, on its fulfilment of the legal obligations that derive from EU constitutional provisions and the ratification of international instruments such as the CRPD.

4.1 Structural Funds spending

Concerns have been harboured regarding how EU funds, namely Structural Funds, are still employed for expanding or renovating institutions (Open Society Foundation 2012) at the national level. Evidence suggests that EU funds are still being used for the renovation of institutions for people, including children, with disabilities (Ibid.) instead of funding the creation of alternative, family-based services. For instance, particularly Central and Eastern European countries (CEECS) employ EU funds to build or renovate institutions. Countries such as Hungary, Latvia and Bulgaria have funded projects that included financial investments in institutions (ECCL 2013:9). In the Bulgarian case, some institutions for children with disabilities were closed, yet local authorities failed to take action to make mainstream public services inclusive for disabled children, while ESF support was employed for services within the residential facilities for children, not in the mainstream (ECCL 2013).

The key stakeholders active in this area, such as Eurochild (2012b), prioritise the need to shift from the medical model regarding the care of children with disabilities – namely treating children as patients with illnesses in institutional care – to a model that treats children as individuals with human rights entitlement. To this end, the key solutions to be advanced are the prevention of the abandonment of children with disabilities by their families, as well as the provision of family or community-based specialist care alternatives (Eurochild 2012b: 5). With respect to the EU, the key challenge faced is the need to ensure that EU funds are deployed to support alternative care solutions, rather than institutionalisation, in line with the EU's child rights commitments, as they transpire from the CRC, and legal obligations, as reflected in the CRPD provisions. In this respect the Commission, which oversees the disbursement of EU funds, plays a key role in ensuring that EU funds are spent in line with EU legal obligations and values, such as human rights protection (Article 3 TEU). Better monitoring and oversight of how EU financial support is employed at the national level would render EU efforts to assist the de-institutionalisation process in the Member States more effective.

The inclusion of the *ex ante* conditions in the Common Provisions Regulation is intended to address this deficiency in EU funding support for institutional care. While it is still too early to evaluate the effectiveness of these conditions in ensuring that EU funds are, indeed, no longer employed for building new or refurbishing old institutions, it is evident that the EU has now more legal and financial clout to steer the de-institutionalisation process at the national level. Furthermore, the EU has more leverage to ascertain that the use of EU funding is compliant with international instruments, given that the general *ex ante* conditionality in the Common Provisions Regulation stipulates the need for Member States to provide evidence – before being allocated EU funding – that there is an effective monitoring structure in place for the implementation of the CRPD (European Commission 2014b). In other words, the EU can ensure, via its funding requirements, that EU Member States comply with their legal obligations arising from the CRPD, and therefore, that their actions are conducive to facilitating independent living and community inclusion of persons, including children, with disabilities.

4.2 Fundamental rights

Another hurdle faced by the Union in its actions to advance the de-institutionalisation process is ensuring that the employment of EU funding, such as Structural Funds, is consistent with the EU Charter of Fundamental Rights. After the entry into force of the Lisbon Treaty, all EU actions have to comply with the provisions and rights enshrined in the EU Charter, whilst the Charter has acquired the same legal status as the treaties. The EU Member States have to respect the EU Charter when implementing EU law at the national level (Article 51). This key challenge was highlighted by the European Ombudsman, Emily O'Reilly, who opened an investigation in 2014 into respect for fundamental rights in the implementation of the EU's cohesion policy – the EU's regional policy aimed at addressing the economic disparities of the Union's regions – via the Structural Funds. The Ombudsman's inquiry was particularly pertinent given the large number of complaints received by that office concerning the employment of EU funding to 'institutionalise' persons with disabilities, including children (European Ombudsman 2014a). The key concern expressed by the European Ombudsman was that the Commission lacks the necessary means to ensure that the fundamental rights in the EU Charter are respected when EU funding is employed at the national level (European Ombudsman 2014b). The answers supplied by the Commission to Ombudsman O'Reilly's inquiry specify that the *ex ante* conditionalities in the Commission Provisions Regulation ensure that requirements concerning anti-discrimination, gender and disability have to be fulfilled by the Member States when using EU Structural Funds (European Commission 2014a), yet there is no explicit obligation to comply with all provisions in the Charter, particularly those relevant to children. Furthermore, by drawing on the Court's case law, the Commission highlighted that, with respect to cohesion policy, the concept of 'implementing EU law' requires "a certain degree of connection above and beyond the matters covered being closely related or one of those matters having an indirect impact on the other" (European Commission 2014a: 4). In other words, it is not explicitly clear whether national measures, adopted as part of the implementation of EU cohesion policy, are intended to implement EU law, and hence, whether they would need to comply with the Charter. Indeed, the Commission admitted that the principles of non-discrimination and equality between men and women have been reinforced regarding the implementation of EU cohesion policy (European Commission 2014a:11), and that, therefore, there are no direct obligations on the Member States to comply with the Charter provisions when addressing the issue of de-institutionalisation, for instance. This indicates that the Union in general, and the Commission in particular, need to give proper consideration to the Charter and its standards (Butler 2012, 2014) with respect to how EU funding is spent in cohesion policy, which includes the de-institutionalisation of children. By downplaying the role of the fundamental rights provisions in the Charter regarding Member States' implementation of cohesion policy, the Commission undermines the weight it attaches to the process of de-institutionalisation at the national level, as well as to the broader provision of national child care in line with the CRC and CRPD principles.

4.3 Involvement of civil society actors

The more inclusive involvement of key stakeholders, such as children's organizations, in implementing the de-institutionalisation process at the national level is another obstacle encountered by the EU. For instance, the reform template that emerged from the EU's intervention in child protection in Romania during the enlargement process consisted of employing EU financial support to fund projects by local authorities, with limited roles played by NGOs. In the same vein, children's organizations in the Member States play a minor role in the employment of Structural Funds to finance community-based services and closure of residential institutions. For instance, according to the current financial framework of EU Structural Funds, NGOs are prevented from providing community-based services (ECCL 2013), although it is a legal requirement to have NGOs involved in the programming and implementation of Structural Funds. The limited NGO involvement has negative consequences at the national level as local authorities often lack the capacity and knowledge to provide such services. For instance, in the de-institutionalisation process in Bulgaria, NGOs have been excluded from applying for Structural Funds projects despite the key role played by civil society organizations in the closure of institutions (ECCL 2013:13). Children's NGOs possess significant know-how and practical experience in assisting transition processes from institutional care to community-based care. To this end, NGOs could be more effectively involved in the key stages of planning, implementation and evaluation of Structural Funds at the national level.

Furthermore, children's NGOs could play a more strategic role in delivering child care services. For instance, the de-institutionalisation process in Bulgaria entailed the availability of social services, such as foster care, to provide alternative care solutions to children leaving institutional care. Nevertheless, children's organisations are excluded from the provision of foster care services in Bulgaria, despite having played a crucial role in its development in the first place (National Network for Children 2012). This situation outlines that municipal administrations, and local authorities more generally, by lacking the necessary experience in providing specific child care services and by failing to involve civil society actors in the provision of these services, jeopardise the de-institutionalisation process and the provision of alternative child care solutions. Therefore the involvement of local NGOs in the planning of de-institutionalisation as well as provision of community-based services, as financed by EU funds, would ascertain that EU instruments are adequately deployed in assisting de-institutionalisation processes at national level. Indeed, EU institutions need to collaborate more closely with European and national civil society actors that have expertise on fundamental rights, including the process of de-institutionalisation. In brief, the EU's policy on de-institutionalisation would benefit from a more strategic employment of the expertise and practical knowledge that local children's organisations possess.

4.4 Integrated approach

The absence of an integrated approach, both at national and European levels, to addressing the key causes conducive to children's institutionalisation is another challenge. The EU Member States have the primary responsibility for the regulation and functioning of national child protection systems. The most common factors leading to children's abandonment in institutions are poverty and social exclusion (Save the Children 2009, 2014). However, these are rooted in complex economic and social factors that require concerted action on the part of key national government departments. At the same time, governments lack the political will to invest heavily in family support services and community-based care alternatives, and therefore, most often, institutions seem to be the only alternative care solution[14]. The EU, therefore, could play a pivotal role in supporting Member States' efforts to address the deep seated causes of children's institutionalisation by embracing an integrated approach to tackling these factors. The EU could achieve this by advocating that the *ex ante* conditionalities for implementing projects funded by Structural Funds are indeed met, and that national authorities take action aimed at preventing the continuation of institutionalisation. The EU has limited legal competence to intervene in the regulation and operation of child protection systems and more generally, children's rights provision at the national level. However, the EU has key legal and financial tools, such as anti-discrimination legislation and the Structural Funds, which could be deployed more effectively to ascertain that national governments adopt strategic actions to root out the causes that lead to child abandonment. Thus, the EU could play a central role in supporting Member States to adopt a holistic approach to the issue of institu-

14 Evidence demonstrates that institutional care is far more expensive than the cost of providing alternative care solutions (Save the Children 2009: 12).

tionalisation by targeting the risk factors conducive to child abandonment. For instance, EU actions could be channelled towards assisting national authorities in targeting those families at risk of child abandonment.

More recently, the European Commission conducted a public consultation in the summer of 2014 entitled EU Guidance on Integrated Child Protection Systems (see also Lind-Haldorsson and O'Donnell's chapter in this volume). The theme of integrated child protection systems had initially been addressed within the context of the EU Forum on the Rights of the Child in 2012 and 2013. The Commission's key objective here is to provide national authorities with concrete guidelines on the adoption of an integrated child protection system whereby "child protection is not just a matter of one department, but a horizontal concern across sectors", as Viviane Reding, the Commissioner for Justice, Fundamental Rights and Citizenship put it (European Social Network 2014). At the time of writing, the Commission has not yet adopted a policy document on the EU's guidelines or recommendations regarding integrated child protection systems. While the soft law instruments that the EU might adopt in this area (e.g. the forthcoming Guidelines on Child Protection Systems, see Lind-Haldorsson and O'Donnell's chapter in this volume) could support national efforts in endorsing a more holistic approach to child protection systems in practice, it would still be the Member States' decision whether they wish to pursue the EU guidance in this area or not. Therefore, the EU could make a difference on national child protection systems and the issue of de-institutionalisation if, apart from its soft law instruments, it could deploy more effectively its legal and financial instruments in targeting the key factors, such as poverty and social marginalisation, that lead to child abandonment in the first place. All in all, EU actions could have an added value if the current available EU instruments would better target those national factors conducive to children's institutionalisation in the Member States.

Conclusion

This chapter has examined the emergence of children's de-institutionalisation as an EU policy issue – during the Eastern enlargement process – and the key aspects as well as shortcomings of the current EU policy in this area. It was shown that, indeed, the EU has come a long way in addressing the process of children's de-institutionalisation by using a comprehensive set of legal, policy and financial instruments. Furthermore, having endorsed the main international instruments in this area, particularly the CRC and CRPD, the EU's actions to tackle the situation of children in institutional care are more likely to reflect the international standards that guide de-institutionalisation processes. Given the complexity of this process itself, the EU has been successful in developing a comprehensive policy in this area; however, there are still significant challenges – such as the use of Structural Funds, fundamental rights protection, involvement of civil society groups and an integrated approach to child protection – that the EU has to address. What this chapter has illustrated, more specifically, is that the EU has taken up children's de-institutionalisation as an objective that can be addressed by a variety of EU instruments as part of both EU internal and external policies spheres. It remains to be seen whether, indeed, the EU institutions have the will to employ more effectively the available EU competencies, as well as legal and financial instruments, to change the situational of children in institutional care for the better.

References

Alt, H. and Alt, E. (1959) Russia's Children, New York, Bookman Associates.

Browne, K. et al. (2005) A European Survey of the number and characteristics of children less than three in residential care at risk of harm, in: Adoption and Fostering 29, 4, pp. 23-33.

Browne, K. et al. (2006) Overuse of institutional care for children in Europe, in: British Medical Journal 332, 25, pp. 485-7.

Browne, K. (2009) The Risk of Harm to Young Children in Institutional Care, London, Save the Children.

Burson-Marsteller (2005) Family Matters. A Study Institutional Childcare in Central and Eastern Europe and the Former Soviet Union, available from http://p-ced.com/reference/Family_Matters_summary.pdf.

Butler, I. de Jesus (2012) Ensuring Compliance with the Charter of Fundamental Rights in Legislative Drafting: The Practice of the European Commission, in: European Law Review 37, 4, pp. 397-418.

Butler, I. de Jesus (2014) A Fundamental Rights Strategy for the European Union, Policy Brief, Brussels, Open Society European Policy Institute.

COFACE (2012) Free our people, end institutionalisation! November, public letter, available from http://www.coface-eu.org/en/Projects/De-Institutionalisation/.

Courtney, M.E. and Iwaniec, D. (eds) (2009) Residential Care of Children: Comparative perspectives, Oxford, Oxford University Press.

ECCL (2012) Wasted Time, Wasted Money, Wasted Lives – A Wasted Opportunity?, Report, available from http://community-living.info/documents/ECCL-StructuralFundsReport-final-WEB.pdf.

EEG (European Expert Group on the Transition from Institutional to Community-based Care) (2014) Toolkit on the Use of European Union Funds for the Transition from Institutional to Community-based Care, revised edition, June, available from http://deinstitutionalisation guide.eu/wp-content/uploads/Toolkit-on-the-Use-of-European-Union-Funds-for-the-Transitio n-from-Institutional-to-Community-based-Care-English.pdf.

Eurochild (2010) Children in Alternative Care - National Surveys, 2nd Edition, January, available from http://www.crin.org/docs/EuroChild%20Children%20in%20Alternative%20Care.pdf.

Eurochild (2011) How the economic and financial crisis is affecting children & young people in Europe, January, available from http://www.eurochild.org/fileadmin/public/05_Library/Thematic_priorities/02_Child_Poverty/Eurochild/Eurochild_Crisis_Update_Report_2012.pdf.

Eurochild (2012a) De-institutionalisation and quality alternative care for children in Europe – Lessons learned and the way forward, October, available from http://www.bevaikunamu.lt/wp-content/uploads/2013/12/DI_Lessons_Learned.pdf.

Eurochild (2012b) Deinstitutionalisation Myth Buster, report, available from http://www.eurochild.org/fileadmin/public/05_Library/Thematic_priorities/06_Children_in_Alternative_Care/Eurochild/DI_Myth_Buster_web_use.pdf.

European Commission (1997) Agenda 2000 – Commission Opinion on Romania's Application for Membership of the European Union, DOC/97/18, Brussels, 15 July.

European Commission (2002) Regular Report on Romania's Progress Towards Accession, SEC(2002) 1409, Brussels, 9 October.

European Commission (2003) Equal opportunities for people with disabilities: A European Action Plan 2004-2010, COM(2003) 650 final, Brussels, 30 October.

European Commission (2005) Romania. 2005 Comprehensive Monitoring Report, SEC (2005) 1354, Brussels, 25 October.

European Commission (2009) Report of the Ad Hoc Expert Group on the Transition from Institutional to Community-based Care, Brussels, European Commission.

European Commission (2010) European Disability Strategy 2010-2020: A Renewed Commitment to a Barrier-Free Europe, COM(2010) 636 final, Brussels, 15 November.

European Commission (2013) Towards Social Investment for Growth and Cohesion – including implementing the European Social Fund 2014-2020, COM(2013) 83 final, 20 February.

European Commission (2014a) Comments of the Commission on the European Ombudsman's Own-initiative inquiry, Ref. OI/8/2014/AN, available from http://www.ombudsman.europa.eu/en/cases/correspondence.faces/en/58451/html.bookmark.

European Commission (2014b) Guidance document on ex-ante evaluation for the European Structural and Investment Funds, part I, part II, 13 February, available from http://ec.europa.eu/regional_policy/information/guidelines/index_en.cfm#2.

European Council (1993) Conclusions of the Presidency SN 180/93, Copenhagen, European Council, available from http://www.cvce.eu/obj/conclusions_from_the_copenhagen_european_council_excerpt_on_the_eu_accession_criteria_21_22_june_1993-en-24104be4-664b-41b8-8e16-756c57868498.html.

European Ombudsman (2014a) Press release No. 14/2014 EU 'cohesion' policy: Ombudsman investigates protection of fundamental rights, 21 May, available from http://www.ombudsman.europa.eu/en/press/release.faces/en/54420/html.bookmark.

European Ombudsman (2014b) Letter to the European Commission opening own-initiative inquiry OI/8/2014/AN concerning the respect for fundamental rights in the implementation of the EU cohesion policy, 19 May.

European Parliament (2009) International Adoption in the European Union, Final Report, IP/C/LIBE/2008-003, 27 March.

European Social Network (2014) Towards Integrated Child Protection, available from http://www.esn-eu.org/news/308/index.html.

Hodges, J. and Tizard, B. (1989a) IQ and behavioural adjustment of ex-institutional adolescents, in: Journal of Child Psychology and Psychiatry 30, 1, pp. 53-75.

Hodges, J. and Tizard, B. (1989b) Social and family relationships of ex-institutional adolescents, in: Journal of Child Psychology and Psychiatry 30, 1, pp. 77-97.

Iusmen, I. (2013a) Policy Entrepreneurship and Eastern Enlargement: the Case of EU Children's Rights Policy, in: Comparative European Politics 11, 4, pp. 511-529.

Iusmen, I. (2013b) The EU and International Adoptions from Romania, in: International Journal of Law, Policy and the Family 27, 1, pp. 1-27.

Iusmen, I. (2014) Children's Rights, Eastern Enlargement and the EU Human Rights Regime, Manchester, Manchester University Press.

Ivanova, V. and Bogdanov, G. (2013) The Deinstitutionalization of Children in Bulgaria – The Role of the EU, in: Social Policy & Administration 47, 2, pp. 199-217.

Jacoby, W., Lataianu, G. and Lataianu, C.M. (2009) Success in Slow Motion: The Europeanization of Romanian Child Protection Policy, in: Review of International Organizations 4, 2, pp. 111-133.

Lataianu, C. (2001) Social Policies for the Protection of Abandoned Children: Institutionalisation and Alternatives to Institutionalisation of Children in Post-Communist Romania, Bucharest, BCS.

Lucarelli, S. and Manners, I. (eds) (2006) Values and Principles in European Union Foreign Policy, London, Routledge.

Maclean, K. (2003) The impact of institutionalization on child development, in: Development and Psychopathology 15, pp. 853-884.

Manners, I. (2002) Normative Power Europe: A Contradiction in Terms?, in: Journal of Common Market Studies 40, 2, pp. 235-258.

Manners, I. and Diez, T. (2007) Reflecting on Normative Power Europe, in: Berenskoetter, F. and Williams, M. J. (eds) Power in World Politics, London, Routledge, pp. 173-188.

Mansell J. et al. (2007) Deinstitutionalisation and Community Living – Outcomes and Costs: Report of a European Study, Canterbury, Tizard Centre, University of Kent.

Mulheir, G. and Browne, K. (2007) De-Institutionalising and Transforming Children's Services: A Guide to Good Practice, Birmingham, University of Birmingham Press (in collaboration with EU, WHO, CHLG and Hope and Homes for Children)

National Authority for Child Protection and Adoption (2004) Children First, PHARE 1999 Programme for Development of Child Welfare Services in Romania, Bucharest, National Authority for Child Protection and Adoption.

National Authority for the Protection of Child's Rights (2006) Child Welfare in Romania, Bucharest, National Authority for the Protection of Child's Rights.

National Network for Children (2012) Which are the problem areas in the deinstitutionalization, Report, available from http://nmd.bg/en/Position/which-are-the-problem-areas-in-the-deinstitutionalization/.

Nelson, C., Zeanah, C. and Fox, N. (May 2009) The Effects of Early Deprivation on Brain Behavioural Development, Bucharest Early Intervention Project, Oxford, Oxford University Press.

Open Society Foundation (2012) Petition to the European Parliament, available from http://www.opensocietyfoundations.org/sites/default/files/petition-eu-parliament-20121018.pdf.

Padoa-Schioppa, T. (2001) Europa, Forza Gentile, Il Mulino, Bologna.

Save the Children UK (2007) Child Protection and Care Related Definitions, October, available from http://resourcecentre.savethechildren.se/sites/default/files/documents/5608.pdf.

Save the Children (2009) Keeping Children out of Harmful Institutions, London, Save the Children Fund.

Save the Children (2014) Institutional Care: the Last Resort, Policy brief, available from http://resourcecentre.savethechildren.se/library/institutional-care-last-resort-policy-brief-2014.

Schimmelfennig, F. and Sedelmeier, U. (2004) Governance by conditionality: EU rule transfer to the candidate countries of Central and Eastern Europe, in: Journal of European Public Policy 11, 4, pp. 661-79.
UNICEF (2007) Child Protection Information Sheets, New York, UNICEF.
UNICEF (2010) A Consultation on Definitions of Formal Care for Children, Report, available from http://view.officeapps.live.com/op/view.aspx?src=http%3A%2F%2Fwww.crin.org%2Fdocs%2FDefinitions%2520for%2520Formal%2520Care.doc.
Whitman, R.G. (ed.) (2011) Normative Power Europe: Empirical and Theoretical Perspectives, Basingstoke, Palgrave Macmillan.

"When we buy a young boy …": Migrant Footballers, Children's Rights and the Case for EU Intervention

Eleanor Drywood

1. Introduction

The title of this chapter is drawn from a quotation by the long-standing manager of Arsenal FC, Arsène Wenger, in which he rigorously defends the football industry against accusations that the recruitment of talented children from abroad to play in Europe's professional football leagues is a form of modern slavery:

> …I'll show them what we do and how we treat the boys … In some places in Brazil some boys do not have the same conditions or treatment that we have. Medically, psychologically, and 'footballistically'. It is ridiculous [to call it child slavery] … When we buy a young boy we train him and give him a chance to play. We promote, we educate and we integrate. That's why we have success.

Arsène Wenger, Manager, Arsenal FC[1]

What is striking about this quotation is that hidden amongst the impressive list of benefits offered by professional football clubs to young recruits is the phrase 'when we buy a young boy'. The casualness of its use suggests a normality to the idea that a football club can 'own' a child. Wenger is also selective in focusing only on success stories at a handful of elite clubs and ignoring the murky underworld that is fuelled by a market in young foreign players. This is a phenomenon associated with unscrupulous agents, manipulative practices and high levels of exploitation in developing regions of the world. It is also one in which many young children are promised a lucrative career in football leagues across Europe, yet very few go on to succeed in the professional game. In 2001, and in response to concerns surrounding these practices, football's global governing body, the Federation of International Football Associations (FIFA), banned the international signing or transfer of players under the age of 18 (Article 19 FIFA's Regulations on the Status and Transfer of Players (RSTP)). This made it (theoretically, at least) impossible for clubs to sign players from abroad until they became adults (subject to limited exceptions). There is much evidence, however, that this prohibition remains ineffective and that a buoyant trade in child footballers from abroad contin-

1 As cited in Jones 2009.

ues to thrive. As a 2014 expose in the UK's Telegraph newspaper explains: '[t]he intensity of the quest for fresh recruits is such that some clubs knowingly take risks by bringing in underage players or by acquiring them via murky means' (Brown 2014). The purpose of this chapter – the first analysis of this area in academic literature – is twofold. First, it will establish the phenomenon surrounding the recruitment of young foreign footballers to Europe's professional game as an important area of scrutiny in children's rights studies. Second, through an analysis of the European Union's (EU) expanding activities in relation to both sport and children's rights, it will argue that the supranational body can, and should, be more proactive in addressing the failure of football's governing bodies to address the injurious children's rights consequences of the current football transfer system.

The chapter begins with an overview of the social phenomenon surrounding the recruitment of young players from abroad to Europe's football leagues. Through the discussion, reference is made to practices that represent a threat to the well-being and rights of the children involved, as understood with reference to the United Nations Convention on the Rights of the Child (CRC). The aim of this section is to establish that, for all the very positive potential effects that participation in elite football may have for some children, the operation of the football transfer system raises some serious questions surrounding the rights and welfare of young foreign players.

It is then argued that the current European football transfer system was born of the Court of Justice of the European Union's (CJEU) decision to apply free movement law to the football profession in the seminal case of *Bosman* (Case 145-93, [1995] ECR I-4921), and that the supranational organisation therefore bears some responsibility to mitigate the ill effects of the buoyant trade in young footballers from abroad that has thrived under this set up. Whilst it is acknowledged that the precise impact of the *Bosman* ruling remains debated, this decision, at the very least, brought the football transfer system within the scope of EU law, such that – read in conjunction with its growing children's rights agenda – it is unconscionable for the supranational body to ignore the issue of young migrant footballers.

A crucial part of this paper is to scrutinise attempts by football's governing bodies to stem this practice through a prohibition on the international transfer of minors. There is a prominent rhetoric from football's global regulator, FIFA, and sport's highest judicial body, the Court of Arbitration for Sport (CAS), espousing the importance of protecting minors and the need for the aforementioned outright ban to be applied effectively. Yet, the evidence is that clubs continue to recruit minor players from abroad in significant numbers. As the Wenger quotation above demonstrates, there are many within football who are strongly opposed to the current prohibition on the international transfer of minors. The possibility of discovering the next global superstar, for relatively little financial outlay, ensures that clubs will reluctantly cede to a ban on this type of recruitment. The argument ventured here, therefore, does not posit any single legal solution; instead, it suggests that the EU has the political leverage, the legal competence and the range of policy tools at its disposal to spearhead activities aimed at exploring more effective responses to the negative impact of the football transfer and recruitment system on the rights of migrant child players.

2. Children's Rights and Young Migrant Footballers

Current recruitment and transfer practices within the football industry, particularly in relation to young foreign players, raise a number of pertinent children's rights and welfare questions. At one end of the spectrum are the deeply worrying, headline grabbing stories of rogue agents operating in developing countries, duping vulnerable young players out of large sums of money on the promise of a career in football that never materialises (Meneses 2013; BBC World Service 2014; BBC News 2014; Brown 2014). These practices, often likened to child trafficking, or described as a modern form of slavery,[2] certainly encompass numerous rights violations and leave a question mark over the extent of complicity on the part of a multi-million pound sporting industry that benefits so lucratively from the discovery of the next African, South American or Asian superstar. On the other hand, there are success stories: young migrant players who secure a contract with a European club, fulfilling their dreams of a career in professional football – perhaps most famously, Lionel Messi who, recruited by FC Barcelona at the age of 13 from his native Argentina, has enjoyed a prolific career in Europe and is now one of the most decorated players in global football. These success stories nonetheless pose important children's rights questions, albeit subtler (but ultimately thornier) ones, around the ethics of the football industry: is removing a child from his home and family and transporting him across the world for the sporting and commercial gain of a football club ever justifiable? Understanding and conceptualising the complex range of children's rights issues at play here is a challenge. What follows is the first mapping out of this social phenomenon from the perspective of children's rights studies. Whilst there is only limited research on this topic, recent years have seen growing

2 Whilst these practices are often referred to as trafficking and slavery in the colloquial sense, it is not clear that they would fall within either definition in the strict legal sense: see Article 1(1)of the Slavery Convention 1926, Article 2.1 of the ILO Convention (No. 29) concerning Forced or Compulsory Labour and the Protocol to Prevent, Suppress and Punish Trafficking in Persons, Especially Women and Children, Supplementing the United Nations Convention Against Transnational Organised Crime.

media interest in the practices surrounding the recruitment of young players from abroad, the resulting journalistic investigations offer valuable insights for the social phenomenon at the heart of this analysis. The available evidence is presented with reference to the CRC, the accepted global touchstone for children's rights values, to highlight where current recruitment practices present children's rights issues.

2.1 The experiences of migrant child footballers

In recent years, the phenomenon of rogue football agents operating in developing regions of the world, and in particular Africa, has attracted media attention. These individuals are shown to be targeting young players, luring them to Europe with the promise of a trial at an elite European club, often using a process similar to people traffickers. Emboldened and inspired by superstars such as Cameroonian Samuel Eto'o and Ivorian Didier Drogba, who have enjoyed highly lucrative careers at top European clubs, young players and their families can be highly vulnerable to approaches by rogue agents. This is addressed in the 2012 documentary *Slaves to Football*:

> In Africa, millions of young boys dream of escaping poverty by becoming professional footballers. But where there are dreams, there are people willing to exploit the dreamers. All over Africa, scammers posing as football agents are duping the families of young men out of their savings for the promise of professional football careers in Europe and elsewhere. (Von Einsiedel 2010)

A study commissioned by the European Commission in 2009 looked at available evidence to chart this phenomenon (KEA/CDES/EOSE 2009: 121). According to their findings, the process begins when an intermediary spots a player and promises to facilitate his recruitment to a European Club. These players frequently receive coaching at informal 'academies', which provide the most basic facilities and rudimentary training, whilst often working in conjunction with rogue agents (Von Einsiedel 2010). The prevalence of these academies is astonishing: as an example, there are an estimated 500 in Accra alone and 'thousands more spread across Ghana' (McDougall 2008). According to the European Commission report, the next step is that the intermediary pressures the player's family for money, the result often being that they sell their possessions or take out a loan having been convinced of a quick return on their investment (KEA/CDES/EOSE, 2009: 121). *Slaves to Football* suggests that many of these players never make it to Europe, the promised trial materialising at clubs offering less lucrative careers in places such as the Cape Verde Islands (Von Einsiedel 2010). Those that do travel to Europe, following illegal and dangerous journeys, are 'put to the test' by several clubs

... until the intermediary is satisfied or gives up the process' (KEA/CDES/EOSE 2009: 121).

Those young players who fail to secure a contract with a club are often abandoned by the agent, with reports of a growing homeless population of young footballing hopefuls across Europe (McDougall 2008), particularly in cities with a former colonial link to regions of Africa such as Paris and Brussels. An ex-Cameroon youth international, Jean-Claude Mbvoumin, has set up a charity, Culture Foot Solidaire, based in Paris, supporting these young players. He outlines the situation these children face when they fall prey to an unscrupulous agent:

> So few make it, but they all come, more and more each year, and they are getting younger all the time. Thousands of kids to France. Everything is fluid in Africa – borders and passports. An increasing number of boys are coming by plane, not just the boats through the Canary Islands. One-month visas are easy to get with bribes in Africa, but after they fail their trials they stay on. They have nothing to go back to. These kids are as young as 14, they end up on the streets, worse off and in more danger than they could ever be at home. (Cited in Mcdougall 2008)

Given that, on the whole, these young men have travelled illegally to Europe using false documents they then become irregular migrants with no right to work and no income source. Furthermore, many are embarrassed by the prospect of returning home because of the sacrifices their families have made for a career that has failed to materialise (KEA/CDES/EOSE 2009: 121). They find themselves, as depicted in the documentary *Slaves to Football*, with "no passport, no permit and destroyed psychologically" (Von Einsiedel 2010). Jean-Claude Mbvoumin is keen to add that whilst most of the available information focuses on Africa, this is not a problem limited to this region, stating that it affects South America and eastern Europe as well (as cited by Aarons 2011). Indeed, in 2013 Juan Pablo Meneses published a book exposing the exploitation of young footballers in South America, highlighting the highly aggressive recruitment tactics utilised by European leagues in this region (Meneses 2013).

At the other end of the spectrum, there are huge success stories surrounding migrant players who are taken on by European clubs. In 2013, rival Spanish teams FC Barcelona and CF Real Madrid both signed prodigious talents from Japan aged just ten years, prompting a flurry of YouTube clips proclaiming the two players as the next stars of European football (South 2013). Players recruited to the top teams in Europe are placed in elite football academies, offering state of the art training facilities and bespoke educational programmes (Longman 2011). The potentially huge benefits to children who are able to access these cannot be ignored: the opportunity to play the game they love, with the accompanying benefits to health and well-being, alongside the possibility of a lucrative career. Indeed, as Arsène Wenger argues in the quotation that began this chapter, the experiences of many of these young players fly in the face of accusations of trafficking and slavery.

On the other hand, it cannot be presumed that all young migrant players who secure a professional contract are safeguarded from exploitative practices and situations that threaten their security and well-being. Even if they are amongst the privileged few who are taken on by a clubs, feelings of isolation and loneliness can be more common amongst migrant players who are often living apart from their families, in culturally and linguistically unfamiliar environments. This is something that Jean-Claude Mbvoumin of Foot Solidaire argues ought to be addressed by the industry:

> When you're discovering a new country, when you're injured, when you're at the end of your tether, you're alone because you're far away from your family. You're left to fend for yourself. (FIFA 2008)

Furthermore, whilst players dream of a career at a top European team, many end up in the lower leagues of less prestigious footballing nations. Here, the training and conditions offered are vastly different from the elite academies of the richest clubs. Often players are pressured into short-term contracts with precarious conditions that disadvantage them (KEA/CDES/EOSE 2009: 121).

2.2 The children's rights issues at play

The experiences of young migrant footballers outlined above vary considerably. At one extreme, there is growing evidence of a set of practices that – in addition to being criminal, with their slavery and trafficking-like characteristics – entail egregious violations of principles found in the United Nations Convention on the Rights of the Child. For example, the obligation on states parties to combat the sale and trafficking of children (Articles 11 and 35) and the range of provisions to protect children from various forms of exploitation, including economic (Articles 32 and 36). Furthermore, without appropriate support in place, uprooting a child from their home to move abroad at a young age can adversely impact their right to maintain contact with their parents (Article 9) and quite possibly interrupt their schooling in a way that is inconsistent with their right to education (Article 28). The failure of the football industry to engage with these practices is, of course, highly problematic and points to the need for intervention from outside the game.

Furthermore, as important as addressing these striking violations of the rights of the child is, they should not allow us to ignore the more controversial questions raised by the success stories: that is, those young people who succeed in securing a professional career with an elite club following migration to Europe. Is the very fact of allowing minors to play professional football incompatible with children's rights principles? This question goes to the heart of debates on child labour (see further: Ferreira in this book) and whether commercial and, in this case, sporting gain for adults on the back of work carried out by children is justifiable. These arguments engage the principles found in Article 33(1) CRC which protect children from 'work that is likely to be hazardous or to interfere with the child's education, or to be harmful to the child's health or physical, mental, spiritual, moral or social development'. There has been quite limited debate on the application of child labour legislation to sport (see, as an exception: Donnelly 1997). Broadly speaking, where young players register with a football academy, the vocational and educational nature of the programme they are offered allows the activities to fall outside the scope of employment. However, a residual question mark hangs over the impact of the clear sporting and commercial gain (current or future) for clubs when they invest in young players on debates around exploitation and abuses of power in the context of children's rights. Interestingly, Michel Platini, the President of UEFA, European football's governing body, views the participation of migrant children in professional football as unjustifiably exploitative:

> Paying a child to kick a ball is not that different from paying a child to work on a production line. Both amount to exploiting child labour. And when you pay a child or their parents to travel overseas, when you uproot them from their home environment, when you make them emotionally disorientated, I call that child trafficking ... Some people talk about the free movement of workers. I am talking about the protection of children. Some talk about competition law. I am talking about the right to respect human integrity; a child's right to grow up surrounded by their friends and family. (Michel Platini, UEFA President, Speech to European Parliament, February 2009)

Furthermore, although players who register with elite football academies largely escape the egregious children's rights violations that can occur as part of the football recruitment process, their successes nonetheless fuel these more insidious practices. As long as elite clubs continue to recruit young foreign players from overseas and these players enjoy high profile careers, a market will exist for unscrupulous agents and abusive practices.

Of course, whilst considering these questions, the fact that FIFA has had a prohibition on the international signing and transfer of players under the age of 18 in place since 2001 should not be forgotten. The fact that this sort of recruitment continues to take place – and is fuelling a set of practices that raise important and significant children's rights questions – underlines the need for a more effective interrogation of the phenomenon and its regulation. In light of this, the attention of this analysis now turns to the role that the EU – working alongside the football industry – can play in spearheading and facilitating this process. The essence of the argument that follows is that the EU, through its landmark ruling in the *Bosman* case, brought the football transfer system within the scope of EU law. The result is a set of consequences for young migrant players that, whilst almost certainly unintentional, have fuelled the children's rights issues outlined above. The EU has, in recent years, affirmed its commitment to an increasingly ambitious children's rights agenda across the range of its activities – this, it is argued, compels a response to the issue of young migrant footballers from the supranational body.

3. Football's Transfer and Recruitment System: Creating a Market For Young Migrant Footballers

To understand the current – highly liberalised and highly commercialised – football transfer system, brief consideration must be given to its roots as part of a restrictive employment agreement which 'shackled' players to clubs 'like a ball and chain' (Maguire 1999: 102). Following the decision of the FA to professionalise the sport in 1885, a system of player registration was introduced to prevent individuals from appearing for several different clubs in the same season (see further: Magee 2006-7). This situation operated heavily in favour of clubs, however: once a player was registered, he was unable to move employers without the consent of the club who held his registration, even following the expiry of his contract. Clubs soon realised the potential to sell registrations, receiving a monetary sum as consideration for releasing the player – what is known as a transfer fee (see further: McArdle 2000: 19). As Monroe states: the system "was designed to protect smaller clubs by preventing players from club hopping, instead [it] resulted in the registration becoming something to be bought and sold" (Monroe 1999: 31). Pearson observes that, in some instances, this not only restricted the freedom of players to choose their employer, but, at its extremes, also prevented footballers from playing professional football completely (Pearson 2015). This situation was played out elsewhere in Europe: whilst the discussion here has considered the jurisdiction of the English FA, developments in France and Germany followed a similar trend (KEA/CDES/EOSE 2009: 29). Indeed, the international transfer system became irreversibly 'Europeanised' with the CJEU's landmark ruling in the case of *Bosman* (1995). This decision laid the groundwork for a professional game that now – intentionally or otherwise – effectively incentivises clubs to recruit talented players from abroad at as young an age as possible.

Jean-Marc Bosman was an out of contract player with RC Liège in Belgium who wanted a transfer to French side FC Dunkurque. Liège would not allow Bosman to leave unless Dunkerque paid them a transfer fee; however, the two clubs were unable to reach an agreement. A reference was made to the CJEU in respect of Bosman's case, with the player arguing that his freedom of movement rights as a Community worker (ex-Article 48 EEC, now Article 45 Treaty on the Functioning of the European Union (TFEU)) were breached by a transfer system that effectively prevented him from taking up work in another EU Member State. The Court accepted Bosman's argument and ruled that, once a player's contract had expired, his original club could not demand the payment of a transfer fee, the latter only being permissible where the player moved clubs during their contracted period (*Bosman* decision: paras. 92-104). In effect, in one fell swoop, the Court had put an end to the payment of transfer fees across Europe.[3] The precise impact of *Bosman* on the football transfer system is complex and continues to be debated to this day; however, some effects of this decision are clear. First, it put players very much in the driving seat when it came to negotiating a transfer. Not only were they able, when out of contract, to move clubs without the need for their former and prospective employer to agree on a transfer fee, they were also in a stronger bargaining position in relation to salaries and signing on fees as their new club had not had to pay anything to secure their services. It is, therefore, often observed that the market liberalising effect of *Bosman* ushered in an era in which players are able to demand vast sums of money in return for their footballing services (KEA/CDES/EOSE 2009: 26).[4]

The CJEU made a second important ruling in *Bosman* (1995), namely that nationality based quota systems – which had previously existed in some domestic leagues and European football competitions, limiting the number of 'foreign players' that could be fielded by a team – also constituted an obstacle to freedom of movement of workers (*Bosman* decision: paras. 116-120). A number of arguments had been raised to support nationality based quotas including, interestingly for this discussion, that they safeguarded against an influx of foreign (both European and non-European) players and the risk that this may stifle youth development at a local level. The Court rejected this argument; instead pointing out that by opening up the job market in other EU

3 For accuracy, it should be noted that, as a free movement of workers case under EU law (ex-Article 48 EEC, now Article 45 TFEU), this ruling initially applied only to transfers between clubs in different Member States. Further changes in 2001 applied the Bosman principles to players moving between two clubs in the same country (see FIFA's RSTP). This is not to say that payments are no longer made to former clubs upon the transfer of a player, and these are often informally referred to as transfer fees. Following Bosman the football industry agreed upon a new system with the following features: compensation is paid to the club that trained the player each time he transferred up until the age of 23 (Article 20 RSTP); where a player breaches their contract without just cause a compensation fee will be paid to the original employing club (Article 17 RSTP).

4 This is not to suggest that Bosman is the only factor that has contributed to the increased earning power of footballers in over the past 20 years, merely that it was a key development in this trend. See further: KEA/CDES/EOSE 2009 KEA 2013.

Member States the abolition of quotas increased future employment opportunities (*Bosman* decision, para. 134). A further justification for the quotas was that they would prevent the richest clubs from signing the best players from abroad, thus threatening the competitive balance of the sport. It was accepted that the preservation of competitive balance in sport was a legitimate objective; however, the Court was of the view that the existing quotas did not achieve that aim as there are no rules limiting the possibility for clubs to recruit the best national players, thus undermining its achievement (*Bosman* decision: para. 135).

The most obvious impact of this aspect of the ruling in *Bosman* is the striking internationalisation of the football profession. Whilst the *Bosman* ruling itself initially applied only to transfers within the EU, it stimulated a shift in the culture surrounding football recruitment whereby clubs began to think globally when recruiting players. A recent analysis of the players in the first team squads of clubs in top division leagues in Europe revealed that the percentage classed as 'expatriate' has risen steadily over recent years and now stands at 37% (Poli/Besson/Ravenel 2014: 6). Similarly, the proportion of players who have experienced some sort of international migration during their career is 49%. Indeed, in the English Premier League, a team has not named a squad made up entirely of English players since February 1999 (Taylor 2011). Put quite simply, the migrant footballer has become a very common – and growing – phenomenon, with most players accepting that a move abroad will probably be required at some point in their career.

Furthermore, football's governing bodies' attempts to mitigate the effects of *Bosman*'s removal of nationality-based quotas have arguably created a situation which encourages clubs to ensure that, where they do recruit players from abroad, they do so at as young an age as possible. In 2005, UEFA introduced its 'homegrown players' rule, requiring each club to have four club-trained players and four players trained by a club in the same national football association in its 25-man squad. A player is 'homegrown' if, regardless of their nationality, they have been trained by their club (or by another club in the same national association) for at least three years between the ages of 15 and 21 (Freeburn 2009). Since the 2006-7 season, this rule has applied to all European club level competitions and, latterly, in many domestic leagues. The purpose of this rule is, according to UEFA, to encourage the local training of young players and to prevent richer clubs from 'hoarding' the best international talent (UEFA 2014). Ironically, however, if the protection of young players is UEFA's priority, what the rule effectively does is incentivise clubs to recruit players from abroad at as young an age as possible: if a player joins a club before the age of 15, he will satisfy the homegrown player rule by his 18th birthday. This concern was raised by the European Parliament's *Resolution on the Future of Professional Football in Europe*, in which it stated that "additional arrangements are necessary to ensure that the home-grown players initiative does not lead to child trafficking, with some clubs giving contracts to very young children (below 16 years of age)" (European Parliament 2007: para. 35).[5]

Two key points have emerged from this discussion of the football transfer system. The first is that, following the *Bosman* decision in 1995, various factors have combined to create an environment in which a market in young footballers from abroad is likely to thrive. There is a relatively low financial outlay in recruiting players from overseas, particularly those who, at a young age, have none of the high costs associated with more established players. Furthermore, if the footballing services of that child can be secured before they turn 15, they are an even greater asset to their club, effectively becoming a 'local' player on turning adult. The second point to observe is that EU intervention contributed to this trend. In a general sense, this decision linked EU law and the structure of the football transfer system inextricably and indefinitely. More specifically, whilst a potentially problematic impact on the rights and welfare of young aspiring footballers overseas was almost certainly not an intended consequence of the *Bosman* ruling, it appears to be its by-product.

The next section will go on to discuss attempts by football's governing bodies to allay fears surrounding aggressive recruitment of young players from abroad in the post-*Bosman* era and highlight the current weaknesses of these regulations, before the final section argues that the EU has a role to play in addressing these shortcomings.

4. Attempts by Football's Governing Bodies to Regulate the Trade in Young Migrant Footballers

Following *Bosman*, football's governing bodies and representatives of both the international players' union (FIFPRO) and the domestic leagues, worked with the EU to establish a new set of rules governing transfers. Central to these negotiations was the status of young migrant footballers. The result was FIFA's Regulations for the Status and Transfer of Players (RSTP), introduced in 2001, which prohibit the international transfer of players under the age of 18 (Article 19), subject to certain exceptions. These regulations apply globally and, therefore, bind all players and clubs registered with any national football association who take part in official competitions. The provision applies not only to players moving between clubs, but also to initial registra-

5 It should be noted that there is limited empirical evidence of the actual impact of the rule on clubs' recruitment strategies (Dalziel et al 2013: 63).

tions (Article 19(3) RSTP). Therefore, the regulations (in theory at least) prevent any registration of non-national minors from abroad, a significant limitation on the capacity of clubs to recruit talent on a global scale. Furthermore, FIFA have gradually introduced a series of further checks in an attempt to identify unscrupulous practices on the part of clubs and agents and ensure compliance with Article 19. Since 2009, all international transfers and first registrations of minors are considered by a sub-committee of FIFA's Players' Status Committee.[6] This is facilitated by a computer based transfer matching system, which requires clubs to input information on all non-national players who are the subject of a transfer or first registration. This information relates to proof of residence for the player and players' parents, as well as the academic education and football training that will be offered by the receiving club. Without the approval of the sub-committee the transfer cannot go ahead.

Evidently, however, there remains a buoyant trade in young international footballers, and as long as clubs continue to sign these players the exploitative practices surrounding this market are likely to remain. It is not always clear how clubs manage to circumvent the prohibition on transfers of minors: most reports of this practice in the news media simply state that a signing has taken place, with FIFA's ban (and its ineffectiveness) rarely mentioned. Of course, the possibility exists that forged documents are used, or that administrative errors occur (some, presumably, less accidental than others).[7] Equally, however, some attention should be given to a number of exceptions to the general prohibition on the international transfer of minors that are enumerated in Article 19 RSTP. Whilst each of these exceptions serves an important purpose by allowing young players to pursue a career in professional football in fairly uncontroversial circumstances, they nonetheless open up possibilities for manipulation by clubs desperate to sign young overseas players. This section will begin by discussing each of these exceptions and (where applicable) pointing to the ways in which they weaken the overall prohibition. Following that, cases in which FIFA have taken action against clubs for breaching Article 19 RSTP will be outlined. Here it is noted that the Court of Arbitration for Sport (the final court in disputes relating to FIFA Regulations) has interpreted Article 19 RSTP strictly, giving a high priority to the aim of the provision in protecting minors. This section will demonstrate that a promi-

6 Details on how these procedures protect minors is found on FIFA's website (2011): http://www.fifa.com/aboutfifa/organisation/footballgovernance/news/newsid=1493936/ (2014-13-10).

7 Indeed, in some places it is suggested that when they were recently sanctioned for a breach of Article 19 RSTP, Barcelona FC took advantage of the possibility of registering their players with either the Spanish FA or the Catalan FA for the purposes of the transfer matching system. See further: http://www.asser.nl/Default.aspx?textid=40903&site_id=11&level1=&level2=13914 (2014-13-10).

nent rhetoric espousing the importance of protecting minors through an uncompromising stance in relation to foreign recruitment is evident at the highest echelons of football governance and from sport's judicial bodies, yet there is a significant mismatch with the effectiveness of this stance in reality. This is the basis for the argument that a form of legal or policy intervention is required to stimulate work towards a more effective regulatory response.

4.1 The Article 19 RSTP exceptions

The first exception to Article 19 RTSP is that, within the EU/EEA, a lower threshold is set and players may move between countries from the younger age of 16 (Article 19(2)(b) RSTP). This allows intra-European migration of footballers at a younger age than the wider prohibition. Furthermore, it should be noted that this exception is not restricted to EU citizens (that is nationals of one of the Member States (Article 20(1) Treaty on the Functioning of the European Union)), instead extending to the transfer of a player of any nationality between two clubs within the EU/EEA. Anecdotally, there are suggestions that agents of young players from outside Europe make use of countries within this area who have more relaxed nationality laws, or ones where there is a ready trade in false passports, to gain access to the territory.[8] Once a player is legally resident in an EU/EEA country, or they have signed with a club within that area, they can then access the remainder of the territory whilst under the age of 18.

Second, an exception exists in relation to players who live near a national border and intend to register with a club in a neighbouring country, a group that will be termed 'frontier players'.[9] This provision applies anywhere in the world, but is obviously particularly relevant within Europe where the EU's free movement laws have made travel between Member States for work especially commonplace. The relevant provision states that both the player's home and the registering club must be within 50km of the border, and that the distance between these two locations must not exceed 100km (Article 19(2)(c) RSTP). This is a fairly unremarkable exception to the wider prohibi-

8 It is not appropriate to cite an authority on this point, given the evidence is anecdotal. However, the suggestion has been made that Bulgarian passports can be obtained by young aspiring players with relative ease, thus granting them access to all clubs in Europe.

9 This term evokes the concept of a frontier worker in EU law. Broadly conceived, this refers to someone who works on one side of a border but lives on the other, and returns home at least once a week and is, therefore, entitled to special provisions in relation to access to social security benefits (Article 1(b) Regulation (EEC) No 1408/71 of the Council of 14 June 1971 on the application of social security schemes to employed persons and their families moving within the Community (OJ L 149, 05/07/1971, 0002-0050)

tion: it envisages a scenario in which there is technically an international dimension, but in reality any such registration would not require a player to be uprooted from their family and home. Indeed, at elite level, it is far from unusual for a young sportsperson to travel a distance of 100km within one country; this provision simply ensures that players living near a border are not denied the opportunity to access local clubs, for the mere reason that travel just happens to involve crossing a border.

The final exception found in Article 19 RSTP applies when the player's parents move to the country in which the new club is located for reasons not linked to football (Article 19(2)(a) RSTP). On the one hand, it is an appropriate exception: it would be problematic if FIFA's ban on international transfers and registrations of minors created barriers to the opportunities offered to the children of recently arrived migrant families. On the other hand, this provision seems to provide a way of circumventing FIFA's regulations. As happened in the case of *Cádiz* (CAS 2005/A/955), discussed below, the 'reasons not linked to football' can be created after the club has expressed an interest in the player and – if these are believed by the Players' Status Committee – the transfer of a minor will proceed as an exception to Article 19 RSTP. Clearly, where facts that contradict the contention that the decision to migrate preceded the club's interest in the player come to light, the club and player risk contravening Article 19 RSTP and the transfer will be banned, as happened in *Cádiz*. However, although there is little research on this point, anecdotally it is suggested that this provision provides the most common route around FIFA's prohibition on the international transfer of minors. For a fuller understanding of how FIFA's prohibition on the international transfer of minors operates and how Article 19 RSTP has been interpreted by sport's highest judicial body, the Court of Arbitration for Sport, the principle cases in the area will now be discussed.

4.2 A children's rights rhetoric from FIFA and CAS?

In February 2005, Carlos Javier Acuña Caballero, a 16 year old Paraguayan player with Club Olympia de Paraguay, signed a contract with the Spanish club Cádiz CF. He had been scouted by an agent at an under-20s international tournament in Colombia the previous month. The Paraguayan FA blocked Acuña's transfer on the basis of non-compliance with FIFA's Regulations on the Status and Transfer of Players, including Article 19 RSTP: at 16 years of age, Acuña was a minor and fell within the prohibition on international transfers (here from Paraguay to Spain). At the club's request, the Spanish FA appealed to the FIFA's Players' Status Committee. The evidence put to the Committee was that the Cabellero family were in financial difficulty and so intended to move to Spain for Mrs Cabellero, Carlos's mother, to take up a job in a restaurant. In other words, the club argued that the family's move to Spain was for reasons unrelated to football, thus bringing the player's situation within one of the exceptions permitted by the RSTP.

The Players' Status Committee was not satisfied with the explanation of the family and Cádiz CF, ruling that the transfer would breach FIFA regulations, a decision that the Club subsequently appealed to CAS. Before the Court, the appellants first attempted to have FIFA rules on the protection of minors declared void, arguing that they conflict with mandatory provisions of public policy, relying in particular on several provisions of international law, Swiss law and Spanish law.[10] CAS rejected this argument, ruling that limiting the international transfer of minors is a legitimate objective and, given that the regulations provide for 'some reasonable exceptions', they are proportionate to that aim (*Cádiz* decision: Para. 7.2.2.). In its ruling on this point, CAS endorsed the importance of 'protect[ing] young players from international transfers which could disrupt their lives, particularly if, as often happens the football career fails, or, anyway, is not as successful as expected' (*Cádiz* decision: Para. 7.2.2.). Furthermore, the Court, having heard evidence afresh, was of the view that that the accounts of the player, his mother and Cádiz FC were not credible – the ruling on the facts being that the mother was offered her job a week after the contract between her son and the club was agreed. The transfer, therefore, did not fall within the exception, the Court ruling that the family had in fact moved to Cádiz exactly because of the player's football career.

Overall, the *Cádiz* case represented a robust defence of the purpose behind Article 19 RSTP: no one reading the case would be in any doubt as to the importance placed by CAS on the protection of minors as a legitimate objective, justifying restriction on players' international movement. This was lent further force by the subsequent decision in *Midtjylland* (CAS 2008/1/1485). FC Midtjylland, a Danish Premier League Club, has an established cooperation with FC Ebedei, a Nigerian club based in Lagos. This agreement gives Midtjylland the purchase option on talented players from the Nigerian club. Over the course of the 2006-7 season, six Nigerian players aged 16 and 17 were registered with the Danish club. The issue in this case was that the players were granted licences by the Danish FA as *amateur* players and the club argued that as non-professionals they fell outside the scope of Article 19 RSTP. There was no dispute that the players fell within the Danish FA's definition of amateur players: they had been issued with student visas by the Danish Immigration Service and were studying at public schools (albeit part-

10 The Court gives short shrift to this argument so the reported decision is not particularly expansive on its substance. However, the club and player seem to have argued that the players' right to pursue his profession is not upheld and the principle of non-discrimination on the grounds of sex, nationality and race is contravened (see Para. 3).

time to allow for their football training) and received only a modest contribution towards board, lodgings and pocket money. In deciding that Article 19 RSTP did apply to the amateur players in question, the Court advocated a purposive reading of the provision, in light of its clear intention to protect young people:

> Any other construction would be contrary to the clearly intended objective and spirit of the regulation … to apply Art 19 of the RSTP restrictively … could result in obviating protection of young amateur players from the risk of abuse and ill treatment which was clearly not within the anticipation of the scope of the regulation. (*Midtjylland* decision: Para. 7.2.5)

A further outcome of the *Midtjylland* case was that CAS confirmed FIFA's Players' Status Committee will accept two further exceptions to Article 19, limited to the situation of students who are signed from abroad. This is the case where: relocation is for the purposes of studies, not football related activity; or relocation is in the context of an agreement between the football association of origin and the new club, within the scope of a development programme subject to strict conditions (e.g. the provision of education, for a limited duration etc.). In relation to the facts before them, CAS ruled that the Nigerian players did not fit into either of these categories, so their transfers were not permitted.

In April 2014, FIFA's Disciplinary Committee sanctioned FC Barcelona and the Spanish Football Federation (RFEF) for breaches relating to the international transfer and registration of players under the age of 18.[11] The sanctions arose from investigations through FIFA's Transfer Matching System and related to activities during the period 2009 to 2013 concerning ten minor players. The most high profile of these was Seung-Woo Lee, signed by Barcelona in summer 2011 at the age of 13 and touted as the 'Korean Messi'. Now 16, Lee is a star of Barcelona's youth team and has signed a contract to remain at the club until 2019, reportedly turning down a number of lucrative offers to play elsewhere in Europe.[12] The punishment imposed on FC Barcelona was a transfer ban at both national and international level for one year and a fine of 450 000 Swiss francs (approximately €370 000). The club was also given a period of 90 days to regularise the situation of the relevant minor

11 At the time of writing, the full decision of the Disciplinary Committee has not been made public, with the fullest account offered by a press release on FIFA's website: http://www.fifa.com/aboutfifa/organisation/news/newsid=2313003/ (2014-23-10). Further information is provided in the official response from Barcelona FC, published on their website: http://www.fcbarcelona.com/club/detail/article/official-statement-from-fc-barcelona-on-the-sanction-imposed-by-fifa-s-disciplinary-commission (2014-23-10). A useful analysis is provided by van Maren and Marino 2014.

12 As an aside, it is interesting to note that, regardless of how he came to sign for Barcelona at the age of 13, the option to move elsewhere in Europe club became available to him when he turned 16 as transfers within the EU/EEA are permitted under Article 19 RSTP from this age upwards..

players. The Spanish Football Federation was fined 500 000 Swiss Francs (approximately €410 000) and given one year in which to reform its regulatory system for the international transfer of minors. In the press release published on FIFA's website, the governing body noted the 'serious' nature of the infringements as justification for the heavy penalty imposed. Furthermore, FIFA stated that that 'the protection of minors in the context of international transfers is an important social and legal issue that concerns all stakeholders in football'.[13]

The sanction imposed on FC Barcelona appeared, at first sight, to be significant on a number of fronts. First, whilst few had any doubts that, with a reported annual turnover of more than €400 million, FC Barcelona would have little problem meeting the financial penalty, the imposition of a transfer freeze had the potential to place a significant burden on the club. At the end of the 2013-14 season, the first team squad was widely considered to be in need of strengthening in certain key positions and the club had been linked with a number of high profile transfer targets (van Maren and Marino 2014). At the time the sanction was announced, the possibility that the club would not be able to make these reinforcements was significant enough to be seen as a threat to its likely success in domestic and European competitions for the following season, no trifling matter for a club of Barcelona's reputation and stature. Secondly, this is the first high-profile case brought under Article 19 RSTP against a leading European club, such as FC Barcelona. The cases against Cádiz FC and FC Midtjylland concerned teams that do not enjoy the same global sporting profile as Barcelona. In the Midtjylland case, before CAS, the Danish club argued that they were unfairly discriminated against by FIFA who, it was alleged, was targeting smaller clubs whilst ignoring infringements of Article 19 RSTP by large European teams, citing FC Bayern München as an example. This argument was rejected by the Court, who referred to the legal principle that 'no one can claim for equal treatment by referring to someone else who had adopted illegal conduct without sanction' (Midtjylland decision: Paras. 7.5.1-7.5.6).

However, the argument illustrates that there is a belief that larger clubs are immune from sanctions for violation of Article 19 RSTP, a perception that is significantly challenged by the case against FC Barcelona. Thirdly, La Mesia is a highly respected football academy, with a reputation for nurturing young players in a holistic manner which places high value on educational opportunity and personal development, as well as elite football training (Longman, 2011). As such, the message sent out by the sanctioning of this club is that transfer of minor players from abroad will not be tolerated regardless of the level of opportunity offered – and regard for individual welfare – when the player arrives in Europe. This case was not about targeting just the more

13 See the FIFA website: http://www.fifa.com/aboutfifa/organisation/news/newsid=2313003/ (2014-02-02).

exploitative practices associated with the recruitment of young players from abroad; instead the decision to sanction Barcelona suggests that FIFA, consistent with the wording of Article 19 RSTP, views any transfer of a minor from outside Europe as problematic. Indeed, FIFA's press release emphasises the level of importance attached to the protection of minors by the Disciplinary Committee:

> … the protection of minors in the context of international transfers is an important social and legal issue that concerns all stakeholders in football. Above all, the committee highlighted that while international transfers might, in specific cases, be favourable to a young player's sporting career, they are very likely to be contrary to the best interests of the player as a minor. On the basis of this analysis, the committee concluded that "the interest in protecting the appropriate and healthy development of a minor as a whole must prevail over purely sporting interests". (FIFA 2014)

Accordingly, it seems that FIFA, in imposing such a significant and high profile sanction in the interests of upholding the protection of minors, has sent out a clear message in relation to the recruitment of young players from abroad. FC Barcelona, however, vehemently defended their actions, stating that: 'FCB [FC Barcelona] creates people before they create athletes, a fact that has not been considered by FIFA, which has applied a penalty ignoring the educational function of our training programme'.[14] The club appealed FIFA's decision and – crucially – the transfer ban was suspended until the appeal could be heard. This decision significantly reduced the force of the initial sanction. It allowed the club to make a number of signings during the summer of 2014, such that the squad could be reinforced in a way that built capacity for any future reinstatement of the ban. Whilst FIFA rejected the appeal, the potency of the initial sanction was lost: the transfer ban with immediate effect would have hurt FC Barcelona on the field far more than one that can be planned for. Barcelona subsequently appealed the case to CAS who, in late December 2014, days before the first transfer window of 2015 opened, announced that the appeal had been rejected and that the ban would enter into force immediately. The result is that FC Barcelona will be unable to sign any players for the duration of 2015. In order to ensure that the ban was in place for the start of the transfer window, CAS released the decision without its reasoning, which at the time of writing remains unpublished, so further comment on the case is not possible.

One thing that appears to be certain is that, in spite of a clear stance from FIFA and CAS that the wording and spirit of Article 19 RSTP must be upheld, the current market in young footballers from abroad continues to thrive. There is ample evidence that current recruitment strategies are well embedded in a number of regions across the world and that clubs will search out legal loopholes to ensure they can continue to tap these markets. In spite of

14 As cited by Riach 2014.

this prominent rhetoric from both FIFA and CAS in support of a provision that claims to protect minors, it is clear that systemic issues within the football industry are fuelling practices that run counter to both the content and spirit of Article 19 RSTP. Aside from these cases, brought by FIFA and upheld by CAS, there appears to be little work to challenge a culture which both accepts and nurtures a high level of recruitment from abroad by clubs at every level of European football. In light of the football industry's failure, then, to tackle on its own this phenomenon, the argument now turns to the role of the EU, as both a legal and political body, in mobilising a response that meets the children's rights challenges presented by this phenomenon.

5. Making the Case for EU Intervention

Previous sections have demonstrated that a prohibition on transfers of footballers under the age of 18 from outside the EU (and under 16 within the EU) has not curbed a buoyant trade in young people from abroad who dream of playing in Europe's football leagues, but who experience extremely varied degrees of success. This final section argues that the EU has a role to play in exploring, highlighting and combating the more damaging consequences of this phenomenon. To begin, it is important to underline that this argument does not suggest the football industry itself does not have a fundamental role to play in addressing this issue – indeed, any changes to the regulation of the transfer system or other measures to promote the rights of children in this scenario would require the full support and cooperation of relevant governing bodies. However, in light of the limited progress made thus far by FIFA's attempts to regulate the international transfer of minors – and given the EU's increased activities in recent years in relation to both children's rights and sport – it is argued that the supranational body, working alongside stakeholders from within the industry, has a role to play in spearheading a more effective response. The discussion that follows is necessarily sensitive to the limited legal competences enjoyed by the EU in relation to both children's rights and sport, and considers the range of legal and policy options open to the EU, including those which move beyond a traditional legally binding regulatory approach. Crucially, this allows suggestions to be made for a role for the EU which has at its heart the need to work with the football industry to address this issue.

5.1 The rationale for EU intervention from a children's rights perspective

Whilst the EU has historically played a very hands-off role, recent years have seen an increase in activities targeting young people in a wide range of legal and policy areas and the emergence of an explicit agenda in relation to children's rights (Commission 2011). Justification for supranational intervention in this arena clusters around two central arguments, both of which support the contention ventured here that the EU has a role to play in addressing the impact of the transfer system on the rights of young migrant footballers. First, there is a case for EU action in relation to children's rights where supranational intervention has added-value: that is, where the EU is able to achieve a more effective result through a single response, than each Member State would acting alone (Stalford 2012: 7). Often this occurs in relation to issues that have a cross-border or cross-jurisdictional element, such as divorce and parental responsibility disputes arising from international family breakdown (Stalford 2012: 89). This argument is certainly relevant here: football is heavily regulated at international level by both FIFA and UEFA and the transfer system operates, certainly since *Bosman*, in an inherently cross-national manner. Here, however, the added-value of EU intervention lies equally potently in the coherence of a coordinated approach and the efficiency of working together to confront a problem that manifests itself across a number of Member States, with all of Europe's professional football leagues boasting players recruited from abroad.

Secondly, the EU, in acting within established areas of competence, can create policy 'spill-overs' which operate to the detriment of young people, such that where this happens there is clear justification for supranational intervention in the children's rights arena (Stalford and Drywood 2009: 146). Broadly speaking, protection of fundamental rights by the EU is constitutionalised in Article 6 Treaty on the European Union (TEU). This protection manifests itself in a number of ways, but at its heart lies the basic proposition that the EU must ensure its powers are exercised in a way that respects the rights recognised in a number of instruments, most explicitly the Charter of Fundamental Rights of the European Union and the ECHR (Article 6 TEU). This is supplemented by a reference to the Union's role in contributing to protection of the rights of the child found in Article 3 TEU, a provision which, rather than creating additional legislative powers, instead outlines a set of values and principles which inform the exercise of existing EU competences. The Court has ruled that the United Nations Convention on the Rights of the Child informs general principles of EU law and can, therefore, be used to review the legality of the acts of the institutions, as well as the implementation of Union law, or indeed any activities that fall within the scope of

Union law (Case C-540/03 *Parliament v Council* [2006] E.C.R. I-5769). As an example, in *Dynamic Medien* (Case C-244/06 [2008] ECR I-505), the Court found that protection of the child was a legitimate interest justifying a breach of free movement of goods principles. Equally, the Court recognised in its decision in *Bernard* (Case C-325/08 [2010] ECR I-02177) that the post-*Bosman* system of replacing transfer fees with the payment of compensation to a footballer's former club to reflect their investment in the player's training in principle constituted a breach of free movement provisions, but could be justified on the basis that it encourages the recruitment and training of young players. In other words: the Court has made it clear that protection of the rights of the child informs the exercise of free movement law and, indeed, can act as a brake on the pursuit of this objective. Given the current football transfer system has been significantly shaped by the *Bosman* ruling – and the decision to apply free movement law to this aspect of sporting regulation – a link is formed between its impact on the status of individual players and the constitutionalised obligation to respect fundamental rights. It has been shown that, through its liberalising effect on the transfer system, the *Bosman* ruling contributed to an environment in which the recruitment of young players from abroad has thrived. Indeed, trends such as the internationalisation of professional football and the emphasis on recruiting players at a young age in order to acquire cheap talent, or as a response to the homegrown players rule, are arguably – directly or indirectly – linked to the CJEU's decision in *Bosman* to apply free movement provisions to the football transfer system. It can, therefore, be argued that the EU's role in aggravating a children's rights issue creates an obligation to pursue activities that mitigate these ill effects.

That said, it should not be assumed that an argument which 'constitutionalises' the need for EU action in this area also suggests that this ought to take the form of judicial intervention or binding legislation, something that would be legally difficult given the EU enjoys no standalone legislative competence in relation to children's rights. A central characteristic of EU children's rights activities, as they have developed over recent years, is the deployment of a number of alternative 'soft' modes of governance that offer effective tools to address the detrimental impact that 'hard' law can have on the status of young people (Stalford and Drywood 2009; Drywood 2010). So, whilst it is the connection to free movement law that provides the 'hook' for EU intervention – since respecting free movement seems to have increased the likelihood of young players being recruited from abroad – the impact of this does not have to be mitigated through the hard law approaches traditionally associated with the internal market. Furthermore, as will be argued in the following section, the most appropriate legal basis for EU activity to address the impact of the transfer system on young migrant footballers is Article 165 TFEU; a competence which grants powers to act in support of, to coordinate and to supplement Member State actions in the field of sport. This type of competence is typically associated with the adoption of broad guidelines or incentive measures, or facilitating the exchange of information about best practice (Dashwood et al 2011: 104) and, therefore, primarily provides a legal basis for soft law activities. Furthermore, it has been observed that the range of soft law tools at the Union's disposal is well suited to politically or culturally sensitive areas that require a more participatory and consensus-based form of supranational governance (Trubek/Trubek 2005; Beveridge/ Velluti 2008), suggesting that this approach is well suited to an issue that requires the delicate balancing of a number of competing agendas and respect for the deeply engrained principle of sports' governing bodies' autonomy.

5.2 The rationale for EU intervention from a sports perspective

The EU's competence to support, coordinate and supplement activities in relation to sport was introduced by the Lisbon Treaty. Crucially, this provision includes the direction that 'Union action shall be aimed at … protecting the physical and moral integrity of sportsmen and sportswomen, *especially the youngest sportsmen and sportswomen*' (Article 165(2) TFEU; emphasis added). Read in conjunction with supranational obligations in relation to children's rights, outlined above, it is argued that there is a clear basis for EU intervention in relation to the impact on young people of a trade in migrant footballers where there is a political desire to push an agenda forward. Further, it is argued that this political desire is, indeed, present for two principal reasons: first, that sports policy at EU level has, in recent years, been shaped by a move towards the promotion of social, and not solely economic, objectives; second, that there is strong evidence of a desire to address the specific situation of young migrant footballers from within both the Commission and the European Parliament.

Whilst the EU initially entered the arena of sports law in the early 1970s as a by-product of its competences in other areas, particularly free movement and competition law (Case 36/74 *Walrave*[1974] ECR 1405; Case 13/76 *Donà* [1976] ECR 1333; Case 222/86 *Heylens*[1987] ECR 4097; *Bosman*), more recent years have seen the emergence of a genuine supranational sports policy, that is a more holistic and coherent agenda that addresses sport as a policy area in its own right (rather than merely as an accidental subject of EU law). Crucially, the institutions have made efforts to move away from an engagement with sport in a purely economic context and to emphasise its social value. A critical reason for this was that the *Bosman* decision – and particularly the effect it had upon the earning powers of footballers – gave a sense that the EU's impact in the sporting arena was not necessarily a positive one, and quite possibly inconsistent with its emerging social and citizenship based objectives:

> The EU was seen as a venue through which the full commercial potential of sport could be exploited at the expense of the real values of the game. As such, the EU was not reconnecting itself with its citizens, it was taking the people's game further away from them. A body of opinion emerged within the EU seeking to give the socio-cultural and integrationist qualities of sport a higher priority and for sport to be afforded a higher level of protection from EU law. (Parrish 2003: 14)

When the Treaty of Amsterdam was signed in 1997 a short Declaration was annexed to the document emphasising 'the social significance of sport' and calling on EU bodies 'to listen to sports associations when important questions affecting sport are at issue' (OJ C 340/136 10.11.1997). The most explicit articulation of the scope and content of EU sports policy is now found in the Commission's *White Paper on Sport* (Commission 2007), a document which addresses the economic dimension of sport and its organisation, but places the most significance on its societal role. Indeed, a strong feature of the White Paper is the prominence given to the protection of minors and the need to combat exploitation of young people in professional sport. The Commission highlights bad practices by some agents, including the exploitation of young players, as damaging the sport and raising questions about its governance, going on to state that the health and security of minor players must be protected (Commission 2007: 15). Furthermore, the potentially fraught status of young migrant footballers who are unsuccessful in securing a professional career is acknowledged and identified as a concern:

> The most serious problem concerns children who are not selected for competitions and abandoned in a foreign country, often falling in this way in an irregular position which fosters their further exploitation. Although in most cases this phenomenon does not fall into the legal definition of trafficking in human beings, it is unacceptable given the fundamental values recognised by the EU and its Member States. It is also contrary to the values of sport. (Commission 2007: 16)

The European Parliament has also drawn attention to the practices referred to above, itself preferring to categorise them as trafficking (European Parliament 2007). The Parliament makes a direct link between the recruitment of very young players and the introduction of the homegrown players rule and raises concerns over the status of 'trafficked' players from the point of discovery, through to recruitment and reception and their welfare in the event that they are not selected by a European team (European Parliament 2007: Paras. 35-38). It also highlights the importance of educational provision for young players (European Parliament 2007: Para. 39). The level of awareness shown by the institutions in relation to the children's rights issues relating to the status of young migrant footballers, and the prominence given to these concerns in key policy documents, establishes a clear political desire to address this question at EU level.

5.3 Softly, softly: The use of alternative modes of EU governance in the context of children's rights and sport

This, of course, leads on to the question of what form EU intervention on this issue would take. As has been suggested, the relevant legal bases in relation to both children's rights and sport support the use of 'soft' modes of governance and, indeed, these are activities which the supranational body has deployed effectively in both areas in the past. Whilst an in-depth outline of potential EU activities to promote the rights of young migrant players in the football industry is beyond the scope of this chapter, some brief elaboration is merited in order to further bolster the central argument that the EU has a role to play in addressing this issue.

First, as has been argued above, it would be neither legally possible, nor politically appropriate, for the EU to target a children's rights agenda in the context of the football transfer system through binding legal measures. Indeed, Garcia observes that in the post-*Bosman* era, much progress was made by the Commission in terms of the EU's role in regulating the football industry, not through the imposition of formal sanctions, but rather as a result of negotiations with the relevant governing bodies (Garcia 2007a). He further argues that football's European governing body, UEFA, now sees the EU as a 'long term strategic partner' and cites one reason for this being that the two bodies enjoy a shared set of social values and a belief in their contribution to sport (Garcia 2007b: 216). The idea of the EU as an agenda-setter in the context of the football industry very much accords with the approach taken in relation to a number of children's rights questions. In this context, the powerful political status enjoyed by the supranational body has provided a focal point for discussions and negotiations surrounding any coordinated activity where a complex range of stakeholders are involved. Stalford has observed that:

> The EU offers a unique forum and source of funding to bring together a range of actors at international, European and domestic level to share experience and best practice on such issues, set mutually-agreed benchmarks, and stimulate wide dissemination, awareness-raising and policy exchange. (Stalford 2012: 7)

The task of bringing together governing bodies, football clubs and players' representatives, alongside experts on children's rights on the issue of recruitment of young players from abroad is a challenge, particularly, given the lack of consensus from within the football industry in relation to the appropriateness and efficacy of the current prohibition on international transfers of minors. A supranational body such as the EU enjoys a status which can achieve this and, crucially, possesses the funding to explore a range of options to improve the children's rights situation for young migrant players.

Second, as was highlighted in an earlier section, evidence in relation to the children's rights consequences of recruitment of young foreign players to European football is limited. This remains a chronically under-researched area with much of the evidence that policy-makers have to work with resulting from small scale investigations by journalists (for example: Brown 2014) or ones with a narrow regional focus (for example: Menses 2013). If effective responses to this situation are to be agreed upon, a solid – and fuller – evidence-base is needed. Crucially, this would need to be commissioned by a body with the political leverage to ensure the cooperation of relevant stakeholders. The Commission and European Parliament have previously overseen large-scale pan-European research into aspects of sports regulation, such as a 2009 study on sports agents in the European Union (KEA/CDES/EOSE 2009). Furthermore, the EU's Fundamental Rights Agency provides expert advice to the institutions and has produced reports on the status of groups of migrant children to assist policy-makers.[15] Alongside assisting policy-makers working with stakeholders within the football industry on this issue, any such research would have a further awareness-raising function, thus increasing pressure on the football industry to address it.

Thirdly, as the EU continues to engage with the football industry, primarily through economic aspects of its regulation, the rights of children impacted by these legal and policy developments must be mainstreamed into its activities. Children's rights mainstreaming has been defined as '[t]he incorporation of children's rights, needs and welfare, according to the principles of the UNCRC, at all stages and at all levels of EU law and policy-making' (Stalford and Drywood 2009: 163). So, for example, if any future legal developments in relation to the free movement of persons or competition law were to impact on the football transfer system (in the way that *Bosman* and subsequent rulings did), the mainstreaming principle requires all institutions, legislative and judicial, to uphold children's rights principles through these activities. Increased awareness at institutional level of the impact of EU activities on the status of young migrant players, through the research activities suggested above, would facilitate the mainstreaming of children's rights when the supranational body exercises its competence in relation to the football industry. Crucially, therefore, EU actions suggested here in relation to the rights of young migrant players in the European football industry must be viewed holistically – as a package of tools at the EU's disposal which can be used to increase awareness of the problem and identify ways of improving it – but which require the participation and cooperation of the football industry itself if they are to yield any practical effects.

---

15 See http://fra.europa.eu/en/publications-and-resources for a list of FRA publications (2014-13-10).

6. Conclusion

This chapter had two aims. The first, broader, priority was to establish the phenomenon surrounding the recruitment of young foreign players to European football clubs as an important area of analysis within children's rights studies. This was done by weaving together evidence relating to the treatment and experiences of children with relevant provisions of the CRC. This demonstrated that a set of egregious children's rights violations occur in the name of recruiting children to European football clubs. Surprisingly, with the exception of a few newspaper pieces, this phenomenon has received very little attention from either the NGO/charitable sector or policy-makers at any level. Equally, the football industry itself has failed to engage with the failure of its 2001 ban on the recruitment of young foreign players and the insidious consequences of a continued trade in migrant footballers. To fully confront this problem a difficult question needs to be tackled: that is, the extent to which it is acceptable for football clubs to profit in sporting and commercial terms from their current reliance on young, foreign players. There is conflict within the industry on this point and a failure from those outside of it to provide a platform for its discussion. Certainly, this complex question requires further unpacking in academic terms; subjecting the full gamut of experiences of young migrant footballers to a children's rights-based analysis is a priority for future research. Fascinating questions await surrounding the relationship between child labour and elite sport; the suggestion that the aggressive recruitment of young foreign players is a form of modern slavery; and the appropriateness of an outright ban on minor footballers from abroad participating in Europe's leagues. This chapter – as the first significant analysis of this phenomenon – has laid down a challenge to both academic commentators and policy-makers to grapple with these questions.

But if we are to criticise the failure of those outside the football industry to confront this problem, where should we target out efforts? The second central argument of this chapter is that the EU is – both legally and politically – the appropriate body to stimulate a more effective response to the children's rights issues arising from current practices around the recruitment of young foreign players. However, rather than suggesting merely that an inherently cross-border phenomenon such as this would be more *effectively* dealt with via European-level intervention, the argument is rather that the supranational body ought to be *compelled* to spearhead activities to confront this problem because of its growing agendas in relation to both sport and children's rights. Following the CJEU's decision in *Bosman* two decades ago, the football transfer system has operated at a European level and has submitted to the scrutiny of EU law, the latter having a significant impact on its current operation. This is the environment in which a trade in child footballers from abroad operates – often in a duplicitous and exploitative manner that has significant and devastating consequences for children's enjoyment of their rights under the CRC. Can the EU, then, really ignore this situation given the constitutional status of its commitment to protecting the rights of the child (Article 3 TEU) and to promoting the principles enshrined in the CRC (Commission 2007: 4)? Of course, this would mean going into battle with those in the football industry who vehemently defend their treatment of young migrant footballers – and who show little willingness to submit to the ban on underage transfers of foreign players. This is a significant challenge; the football industry is not famed for welcoming external scrutiny of its rules and regulations. However, the EU has held its nerve in asserting its competence to subject the economic aspects of football regulation to free movement of persons and competition laws – decisions which, at the time, were phenomenally unpopular within the industry. We might, therefore, question the promises and rhetoric of the ever expanding children's rights agenda if the EU turns a blind eye to this issue.

References

Aarons, Ed (2011) African Football Trafficking a 'Growing Problem' BBC Sport, http://www.bbc.co.uk/sport/0/football/15296412 (2011-14-10).

Beveridge, Fiona and Velluti, Samantha (eds) (2008) Gender and the OMC: Perspectives on Law, Governance and Equality in the EU, Farnham, Ashgate.

BBC News (2014) Fifpro: Young Players Abandoned If They Don't Succeed, Says Union (12 April 2014),.News Report, http://www.bbc.co.uk/sport/0/football/27000050.

BBC World Service (2014) Child Footballers! The Search for the Next Messi (11 April 2014), Radio Broadcast, http://www.bbc.co.uk/programmes/p01wtd03 (2014-10-20).

Brown, Oliver (2014) The Dark Side of Football Transfers, The Telegraph, http://s.telegraph.co.uk/graphics/projects/football-the-dark-side-of-transfers/index.html (2015-01-01).

Chappelet, Jean-Loup (2010) Autonomy of Sport in Europe, Strasbourg, Council of Europe

Commission (2011) An EU Agenda on the Rights of the Child (COM (2011) 60 final), Policy Document.

Commission (2007) White Paper on Sport (COM (2007) 39 final), Policy Document

Dalziel, Murray et al (2013) Study on the Assessment of UEFA's 'Home Grown Player Rule' (Negotiated Procedure EAC/07/2012), Research Report. http://ec.europa.eu/sport/library/studies/final-rpt-april2013-homegrownplayer.pdf (2014-13-10).

Dashwood, Alan et al (2011) Wyatt and Dashwood's European Union Law, Oxford, Hart.

Donnelly, Peter (1997) Child Labour, Sport Labour: Applying Child Labour Laws to Sport, in: International Review for the Sociology of Sport 32, 4, pp. 89-406.

European Parliament (2007) European Parliament Resolution of 29 March 2007 on the Future of Professional Football in Europe (2006/2130(INI)), Policy Document.

FIFA (2014) http://www.fifa.com/aboutfifa/organisation/news/newsid=2313003/ (2014-13-10).

FIFA (2008) http://www.fifa.com/aboutfifa/socialresponsibility/news/newsid=920094/ (2014-13-10).

Freeburn, Lloyd (2009) European Football's Home-Grown Players Rules and Nationality Discrimination under the European Community Treaty, in: Marquette Sports Law Review 20, 1, pp. 177-221.

Garcia, Borja (2007a) From Regulation to Governance and Representation: Agenda-Setting and the EU's Involvement in Sport, in: Entertainment and Sports Law Journal 5, 1.

Garcia, Borja (2007b) UEFA and the European Union: From Confrontation to Cooperation, in: Journal of Contemporary European Research 3, 3, pp. 202-223.

Gardiner Mark et al (2012) Sports Law (4th Ed.), London, Routledge.

James, Mark (2013) Sports Law, Basingstoke, Palgrave Macmillan.

Jones, Dean (2009) Wenger Dismisses Platini Transfer Plan, The Independent, http://www.independent.co.uk/sport/football/premier-league/wenger-dismisses-platini-transfer-plan-1785287.html (2014-14-10).

KEA/CDES/EOSE (2009) Study on Sports Agents in the European Union (A Study Commissioned by the European Commission DG for Education and Culture), Research Report http://ec.europa.eu/sport/library/documents/study_on_sports_agents_in_the_eu_en.pdf (2014-13-10).

Longman, Jeré (2011) The Catalan Way to Grow Players on Home Soil, The New York Times, http://www.nytimes.com/2011/05/27/sports/soccer/la-masia-a-model-for-cultivating-soccer-players.html?_r=1&adxnnl=1&adxnnlx=1415819298-BQRgetw0iHsNOy/yVEnmMw& (2014-14-10).

Magee Jonathan (2006-7) When is a contract more than a contract? Professional Football Contracts and the Pendulum of Power, in: Entertainment and Sports Law Journal, 4, p. xxvi.

Maguire, Jospeh (1999) Global Sport: Identities, Societies, Civilizations, Oxford, Polity Press.

McArdle, David (2000) From Boot Money to Bosman: Football, Society and the Law, London, Cavendish.

McDougall, Dan (2008) The Scandal of Africa's Trafficked Players, The Observer. http://www.theguardian.com/football/2008/jan/06/newsstory.sport4 (2014-13-10).

Meneses, Juan Pablo (2013) Niños Futbolistas, Barcelona, Blackie Books.

Morrow, Stephen (1999) The New Business of Football: Accountability and Finance in Football, London, Macmillan Press.

Parrish, Richard (2003) Sports Law and Policy in the European Union. Manchester, Manchester University Press.

Pearson, Geoff (2015) Sporting Justifications under EU Free Movement and Competition Law: the Case of the Football 'Transfer System, in: European Public Law, forthcoming.

Poli, Rafaele, Besson, Roger and Ravenel, Loïc (2014) CIES Football Observatory Demographic Study, Research Report, http://www.football-observatory.com/IMG/pdf/ds2014_abstract-2.pdf (2014-13-10).

Pringle, Keith (1998) Children and Social Welfare in Europe, Oxford, Oxford University Press.

Riach, James (2014) Barcelona Hit with a Year-Long Transfer Ban for Breaching Rules on Youngsters, The Guardian, http://www.theguardian.com/football/2014/apr/02/barcelona-transfer-ban-fifa-fine (2014-14-10).

Snyder, Francis (1993) The Effectiveness of European Community Law: Instruments, Processes, Tools and Techniques, in: Modern Law Review 56, 1, pp. 19-54.

South, Pete (2013) Real Madrid Sign 9-Year-Old to Rival Barca Protégé, Blog Post, http://www.givemesport.com/388442-real-madrid-sign-9yearold-to-rival-barca-protege (2014-14-10).

Stalford, Helen and Drywood, Eleanor (2009) Coming of Age? Children's Rights in the European Union, in: Common Market Law Review 46, 1, pp. 143 – 172.

Stalford, Helen (2012) Children and the European Union, Oxford, Hart.

Taylor, Louise (2011) Aston Villa's All-English Team A Distant Premier League Memory, The Guardian, http://www.theguardian.com/football/blog/2011/feb/25/premier-league-foreign-players-aston-villa (2014-14-10).

Trubek, David and Trubek, Louise (2005) Hard and Soft law in the Construction of Social Europe: the Role of the Open Method of Coordination, in: European Law Journal 11, 3, pp. 343-364.

UEFA (2014): http://www.uefa.com/news/newsid=943393.html (2014-13-10).

Van Marin, Oskar and Marino, Giandonato (2014) International Transfers of Minors: The Sword of Damocles over FC Barcelona's Head?, Blog Post http://www.asser.nl/Default.aspx?textid=40903&site_id=11&level1=&level2=13914 (2014-14-10).

Von Einsiedel, Orlando (2010) Slaves to Football (People and Power), Documentary, Aljazeera. http://www.aljazeera.com/programmes/peopleandpower/2010/03/201033611552168 50.html (2014-13-10).

Networked Children, Commercial Profiling and the EU Data Protection Reform Agenda: In the Child's Best Interests?

Joseph Savirimuthu

Introduction

There is a powerful meme – empowering children. This meme is being given a new lease of life as children are regarded as central to the pursuit of EU economic, social and cultural goals. The idea of empowering children is likely to be welcomed by many, not least by those who have long battled to encourage policymakers to take into account children's needs and interests in the networked environment (Savirimuthu 2012: 31-38; Commission 2011b). Arguments in the 1990s and those which continued into the turn of this century about using regulations to create a safe environment for children remind us that many significant concessions made in accommodating children's needs and interests were not easily obtained. Policymakers and stakeholders turned to empirical studies and ground-breaking initiatives under the Safer Internet Programme, and together crafted a delicate balance between online child safety concerns and children's engagement and participation in the networked environment (Commission 2011a, 2011b). In just over two decades, significant progress has been made in creating a safe networked environment for children. That is not all. Children have emerged as major consumers of social media and new technologies (OfCom 2014: 39-42). Empowerment of children, during this period, has increasingly become entwined with the pursuit of economic objectives and the single market.

It is easy to be dazzled by the rhetorical and ideological appeal of empowering children and overlook the negative outcomes. Concerns have, for example, been expressed that a combination of an inability to constrain business interests and a failure to provide adequate safeguards for children in the realm of food advertising and marketing, are undermining children's health and well-being (Bailey 2011: 63-69). The uneasy intuition one feels about policymakers pushing through the *raison d'être* for empowerment, which at times shows scant appreciation of adverse social costs, is resurfacing in another sphere of public policy – empowering children to manage their personal data as a basis for promoting innovation and economic opportunities in the digital economy. Empowerment is now regarded as the flagship of the Commission's European Strategy for a Better Internet for Children (Commission 2012a) (the EU Strategy). Many have remarked favourably on this EU Strategy, in view of previous Commissions' efforts in the realm of online child safety (O'Neill, Staksurd and McLaughlin 2013). Formulated in 2012, the EU Strategy now paves the way for a more ambitious agenda against the background of a new policy and constitutional landscape in post-Lisbon Europe (Commission 2010; Commission 2011). It is worth noting that the EU was already at the forefront of promoting children's rights before the coming into force of the Lisbon Treaty (Savirimuthu 2012). The major difference then was that discourse about children's rights was framed in terms of obligations to respect *human* rights more generally.

Protection of *children's* rights is now explicitly recognised as an objective of the EU (Article 3 TEU). The integration of the European Union Charter of Fundamental Rights (OJ C 83, 30.3.2010, p. 389-403, hereafter the Charter) into the EU regulatory framework ensures that fundamental rights have "the same legal value as the Treaties" (Art 6 TEU). It contains a number of provisions that are relevant to children's virtual lives. Article 8 of the Charter, for example, makes explicit the protection of personal data as a fundamental right of all individuals. Data protection rules and norms must now empower children. Children will now be able to exercise their rights to information self-determination as individuals and citizens in the digital economy. This has to be read in conjunction with Article 24 of the Charter which states that in all actions relating to children, the child's best interests must be a primary consideration. The dilemma facing policymakers in translating Article 24 of the Charter into meaningful policy adjustments must now be considered alongside other developments. At present, under current data protection rules, children are not regarded as a group of individuals meriting specific "protection and care as is necessary for their well-being" (Article 24 Charter). Rather, children fall within the age-generic provisions of EU secondary legislation which, protect the personal data of all "natural persons" (Directive 95/46/EC, Official Journal L 281, 23/11/1995, Arts 1 and 2(a), hereafter the 1995 Directive) and Directive 2002/58/EC Official Journal L 201, 31/07/2002 (hereafter, the e-Privacy Directive).

The proposals to reform current data protection rules explicitly identify children as legitimate rights bearers with specific needs and interests (Commission 2012b). While such proposals are to be welcomed, when viewed as whole they raise some intriguing practical and conceptual challenges for data protection regulations (Fuster and Gutwirth 2013: 531-539). Of particular interest in this chapter are the premise and consequences of aligning children's right to information self-management with innovation under the EU's model of empowerment. For practical reasons, the chapter does not rehearse the tensions between the concept of children's rights and paternalism on the one hand and autonomy and protection on the other (Savirimuthu 2012: 10-

12 and 193-197, Fortin, 2009: 19-29). The discussion will concentrate instead on the outcomes of empowering children within the context of data protection law. It undertakes a critical assessment of pillar 2 of the EU strategy and will show that the current use of the 1995 Directive and e-Privacy Directive to reinforce these fundamental rights in a manner that is consistent with children's best interests should not underestimate the impact of particular features of networked environments on children's autonomy, agency and expression.

The analysis presented below proceeds on the following presumption: if children's needs and expectations are to be better addressed in a principled and credible manner, policymakers must take into account the specific features of networked environments that expose regulatory and structural imbalances that contribute to individuals' ability to assert control over their personal information. This chapter suggests that the assumptions we make about empowerment and its value in enhancing children's rights to information self-determination cannot be easily reconciled with the fact that networked environments modulate visibility, exposure and information sharing practices (Cohen 2013: 1916; Boyd and Marwick 2014: 1062). Nowhere is this mismatch between the EU Strategy's vision of empowering children and the reality of networked environments more clearly evidenced than by the construction of business models, which view personal information as a commodity to be exploited for no purpose other than to gain competitive advantage in the networked economy. A case in point is the practice of aggregating personal information for generating profiles of children and serving them with advertisements based on their browsing habits and online interactions. The protective potential of both the 1995 Directive and the e-Privacy Directive is being outpaced by the speed and scale of the transformative nature of social media and new technologies on society and the emergence of the personal data ecosystem. The extension of the empowerment meme as a policy objective in data protection law is problematic since it is far from clear how innovation potential and economic dynamics are to be reconciled with children's fundamental rights to privacy and protection of their personal data, without effective protection mechanisms being installed at the outset. This prompts questions as to whether the adjustments made in the proposed reforms would be sufficient to advance children's best interests as envisaged in the Charter.[1]

The specific aim of this chapter is to articulate why there is a need to begin a serious dialogue on how children's best interests can be better integrated into EU data protection legislation in a manner that is compatible with children's reasonable expectations and their rights under the Charter, while being alive to the political, economic, and social drivers of the broader policy agen-

---

1 Compare Commission 2012b in particular recitals 29, 38, 46 and European Parliament and of the Council amendments / COM/2012/011 final - 2012/0011 (COD), recitals 29, 38, Article 8 and Article 32(a).

da in the EU. Section 1 begins with some preliminary observations on the vision proposed by the EU Strategy, noting the political faith in self-regulation coupled with the restricted objective of encouraging children to exercise greater responsibility over their personal data to minimise risks of peer victimisation and online sexual solicitation. Section 2 considers the implications of new technologies and the design of communication spaces for children's autonomy over their personal data and privacy. Section 3 examines whether policymakers' confidence in the ability of EU data protection legislation to adequately protect children's personal data is both principled and credible. It will be suggested that the structural and substantive logic of existing and proposed law continue to be instructed by businesses' desire to extract maximum value from personal information. Section 4 confronts the data protection challenges from a fresh, rights-based perspective; it asks, 'what if' businesses meet the standards of the Convention on the Rights of the Child (CRC). The discussion will leave the conclusions open-ended but will suggest that requiring businesses to act in accordance with CRC values may prove to be a subtle strategy towards creating a mindset that could ultimately achieve two immediate outcomes. First, it may help resolve the protection/empowerment balance inherent in children's rights and explicit in the Charter, in particular Articles 24, 7 and 8. Second, knowing that businesses voluntarily integrate CRC standards may be a far more effective and sustainable strategy than threats of legislative intervention, monetary penalties and investigations. The chapter concludes that steering data protection rules towards embracing fundamental CRC values through design solutions and codes of practice may help demonstrate and realise a principled and sustainable approach towards furthering children's best interests.

1. The EU Strategy and Information Self-Determination

It is of course right that there should be an EU Strategy for the Internet that seeks to ensure that children in the networked environment do not find their trust and confidence impaired by threats to their safety. Why should children be exposed to risks to their health and well-being by the mere fact of using the Internet or other communication devices such as smartphones and computers? The EU Strategy has 4 main pillars; these aim to:

i. stimulate the provision of high quality creative and educational online content for children and young people;
ii. raise levels of awareness of the opportunities and risks associated with use of the internet and equip young people with the skills needed to use the internet safely and responsibly;

iii. create a safe online environment for children; and
iv. combat the distribution of child sexual abuse material via the internet and use of the internet for the purposes of child sexual exploitation (Commission 2012a: 7-16).

A host of familiar approaches and measures previously adopted are regarded as being relevant to reaching the objectives set out in the 4 pillars (Commission 2012a: as above). These involve calls for greater coordination between industry, Member States and the Commission in implementing child safety policies and initiatives to support parents and children.

1.1 Framing the Problem: The Model of Empowerment

The EU Strategy requires data protection and privacy risks encountered by children to be specifically addressed (Commission 2012a: 5, 11-13). The Commission does not disguise the imperatives driving this multi-faceted conception of children and stresses that empowering children is not simply a rhetorical turn:

> Paying attention to the demands of children opens up a wide range of business opportunities. The global digital content market is predicted to cross 113 billion Euros in 2028. The market worth of mobile apps was 5 billion euros, and is expected to grow up to 27 billion euros by 2015, mainly driven by games and with more than 5 billion mobile subscriptions worldwide. The global video game market is predicted to reach sales of over 62 billion euros. With the wide proliferation of tablets, smart phones and laptops that children use heavily, the potential market for interactive creative and educational online content for both young children and teenagers is substantial. Online and mobile apps and games provide unprecedented opportunities for business development, in particular for SMEs and creators, as they allow for direct contact with potential users/clients. Children themselves could become online creators and start-up businesses. (Commission 2012a: 3)

There are some subtle social and economic engineering undercurrents that should not go unobserved. First, it should be noted that the Commission is clearly aware of the need to calibrate current political, economic and social frameworks with the transformative nature of networked environments and technologies. Unlocking the value of personal data is regarded as a policy that is intended to stimulate innovation and provide new economic opportunities. Second, there is an assumption that these policy objectives cannot be attained unless orthodox approaches to privacy and data protection are made more adaptable and flexible without undermining individuals' fundamental rights (Commission 2012a: 3-8 and 15). It would not have gone unnoticed that against this background, the EU Strategy's conception of children in networked environments have been undergoing a reassessment of late, in terms of their legal status, their expectations as citizens and equally important, policymakers' expectations of them as consumer citizens in the digital economy. This expansive view of children has been based on the wisdom that aligning children's interests as consumers with those of the market will give rise to considerable economic and cultural opportunities. The EU Agenda for the Rights of the Child (2011), it will be recalled, sets in place a blueprint for advancing children's needs and interests not simply as individuals with constitutional rights but also as legitimate actors in the social and economic sphere (Commission 2011b). Investment in children is increasingly regarded as a policy priority (Piper 2010: 1 and Commission 2011b: 3-4).

Let us for the moment accept uncritically the premise that a new model of empowerment is needed to unlock the value of children's personal data. What safeguards does the Commission envisage as being necessary to protect the rights of children under the EU Strategy? Pillar 2 provides some possible answers to this question. The Commission begins by suggesting that all children should be empowered and those who are vulnerable protected:

> Children have specific needs and vulnerabilities and their difference has to be recognised. The internet and ICT provide children with a wide range of opportunities to play, learn, innovate and be creative, to communicate and express themselves, to collaborate and engage in society, to be more aware of the world around them, and to develop essential skills, and exercise their rights. But children also need to be protected. (Commission 2012a: 3)

Section 2.3.4 of the EU Strategy contains some measures regarded as providing adequate safeguards to possible problems resulting from empowering children. There is, first of all, an acknowledgment that industry, Member States and the Commission will need to work together to ensure that as personal data is collected and used, and that businesses will engage fully with children and equip them with information and tools to help them make meaningful choices and decisions (O'Neill, Staksrud and McLaughlin 2013: 11-18). The EU Strategy also identifies two particular data mining practices that need ongoing oversight. The heading to Section 2.3.4 provides a clue to the mischief intended to be addressed – "Online Profiling and Overspending".[2] We get a sense of the Commission's thinking of the risks posed by profiling and advertising and the steps to be taken in the following extract in the EU Strategy:

2 See the efforts made in the UK: OFT investigates free children's web and app-based games. Press Announcement, United Kingdom Office of Fair Trading, April 12, 2013: http://www.oft.gov.uk/news-and-updates/press/2013/33-13. The OFT's Principles for online and app-based games, United Kingdom Office of Fair Trading, OFT1519: http://www.oft.gov.uk/shared_oft/consumer-enforcement/oft1519.pdf. Annex to the OFT's Principles for online and app-based games, United Kingdom Office of Fair Trading, OFT1519a: http://www.oft.gov.uk/shared_oft/consumer-enforcement/oft1519a.pdf. Online games industry given two months to get house in order following OFT investigation, Press Announcement, United Kingdom Office of Fair Trading, January 30, 2014: http://www.oft.gov.uk/news-and-updates/press/2014/05-14.

> Children, especially younger ones, do not have a developed ability to engage critically with advertising messages. In virtual worlds, children can often pay for virtual goods via their mobile phones, by calling or texting, and therefore with no prior parental permission necessary. Children may also seek to access online gambling or gaming sites. They can download ringtones for their mobile phones or accidentally access the internet on their mobiles. All this may incur high charges. The aims are to make sure that standards for advertising on websites for children allow a level of protection comparable to that of advertising in the audiovisual services and that, with regard to behavioural advertising, no such segments are created to target children, and to ensure that spending online or on mobile phones by children does not generate unforeseen high costs. (Commission 2012a: 12-13)

Finally, the Commission proposes a model of empowerment which defines the way children, their parents and industry negotiate the way personal data is to be managed (Commission 2012a: 8 -13). The expectation here is that children, under this model, will eventually have: (i) greater control over their personal data; and that (ii) businesses will be required to obtain their consent before personal data belonging to them is processed in certain instances.[3] These two measures can be described as the 'control' and 'notice and consent' models respectively. 'Control', implies that children will not only be provided with information to help them understand the way their personal data will now be collected but that they will be provided with tools, such as privacy settings, to help them regulate the flows of their personal data. The role of 'consent' is, like 'control', regarded as central to empowering children and is viewed as enabling them to make informed decisions and choices in respect of the way they use their personal data (Commission 2012a: 4 and 15). The ascription of responsibility to children in the way personal information is to be managed has two aspects. The first involves unlocking the innovation potential of personal data and the second, as the Commission observes, to promote development and civic engagement:

> Young children need 'online playgrounds' where they can both play and learn; teenagers could benefit from creative and educational games to stimulate their imagination and support their positive use of the internet. (Commission 2012a: 7)

1.2 The Problem with Empowerment

Children's rights, the EU Strategy and the Agenda for the Rights of the Child become linked symbiotically with the Commission's Growth Strategy, Europe 2020. Stalford observes that the elevation of the children's rights agenda in the EU corresponds with the recognition that a failure to invest in children

3 The Commission does not make explicit, instances when children's ability to consent will not require parental oversight and appears to leave open the circumstances where children will be deemed to have full autonomy.

now will have long-term institutional, social and economic ramifications (2013: 9). The economic and social opportunities derived from conceptualising children as autonomous individuals capable of making lifestyle choices are considerable. The issue of commercial marketing to children is an ever-present problem and one which remains a highly contested terrain in public policy. While it is beyond the scope of the study to re-visit this debate fully,[4] it may at first blush seem that the Commission has anticipated concerns regarding likely adverse policy outcomes when it places children's rights to information self-determination at the heart of its strategy towards maximising the opportunities for economic growth and innovation (Commission 2012a: 7-8). Well-informed children, acting as responsible citizens should be allowed to determine how, when and by whom their personal data can be accessed and used. By fostering trust and empowering children, innovation opportunities can be realised and children and society generally will benefit from increased choices and access to a wide range of goods and services.

One does not doubt that personal data management and responsible use of the Internet and social media are relevant to children's developmental and educational opportunities too (Commission 2012c: 6). The recent qualitative study in the EU Kids Online project illustrates how engagement in the networked environment continues to enhance children's developmental processes through access to wide range of media, participation, formation of relations and experimentation (Vincent 2015; EU Kids Online 2014).

To safeguard children, society has long relied on the agency of privacy, data protection laws and responsible adults to help resolve some difficult dilemmas surrounding children's autonomy (Savirimuthu 2012: 10-12; Richards 2015: 64). Those dilemmas, although real, have long been mitigated through a combination of social and legal norms. Schools and homes continue to be regarded as spaces for nurturing, human development and fulfilment of children's potential. Parents and educators recognise the value of children enjoying private spaces for development, and would readily respect children's 'right to be left alone'. The EU Strategy's model of empowerment obscures the interplay between these social dimensions and underestimates some intractable dilemmas networked environments pose for children. Networked environments collapse contexts, redefine social norms and create the illusion of autonomy (Cohen 2012: 101-106). Understanding the social dynamics of networked environments, the scale and effects of monitoring, the range of personal data collected and observations made or inferences drawn, and uses of personal data, are crucial to grasping the problems and solutions

4 The Communication spends time focusing on the measures that need to take to safeguard children from inappropriate advertising and the financial implications for children and their parents. Advertising and commercial practices targeting children are now regulated by the Unfair Commercial Practices Directive 2005/29/EC. A sceptical view of the Directive 2005/29/EC can be found in Garde 2011 pp. 149-171.

that will be needed if the model of empowerment preferred by the Commission is to provide adequate safeguards for children's fundamental rights (Commission 2012c: 2-4).

Three specific concerns emerge from the Commission's framing of problems and the prescriptions offered. First, the premise that information self-management facilitates innovation does not give sufficient importance to the way communication platforms are designed to remove barriers to accessing personal information through a combination of promoting norms of visibility, information sharing and contractual instruments. Networked environments are far from neutral. Communication platforms have *ex ante* features, which favour the interests of business and constrain the choices of individuals and their ability to assert control over their personal information (Cohen 2014). Neither does the Commission give enough emphasis to the real imbalance that exists between individuals and those who collect their personal information. Increased awareness of the value of privacy and skills to manage personal data, will no doubt empower children in the sense that they may be able to make informed decisions about which information they should disclose, to whom and in what contexts. There is considerable body of opinion and studies however that point to features in networked environments, which undermine individuals' ability to retain control over their personal information (Steijn 2014; Hildebrandt 2009). Some degree of effective and principled regulatory oversight is still needed to ensure that these communication spaces do not continue to violate children's reasonable expectations for quiet enjoyment.

Second, the EU Strategy's entire focus on misleading advertising practices, peer victimisation and online sexual victimisation is in itself surprising. No one will disagree that many incidents involving children being victimised by their peers or approached by adults intent on engaging in sexual activity could have been avoided if children did not disclose particular information or engage in conversations that were risky. We need, however, to expand our understanding of 'harms' to also include other scenarios: loss of control over the collection and use of personal data; innocuous items of information that can be aggregated to create profiles which may lead to differential treatment; indiscretions committed by children in their naivety and immaturity that are unlikely to be forgotten and may come back to haunt them in years to come; and real risks of personal data being manipulated or used out of context.

Third, the solutions proposed by the Commission, suggests that answers to some fundamental questions have not been fully thought through. For example, we could ask why it is that children either do not realise the privacy risks associated with their online activities or struggle to manage their personal data in networked environments (Solove 2013: 1883-1889)? Given children's reasonable expectations regarding the use of technology and opportunities for identity experimentation, play and learning, is it right that we divest all responsibility for the design of communication platforms to industry? How do we promote transparency, accountability and fairness in a way that is meaningful to children (Cohen 2012: 234-239)? How should we conceptualise spatial privacy in networked environments? What is privacy for? While it is not doubted that data collection and processing practices facilitate innovation and make possible new services, content and goods to children, it is equally important that the challenges in retaining control over personal information and the adverse impacts of aggregation are not only acknowledged but also addressed.

The policy prescriptions envisaged in the model of empowerment provides us with a glimpse of how assumptions and reasoning that prioritise economic benefits and consumer interests underestimate the extent to which data protection rules can or are able to respond to the needs and expectations of children. This is a point worth remembering when attempts are made to articulate the interplay between Articles 24, 8 and 7 of the Charter on the one hand and the operation of EU data protection law in networked environments on the other. Information self-determination in the context of online profiling or targeted advertising is not simply a matter of protecting vulnerable or impulsive children from visiting websites to engage in age-inappropriate activities or entering into a spending spree due to deceptive or misleading businesses practices. To those who are accustomed to the operation of data protection rules, it will not have gone unnoticed that the model of empowerment conceals a number of problems that EU data protection legislation has long struggled to resolve: individuals continue to underestimate harms to their reputation resulting from disclosure; privacy and information sharing policies are difficult to read and understand; tracking every digital footprint is time consuming, complex and expensive; and making informed yet highly speculative decisions about future harms is extremely difficult. Of course, the management of privacy, control over personal data and determination of contexts in which information can be disclosed is not a new problem. But what has changed dramatically are the nature and sheer scope of networked environments. The persistence and sophistication of new data mining technologies create conditions that require critical conversations about how children's expectations of privacy can be promoted. The next section draws out particular features of networked environments and information collecting practices that raise serious concerns about the empowerment model, as a prelude to understanding what strategies are available to address children's needs and expectations.

2. Networked Publics: Communication, Visibility and the Autonomy Trap

The Commission in the EU Strategy portrays a far from problematic view of the significance of communication platforms and its design features for children's ability to manage their personal data within the context of profiling and advertising practices. The recent Net Children Go Mobile reports for example, while highlighting the benefits derived from interaction between children's developmental processes and digital activities, expect that greater information awareness will promote control and information self-determination (O'Neill and Dinh 2015; Livingstone et al., 2012; Livingstone and O'Neill 2010). Both conceptions fall into the 'autonomy trap' as the emphasis on notice, consent and control assume that communication spaces are neutral environments, and underestimates the way in which the collapsing of contexts (e.g. Home/School, Work/Play, Public/Private) and processing of personal information redefines autonomy (Schwartz 2000: 821; Kang 1998: 1198). It may be helpful to begin by considering the particular dimensions of networked environments and information collecting practices that justify concerns being expressed about the role and value of empowering children to take full responsibility for their personal data.

2.1 Information Collection in Networked Environments

Four types of business activities in the networked environment have a direct impact on children's ability to manage their personal information: (1) information collection; (2) information processing; (3) information dissemination; and (4) invasion (Solove 2002: 1153-1154). For example, personal information is easily collected when individuals go online, browse websites and access content and interact with friends. Tablets, software applications (apps) and mobile phones now enable information to be collected from multiple venues and devices. Wi-fi is ubiquitous in most places and blurs private and public spaces of activity. Powerful analytic software is used to analyse personal data with a view to determining individuals' preferences, tastes and choices. Knowledge created from personal data can now be used for a wide range of purposes. An online business may use information collected from website visitors to provide services and goods relevant to their needs and preferences. Information relating to personal browsing habits and content accessed can be used to predict and, importantly, shape choices and values. Information generated from an individual's use of the internet or services can also be sold to or shared with advertisers. The economic opportunities created from unlocking the value of personal data are all legal, subject to some safeguards provided by the law. That said the acts of profiling and targeting of children in particular with customised advertisements has long been an area of concern for privacy advocates.[5] In most cases, user consent to the use of the services or accessing content on websites is deemed to constitute assent to information collection, use and sharing practices.

Knowledge of the scale of data mining activities such as these still leave unexplained why the model of empowerment on which EU data law and policy is based can be seen as giving rise to the 'autonomy trap'. Marwick and Boyd articulate the notion that communication spaces constrain and shape individuals' management of their personal data (2014: 1065). I want to use their interpretation of 'networked publics' to show that children do desire to preserve their privacy and manage their personal information but encounter considerable difficulties asserting their 'right to be left alone' or rights to self-determination of their personal data. The dilemmas children face in managing their privacy and asserting meaningful control of their personal information flows from the design of communication spaces, which produces three consequences: (i) information self-management practices become defined by technological functionality; (ii) networked norms of visibility create audience dynamics that are difficult to resist; and (iii) access to personal data is used to redefine individual autonomy (Marwick and Boyd 2014: 1063).

2.2 Networked Publics

A significant proportion of children have Facebook, Twitter and Instagram accounts. Smartphones and tables have apps that increase the convenience and 'real-time' experience of interaction. Apps enable children to update their social network profiles, receive regular updates of postings by friends and contacts and develop their identities (Livingstone 2008: 393-411). Scholars seeking to resolve the privacy conundrum have drawn insights from the dynamics of digital natives in 'networked publics' (O'Neill and Dinh 2015; Livingstone et al. 2012; Livingstone and O'Neill 2010). 'Networked publics' can be described as communication spaces constructed through networked technologies such as smart phones, tablets, laptops and computers. These communication spaces are distinctive in the sense that they mediate interac-

5 See for example, Schwartz 1999: 1644; Sweeney1997: 100; Zarsky 2003; De Hert and Papakonstantinou 2012. More recently, Article 29 Working Party has issued an opinion and an Advice Paper: Opinion 2/2010 on online behavioural advertising and Advice paper on essential elements of a definition and a provision on profiling within the EU General Data Protection Regulation, available at http://ec.europa.eu/justice/data-protection/article-29/documentation/other-document/index_en.htm.

tions between people and imagined communities. Networked publics, whether these emerge on Twitter, Instagram or Facebook, represent a type of communication space. Each communication space has its own technological affordances or features that allow individuals to share information, build relations and participate in conversations in communities (Schmidt 2014: 3-14). Some illustrations can be provided to emphasise how flows of information are modulated by the design of communication spaces and tools. For example, Twitter provides @ for users to tweet information. Individuals can use text or hashtag (#) to start conversations or participate in discussions. People who follow each other on Twitter can also use the direct message facility ('DM') to have private conversations with each other. Messages are limited to 140 characters and can contain hashtags, photos and links. Facebook, another site favoured by children, also provides technological affordances for individuals to participate in networked publics but does not restrict the size of posts or length of conversations. Like Twitter, the communication space designed by Facebook is accompanied by the expectation that individuals connect with 'Friends'. This expectation of reciprocal social relationships distinguishes Facebook from Twitter. Only 'Friends' can connect and share information with each other on Facebook. When individuals connect with each other on Facebook, technological affordances structure the flow of personal information, which enable the individual to see each other's post on their 'News Feed'. Individuals can also use technological settings on Facebook to define their audiences, determine which posts are accessible and by whom, and use search tools on the site to find new 'Friends'. Technological affordances such as 'tagging', 'Like', and comment boxes allow individuals to interact with each other. Facebook provide users with timeline and notification facilities to enable users to obtain real-time experience with their connections and obtain regular updates. Increasingly, social media can be accessed through devices other than desktops.

Hyper-connectivity is an integral part of shaping audience dynamics and promoting norms of visibility and information sharing practices. Any credible attempt to empower children must account for the way networked environments modulate norms of visibility and information sharing. The design of communication spaces also structure behavioural norms, leaving users with the responsibility of defining the way their information is accessed or viewed (Johnson and Jajodia 1998: 26-34). Affordances such as 'tweet', 'tag', 'Like; or # create tools through which individuals engage in participatory activities, explore spaces for identity and experimentation while maintaining control over their personal data. These affordances also pose children with the dilemma of managing the boundaries of 'publicness' (Marwick and Boyd 2014: 1062). It is true that privacy settings enable users to control who participates in their networks. However, consent to terms on social networking sites enables service providers to access vast amounts of personal information. In networked publics, since notice and consent are effectively meaningless, children are left with the predicament of making complex and undesirable trade-offs, resorting to social stenography techniques or accepting that the cost of obscurity is exclusion from participation in communities.

In summary, an awareness of the role played by these structural dimensions is critical to understanding why the Commission's model of empowerment may be the wrong solution to a real problem. The structural dimensions of online environments shape and influence the way children define their spaces for intimacy, identity and engagement. By failing to give sufficient weight to the nuances of children's information sharing practices and their desire to participate in networked environments, the Commission appears to have formulated a strategy for the future based on contestable premises and conceptions of information self-determination that do not quite match the complexities of networked environments. The result of this approach is that reliance is ultimately placed on data protection rules to alleviate any regulatory tensions and leaves open the question of how businesses will address children's expectations and needs.[6]

Having raised some questions about the shortcomings of the model of empowerment we can now turn to consider whether even a sympathetic reading of the 1995 Directive and the e-Privacy Directive can help redress the asymmetrical relations that define children and social media companies and if not, whether the proposed data protection reforms may provide the solution to the problems identified in this section. It should not have gone unnoticed that notwithstanding the ambitions mapped by the EU Strategy, if the regulatory strains are to be taken up by data protection rules, it will have to be guided by insights and values other than those provided by the market.

3. The EU Data Protection Directives, the Protection of Children's Personal Data and Networked Environments

We are very much at the initial phase of thinking through the appropriate regulatory responses to the challenges posed by the personal data ecosystem.

---

6 Commission 2012a at p.13 states "build on self-regulatory standards such as those defined by the European Advertising Standards Alliance for behavioural advertising". This recommendation ignores the safeguards proposed by Article 29 Working Party Opinion 16/2011 on EASA/IAB Best Practice Recommendation on Online Behavioural Advertising, available at: http://ec.europa.eu/justice/data-protection/article-29/documentation/opinion-recommendation/files/2011/wp188_en.pdf. Also see EDPS Opinion on the Communication from the Commission – "European Strategy for a Better Internet for Children" (17.07.2012) http://www.edps.europa.eu/EDPSWEB/webdav/site/mySite/shared/Documents/

The business models of social media organizations such as Facebook, Twitter, Tumblr and Instagram are constructed to build databases of personal information with the purpose of creating new value or selling the information available to advertisers. It is not a coincidence that companies such as Google, Facebook, Microsoft, Apple, Twitter, Yahoo and AOL have been actively making acquisitions and aggressively seeking "new ideas, products, and services to market, and managers are seeking ways to appropriate, control, and valorize the creativity of the common" (Zwick, Bonsuand and Darmody, 2008: 174). Innovation and competitive advantage are inextricably linked to leveraging the value of personal data. During the World Economic Forum in 2010, leading IT businesses from the developed economies, privacy advocates and other stakeholders participated in an initiative entitled, 'Rethinking Personal Data' (WEF 2010). The discussions revolved around the challenge of creating a framework that optimised the economic potential of personal data while ensuring that adequate safeguards were put in place. An overriding theme at the event was that data protection laws had to be both adaptable and flexible.[7]

The EU Strategy appears to be like-minded, which is to unlock the value of personal data. Even though personal information is not regarded as property, this has not prevented it from becoming a valuable asset for innovation, marketing and revenue generation (Purtova 2011). This is an important development in the digital economy. Revenue generated from the sale of communication devices and smart phones is being overtaken by those generated from advertising and marketing. The mobile advertising revenue expected from increased use of mobile apps for search, content and social activities is estimated to reach £73.82bn by 2020.[8] Online profiling and advertising practices are regarded as central to unlocking the value of personal data belonging to consumers. We do not need to be privacy or child safety scholars to realise that calls for industry to exercise self-restraint "with regard to behavioural advertising, [so that] no such segments are created to target children" is far from being a policy that will guarantee the pursuit of children's best interests (Commission 2012a: 13). If the Commission's purported child-centred focus can be queried, might similar doubts about the ability of EU data protection law to constrain the undesirable consequences that may follow from the problems of aggregation and behavioural advertising? Data protection rules are not based on requiring industry to positively advance the interests of individuals (Purtova 2014: 204-221). Its legacy and continued relevance lies in the uneasy relations between the pursuit of economic objectives and ensuring

7 See also Department for Business (2015): Innovation & Skills UK vision for the EU's digital economy; and Kunster and Thomas et al. (2013)..

8 ABI forecast available at https://www.abiresearch.com/market-research/product/1019237-mobile-security/.

that fundamental rights are not eroded, as the following observation makes clear:

> two of the oldest and equally important ambitions of the European integration process: the protection of fundamental rights and freedoms of individuals and in particular the fundamental right to data protection, on the one hand, and the achievement of the internal market – the free flow of personal data in this case – on the other. (Commission2010b)

Balancing these two goals has never been straightforward.[9] As new technologies and networked environments increase business access to individuals' personal data, concerns have been expressed about the impact of such activities on individuals' fundamental rights (De Hert and Papakonstantinou 2012: 42). A study conducted in 2012 of apps available on Apple's iTunes app store, Google's Play App store, and Amazon's Kindle Fire App store revealed the lack of transparency and varying degrees of compliance with privacy obligations.[10] Turow, for example, observes that the design of communication spaces embeds a power structure through which audience expectations are shaped and defined to serve the pursuit of economic objectives (2011: 174-189). This is a valid observation, not least because it underlines the constant resource demands placed on data protection officials to enforce its rules:[11]

> The fragmented nature of the app ecosystem, the wide range of technical access possibilities to data stored in or generated by mobile devices and the lack of legal awareness amongst developers create a number of serious data protection risks for app users. These risks range from a lack of transparency and lack of awareness amongst app users to poor security measures, invalid consent mechanisms, a trend towards data maximisation and elasticity of data processing purposes. (Article 29, 2013: 27)

Data protection laws have by necessity rather than by design developed solutions through a complex process of rule-making, investigation and negotiation. We see some of the limits to this rule making, particularly within the context of online profiling and targeted advertising. The structure of data protection law and its role in mediating ongoing tensions between innovation and individual rights, as well as the ongoing problems of transparency, ac-

---

9 It is also worth noting that data protection is regarded as being concerned with internal markets (first pillar) and law enforcement and judicial co-operation (third pillar) rather than across all three pillars. See background provided by Simitis 1987; Gutwirth 2012; Gellert and Gutwirth, 2012).

10 Future of Privacy Forum, FPF Mobile Apps Study (June 2012) 1-5, available at http://www.futureofprivacy.org/wp-content/uploads/Mobile-Apps-Study-June-2012.pdf. See also FTC staff report Mobile Apps for Kids: Current Privacy Disclosures are Disappointing (Feb. 2012) available from http://www.ftc.gov/os/2012/02/120216mobile_apps_kids.pdf.

11 The Article 29 Working Party is an independent body of the European data protection authority. One of its roles is to advise the European Commission on issues related to personal data protection.

countability and proportionality can be highlighted by turning to its unique rules.

The principal argument canvassed here is that EU data protection Directives provide a set of default rules that leans towards promoting information access. Checks on non-compliance are however left to negotiations, threats of sanctions and monetary penalties.[12] The economic logic of monetizing personal information is to a large extent also reflected in the limits placed on data protection rules to control information flows, with the result that significant externalities end up being placed on individuals, requiring them to make complex trade-offs (Brownsword 2009; Federal Trade Commission 2012).

The discussion below will show that the model of empowerment, with its emphasis on control and consent as a ground for processing personal data may be sound in theory but its application and implementation leaves much to be desired.

3.1 Personal Data

The EU data protection legislation governs the processing of 'personal data', which has been defined as:

> Any information relating to an identified or identifiable natural person; an identifiable person is one who can be identified directly or indirectly, in particular by reference to an identification number or to one or more factors specific to his physical, psychological, mental, economic, cultural or social identity. (Article 2(a) 1995 Directive)

This broad definition of personal data has kept pace with the way new generation of technologies capture information created by and about individuals.[13] Customisation, the development of sophisticated marketing and advertising techniques and the ease with which personal data is made accessible has led to an exponential growth in markets for collection, storage and processing of personal data. The "database privacy problem" that Solove highlights foreshadows the transformative nature of new technologies (Solove 2001: 1399).[14] The breadth of the definition of personal data under Article 2(a) of

---

12 See Article 29 Working Party letter to Google requiring it to review its privacy policies: http://www.cnil.fr/fileadmin/documents/en/GOOGLE_PRIVACY_POLICY-_RECOMMENDATIONS-FINAL-EN.pdf and Google's undertaking following the investigation by a number of national data protection authorities: https://ico.org.uk/media/action-weve-taken/undertakings/1043170/google-inc-privacy-policy-undertaking.pdf.

13 See for example, World Economic Forum, Personal Data: The Emergence of a New Asset Class, 2011, available at http://www.weforum.org/projects/rethinking-personal-data; and Zarsky 2004.

14 Solove, D (2001) *Privacy and Power: Computer Databases and Metaphors for Information Privacy*, pp. 1404-1407 (p. 1399: "The Big Brother metaphor is definitely effective at cap-

the 1995 Directive corresponds with the emergence of personal data as a new class of assets (Zarsky 2004: 45). Recital 26 of the 1995 Directive provides that when determining whether a person is identifiable, account must be taken of "all the means likely reasonably to be used either by the controller or by any other person to identify the said person". Digital technologies not only enable information, which is volunteered by individuals, to be collected but also those which are based on inferences and predictions derived from aggregated personal data.

For example, 'personal data' for the purposes of Article 2(a) of the Directive will include not only biographical or other personal information but also web searches, browsing history, devices used, activities on social media sites, emails, phone calls and user-generated content.[15] As society becomes increasingly connected with a range of technologies "behaviour is increasingly monitored, captured, stored, used and analysed to become knowledge about people, their habits and their social identity" (Van der Hof and Prins 2011: 111).

3.2 Conditions Imposed on Processing Personal Data

Articles 6 and 7 of the 1995 Directive provide a core set of obligations and safeguards in relation to the processing of personal data. Article 7, sets out a number of grounds where processing activities are regarded as legitimate. For example, processing of personal data by a party (known as the 'data controller') is lawful when an individual (known as the 'data subject') has given unambiguous consent (Article 7(1)(a) 1995 Directive). However, consent is not the only ground under which personal data can be processed. Processing undertaken to conclude a contract to which the data subject is a party or where processing of personal information is one which is imposed by law on a data controller is regarded as legitimate. While these grounds are regarded as legitimate *a priori*, Article 7(1) (f) of the 1995 Directive states that processing in the absence of consent is legitimate as long as it is regarded as:

> ...necessary for the purposes of the legitimate interests pursued by the controller or by the third party or parties to whom the data are disclosed, except where such interests are overridden by the interests for fundamental rights and freedoms of the data subject which require protection under Article 1 (1).

---

turing certain privacy problems, but not all privacy problems are the same. I argue that the metaphor fails to capture the most important dimension of the database problem: the nature of our relationships with public and private bureaucracy and the effects of these relationships on human dignity and freedom.")

15 Article 29 Working Party Opinion 4/2007 on the concept of personal data (WP 136) pp. 16-17.

Processing of sensitive personal data relating, for example, to a person's race or ethnic origin, political opinions, health and sexual life have stricter requirements (De Schutter and Ringelheim 2008: 362) The fact that the grounds of processing are legitimate under Article 7 does not necessarily bring the matter to an end. Article 6 introduces a set of normative criteria, which the data controller is expected to respect. The values and standards which processing of personal data activities must adhere to are: fairness and lawful processing, minimality, purpose specification, information quality, data subject participation and control, disclosure limitation and information security. While there is some agreement regarding the circumstances when processing is lawful, determinations regarding the fairness of processing are not entirely straightforward. Recital 36 lends some colour to the scope of the inquiry, and provides that:

> if the processing of data is to be fair, the data subject must be in a position to learn of the existence of a processing operation and, where data are collected from him, must be given accurate and full information, bearing in mind the circumstances of the collection.

Fairness has been interpreted as requiring data processing practices to be transparent and not disproportionate in view of the purposes for which the personal data was originally collected.[16] Both transparency and proportionality are regarded as an integral part of the balancing of the data subject's and data controller's interests. The principles of minimality and purpose of limitation are an obvious expansion of the principle of fairness. Article 6(1) (c) of the 1995 Directive provides that processing must be "relevant and not excessive in relation to the purposes for which they are collected and/or further processed". The purpose limitation principle engages both fairness and lawfulness, and states that "personal data shall be collected for specified, lawful and/or legitimate purposes and not subsequently processed in ways that are incompatible with those purposes."

There are three elements to the purpose limitation principle. First, data controllers are required to notify the data subject of the purposes for which processing is undertaken. Second, data controllers are required to adhere to the reasonable expectation of data subjects that the processing is compatible with the original purposes for which personal data was collected. Third, the purposes of processing must be lawful. The principle of information quality, which again overlays the grounds under which Article 7 processing is permitted, imposes a series of requirements, namely, that the personal data that is collected and processed is valid, relevant and complete. There is an expectation that data controllers take reasonable steps to ensure the quality of data (Article 6(1) (d)). Finally, even though Article 6 does not explicitly state the primacy of data subjects' reasonable expectation of control over the pro-

16 ECtHR, *Leander v. Sweden*, No. 9248/81, 26 March 1987, para. 58. Decision of 9.11.2010 in Joined Cases C-92/09 *Volker und Markus Schecke GbR* and C-93/09 *Hartmut Eifert.*

cessing of personal data, we can extrapolate from Articles 7, 8, 12 and 14, 'consent' type obligations and rights, a principle of information self-determination (Rouvroy and Poullett 2009: 51). For example, even if a data controller can lay claim to processing without relying on Article 7(1) (a), as may be the case when Article 7(1) (f) is relied upon, the principle of self-determination may provide the data subject with an expectation that certain wishes are respected. For example, the data subject could request access to information relating to decisions reached as a result of automated processing of personal data (Article 12(a)). Article 14(b) provides the data subject with the right to object to the processing of personal data for direct marketing purposes. This cursory overview of the EU data protection rules raises questions as to whether they impose adequate and sufficiently tailored constraints on industry data collection practices which correspond with the Commission's children's rights strategy.

3.3 Profiling and Behavioural Advertising: A Closer Look

The creation of user profiles through automated processes and targeted advertising are regulated by EU data protection law. For example, Article 15 of the 1995 Directive deals with the automated practice of constructing user profiles based on volunteered information, online activities and inferences derived from browsing history and clickstream activity. Increasingly, the development of sophisticated data analysis technologies and design of communication platforms have not only allowed for user profiles to be constructed but have also enabled advertisers to use such information to target individuals based on their personal characteristics such as age, gender, lifestyle interests and preferences and online activities. The 1995 Directive does not deal with the act of installing software onto communication devices with a view to engaging in processing of personal data. This software, also known as 'cookies', enables websites to monitor an individual's browsing activities, preferences and sites visited by users. Directive 2002/58/EC (as amended), also known as the e-Privacy Directive, deals with a particular form of information collecting practice.[17] The e-Privacy Directive transposes the data protection principles and safeguards set out in the 1995 Directive. Article 5(3) of the e-Privacy Directive permits:

---

17 The Directive states that users must give their consent before software can be stored on their terminal equipment, or that access to such information may be obtained. In order to do this, users must receive clear and comprehensive information about the purpose of the storage or access. These provisions protect the private life of users from malicious software, such as viruses or spyware, but also apply to cookies.

> …the storing of information, or the gaining of access to information already stored, in the terminal equipment of a subscriber or user is only allowed on condition that the subscriber or user concerned has given his or her consent, having been provided with clear and comprehensive information, in accordance with Directive 95/46/EC, inter alia, about the purposes of the processing.

At first sight, it would seem that the 1995 Directive and the e-Privacy Directive would resolve concerns raised by online profiling and behavioural advertising. There are four possible arguments in favour of this view. First, control is achieved since processing of personal data will only be legitimate if one of the grounds set out in Article 7 is present (see above). Second, consent of the user and 'consent type' provisions provide an important regulatory oversight over the collection practices. Third, the principles of proportionality, purpose limitation and fairness will limit potential misuse of personal data. Fourth, the principle of information self-determination will align data controllers' processing activities to the expectations of the data subject. It is agreed that 1995 Directive has a number of provisions that directly address data protection concerns. However, the existence of these substantive safeguards does not imply that industry behaviour is constrained in practice. Additionally, the substantive principles are widely drafted and the particular type of activity covered by Article 15 is significantly limited (Robinson, Graux, Botterman and Valeri 2009: 40). As an example, consider Article 15(1) of the 1995 Directive, which provides that every person has the right:

> …not to be subject to a decision which produces legal effects concerning him or significantly affects him and which is based solely on automated processing of data intended to evaluate certain personal aspects relating to him, such as his performance at work, creditworthiness, reliability, conduct, etc.

Data subjects control over profiling is limited. Consider for example, Jenny,[18] who purchases five pizzas from a supermarket every Friday. The supermarket's computer processes the information and automatically sends Jenny some discount vouchers. Although automated processing has taken place, it would not give rise to legal effects. Neither would profiling – 'Jenny likes pizzas' – be regarded as involving an evaluation of "personal aspects relating to [her]". The decision to send Jenny discount vouchers is arguably based on objective or factual data. Similarly, automatically generated ads based on information posted on Jenny's profile page on Facebook or photos uploaded on Instagram would fall outside the mischief of Article 15. An example of a situation where automated processing produces legal effects, would be inferences drawn from Jenny's volunteered information on Facebook that she is likely to engage in criminal activity, based on racial, geographical or demographic data.

18 Jenny is a hypothetical young girl (child) used here for the sake of the argument.

A point worth emphasising is that EU data protection rules do not regard protection of personal data as an absolute right and neither is the data subject's consent essential as a ground for processing under Article 7. That said, as noted previously, Member States do provide data subjects with an opportunity to object to unsolicited direct marketing and particular forms of automated processing.[19] Behavioural advertising which relies on constructing profiles based on browsing behaviour is not covered by Article 15 of the 1995 Directive, as tracking is only made possible when software is installed onto users' computers. Article 5(3) of the e-Privacy Directive requires that users be provided with "clear and comprehensive information" and must give their prior informed opt-in consent before any cookies are set on their "terminal equipment" (e.g., computer or mobile device). This is an important safeguard, in theory. Under the previous 'cookies' rule businesses were only required to provide notice and an opt-out mechanism.[20]

The Privacy and Electronic Communications (EC Directive) (Amendment) Regulations 2011, which implements the EU rules on cookies, requires third parties delivering ads to web users, with a view to monitoring their user behaviour, to provide clear and comprehensive notices. Explicit consent is required when third parties capture all browsing activity.[21] The reality however is very different. Websites provide pop-boxes for individuals to accept the terms of service before cookies are installed. It is common to find websites providing a hyperlink to a separate page for individuals to review the privacy policy. Most users merely click the 'I Agree' box to access content and services. Where an individual does not accept the installation of cookies, access to the contents on the site is either restricted or blocked. It should not be overlooked that the mere fact a web user opts-out of online behavioural advertising does not bring to an end other forms of generic online advertising. There are other limitations to the e-Privacy Directive. Websites for example can store personal information and can collect, store and process information, which they deem to be strictly necessary in the event that services have been expressly requested.[22] On a practical level, due to the range of data collection and sharing practices, the idea of information self-determination in a networked environment may at best be unrealistic since individuals lack the time, resources and skills to identify and track their extensive digital trails being monitored by websites. This is particularly salient in relation to chil-

19 Section 12(2) Data Protection Act 1998 requires the data controller to inform the data subject if decisions have been taken through automated processing of personal information.

20 The Privacy and Electronic Communications (EC Directive) (Amendment) Regulations 2011 implemented the new rule in the UK.

21 The Advertising Standards Authority regulates online behavioural advertising in the UK.

22 See study by Mayer, J. R. and Mitchell, J. C. *Third-Party Web Tracking: Policy and Technology*, PROC. 2012 IEEE SYMP. ON SECURITY & PRIVACY 413, 415 (2012), available at https://cyberlaw.stanford.edu/files/publication/files/trackingsurvey12.pdf.

dren. Given the scale of collection and ready availability of technologies to process and analyse information, it would be impossible for data subjects (and certainly children) to detect violations of these data protection regulations or misuse of their personal information.[23]

Finally, the Commission's suggestion in the EU Strategy that data controllers observe the 1995 Directive rules, assumes that there are effective accountability mechanisms to restrict self-seeking behaviour and commercial interests. Ascertaining whether data protection obligations have been breached is far from straightforward and is contingent on individuals establishing that the grounds for legitimate processing are not present and, if legitimate, do not meet the thresholds of the guiding principles. Further complications may arise by virtue of the fact that the terms of service and privacy policies used by social media businesses and organizations invariably result in individuals ceasing to retain much control over their personal information. As Marwick and Boyd point out, many individuals turn to self-help strategies and "develop innovative mechanisms for achieving privacy in response to the technical architectures and social dynamics that underpin networked publics" (2014: 1052).

3.4 Proposals for Reform: The General Data Protection Regulations

Negotiations for the proposed reform to Directives 95/46/EC and Directive 2002/58/EC are reaching a conclusion.[24] The General Data Protection Regulations ('Regulations') aim to provide an overarching framework regulating the processing of processing of personal data in keeping with the needs of modern economies and societies. The Regulations still keep intact the sub-

23 See Reference for a Preliminary Ruling from High Court of Ireland (Ireland) made on 25 July 2014 *Maximillian Schrems v Data Protection Commissioner* (Case C-362/14), 2014 O.J. (C 351) 5.

24 The Draft Regulation is being considered by the European Parliament, the European Commission and the Council of the European Union. Governments, industry and organizations are engaged in ongoing discussions and lobbying. The Draft Regulation will be adopted through the legislative procedure, with both the European Parliament and the Council of the European Union jointly adopting the legislation. On the position of the European Parliament see http://register.consilium.europa.eu/doc/srv?l=EN&f=ST%207427%202014%20REV%201, the 'Albrecht' Draft Report 2012/0011(COD), available at http://www.europarl.europa.eu/meetdocs/2009_2014/documents/libe/pr/922/922387/922387en.pdf and LIBE Committee, Compromise Amendments on the General Data Protection Regulation (voted on 21 October 2013), http://www.europarl. europa.eu/meetdocs/2009_2014/documents/libe/dv/comp_am_art_01-29/ comp_am_art_01-29en.pdf.

stantive principles under the 1995 Directive while including the principles of transparency and data security. For present purposes, the Chapter will highlight those that relate to the EU Strategy and the model of empowerment. 'Privacy by design' is envisaged as a measure to provide for more effective protection of the rights of data subjects, particularly children. The Commission has proposed the definition of a child for the purposes of data protection to be an individual under 18 years. The Regulations also require data controllers to adopt measures that incorporate plain language, so that the question of whether consent has been obtained is not in doubt, particularly where children are involved. More specifically, social media services will require consent of parents where the child is under 13 years old (Jasmontaite and De Hert 2015: 22-24). Article 8(1) of the Regulation states that information society services directed to a child below the age of 13 are lawful only if the child's parent gives consent. For example, 'personal data', which is processed for profiling or behavioural advertising purposes will now be subject to safeguards under the Regulation. Article 4(8) of the Regulation makes explicit the meaning of consent for the purposes of data protection:

> the data subject's consent means any freely given specific, informed and explicit indication of his or her wishes by which the data subject, either by a statement or by a clear affirmative action, signifies agreement to personal data relating to them being processed.

Article 20(2) of the Regulation would possibly benefit from being made clearer. There needs to be specific provision making clear the obligation that children and their parents should be provided with meaningful information, such as the types and range of profiling activity, the information collected, the use made of the information, information sharing arrangements purposes and the grounds upon which the processing can be said to be compatible with the 'best interests of the child' principle. There is an important caveat to this recommendation. It is not entirely clear the basis upon which policymakers feel confident in assuming that children or their parents can or should assume responsibility over the management of the child's personal data. Could we really expect parents and their children to monitor how companies are processing personal information?

That said, Article 20 of the Regulation is to be welcomed since it now introduces a specific right of an individual not to be profiled and as a result modifies Article 15 of the 1995 Directive. However, the limitations identified under Article 15 of the 1995 Directive are still present. For example, data controllers can still collect and categorise personal information under Article 20(2) of the Regulation, if it is undertaken for the purposes of entering into a contract to which the data subject is a party. Under the Regulation data controllers need only provide 'suitable' rather than 'effective' safeguards, which protect the legitimate interests of the data subject. Profiling is still permitted where it is shown that "processing is necessary for the purposes of the legitimate interests pursued by a controller". The absence of any definition of profiling is very likely to perpetuate the asymmetrical relationship between children and data controllers. In short, the benefits to children under the Regulation are likely to be marginal, since automated processing which involves assessments or predictions based on factual data, relating to preferences, interests and movements will still be permissible.[25]

Even though the final text for the Regulation has yet to be realised, concerns have already been expressed in relation to the safeguards children can expect with regard to the management of their personal information. For example, Purtova suggests that the legitimate interests of the data controller and contractual terms may embed the imbalance and power structures that already exist as between data subjects and data controllers (Purtova 2014: 204-221). It is worth recalling that the legitimate interests ground for processing under Article 7(f) of the 1995 Directive can only be overridden if proven to erode fundamental rights.[26] Article 6(1) (f) of the Regulation leaves data controllers with the task of balancing their 'legitimate interests' against the interests of data subjects to protection of their fundamental rights and freedoms. Suggestions that individuals' in networked environments can fully assert control over their personal data do not give enough weight to the significant imbalance that exists between social media companies and individuals. Networked publics force individuals to make complex trade-offs between the desire for privacy and the need to communicate and participate (Bruns 2013: 14). There is a much broader aspect to the issue of empowerment that data protection rules have yet to fully engage with, namely, whether more can or should be done to ensure that industries assume greater responsibility in the way children's personal data is collected and used (Acquisti, Brandimarte and Loewenstein 2015: 509-514). Finally, van der Hoff, while acknowledging that great strides have been taken in bringing to the forefront of public and industry consciousness the needs and reasonable expectations of children, has questioned whether the aspirations will materialise into meaningful measures (2014: 139-140). As Gillespie observes, communication platforms are business models which continuously:

25 It is however not entirely clear whether Recital 58 of the regulation, which discourages profiling of children will be explicitly stated in the final text of Article 20 of the Regulation. See also the Article 20 Working Party Opinion 02/2013 on apps on smart devices, February 2013, www.cbpweb.nl/downloads_int/wp202_en_Opinion_on_Mobile_Apps.pdf, p. 26, and Opinion 2/2010 on online behavioural advertising, 22 June 2010, p. 17: http://ec.europa.eu/justice/policies/privacy/docs/wpdocs/2010/wp171_en.pdf.

26 Decision of 24.11.2011 in Case C-70/10 (Scarlet Extended v SABAM), Decision of 16.2.2012 in Case C-360/10 (*SABAM v Netlog*), CJEU in Case C-524/06 *Heinz Huber v FRG* [2008] ECR I-9705, ECtHR, and *Marper v the United Kingdom*, Nos. 30562/04 and 30566/04, 4 December 2008; see also, for example, ECtHR, *MM v the United Kingdom*, No. 24029/07, 13 November 2012, Joined Cases C-293/12 and C-594/12, *Digital Rights Ireland Ltd v Minister for Communication et al.* and *Kärtner Landesregierung et al.*, judgment of 8 April 2014.

> have to strike their own balance between safe and controversial, between socially and financially valuable, between niche and wide appeal. And, as with broadcasting and publishing, their choices about what makes it onto the platform, how it is organized, how it is monetized, what can be removed and why, and what is technically possible or prohibited, are all real and substantive interventions into the contours of public discourse. (2010: 409-410)

Gillespie is also alluding to the carefully crafted relationship social media companies and organizations have with end users, advertisers and professional content producers (Ibid.). Any expectation of empowerment over personal data or privacy, and tensions created from monetizing content on social networking sites is diffused through carefully constructed terms of service and appeals to the rhetoric of placing the individual in charge.

The EU model of empowerment, against the background of EU data protection law, still leaves us with a conundrum: how should children's needs and reasonable expectations be integrated into data protection rules? Is it right that participation in online playgrounds means that children forego their reasonable expectations to privacy and rights to self-determination of their personal data? In the next section we can explore some ideas regarding the integration of children's needs and expectations into EU data protection legislation in a manner that is compatible with children's reasonable expectations and rights while being alive to the political, economic, and social drivers of the broader policy agenda in the EU.

4. A Counterfactual Analysis: What if…?

Both the EU Strategy and reform of EU data protection legislation face the challenge of enabling data controllers to fully realise the economic value of personal information, whilst at the same time ensuring that data subjects' fundamental rights are not eroded. Policymakers have been extremely keen to proclaim the importance of taking into account children's needs and expectations but fall short of articulating how economic and developmental issues that impact children can be better addressed. Positioning children's rights has been a constant preoccupation of policymakers in the realm of the networked environment ever since convergence enabled children to take advantage of the Internet and access an array of online services.[27] Even though promoting

27 See the Principles for the Safer Use of Connected Devices and Online Services by Children and Young People in the EU, available at: www.rcysostenibilidad.telefonica.com/blogs/wp-content/uploads/2012/01/ICT_Principles.pdf, European Framework for Safer Mobile Use by Young Teenagers and Children; http://ec.europa.eu/information_society/activities/sip/self_reg/phones/index_en.htm.

trust and confidence posed enormous challenges, solutions were eventually found by first, resisting the urge to devise policies founded on out-dated notions of the way children mediated their online interactions (Livingstone and Bulger 2013). Second, it was accepted by policymakers that responsibility for online child safety governance should be implemented by three groups of actors, and not just children and their parents: (i) those who make the technologies; (ii) those who make consumption of the technologies and services available; and (iii) those who consume the technologies and services.[28]

In the remainder of the discussion, I would like to highlight how data controllers, principally those who make the technologies and those who provide the services could use the CRC as a framework for initiating further discussions with all stakeholders with a view to developing principled and workable solutions. What follows is a sketch of some of key principles and strategies that could form the basis of future discussions when grappling with the interplay between Articles 24, 8 and 7 of the Charter within the context of data protection rules.

4.1 Applying the Convention on the Rights of the Child to the protection of children's personal data

The CRC continues to provide "basic standards that apply without discrimination to all children worldwide" as well as informing frameworks for governance (Livingstone and Bulger 2013: 2). Livingstone and O'Neill argue that even though the CRC does not provide strong guarantees and its rules are unevenly implemented, it does provide an admirable touchstone and logic that is difficult to ignore (2014: 19-38). The CRC sets out basic standards and specifies minimum standards that help steer policymakers towards developing principled and sustainable strategies. There is general consensus that its well-established principles are coherent and conceptually defensible. The Commission's Communication *An Agenda on the Rights of the Child* ascribes to this view in its statement that "[t]he standards and principles of the CRC must continue to guide EU policies and actions that have an impact on the rights of the child" (Commission 2011a:3). The CRC's emphasis on the value of personhood, encapsulated in the best interests of the child principle, is indispensable to the information management dilemmas facing children in networked publics, even where conflicts in interests may arise between data controllers and data subjects. Forging a consensus and devising credible and

28 On the issue of self-regulation and co-regulation see Rubinstein, I. (2011) Privacy and Regulatory Innovation: Moving Beyond Voluntary Codes. In: *A Journal of Law and Policy for the Information Society* 6 I/S pp. 355-423.

sustainable strategies is an immediate challenge. One advantage policymakers have and which was unavailable during the mid-1990s is that we have come to utilise various regulatory techniques and strategies in reaching our goals. The success of the online child safety governance model cannot be disassociated from the value placed by all stakeholders to the norms and principles of the CRC and its continued influence.

The provisions in the CRC have natural affinity with the participatory opportunities provided by the Internet and communication technologies. Personhood, in view of the CRC will also include freedoms such as autonomy, dignity, identity and privacy as they are essential to enabling children to develop into rational mature adults. The CRC can be seen as providing minimal standards, which organizations and adults in society are expected to adhere to, where these impact children. The best interests of the child principle also encourages businesses to take positive measures that promote well-being, development and fulfilment. As the Committee on the Rights of the Child reminds us, we must not readily assume that the opportunities for economic growth will result in children's rights being advanced (Committee on the Rights of the Child 2013). The concerns raised in this chapter would be met if:

> ...in the context of business activities and operations ... all business-related policy, legislation or administrative acts and decision-making [are] transparent, informed and include full and continuous consideration of the impact on the rights of the child. (Committee on the Rights of Child 2013: paragraph 26)

What must businesses do? It is perhaps here that the CRC norms can be used to develop a principled and coherent response, which overcomes some of the problems with the EU Strategy and the empowerment model. The communication spaces that define social media business models need to better reflect children's expectations when participating in networked publics. New technologies and access to diverse media enable children to assume multiple roles, and create opportunities for association and expression. Consideration also needs to be given to the value of selfhood. Profiling, online advertising practices and web-tracking practices should not be regarded as simply another transactional opportunity.[29] As Carr observes:

> The self is rarely fixed. It has a protean quality. It emerges through personal exploration, and it shifts with circumstances. That's especially true in youth, when a person's self-conception is fluid, subject to testing, experimentation and revision. To be locked into an identity, particularly early in one's life, may foreclose opportunities for personal growth and fulfilment. (Carr 2015: 206)

29 See empirical work done by Rader, E: *Awareness of Behavioral Tracking and Information Privacy Concern in Facebook and Google* (Conference Paper) available at https://www.usenix.org/system/files/conference/soups2014/soups14-paper-rader.pdf; Bonneau, J and Preibusch, S. (2009) The Privacy Jungle: On the Market for Data Protection in Social Networks, in: *Workshop on the Economics of Information Security* (WEIS), May 2009.

It should also be borne in mind that children do not intuitively regard their online interactions as being subjected to ongoing monitoring. Addressing the needs of children requires an appreciation of the context, which defines children's lifeworld in networked publics (Nissenbaum 2010: 241-243). We can now turn to the pathways which provide a coherent and principled as well as being alive to commercial reality.

4.2 'What if'?

Two avenues could provide the basis for developing opportunities for demonstrating commitment to CRC Principles: (i) Codes of Practice; and (ii) Privacy by Design (PbD).

4.2.1 Codes of Practice

Data protection rules provide a general framework of duties and obligations. The Regulation explicitly identifies children's needs as an important consideration to be taken into account. Codes of practice provide businesses with one instrument through which commitments to CRC can be demonstrated. There are three specific benefits in using codes of practice. First, we need to recognise that children are not a homogenous group of individuals and their needs may vary according to the activity or sector (e.g. education, play, exchanging information and accessing content). Codes of practice provide businesses with a degree of flexibility and adaptability. Second, self-regulation enables businesses to assume direct responsibility for managing children's concerns and needs, and with the added benefit that business practices may even exceed regulatory baselines, for example, as those set out in Articles 6 and 7 of the 1995 Directive. Third, steps can be immediately taken to initiate self or co-regulatory standard setting measures that integrate CRC principles into industry or sector specific codes of practice (Savirimuthu 2012: 242-262). The use of codes of practice is already regarded as an accepted regulatory mechanism under Article 27(1) of the 1995 Directive:

1. The Member States and the Commission shall encourage the drawing up of codes of conduct intended to contribute to the proper implementation of the national provisions adopted by the Member States pursuant to this Directive, taking account of the specific features of the various sectors.
2. Member States shall make provision for trade associations and other bodies representing other categories of controllers which have

> drawn up draft national codes or which have the intention of amending or extending existing national codes to be able to submit them to the opinion of the national authority.

Rather than leave industry to determine what it regards as the standards for accommodating children's needs and interests, CRC principles could be regarded as providing the 'bright-line' of standards, which are commensurate with the information management dilemmas encountered by children. Codes of practice can supplement existing 1995 Directive protections and offer one possible avenue through which we can begin to establish the level of standards deemed to be appropriate for children (Information Commissioner's Office 2010: 17).

4.2.2 Privacy by Design

Policymakers and scholars have turned to engineering solutions to help address information self-management and related dilemmas. This solution is described as 'Privacy by Design' (PbD).[30] PbD is based on the premise that businesses consider privacy anxieties and risks at the outset, rather than leave that question to be addressed after privacy concerns emerge when individuals use the product or services.[31] PbD can be viewed as one regulatory strategy, through which CRC principles and values can be promoted. There is some evidence suggesting that shifting the mindset of product developers and innovators to think about privacy and consumer concerns at the outset may have trust generating properties (Cavoukian 2012). Rubinstein and Good for example, using Google and Facebook as a case study, demonstrated that many of the privacy incidents could have been avoided by introducing design solutions and taking into account consumers use of products and services at

---

30 For a recent overview of the state of play on this issue, see Danezis, G. et al. (2014) *Privacy and Data Protection by Design – from policy to engineering*, EU, ENISA; Castelluccia, C. and Narayanan, A. (2012) *Privacy considerations of online behavioural tracking*, EU, ENISA; Cavoukian, A. and Prosch, M. (2010) *The Roadmap for Privacy by Design in Mobile Communications: A Practical Tool for Developers, Service Providers, and Users*, Office of the Information and Privacy Commissioner of Ontario available online at http://www.ipc.on.ca/images/Resources/pbd-asu-mobile.pdf.

31 Directive 1995/46/EC, recital 46, which deals with the interpretation of Article 17, indicates that security measures cannot simply be added into systems, but should already be incorporated when designing the processing system and the processing itself, a principle known as 'privacy-by-design'. Article 14(3), e-Privacy Directive, can be interpreted in a similar manner; the Commission has the power to set out rules on designing terminal equipment in such "a way that is compatible with the right of users to protect and control the use of their personal data, in accordance with Directive 1999/5/EC and Council Decision 87/95/EEC of 22 December 1986 on standardisation in the field of information technology and communications".

the outset (Rubinstein and Good 2012: 1333-1414). Swire, in his examination of social networking sites, identifies the role played by designs of communication spaces in users' decision to share or withhold information (Ibid.: 103-105). He observes that individuals tend to be relatively uninhibited in social networking sites and the absence of any constraints in the design of communication platforms may at times lead to bad information sharing practices that in some instances result in privacy harms such as loss of reputation, dignity and respect. Both examples illustrate that a balance has to be struck between the use of design and adoption of other strategies such as education.

It should also be borne in mind that engineering solutions are not necessarily the best way of addressing all problems resulting from youth indiscretions and information sharing norms that expose children to privacy harms. Swire also makes another pertinent observation – the model of empowerment may not always be appropriate, as the restriction on flows of information may also collide with fundamental rights such as the freedoms of association and expression (Ibid.). One could interpret Swire's conclusions as reminding policymakers of the dangers of imposing additional regulatory burdens when other optimal measures should be considered. Brown, in a recent study on the UK approach to the introduction of smart meters in households highlighted the economic and social costs from the failure of policymakers to integrate meaningful data protection measures during the product development phase (Brown 2014: 172-184). One conclusion that could be drawn is that failure to implement privacy enhancing protections at the outset may be counterproductive since they may alter business incentives, increase compliance costs, heighten consumer mistrust and ultimately deprive industry from unlocking the value of persona data (Savirimuthu, 2013: 161-186).

The use of engineering solutions to address some social problems within the context of children's engagement with new communication technologies is not new. Design solutions have been long been used by Internet Services Providers to ensure that children do not gain access to illegal or inappropriate content and services. Finding the right balance between integrating privacy values at the developmental phase and at the user phase may appear to be burdensome. This however is not necessarily true. For example, in relation to products such as smartphones, tablets or Apps, developers can easily consider at the outset whether the privacy risks are of such a nature to justify PbD. Even in this sector specific area solutions are already being made available. The UK's Information Commissioner's Office, recently provided guidance to app developers of mobile devices, including game consoles and smart TVs, highlighting simple design solutions that could be adapted to take into account the lifecycle of personal data and users' needs.[32]

32 Information Commissioner's Office, Privacy in mobile apps: Guidance for app developers, available at: https://ico.org.uk/for-organisations/guide-to-data-protection/online-and-apps/. A global survey of mobile apps discovered that over 85% of mobile apps did not provide

It is particularly instructive to note that the specific measures identified in the guidance enable app developers to accommodate the needs of users such as children through a mix of design and awareness creating solutions: (i) use of language that the target audience understands; (ii) stating how personal data is collected and will be used; (iii) ensuring that notices enable meaningful choices to be made; and (iv) layering notices (ICO 2013: 8-9). A broader lesson to be learnt is that targeting the right activity and audience will be important. If implemented correctly at the outset, PbD can avert mistrust and support children who may be vulnerable or impulsive. We can see the value of PbD in recent examples involving concerns relating to in-app purchases made by children, as noted in the EU Strategy. This outcome could have been anticipated by designing payment authorisation and certification solutions, which require prior adult authorization. It is after all conceivable that children engaged in playing games would end up making in-app purchases on mobile phones.

The idea of a counterfactual is not as fanciful as it might seem. The Digital Agenda for Europe, which is one of the European Commission's initiatives under the Europe 2020 Strategy, can be regarded as preferring PbD as an important part of the regulatory toolkit which enable the 1995 Directive rules to promote users confidence and safeguard their fundamental rights (Commission, 2010b: 17). Codes of practice and PbD encourage a process-oriented mindset but in slightly different ways. These pathways direct businesses towards the value of identifying and implementing measures that are not only feasible but principled and responsive to children's needs and expectations.

Acting 'as if' would also shift the responsibility onto businesses to devise, in collaboration with other stakeholders, creative approaches to vesting children with rights to information self-determination, in the sense of what Altman regards as "selective control of access to the self" (Altman 1997: 67). Codes of practice and PbD could be used to deal with the practice of online profiling and web advertising through the provision of information and meaningful choices.[33] Inferring patterns of behaviour with a view to attaining commercial objectives would have to be justified and moderated by assessments on the impact of decisions made on children. Codes of practice could augment current 1995 Directive rules and design solutions. For example, codes of practice could make explicit the specific responsibilities and obligations with a view to demonstrating commitment to recital 58 of the Regulation:

Every natural person should have the right not to be subject to a measure which is based on profiling by means of automated processing. However, such measure should be allowed

---

adequate privacy notices, available at: https://ico.org.uk/about-the-ico/news-and-events/news-and-blogs/2014/09/global-survey-finds-85-of-mobile-apps-fail-to-provide-basic-privacy-information/.

33 See above note.

when expressly authorised by law, carried out in the course of entering or performance of a contract or when the data subject has given his consent. In any case, such processing should be subject to suitable safeguards, including specific information of the data subject and the right to obtain human intervention and that such measure should not concern a child.

Without a principled default position for children, market incentive structures by themselves will fail to provide an effective constraint on industry's desire to leverage the economic value of personal information. Both codes of practice and PbD, it should be stressed, are not the panacea.[34] The aim in this section is to go beyond the model of empowerment and suggest how initiating dialogue and collaboration could help minimise the differences between data controllers and data subjects in a way, which is principled and alive to political and economic realities. More importantly, the discussion leaves open the question of the extent to which CRC principles can be creatively utilised as default principles either in codes of practice or PbD.

Conclusion: Where is Empowerment Taking our Children?

Empowerment is a powerful ideological and rhetorical gambit. As a statement of policy intent it captures our attention. Online playgrounds, like a glass cage, are not neutral environments (Carr 2011: 206). Consent and control are illusions. A fully filled Facebook profile page contains at least forty items of personal data that can be easily processed, used and shared (Grimmelmann 2009: 1149). Once personal data is posted, the reality is that individuals have little or no control over its subsequent use. Consent is rarely meaningful, since many individuals do not read privacy terms when signing up for commercial services. A failure to accept the contractual terms of service will invariably prevent them from participating in networked publics or accessing content or services. Device identifiers, cookies and web beacons, are also redefining spatial privacy in online playgrounds. Every digital footprint is collected, stored and analysed. These technologies now join the list of technologies embedded in networked environments to create a communication space where critical tensions between information self-determination and information access are endemic and mediated in favour of data controllers. The recent experiment by Facebook to gauge the moods of its users by ma-

34 See the correspondence between Article 29 and the advertising industry: Article 29 Data Protection Working Party, Letter to the online advertising industry (OBA) Industry regarding the self-regulatory Framework (August, 2011), available at: http://ec.europa.eu/justice/data-protection/article-29/documentation/other-document/files/2011/20110803_letter_to_oba_annexes.pdf.

nipulating the messages they were presented with on their news feeds illustrates the growing power imbalance between data controllers and data subjects (Kramer et al. 2014). There is no doubt that networked environments create considerable new opportunities – but there are undesirable characteristics that cannot be ignored. Control and consent are far from being ideal proxies for autonomy and empowerment.

The EU Strategy model of empowerment appears to gloss over the reality of networked environments. Data protection policymakers should not overlook the 'autonomy trap' – children will now be placed in the invidious position of making complex trade-offs. Expecting children to make rational choices and behave responsibly at all times is both unrealistic and burdensome. This chapter has identified shortcomings in the model of empowerment in both the EU Strategy and data protection laws. Easy solutions are difficult to find and formulate. The allure of economic and innovation potential in providing children with online playgrounds has perhaps contributed to the rather rash nod towards data protection laws, without providing any principled basis for ensuring that there is a 'bright-line' of children's needs and expectations that cannot be diluted through appeals to contractual terms and business interests.

It is suggested that the model of empowerment is indeed the wrong solution to some real dilemmas encountered by children in networked environments. The alternative approach of integrating CRC principles more explicitly into the design architecture of networked environments and codes of practice may impress upon everyone of society's collective responsibility towards fulfilling children's developmental needs and expectations rather than being content with defining them by market values and preferences. It is true that even if CRC principles were integrated into codes of practice and design solutions, there is no guarantee of compliance. This is why collaboration and engagement with all stakeholders is critical to creating a regulatory space for ongoing dialogue under the mantle of the CRC.

References

Acquisti, Alessandro; Brandimarte, Laura and Loewenstein, George (2015) Privacy and human behavior in the age of information, in: Science 30, January, pp. 509-514.

Altman, Irwin (1977) Privacy Regulation: Culturally Universal or Culturally Specific?, in: Journal of Social Issues, 33, 3, pp. 66-84.

Andrejevic, Mark (2007) iSpy, Lawrence KS, University Press of Kansas.

Article 29 Working Party (2013) Opinion 02/2013 on apps on smart devices WP 202, available at: http://ec.europa.eu/justice/data-protection/article-29/documentation/opinion-recommendation/index_en.htm#h2-3.

Bailey, Reg (2011) Letting Children be Children: Report of an Independent Review of the Commercialisation and Sexualisation of Childhood, London, TSO.

Boyd, Danah and Marwick, Alice (2014) Networked privacy: How teenagers negotiate context in social media, in: New Media & Society, 16, 7, pp. 1051-1067.

Brown, Ian (2014) Britain's Smart Meter Programme: A Case Study in Privacy by Design, in: International Review of Law, Computers and Technology, 28, 2, pp. 172-184.

Brownsword, Roger (2009) Consent in data protection law: Privacy, fair processing and confidentiality, in: Gutwirth, S. et al. (eds) Reinventing data protection?, Dordrecht, Springer.

Bruns, Axel (2013) From Homepages to Network Profiles: Balancing Personal and Social Identity, in: Hartley, J., Burgess, J. and Bruns, A. (eds) A Companion to New Media Dynamics, London, Wiley-Blackwell.

Carr, Nicholas (2015) The Glass Cage: Automation and Us, London, Bodley Head.

Cavoukian, Ann (2012) Operationalizing Privacy by Design: From Rhetoric to Reality, Office of the Information and Privacy Commissioner, Ontario, Canada available online at: http://www.ipc.on.ca/english/Resources/Discussion-Papers/Discussion-Papers-Summary/?id =1254.

Cohen, Julie (2012) Irrational Privacy, in: Journal On Telecommunication and High Technology 10, pp. 241-250.

Cohen, Julie (2013) What is Privacy For?, in: Harvard Law Review 126 pp. 1904-1933.

Cohen, Julie (2014) Configuring the Networked Self. Law, Code, and the Play of Everyday Practice, New Haven, Yale.

Committee on the Rights of the Child (2013) State obligations regarding the impact of the business sector on children's rights, General comment No. 16 CRC/C/GC/16.

Communication from the Commission (2010a) Europe 2020: A Strategy for Smart, Sustainable and Inclusive Growth, COM (2010) 2020, final.

Communication from the Commission (2010b) A comprehensive approach on personal Data Protection in the European Union, COM (2010) 609, final.

Communication from the Commission (2011a) An EU Agenda for the Rights of the Child COM (2011) 60, final.

Communication from the Commission (2011b) Protecting Children in the Digital World COM (2011) 556, final.

Communication from the Commission (2012a) European Strategy for a Better Internet for Children COM (2012) 196, final.

Communication from the Commission (2012b) Proposal for a Regulation of the European Parliament and of the Council on the protection of individuals with regard to the processing of personal data and on the free movement of such data COM (2012) 11, final.

Communication from the Commission (2012c) Safeguarding privacy in a connected world: A European data protection framework for the 21st century COM (2012) 09, final.

De Hert, Paul and Papakonstantinou, Vagelis (2012) The Proposed Data Protection Regulation Replacing Directive 95/46/EC: A Sound System for the Protection of Individuals, in: Computer Law and Security Review 28, 2, pp: 1-13.

De Schutter, Olivier and Ringelheim, Julie (2008) Ethnic Profiling: A Rising Challenge for European Human Rights Law, in: Modern Law Review 71, 3, pp. 358-384.

EU Kids Online (2014) EU Kids Online: findings, methods, recommendations, London, LSE.

Fortin, Jane (2009) Children's Rights and the Developing Law, Cambridge, Cambridge University Press.

Federal Trade Commission (FTC) (2012) Protecting consumer privacy in an era of rapid change – Recommendations for businesses and policymakers, FTC Report, March 2012.

Fuster, Gloria Gonzalez and Gutwirth, Serge (2013) Opening up personal data protection: a conceptual controversy. In Computer Law & Security Review 29, pp. 531-539.

Gellert, Raphaël and Gutwirth, Serge, (2012) Beyond accountability, the return to privacy?, in: Guagnin, D. et al. (eds) Managing Privacy Through Accountability, Basingstoke, Palgrave Macmillan.

Grimmelmann, James (2009) Saving Facebook, in Iowa Law Review 94, pp. 1137-1206.

Gutwirth, Serge (2012) Short Statement about the Role of Consent in the European Data Protection Directive, in: The Selected Works of Serge Gutwirth, available from: http://works.bepress.com.ezproxy.liv.ac.uk/serge_gutwirth/80.

Schmidt, Jan-Hinrik, (2014) Twitter and the Rise of Personal Publics, in: Weller, K. et al. (eds) Twitter and Society, New York, Peter Lang.

Information Commissioner's Office, (2013) Privacy in mobile apps: Guidance for app developers, available at https://ico.org.uk/for-organisations/guide-to-data-protection/online-and-apps/

Johnson, Neil and Jajodia, Sushil (1998) Exploring steganography: seeing the unseen, in: Computer 31, 2, pp. 26-34.

Jasmontaite, Lina and De Hert, Paul (2015) The EU, children under 13 years, and parental consent: a human rights analysis of a new, age-based bright-line for the protection of children on the Internet, in: International Data Privacy Law 5, 1, pp. 20-33.

Kramer A. D. I., Guillory, J. E. and Hancock, T. J (2014) Experimental Evidence of Massive-Scale Emotional Contagion through Social Networks, in: Proceedings of the National Academy of Sciences, 111, pp. 8788-90.

Lamont, Ruth (2014) Article 24 – The Rights of the Child, in: Peers, S. et al. (eds) The EU Charter of Fundamental Rights: A Commentary, Oxford, Hart.

Kang, Jerry (1998) Information Privacy in Cyberspace Transactions, in: Stanford Law Review 50, p. 1193-1294.

Livingstone, Sonia (2008) Taking risky opportunities in youthful content creation: teenagers' use of social networking sites for intimacy, privacy and self-expression, in: New Media & Society, 10, 3, pp. 393-411.

Livingstone, S. and Bulger, M. (2013) A global agenda for children's rights in the digital age: recommendations for developing UNICEF's research strategy, Florence, UNICEF Office of Research.

Nissenbaum, Helen (2010) Privacy in Context: Technology, Policy, and the Integrity of Social Life, Stanford, Stanford Law Books.

OfCom (2014): The Communications Market Report, available at: http://stakeholders.ofcom.org.uk/market-data-research/market-data/communications-market-reports/cmr14/uk/

O'Neill, Brian; Staksrud, Elisabeth and McLaughlin, Sharon (2013) Introduction, in: O'Neill, B. et al. (eds) Towards A Better Internet For Children? Policy Pillars, Players and Paradoxes, Goteborg, Nordicom.

Piper, Christine (2010) Investing in a Child's Future: Too Risky?, in: Child and Family Law Quarterly, 22, pp. 1-20.

Purtova, Nadezhda (2011) Property rights in personal data: A European perspective. Kluwer Law International, The Netherlands.

Purtova, Nadezhda (2014) Who decides on the future of data protection? Role of law firms in shaping European data protection regime, in: International Review of Law Computers and Technology, 28, 2, pp. 204-221.

Richards, Neil (2015) Intellectual Privacy: Rethinking Civil Liberties in the Digital Age, Oxford, Oxford University Press.

Robinson, Neil et al. (2009) Review of the European Data Protection Directive: Technical Report Prepared for the Information Commissioner's Office, Cambridge, Rand.

Rouvroy, Antoinette and Poulett, Yves (2009) The Right to Informational Self-Determination and the Value of Self-Development: Reassessing the Importance of Privacy for Democracy, in: Gutwirth, S. et al. (eds) Reinventing Data Protection?, Dordrecht, Springer.

Rubinstein, Ira and Good, Nathaniel (2013) Privacy by Design: A Counterfactual Analysis of Google and Facebook Privacy Incidents, in: Berkeley Technology Law Journal 28, 6, pp. 1333-1414.

Schwartz, Paul (1999) Privacy and Democracy in Cyberspace, in: Vanderbilt Law Review 52, pp. 1607-1702.

Schwartz, Paul (2000) Internet Privacy and the State, in: Connecticut Law Review 32, p. 815.

Simitis, Spiros (1987) Reviewing privacy in the information society, in: University of Pennsylvania Law Review 135, 3, pp. 707-46.

Stalford, Helen (2012) Children and the European Union Rights, Welfare and Accountability, Oxford, Hart.

Solove, Daniel (2001) Privacy and Power: Computer Databases and Metaphors for Information Privacy, in: Stanford Law Review 53, pp. 1393-1462.

Solove, Daniel (2002) Conceptualizing Privacy, in: California Law Review, 90, pp. 1087-1156.

Solove, Daniel (2013) Privacy Self-Management and the Consent Dilemma, in: Harvard Law Review 126, pp. 1880-1903.

Sweeney, Latanya (1997) Weaving Technology and Policy Together to Maintain Confidentiality, in: Journal of Law, Medicine and Ethics 25, 2 and 3, pp. 98-110.

Swire, Peter (2012) Social Networks, Privacy, and Freedom of Association: Data Empowerment vs. Data Protection, in: North Carolina Law Review 90, 5, pp. 101-143.

Tarleton, Gillespie (2010) The Politics of Platforms, in: New Media & Society 12, 3, pp. 347-364.

Tene, O. (2011) Privacy: The New Generations, in: International Data Privacy Law 1, 1, pp. 15-27.

Turow, J. (2011) The Daily You: How the new advertising industry is defining your identity and your worth, New Haven, Yale University Press.

Van der Hof, Simone and Prins, J (2008) Personalization and its Influences on Identities, Behaviour and Social Values, in: Hildebrandt, M. and Gutwirth, S. (eds) Profiling the European Citizen: Cross-Disciplinary Perspectives, Dordrecht, Springer.

Van der Hof, Simone (2014) No Child's Play: Online Data Protection for Children, in: van der Hof, S., van den Berg, B. and Schermer, B. (eds) Minding Minors Wandering the Web: Regulating Online Child Safety, Dordrecht, Springer.

Vincent, J. (2015) Mobile opportunities: Exploring positive mobile opportunities for European children, London, POLIS, LSE.

Westin, Alan (1967) Privacy and Freedom, New York, Atheneum.

Zarsky, T (2003) Mine Your Own Business: Making the Case for the Implications of the Data Mining of Personal Information in the Forum of Public Opinion, in: Yale Journal of Law and Technology 5, 1, pp. 1-56.

Zarsky, T (2004) Desperately Seeking Solutions: Using implementation-based solutions for the troubles of information privacy in the age of data mining and the internet society, in: Maine Law Review 56, 1, pp. 13-60.

Zwick, Detlev; Bonsu, Samuel and Darmody, Aron (2008) Putting consumers to work, in: Journal of Consumer Culture 8, 2, pp. 163-196.

Child Labour and EU Law and Policy: A Regional Solution for a Global Issue[1]

Nuno Ferreira

Introduction

This chapter will explore the role of the EU in creating and developing labour policies that affect children. The analysis will be framed within the context of the global debates about child labour, and will highlight the role that the EU might play in those debates. The chapter starts by sketching the main lines of the 'child labour' debate, the qualitative and quantitative significance of children in the EU labour market, and the relevant EU competences. It will then touch upon a range of EU labour law instruments that affect children, both as direct addressees – especially the Young Workers Directive – and collateral beneficiaries, including a variety of tools that address sex discrimination. Finally, the chapter will assess the compatibility between the instruments and policies considered and, amongst others, the CRC, the relevant ILO instruments, and the EU Charter of Fundamental Rights. The conclusion will determine the scope for improvement of the current state of affairs, and present policy recommendations.

1. Child labour: A global solution for a global issue?

Whether children – here understood as anyone below the age of 18, in accordance with the CRC – should be allowed to participate in the labour market or in any way engage with the world of work (and to what extent) is an old and contentious debate. The CRC tries to offer some guidance on this matter, by establishing 'the right of the child to be protected from economic exploitation and from performing any work that is likely to be hazardous or to interfere with the child's education, or to be harmful to the child's health or physical, mental, spiritual, moral or social development' (Article 32). This

1 The author wishes to thank the editors of this book and the participants at the 2013 Socio-Legal Studies Association annual conference (York, UK) for their helpful comments and suggestions, and Alison Morley for the thorough copy-editing.

has, however, been insufficient to provide clarity on what precisely are the limits to children's participation in the labour market. For these purposes, the notion of 'child labour' has been developed in relation to those forms of work that are regarded as detrimental to children's physical and mental development and, therefore, should be prohibited. Even understanding 'child labour' in these narrow terms, the ILO estimates that there are currently around 168 million children throughout the world who carry out work that can be classified as 'child labour' (ILO 2015).

Although child labour debates focus mostly on practices that occur outside of the EU, the phenomenon is anything but absent within the EU. Despite the lack of reliable data (a problem exacerbated by the high number of, often young, children working in the informal economy, in domestic environments, in family businesses, and others generally not declared), the number of children in the EU working for pay, profit or family gain could reach 7.5 million (Rodríguez et al. 2007: 4). Leaving aside the insurmountable definitional and logistical difficulties in measuring the extent to which children work (Buck et al. 2011: 175ff), trade unions and media reports have made it clear that the economic crisis and weakening of the social welfare state have rendered 'child labour' in Europe a common phenomenon, affecting particularly migrant and ethnic minority children. Children dropping out of school too early and acting as sibling-carers, sex workers, farm hands, shop assistants for heavy work and, worst of all, members of local mafias (as beggars, prostitutes or drug dealers), are becoming dangerously normalised patterns (ITUC 2011; Allegra 2012; Nadeau 2012). Other less discussed risks concern cross-border young workers engaged in construction work and services, and au pair workers engaged under sui generis agreements often outside the scope of labour law (Rodríguez et al. 2007: 107).

Independently of the statistics and the types of work involved, the attractiveness of involving children with the world of labour will always exist (at least from the perspective of the recipient of the outcome of that work), due to the low costs and abundance of workers available (Van Bueren 1995: 263). It is therefore crucial that policy- and decision-makers have a clear idea of the values and objectives that should guide them in their discourse and action. Any measured answer needs to consider health, developmental, educational, social, economic, political and ethical issues. Global debates have raised various arguments, in favour of either a welfare approach or an autonomy approach. On the one hand, one may argue that children's psychological and physical development may be jeopardised if they are allowed to carry out working activities, especially those entailing particular risks, and that their time should be dedicated to (unpaid) social interactions, education, and a range of activities that may enhance their well-being and nurture their potential. Also, letting children work perpetuates economic, educational and social disadvantages and inequalities, besides generally worsening labour and social standards (Buck et al. 2011: 169). It has been suggested that eliminating 'child labour' and offering universal education can bring about vast economic benefits (ILO 2003). On the other hand, arguments in favour of a more flexible approach to working children relate to children's desire to become independent (namely economically), be helpful to their families, feel part of their social environments, and exercise their 'right to work'to fulfil their needs and construct their identity (Van Bueren 1995: 264; Ochaíta et al. 2000: 25; Hanson and Vandaele 2003; Hanson and Nieuwenhuys 2013; Stalford 2014).

This chapter will situate itself within a welfare approach. It is submitted that the autonomy of children and carers on this matter is legitimately curtailed on the grounds of the children's best interests and the public interest in protecting children from detrimental effects to their physical, mental and moral development, as well as on the grounds of a state's obligation to safeguard the rights of children to physical and mental integrity, health and education. Heed needs to be paid to children's autonomy, right to participation and privacy in this context in order to achieve a balanced overall policy, but these should not outbalance the importance of protecting children from harmful activities. Indeed, it is not sensible to use children's rights to autonomy, participation and privacy as a shield to defend exploitative practices that barely carry any benefit to the children in question and are, in fact, unethical means to create profit for others. Also, whilst the 'child labour' debate on a global scale may be accused of ethnocentrism (Boyden 1997), and a 'regulative approach' (as opposed to an 'abolitionist approach') may deserve attention in developing countries (Hanson and Vandaele 2003), in a European context the peril of ethnocentrism is practically non-existent in respect of 'child labour'. Above all, the socio-economic standards in the EU do not allow for the types of concessions admitted in debates regarding child labour in developing countries; on the contrary, much more demanding policies in this regard need to be implemented in order to reflect the (relative) degree of development across the EU. That may explain why, independently of regional socio-economic-cultural nuances (Rodríguez et al. 2007: 97-99), a social and economic 'abolitionist' outlook on this subject-matter is generally favoured in the prevailing legal and official discourses (including in the 'new' EU Member States: Calvo/Rodríguez 2007: 13-21). Globalisation is making child labour all the more pressing a problem (Buck et al. 2011:187), and being permissive or flexible on this subject is not the way to achieve the objectives of the EU or any of its Member States. Children are, in principle, better placed in educational, family and sport/leisure social settings rather than in work places. This means that the dividing line between (unlawful) child labour and (lawful) child work on the continuum of child involvement with economic production should be pushed towards reducing the scope for child work, thus widening the scope of what should be considered child labour and therefore prohibited. Any deviation from this should be treated as an exception and thoroughly scrutinised. This approach will be discussed in greater detail and borne in mind throughout this chapter.

It is therefore important to devise a tight and well implemented legal framework to tackle issues related to children's involvement with the world of labour. This is all the more so in the light of the increasingly enthusiastic (even if perhaps sometimes only rhetorical) commitment to children's rights and well-being by the EU institutions (European Commission 2011), and reflected in the Treaties (Articles 3(3) and (5) TEU). This commitment to children's rights has also featured in the EU external policy, as both the Commission and the Council have shown some interest in offering children a special place in EU external policies, particularly with regard to the fight against child labour (European Commission 2008; Council of Ministers of the European Union 2010; Vandenhole, this collection). This chapter will focus on EU internal policies and analyse whether the EU has achieved a satisfactory degree of protection for children's rights and interests in the field of labour, and, if not, what else can be done to improve the current state of affairs. With this in mind, section 2 sets the scene by discussing the nature and scope of EU labour law and policy more generally. Section 3 then explores the range of EU labour law tools that have, in different ways, affected children, and section 4 assesses the level of protection offered by these tools to working children and, in particular, their compatibility with other, more fundamental instruments, such as the CRC, ILO Conventions and the EU Charter of Fundamental Rights. Finally, Section 5 suggests the ways in which current EU measures in this area might be improved. This analysis also hints at what role the EU should try to play in addressing child labour in its relationship with non-EU countries.

2. EU labour policy: Competences and evolution

Until 1987, when the Single European Act (SEA) came into force, the EEC Treaty contained extremely weak labour and social law provisions. There was, in fact, a complete lack of competence to legislate with regard to labour standards, as Articles 117 and 118 EEC only contained a 'political programme' (Hartwig 2008: 245), comprising references to common goals and values, and the commitment to promoting collaboration between Member States. With the SEA, Articles 118a and 118b were introduced and the Community became, for the first time, competent to regulate on health and safety related matters in the field of labour. Only minimum standards could be set by directives produced on the basis of this competence, precluding full harmonisation in the field. Article 118a EEC remained unchanged by the 1992

Treaty of Maastricht and it was on its basis that the Community produced the Young Workers Directive (Directive 94/33/EC of 22 June 1994 on the protection of young people at work (hereafter 'YWD') analysed below).

Soon after the introduction of these competences, the 1989 Community Charter of Fundamental Social Rights for Workers (Community Charter) was adopted by 11 out of the then 12 Member States (the UK only adopting it when the Charter was (partly) incorporated into the Treaties by the 1997 Treaty of Amsterdam). This Community Charter enshrines a range of labour-related rights, and it was approved as a 'declaration', hence being considered merely as a (moral) commitment rather than imposing legal obligations as such (Article 28). Still, on the basis of the Community Charter, the Commission launched the 1992 Social Action Programme which included 47 legislative proposals related to the Charter rights. This included several landmark directives such as those on pregnant workers,[2] working time,[3] and, crucially, the YWD.

Subsequent treaties have not significantly amended the relevant provisions, and so EU competence to regulate labour matters has remained largely unchanged since 1997. Subsequent Treaties have, however, increasingly endowed the EU with competences in the field of justice and home affairs, as well as some limited supporting and coordinating competences in the fields of social inclusion (Articles 9 and 151-153 TFEU) and education (Articles 6, 9 and 165-166 TFEU), enabling the EU institutions to legislate in labour-connected fields, as will be seen below. Most significantly, it has been the CJEU that, on some occasions (even if not always with consensually positive results), has pushed forward a social and human rights-driven agenda (namely in relation to gender equality, see 3.1 below). The production of the Charter of Fundamental Rights and its later inclusion into the Treaties,[4] also increased the number of labour-related provisions from which the EU institutions, Member States and individuals may draw to potentially enhance their positions (further explored in 4.3 below). That said, a substantial proportion of the EU's work on labour and child related matters are nowadays dealt with within the context of non-binding (soft-law) instruments and the Open Method of Co-ordination (OMC – discussed at greater length in 3.3 below). EU labour and social policy may therefore be characterised as significant, albeit still considerably limited by the reduced number of competences the EU possesses in this field and the non-binding nature of many of its outcomes.

---

2 Council Directive 92/85/EEC of 19 October 1992 on the introduction of measures to encourage improvements in the safety and health at work of pregnant workers and workers who have recently given birth or are breastfeeding.

3 Council Directive 93/104/EC of 23 November 1993 concerning certain aspects of the organisation of working time.

4 By the Treaty of Lisbon amending the Treaty on European Union and the Treaty establishing the European Community, signed at Lisbon, 13 December 2007.

Bearing this in mind, the next section will consider how the EU devised a range of tools more or less connected with the labour world, which have had an impact on children within the EU.

3. Children in the EU's (internal) labour policy

3.1 Children as incidental beneficiaries

By placing a strong emphasis on the role of the labour force in the creation of an integrated market, the Community inevitably affected families and children. Consequently, although it took several decades for the EU institutions to see children as potential direct and specific beneficiaries of EU law, several of its policies and instruments in the context of labour have had more or less indirect effects on children. Policies on free movement of workers allowed workers' children to move with them, thus letting them enjoy a potentially better standard of life. The 1960s and 1970s were particularly prolific in creating indirect benefits to workers' children, namely by reinforcing the residence rights of workers' family members,[5] as well as of service providers' family members.[6] Although dependent on their parents' right to move and reside as workers, children also acquired specific rights, including the right to study and train in the host Member State under the same conditions as nationals of that State,[7] and the right to remain in that State once the employment relationship or service provision activity of their parents ended.[8] This obviously allowed children to become workers in their own right in the host Member State in due course, thus entitling children to EU labour-related rights, albeit via their parents' exercise of EU law rights. This line of policy was strengthened by instruments that specifically allowed dependent children of workers, service providers, students and others, to work as dependent workers or as self-employed.[9] The rationale for all these provisions benefiting children, however, lies in the fact that they were seen as 'obstacles' to their

5 Article 10 Regulation (EEC) No 1612/68, Council Directive 68/360/EEC, Regulation (EEC) No 1251/70.

6 Council Directive 73/148/EEC.

7 Article 12 Regulation (EEC) No 1612/68, now replaced by Article 10 Regulation (EU) No 492/2011 without any amendment.

8 Regulation (EEC) No 1251/70 and Council Directive 75/34/EEC, now repealed and replaced by Directive 2004/38/EC, in particular Article 12.

9 Council Directives 90/364/EEC, 90/365/EEC and 93/96/EEC on the right of residence, all replaced by Directive 2004/38/EC.

parents' free movement and, therefore, needed to be 'addressed' for the sake of securing the economic benefits of labour free movement – hence children were not autonomous right-holders, but simply possessed 'parasitic' entitlements (McGlynn 2002: 388).

The sex (later, gender) equality agenda has also been at the core of the Community's social policy since its inception. The original Article 119 EEC (now 157 TFEU) on gender equality in pay was complemented relatively early on by secondary legislation and supported by a rich line of European case law. The Community pursued gender equality in the field of employment into the 1980s and 1990s, often following the lead of the Community Courts, in relation to pregnant workers, social security, self-employment and childcare. Along with many other hard- and soft-law instruments, as well as measures beyond the realm of employment, the EU has undoubtedly contributed to greater gender equality, which has improved women's working lives and, consequently, family lives and the amount (and perhaps even quality) of childcare that parents can provide.

What is highlighted here is the indirect relevance of these instruments for children. This range of labour-related instruments indirectly benefited children by ensuring, for example, that the adults caring for them would only have to work for a limited number of hours, possess some flexibility in their working arrangements, enjoy time off work in case of pregnancy/adoption/maternity/paternity, and consequently receive more income and/or time to dedicate to the children. Still, throughout this long period the interests and perspectives of children were "either being sidelined, or addressed only in terms of their future status as 'productive' workers" (Ruxton 2005: 137), something particularly noticeable in the context of the EU's work-family reconciliation policy (James 2012). This was about to change in the 1990s.

3.2 Children as direct beneficiaries

Although it was only in the 1990s that an EU instrument directly addressing working children was developed, children could already have been considered to be (at least potentially) direct beneficiaries of EU labour law and policy in the light of instruments and policies relating to free movement of workers. Indeed, such instruments did directly benefit children, despite not addressing them specifically. From the moment that children may legally constitute workers, they may also exercise their right to free movement – not as indirect beneficiaries of the free movement of their parents, but as direct beneficiaries of their own right to movement as workers (European Commission 2010: 13-15). The extent to which children have exercised this right is, however, unclear (due to lack of data), and most likely minimal, such that, in reality, children remain marginal beneficiaries of the free movement of worker provisions.

The first time that the EU contemplated children as a discrete group in the context of its labour policy was only in 1967, in the form of a Commission's Recommendation on the protection of young workers.[10] Twenty years later, in 1987, the European Parliament called on the Commission to put forward a harmonising instrument on child labour and on Member States to ratify the ILO instruments on the subject-matter if they had not already done so.[11] The Parliament's initiative eventually bore fruit, and in 1992 the Commission presented its proposal for a Council directive on the protection of young people at work on the basis of its 'health and safety' competence (Article 118a EEC), discussed above.[12] The Commission used a range of instruments as sources of inspiration, including the 1959 UN Declaration on the Rights of the Child and the CRC. In its proposal, the Commission highlighted the wealth of evidence to the effect that young workers were more likely than adults to suffer detrimental effects, both physically and psychologically, from occupational risks and working conditions.

The relatively unambitious aims of the proposal were clear from the start. The minimum age for admission to employment was already 15 or 16 in most Member States, so the minimum age (15) proposed by the Commission was not a challenging target. Also, minimum requirements regarding working time and rest periods were already in the process of being established by the 1993 Working Time Directive (WTD),[13] which meant that the proposal did not go much beyond what was already going to be available through the WTD. Moreover, the proposal excluded from its scope the provision of services and self-employment, leaving unprotected all the children carrying out work in those contexts. Such lack of ambition may have been a strategy to achieve the political consensus required to approve the Directive, based on the assumption that the ILO standards were satisfactory and for the most part respected by Member States.

Also, despite the reference to the CRC in the explanatory memorandum to the Commission's proposal, the proposal itself did not make any reference to the CRC or adopt its terminology, namely 'children' as those under the age of 18. Instead, giving preference to the then current classifications of the World Health Organization and ILO, the proposal distinguished between 'children'

10 Recommendation 67/125/EEC of 31 January 1967, OJ 13 February 1967, pp. 405-408.

11 European Parliament, Resolution on Child Labour, Doc. A2-67/87, OJ C 190/44, 16 June 1987.

12 Commission of the European Communities, Proposal for a Council Directive on the protection of young people at work, COM(91) 543 final – SYN 383, Brussels, 17 March 1992, point 3.

13 Council Directive 93/104/EC of 23 November 1993 concerning certain aspects of the organisation of working time.

(under the age of 15) and 'adolescents' (between 15 and 18), all constituting 'young people' (a distinction retained in Article 3 YWD). This distinction, although potentially empowering older children and promoting their autonomy in the light of their increased capacities, risks endorsing an understanding that reduces the rights of older children and deprives them of their due protection. In the light of the more recent strengthening of the EU's children's rights agenda and reliance on the CRC in that context (especially since the 2006 Commission Communication 'Towards an EU Strategy on the Rights of the Child'),[14] it would now make sense to refer to all of these 'young people' as children.

Negotiations between and amongst Community institutions and Member States further watered down the Commission's proposal. For example, the harmonisation of the minimum number of days of *paid* annual leave was removed, leaving only a provision on *some* annual *rest*, thus allowing for minimal, unpaid annual leave. A few aspects of the proposal, however, were improved. For example, light work was defined as work that is not likely to be harmful to the safety, health or development of children, nor to their attendance at school, their participation in vocational guidance or training programmes approved by the competent authority, nor their capacity to benefit from the instruction received (Article 3(d) YWD). The original, much more permissive notion, referred to 'all work which does not cause any abnormal fatigue'. Also, the required age to benefit from the exception afforded to combined work/training schemes and light work was raised to 14 (Article 4(2)(b) and (c) YWD); derogations from the prohibition of light work below a certain age based on national practice and traditions (Article 3(3) of the Commission's proposal) were eliminated as they were clearly excessive; and the maximum duration of work for children carrying out light work went down from 15 to 12 hours term-time per week, and from 3 to 2 hours per school day (Article 8(1)(b) YWD), thus securing time for homework and leisure. In addition, the cultural or similar activities derogation was subjected to further conditions during the negotiations, including not being likely to be harmful to children's safety, health, development or education (Article 5(2) YWD). Moreover, the final wording of the provisions on the general obligations of employers and the vulnerability of young people (Articles 6 and 7 YWD respectively) was strengthened, for example, by imposing on employers the duty to 'adopt the measures necessary to protect the safety and health of young children', rather than simply having to 'take account of any specific risk to the physical and mental health and safety of the young persons'.

Several contentious key issues remained unaddressed. Firstly, occasional or short-term work involving domestic service in a private household or non-harmful work for a family undertaking can be excluded by Member States

14 COM(2006) 367 final, 4 July 2006.

from the Directive's scope of protection (Article 2(2) YWD), despite research indicating that exploitation of working children very often occurs in domestic and family settings (Van Bueren 1995: 266) and that 'occasional' and 'short-term' are vague terms. As Kenner highlights, it may be tempting to justify such an exception with "visions of grape picking and crop harvesting", but "less comfortable Dickensian imagery of domestic exploitation of children" also comes quickly to mind (Kenner 2003: 183). The use of the 'private sphere' notion and public/private distinction to justify such derogations have rendered invisible/acceptable many types of work carried out by children in some Member States, such as domestic work, small errands, baby-sitting, newspaper delivery, gardening and caring for relatives (Larkins 2011). This exception has prioritised the deregulation agenda at the expense of children's health and development, and the legislature should have to justify (and possibly restrict) such a ground for derogation (Bond 1995). Also, "the ideological, economic and pragmatic justifications for the immunity of some forms of this employment all depend upon a questionable belief in an impenetrable demarcation between the realm of the family on the one hand, and the market on the other" (Bond 1996: 291). Although any interference with the family and private realms obviously requires a great degree of justification and is associated with complex issues of parental autonomy and privacy, more precise and limiting wording should have been adopted for exceptions applicable to domestic service in a private household, or to non-harmful work for a family undertaking.

Secondly, allowing derogation from the working time limits of 8 hours/day and 40 hours/week on the basis of 'objective grounds', Article 8(5) YWD offers excessive flexibility to Member States (which is why the EESC proposed the deletion of such an exception).[15] Either no such exception should have been included, or it should have been tempered by the inclusion of the consideration of the best interests of the child, as well as of the legitimacy of the grounds in question and proportionality of the derogation sought. Thirdly, the prohibition of night work between midnight and 4 a.m., which was absolute in the Commission's initial proposal, ended up being weakened by allowing work during that period under certain circumstances and in certain areas (Article 9(2) YWD). Fourthly, the reference to sanctions in the Commission's initial proposal was deleted, and the already-weak provision was renamed 'measures', its wording being amended from requiring penalties to be 'effective, proportionate and dissuasive' to simply 'effective and proportionate' (Article 14 YWD). Even though the YWD is a directive, a more specific and detailed provision could be devised, as will be discussed below (section 5).

15 Opinion on the proposal for a Council Decision on the Protection of Young People at Work (92/C 313/19), 23 September 1992, OJ No C 313/92 P 70, 30 November 1992.

In sum, and anticipating the discussion below, the YWD merely aligned EU law with ILO standards, practically ignoring the CRC and hardly going beyond what most Member States already did. The Directive's aims are worded generally and in positively protective terms: Article 1(3), second paragraph, for example, requires Member States to protect children from economic exploitation and any work that may have a negative impact on their development or education. Also, the YWD contains a non-reducing clause (Article 16), preventing Member States from using the Directive to reduce the domestic levels of protection offered to working children. Such provisions have helped the YWD to become an important piece of labour legislation at EU level, as textbook coverage reflects. Nonetheless, apart from the potentially dangerous exclusion in Article 2(2) (see above), other loopholes have been included in the final version of the YWD (Articles 4 and 5). These include allowing children of any age to carry out cultural or similar activities, allowing children above the age of 14 to work under combined work/training schemes and perform light work, and allowing children above the age of 13 to perform light work specified by national legislation, the last being approved against the will of the Parliament.[16] Finally, Article 13 YWD also allows for a general *force majeure* derogation from working time, night work, rest periods and, at least in relation to children between the ages of 15 and 18, breaks. Whilst this derogation may be appropriate for adult workers, it is not sensible to apply it to working children without any further restrictions (e.g. the best interests of the child, or an explicit legitimacy and proportionality test). Even allowing for concessions due to the fact that the legal basis used regards as a shared competence and only aims to set minimum standards, as well as the fact that social/cultural/economic differences relevant to this debate can be identified across the EU, it is submitted that EU Member States could have aimed higher.

The last step in this second phase of 'children as direct beneficiaries' concerns the Equality Framework Directive.[17] Although working children were already able to potentially benefit from existing EU equality instruments prohibiting discrimination on grounds of sex (discussed above) and race/ethnic background,[18] it is with the Framework Directive that children have become explicit and core beneficiaries of EU equality law. This is a fundamental instrument for children: EU law now enshrines their right to claim equality (interpreted in a broad sense, Article 3) and a significant degree of protection from discriminatory practices against them at work, above all on grounds of age (but also on grounds of sexual orientation, religious belief and

16 Decision of 9 March 1994, OJ No C 91/94 P 89, 28 March 1994.

17 Council Directive 2000/78/EC of 27 November 2000 establishing a general framework for equal treatment in employment and occupation.

18 Council Directive 2000/43/EC of 29 June 2000 implementing the principle of equal treatment between persons irrespective of racial or ethnic origin.

disability). This is not to be used as an argument for allowing children to enter the labour market earlier than permitted by the YWD or any domestic statute (as that would clearly go against the welfare approach adopted in this analysis), but simply to protect from discrimination those children who are of working age. Still, Article 6 dramatically reduces a significant legal hurdle to discriminatory practices. Due to pressure from Member States and the particular (largely perceived) impact of age in the field of work (especially with regard to older workers), Article 6 allows discrimination on grounds of age if occurring for an objectively and reasonably justified legitimate aim, including legitimate employment policy, labour market and vocational training objectives, and if the means to achieve that aim are appropriate and necessary. The fact that discrimination on grounds of age can be justified on the basis of this 'extra' reason clearly contributes to pushing age towards the bottom of the 'hierarchy of grounds' of EU anti-discrimination law.

Case law has confirmed the latitude afforded to Member States in determining public policy objectives which justify derogating from age equality.[19] Nevertheless, in a more recent case, the CJEU held a national rule in relation to pilots' compulsory retirement to be in violation of the prohibition of age discrimination.[20] Also, the CJEU has already had the opportunity to use the Framework Directive to protect the interests of young (but not child) workers: in *Hütter*[21] concerning determination of pay; *Kücükdeveci*[22] concerning calculating the notice period for dismissal; and in *Hennigs and Mai*[23] concerning a national collective agreement providing for differences in basic pay according to age. Other contexts in which the Framework Directive may be used to fight discrimination against working children include the offer of more precarious employment arrangements (e.g., allowing more successive fixed-term contracts for younger workers than for older ones, as advocated in the Netherlands and Spain) and lower salaries (e.g., paying younger workers a proportion of the minimum salary payable to older workers merely on grounds of age, as occurs in Greece and the UK) (Sargeant 2010: 474; Simms 2011: 20-21). Domestic case law also reveals the potential to use age anti-discrimination provisions to protect young workers, as in the UK decision in Wilkinson v Springwell Engineering Ltd, concerning dismissal.[24] Integration into the labour market should clearly not come at the cost of arbitrary dis-

19 For example, C-144/04, *Werner Mangold v Rüdiger Helm*, Judgment of 22 November 2005; C-411/05, *Félix Palacios de la Villa v Cortefiel*, Judgment of 16 October 2007; and C-388/07, *Age Concern England v SSBERR*, Judgment of 5 March 2009.

20 C-447/09, *Prigge and others v Deutsche Lufthansa AG*, Judgment of 13 September 2011.

21 C-88/08, *David Hütter v TechnischeUniversität Graz*, Judgment of 18 June 2009.

22 C-555/07, *SedaKücükdeveci v Swedex GmbH & Co. KG*, Judgment of 19 January 2010.

23 C-297/10 and C-298/10, *Hennigs v Eisenbahn-Bundesamt, Land Berlin v Mai,* Judgment of 8 September 2011.

24 ET/2507420/07.

criminatory practices. In any case, discrimination is only a small part of the range of detrimental treatment that working children may suffer, so not even a generous use of the Framework Directive is able to ensure a high degree of protection for them.

3.3 Post-2000: A bi-cephalous era?

In the post-2000s, the EU's labour law and policy affecting children has been characterised by two completely different 'faces', thus bringing to mind a bi-cephalous being. Indeed, for the last decade or so, the EU's discourse concerning the interconnection between children and the labour market has slowly, but clearly, changed. Symptomatic of this are the instruments related to the Lisbon Agenda, the Europe 2020 Strategy, and OMC processes. Since the 2001 White Paper 'A New Impetus for European Youth' (European Commission 2001) through to the current EU Youth Strategy, EU institutions have looked at children (and youth, i.e. those aged between 15 and 30, although it depends on the specific instrument) as one of two things, thus adopting either one of these 'faces': a problem to be solved (high unemployment rate, lack of qualifications matching the market needs, insufficient entrepreneurship, etc.) and/or as a means to achieve certain results (such as a more green and sustainable economy, or a more ICT-skilled work force). Although the 2001 White Paper placed some emphasis on participation, autonomy and values, in more recent documents the protective, participatory, autonomy and nurturing dimensions seem to be missing for the most part from the EU's discourse. Considering its impact on personal development (including financial autonomy and family life) and social cohesion (including democratic engagement and involvement with civil society) (Simms 2011: 2), the relationship between children and the labour market surely deserves a more empathic and humane analysis.

Admittedly, the EU has been prolific in initiatives regarding youth and its role in society. The EU's overall objectives are noble, including enhancing cooperation between Member States,[25] achieving smart, sustainable and inclusive (in reference to women and ethnic and migrant minorities) growth (European Commission 2010), reducing early school leaving,[26] recognising non-formal and informal learning,[27] and more generally reducing unemploy-

25 Council Resolution of 27 November 2009 on a renewed framework for European cooperation in the youth field (2010-2018).

26 Council Recommendation of 28 June 2011 on policies to reduce early school leaving.

27 Council Recommendation of 20 December 2012 on the validation of non-formal and informal learning.

ment and precariousness. All these measures contribute to the holistic approach commended below (section 5), thus enhancing, albeit indirectly, the EU policies from which children and youth may benefit. Still, the subtext of such instruments and documents is that policies designed for children and youth are means to achieve greater aims (generally improving the labour market and workers' mobility), rather than to promote young people's well-being, quality of life or protection as such. In sum, a more humane perspective is missing. This trend became particularly clear with the 2005 European Youth Pact,[28] designed to use youth to advance the Lisbon Agenda.

Another good example of this is the assertion that

> the Europe 2020 flagship initiative, Youth on the Move, puts young people at the centre of the EU's agenda to create an economy based on knowledge, research and innovation, high levels of education and skills *in line with labour market needs*, adaptability and creativity, inclusive labour markets and active participation in society (emphasis added). (European Commission 2010: 22)

This is not an incidental formulation, since it is reiterated, for example, in the implicit cost-benefit analysis carried out by the Commission in its proposal for a Council Recommendation on Establishing a Youth Guarantee (European Commission 2012b) and in speeches by the European Commissioner for Employment, Social Affairs and Inclusion (Andor 2013). Even potentially child-friendly and socially aware moves, such as the enthusiastic agenda of the Commission on improving education, are marred by a blunt servicing of market needs (European Commission 2012a): the result is the vision of an educational framework at the service of a more economically competitive society, rather than a better society in all respects. The message could not be clearer: young people are perceived primarily as an *instrument and resource* to achieve the goals of EU's policies – in particular economic recovery – and answer businesses' needs for certain skills, not as beneficiaries or addressees of the EU's concerns and priorities. Other elements of such instruments and speeches, for example relating to social protection (European Commission 2010: 17) or training (Andor 2013), do little to combat the utilitarian sub-text, especially if one recalls the restricted competences of the EU in these fields in comparison with the broader competences regarding market integration and labour movement. This restricts such issues crucial to children to the remit of exchange of best practices, peer reviews and mutual learning activities within the context of the OMC, whilst persistently overlooking key issues such as pay and precariousness (as highlighted by the Parliament with regard to the Youth Guarantee).[29] This scenario begs the question: should the EU's governance of children's rights really be concentrating on children as "human

---

28 Annex 1 of Presidency Conclusions of the European Council, Brussels, 22-23 March 2005 (7619/05).

29 Resolution of 16 January on a Youth Guarantee (2012/2901(RSP)). Strasbourg, 16 January 2013.

capital for economic production" (Larkins 2011: 473) or as interested parties whose rights and needs should guide the EU children's agenda?

Although in the examples given above the EU seems to regard children as a means to an end (utilitarian approach), the EU often also sees children and childhood as ends in themselves (humanitarian approach). At the humanitarian end of the utilitarian-humanitarian spectrum of the post-2000 EU policy affecting children in the context of labour, are instruments designed to combat sexual exploitation and human trafficking, produced on the basis of Articles 79(2)(d) and 83(1) TFEU. Sexual abuse becomes sexual exploitation when it possesses a commercial connotation, i.e., when it is connected to, for example, the use of children in prostitution, pornographic publications, and/or trafficking for sexual purposes. Hence the usual link between sexual abuse and sexual exploitation, and the necessary link between sexual exploitation and labour policy. Both child pornography and child prostitution are significant and increasing in Europe (UN 2003; UNICEF 2009: 36).

The EU adopted a hard-law measure in relation to child sexual exploitation for the first time in 2003 with the Council Framework Decision 2004/68 of 22 December 2003, on combating the sexual exploitation of children and child pornography, now replaced by Directive 2011/93/EU. Sexual exploitation and forced labour go hand-in-hand with trafficking. The use of children as slaves or forced labourers, as well as in a range of illicit activities (especially as 'drug mules'), has been on the radar of the UN and the Council of Europe for a few decades now.[30] The EU first addressed this matter through a hard-law measure with the Framework Decision 2002/629/JHA of 19 July 2002 on combating trafficking in human beings, which has been replaced by the current Directive 2011/36/EU. The Preamble to the current Directive is extremely rich in references to children, going as far as recommending a child-rights approach to Member States' anti-trafficking policies. The Preamble makes reference to children as a particularly vulnerable group and to children's best interests as protected by the CFR and the CRC. This Directive has exponentially improved the legal treatment of child trafficking at the EU level, thus constructively building on previous work carried out in conjunction with the ILO (International Labour Office 2009).

Directives 2011/93/EU and 2011/36/EU are mutually supportive, as they address phenomena that often occur in a connected way, e.g., in the case of trafficking of children for sexual exploitation. The Commission's 'The EU Strategy towards the Eradication of Trafficking in Human Beings 2012-16'[31] reflects such interconnectedness, albeit not to a sufficient extent, in particular

30 Council of Europe Parliamentary Assembly Recommendation No. 989 on the Fight against Drug Abuse and Trafficking (1984); UN General Assembly Resolution on Use of Children in the Illicit Traffic in Narcotic Drugs and Rehabilitation of Drug-addicted Minors, A/RES/43/121, adopted on 8 December 1988.

31 COM(2012) 286 final.

with regard to children, as underlined by the Opinions of the Committee of the Regions[32] and the European Economic and Social Committee.[33] These two Directives enhance greatly the protection offered to children who are exploited in a labour context, upon being trafficked and/or in connection to sexual activities. This illustrates a 'best practice' at a global level of how child victims of trafficking and/or sexual exploitation should be protected and their welfare ensured. Also, in the light of the cross-border and global nature of these phenomena, these EU instruments constitute important elements for a framework of cooperation between the EU and non-EU countries, both by using (criminal) law enforcement tools and legal harmonisation.

3.4 Where are we now and where do we go next?

It is therefore possible to identify three distinct, even if chronologically overlapping, phases in the development of EU labour law relating to, or at least affecting, children: a first phase where children were primarily incidental beneficiaries (1957-1990s); a second phase where children became full-fledged direct beneficiaries (1990s-2000s); and a third phase of a bi-cephalous nature (2000s-present). The Lisbon Agenda, the Europe 2020 Strategy and OMC processes are characterised by a considerable degree of instrumentalisation and utilitarianism in the way they deal with children's interests and well-being. More recent (hard-law) labour-related initiatives, such as Directive 2014/36/EU on the conditions of entry and stay of third-country nationals for the purpose of employment as seasonal workers,[34] confirm this conclusion, as the rationale expounded again relates to pursuing a certain vision of economic development and no mention is made of the well-being of child or young workers. The analysis above is yet another sign that there are "conflicting messages about the currency of children's rights at EU level and their vulnerability being diluted or overlooked in the face of competing political and economic objectives" (Stalford and Drywood 2011).

The vast economic benefits for society in general of keeping children in education for longer rather than letting them engage with the world of labour prematurely (ILO 2003) should be borne in mind, but still considered secondary in relation to the paramount interest of children's own well-being. The EU should therefore refocus its children/youth agenda and any policies

32 OJ C 062, 2 March 2013, pp. 22-25.

33 OJ C 044, 15 February 2013, pp. 115-118.

34 Directive 2014/36/EU of the European Parliament and of the Council of 26 February 2014 on the conditions of entry and stay of third-country nationals for the purpose of employment as seasonal workers.

affecting them towards the interests of children/youth themselves, rather than using discourses that more or less implicitly reveal the priority given to market and economic objectives. This is essential if the EU is to have political legitimacy to offer assistance and examples of good practices in this field to partners around the world. The bottom line is that, even if there were no market or economic benefits, fighting 'child labour', delaying children's entrance into the labour market, and improving the working conditions of those children engaging legally with the world of work should still be a political and legal priority. Before looking into ways of doing this, it is important to assess the degree of compatibility between the level of protection currently offered by the EU (in particular via the YWD), on the one hand, and supranational and international instruments, on the other hand.

4. Compatibility with supra-national and international instruments

4.1 The United Nations framework

The ILO, as a UN agency specialised in labour, has been a key international actor in the fight against 'child labour'. Its crucial instruments in this fight are Conventions No. 138 concerning Minimum Age for Admission to Employment (C138), adopted in 1973, and No. 182 concerning the Prohibition and Immediate Action for the Elimination of the Worst Forms of Child Labour (C182), adopted in 1999. These instruments are supported by the ILO's International Programme on the Elimination of Child Labour (IPEC), created in 1992. C138 aims to progressively eliminate child labour and increase the minimum age to be admitted to work so as to ensure children's 'fullest physical and mental development' (Article 1); C182, instead, focuses on the worst forms of child labour, namely those connected with slavery, pornography, illicit activities and (other) work harmful to children's health, safety or morals (Article 3). All EU Member States have ratified both Conventions, so the EU is indirectly bound by them to the extent that they contain human rights standards below which the EU cannot legislate (Article 53 CFR), but not beyond that (Hartwig 2008: 250ff).

The YWD acknowledges the importance of the ILO principles in relation to the protection of young people at work (Preamble Consideration No. 4). Also, as suggested above (section 3.2), the YWD seems to align itself with the ILO instruments in all key aspects (minimum ages, scope for derogation, etc.). The wording adopted by the second paragraph of Article 1(1) YWD is evidence of this, by setting 15 as the general minimum age and linking this minimum age to compulsory full-time schooling (precisely what Article 2(3) C138 has stated since 1973). Also, EU policies more generally combat the worst forms of child labour, by addressing trafficking and sexual exploitation (section 3.3 above).

Still, in relation to a couple of aspects, the YWD may lag behind C138 (the ILO has also held that the YWD lagged behind the ILO instruments, but the Commission has denied this: European Commission 1994). Whilst Article 7(3) YWD allows Member States to derogate from the prohibition of work entailing specific risks in relation to 'adolescents' (ages 15-18) for training reasons, Article 3(3) C138 only allows such types of derogations above the age of 16 (although not limited to training reasons). One may argue that the YWD and ILO provisions in question are not entirely similar (as the YWD provision is linked to training and the C138 provision is not), so a strict parallel cannot be drawn. Still, one should conclude that, in order to ensure Article 7 YWD's compatibility with Article 3 C138, the derogation in Article 7 YWD should only be allowed in relation to children above the age of 16. Also, Article 2 C182, being a more recent instrument, has chosen to align its terminology with the CRC and uses the term 'child' for anyone under the age of 18 (Article 2), unlike the YWD. This reinforces the preferability of the word 'children' over distinguishing between 'children', 'adolescents' and 'young persons'. Moreover, Article 7(1) C182 expressly refers to penal sanctions, although allowing other appropriate sanctions. Paragraph 12 of ILO's Recommendation No. 190 also encourages Member States to punish as criminal offences practices similar to slavery, child prostitution and pornographic activities, and other illicit activities. Whilst EU Directives on sexual exploitation and trafficking favour criminal sanctions, the YWD makes no reference to criminal sanctions, thus leaving Member States free not to use criminal sanctions to punish conduct that may fall within the 'worst forms of child labour' but is not within the remit of the sexual exploitation and trafficking Directives. Even if criminal sanctions are not the most appropriate sanctions in certain instances (for example, when the perpetrators are the child's family members, in which case civil and socio-economic measures may be more suitable), their availability in the context of the YWD would still be an asset. More important, both C138 and C182 clearly apply to both employment and work, thus not being limited to work relationships based on legally recognised employment contracts. The YWD, instead, requires an employment contract or employment relationship as recognised by individual Member States. Whether 'employment relationship' is as broad as 'work' is doubtful; therefore, the EU should ensure the amendment of this terminology at the first possible opportunity.

At any rate, mere compatibility is a very poor aim: the EU, as an organisation encompassing developed countries amongst the richest in the world, should aim higher in terms of social and labour standards. Indeed, in the light of the economic and social progress in the EU, and considering that Article 2(4) C138 states that "a Member whose economy and educational facilities are insufficiently developed may, after consultation with the organisations of employers and workers concerned, where such exist, initially specify a minimum age of 14 years", the EU, *e contrario*, should set the minimum age at 16 or 17. Yet this suggestion raises problems that will be discussed below (section 5).

The UN framework has, however, contributed to the debate about working children not only through the ILO, but also through the CRC. Even before the CRC was approved, the 1924 (League of Nations) Geneva Declaration of the Rights of the Child and the 1959 UN Declaration of the Rights of the Child established that children should be protected against every form of exploitation (Articles 4 and 9 respectively). Article 32 CRC rephrased this obligation in terms of rights and rendered it binding on signatory states, by recognising children's right to be protected from exploitative and harmful forms of work. Also, CRC Articles 11 and 35 on trafficking, 19 on abuse and neglect, and 34 on sexual exploitation, are of relevance to children working under certain circumstances.

Although the CRC had already been approved and all the EU Member States at the time had already signed it by the time the YWD was negotiated and approved, the CRC is not mentioned in the YWD. This is symptomatic of a greater problem: the lack of commitment by EU law and policy to international children's rights (Stalford and Drywood 2011: 199). The absence of any influence of the CRC on the YWD is reflected, as mentioned above, in the choice of terminology, as Article 3 distinguishes between 'young persons', 'children' and 'adolescents', although all of these fall below the age of 18. This lack of terminological consistency is secondary, though – substantive shortcomings may have much deeper consequences.

Some elements in the YWD may be linked to the principle of the evolving capacities of the child, which is a transversal principle in the CRC: Preamble Considerations Nos. 9 and 10 refer to the 'nature of the transition from childhood to adult life' and to the need to guarantee 'working conditions appropriate to [children's] age', and Article 1(3) YWD reinforces the latter idea. This principle could be used potentially to justify a more casuistic and individualised approach to working children, i.e., allowing some children to engage with work earlier and others later, depending on their specific development, capacities and skills. Whilst an attractive thought, as it would allow an effective tailoring of the law to each child's development and the safeguarding of children's interests, this is in fact an impracticable solution: it would require a vast amount of resources to assess each individual case, and it would have the negative side-effect of opening up the system to abuse. The use of set ages (even if just presumed) to determine milestones in the legal rules applicable to children is a recognised necessity, for example in relation to criminal liability. Children who mature early may pursue their interests and foster their development even before they are able to engage with work, for example by becoming involved with (unpaid, voluntary) sport, cultural and social activities.

Strictly speaking, CRC's substantive standards seem to be respected by the EU's legal framework. Significantly, Article 1(3) YWD is compatible with the all-encompassing wording of Article 32(1) CRC. The fact that, contrary to Article 32(1) CRC, the YWD does not use the words 'hazardous' (in relation to work) and 'spiritual' (in relation to children's development) is arguably of no significance, since Article 1(3) YWD's references to 'safety'/ 'health' and 'moral or social development' achieve the same result (McGlynn 2002: 399). Nonetheless, the CRC is much more demanding and specific in relation to the range of enforcement measures (Article 32(2) CRC). These should include legislative, administrative, social and educational measures, including 'appropriate penalties or other sanctions' and not just 'measures' (Article 14 YWD). In the light of the growing alignment of the EU institutions with the CRC, including the CJEU,[35] the YWD could be amended to reflect the broader scope of the CRC.

4.2 The Council of Europe framework

The CoE has also contributed greatly to the framework that currently exists to address issues concerning working children, namely through its human rights instruments and institutions. The link between the regulation of work by children and human (including social) rights is evident, particularly in cases where some degree of exploitation can be identified. As Van Bueren highlights, the exploitation of children 'usually involves cumulative breaches of several fundamental rights, the most common being unlawful interference with family life and the rights to education, health, and leisure, all of which are equally essential for the healthy development and survival of the child' (Van Bueren 1995: 262). Some forms of exploitation of children, especially sexual exploitation and domestic servitude, may also amount to inhuman or degrading treatment and/or to slavery and forced labour (as seen in *Siliadin v France*[36] and *C. N. v United Kingdom*[37]), thereby constituting violations of Articles 3 and 4 ECHR.

35 Beginning in C-540/03, *European Parliament v Council of the European Union*, Judgment of 27 June 2006, and most recently in C-348/09, *P.I. v Oberbürgermeisterin der Stadt Remscheid*, Judgment of 22 May 2012.

36 Application No. 73316/01, Decision of 26 July 2005.

There are no signs of lack of compatibility between the EU law analysed above and the relevant ECHR provisions and ECtHR case-law. Also, bearing in mind the level of protection offered to working children by EU law, the lack of involvement of the EU with direct enforcement of labour law policies within Member States, the use of the ECHR by the EU, and the use of the principle of the margin of appreciation in the application of the ECHR, it is unlikely that the accession of the EU to the ECHR, as foreseen in Article 6(2) TEU, will be of any relevance to the situation of working children in Europe.

Also, within the context of the CoE, it is worth mentioning the 1996 (Revised) European Social Charter. Although 10 out of the 27 EU Member States are not bound by this Treaty, they are bound by the original 1961 ESC, which contains similar, slightly lower, standards (including in relation to working children). The bodies responsible for the enforcement of the ESC have dealt with matters related to working children, namely age limits, the notion of light work, and enforcement.[38] Yet, the ESC weak supervision mechanism, combined with the predominance of the CoE Committee of Ministers over the European Committee of Social Rights (which has tried to uphold higher socio-economic standards), have prevented the ESC from producing substantial changes in reality (Cullen 2000). The ESC remains, however, a significant international instrument setting minimum labour and social standards, including in the EU context, as evidenced by the reference to the ESC in Article 151 TFEU. Articles 7 and 17 ESC specifically regulate the protection of children. It can be asserted that, partly due to its overall flexible wording and consensual content, EU law, and the YWD in particular, complies with the ESC. EU provisions do not regulate pay, which is one of the elements mentioned in Article 7(5) and (7) ESC: the EU's lack of competence in that regard (Article 153(5) TFEU) would not permit it.

Finally, it is worth mentioning the CoE's instruments on trafficking (2005 Convention on Action against Trafficking in Human Beings) and sexual exploitation (2007 Convention on the Protection of Children against Sexual Exploitation and Sexual Abuse). The fact that not all EU Member States have ratified these instruments and, consequently, are not bound by these instruments, makes the EU instruments all the more important to protect children from economic exploitation.

At any rate, the CoE is responsible for setting minimum standards potentially applicable to a large number of countries (currently 47), as opposed to the EU, which is in a much better position to set higher standards across a more limited geographical area. One can thus legitimately expect the EU to go much further than what is prescribed by the ESC and the ECHR.

---

37 Application No. 4239/08, Decision of 13 November 2012.

38 For relatively recent examples, see European Committee of Social Rights, Conclusions 2011 – Albania – Article 7-1, 12 September 2011 (Doc. No. 2011/def/ALB/), and Conclusions XIX-4 – Greece – Article 7-1, 12 September 2011 (Doc. No. 2011/def/GRC/).

4.3 The EU's human rights framework

The EU's labour policy standards in relation to children also need to be confronted with the EU's own (increasingly strong) human rights agenda. The core of the EU's human rights agenda lies in Article 6 TEU's reference to the legally binding value of the CFR (discussed above in section 2), as well as the national constitutional traditions and ECHR constituting general principles of EU law. Crucially, Article 24 CFR establishes the right of children to protection, care and participation, compatibly with the principles of their best interests and evolving capacities. Article 32 CFR prohibits child labour and requires the protection of young people at work, allowing for derogations on grounds of 'more favourable' outcomes for the children in question (perhaps in an allusion to combined work/training or work-experience schemes: Jacobs 2002:74). The CJEU started referring to Article 24 CFR even before the CFR became binding,[39] but there has been no case dealing with Article 32 CFR yet. Despite the broad terms adopted by these provisions, EU law arguably falls short of the standards established in these provisions, particularly in Article 32 CFR. The second paragraph of Article 32 states that "[y]oung people admitted to work must have working conditions appropriate to their age and be protected against economic exploitation and any work likely to harm their safety, health or physical, mental, moral or social development or to interfere with their education." To the extent that exploitation may occur in the context of areas where EU law may be derogated from (including domestic and family settings, and cultural or similar activities), and in the light of the weak enforcement mechanisms imposed at EU level, several aspects of the YWD may be considered in violation of Article 32 CFR. The main obstacle to this, however, is the fact that the Explanations relating to the CFR indicate that Article 32 is based, among others, on the YWD. With such a circular legal mechanism, any scope for using the CFR to improve the situation of working children could be severely curtailed, making a mockery of the 'fundamental rights check-list' system and impact assessment mechanism devised by the European Commission. Still, the CJEU or other institutions may decide to overlook the Explanations relating to the CFR and take a generous approach to Article 32 CFR, perhaps based on a principle of evolutive interpretation.

Article 21 CFR is also relevant to working children, as it prohibits discrimination on grounds, inter alia, of age. This provision does not add anything to what the Framework Directive already does for working children – or at least there is no judicial evidence of the use of this provision to protect the rights of working children beyond the scope of the Framework Directive.

39 C-540/03, *European Parliament v Council of the European Union*, Judgment of 27 June 2006.

Also, Advocate-General Scharpston, supporting the Commission's submission, has even asserted (expounding a legally doubtful reasoning) that 'there is no need to refer to the Charter where EU law is already explicit on the matter. Nor, a fortiori, can the Charter provide grounds for justification of unequal treatment where such grounds would otherwise be absent.'[40] At any rate, in the case of conflict between Article 21 CFR and the Framework Directive, on the one hand, and the YWD, on the other, the Court would most likely consider the YWD provisions justifiable in the light of being backed by ILO instruments and Member States' international commitments (Cullen 2004: 329).

This analysis would be incomplete without a reference to the 1989 Community Charter, discussed above in section 2. This instrument is still held to be valid and relevant, being mentioned in Article 151 TFEU and the Preamble to the CFR, and courts being able to use it as an interpretative tool. Paragraphs 20-23 refer to the 'protection of children and adolescents'. Whilst the Charter's minimum age of 15 and compulsory school age criteria (Paragraph 20) are respected by the YWD, the need to ensure 'equitable remuneration' (Paragraph 21) is not mentioned anywhere in EU (hard-)law. Also, although working conditions, in particular working time, are regulated by the YWD in terms generally compatible with Paragraph 22, there is no provision in the YWD clearly preventing Member States from circumventing working time rules by using overtime (as established in Paragraph 22). Also, despite emphatic soft-law measures in this regard, an entitlement to vocational training (Paragraph 23) is missing from EU hard-law. If one considers that Paragraphs 20 and 22 are mentioned in the Preamble to the YWD, but Paragraphs 21 (on remuneration) and 23 (on vocational training) are omitted, then it becomes clear which of the Charter's 'moral' obligations the EU institutions intended to fulfil. Equitable remuneration and entitlement to vocational training are, therefore, left to the luck of the OMC. As seen above, the OMC attempts to deal with these matters (at least with training), but as discussed in the next section, such crucial matters should not be wholly delegated to the OMC process.

40 Opinion of Advocate General Sharpston delivered on 20 September 2012, in C-363/11, *Epitropos tou Elegktikou Synedriou sto Ypourgeio Politismou kai Tourismou v Ypourgeio Politismou kai Tourismou – Ypiresia Dimosionomikou Elenchou.*

5. Scope for improvement and policy recommendations

As discussed in section 1, there are compelling reasons in favour of delaying the entrance of children into the labour market and, more generally, of preventing children from carrying out work that may in any way affect their psychological or physical full development. Even economic arguments (secondary when one is considering the best interests of children) point towards this policy: investing in education and training, rather than using a young and unskilled work force, is the best way to secure a society made of individuals capable of contributing towards an innovative and sustainable world (European Commission 2012b). The alternative is the perpetuation of a low-paid and low-skilled work force for the sake of short-term gain (but with long-term negative consequences). Fears relating to children's enhanced exploitation within the 'black economy' have not materialised; in fact, some Member States have even reported a significant increase in the employment rate of older children (e.g., Sweden, in relation to 16- to 17-year-olds). These fears should therefore not be used as arguments in favour of retaining the current, somewhat relaxed legal framework, let alone relaxing it further. The previous section explored several aspects where the current EU law on working children needs to be improved to comply fully with international and EU fundamental standards. The involvement of children with the world of labour falls neatly within the competence (even if shared) of the EU, and the EU is in a privileged position to address any lingering issues. Several areas within the EU's remit require attention; this section will, however, concentrate on the YWD substantive standards, due to their particular relevance to most working children.

Overall, the YWD could become stricter, as supported by some Member States (e.g. Greece: European Commission 2004). Firstly, and most significantly, the general minimum age now set at 15 in the YWD should be raised to 16, if not 17, in order to prevent children from starting work too early and to enhance their qualifications – for the sake either of children's preparation for the labour market or of a more qualified society generally, but always with children's best interests as the overall guiding principle. This would be consistent with the need to align the working minimum age with the age of compulsory full-time schooling (Article 1(1) YWD, Article 2(3) C138). This is also in line with ILO Recommendation No. 146 (Article 7(1)), approved in 1973 (at the same time as C138). Although ideally the EU would follow this Recommendation and lead the way world-wide in this context, it cannot be ignored that this suggestion needs to be fitted together with the education system of the Member States, as children may not be left without a place in the education system and without the right to seek employment. Currently, the majority (15) of EU Member States already set the compulsory school age at 16 (for full-time education), whilst one sets it at 14, seven at 15, one at 17, two at 18, and one allows different ages in different parts of its territory (Eurydice 2014). This means that, before the working minimum age could be raised to 16, those Member States which currently set the compulsory school age at 14 or 15 would need to raise it to 16. Since the EU would not be able to adopt any binding measures in this regard due to its limited competence in this field (Articles 6, 9 and 165-166 TFEU), any harmonisation would have to be achieved through the OMC.

Secondly, there is a strong case in favour of reducing the loopholes in the YWD. To begin with, the YWD should (at least potentially) apply to any work, independently of Member States considering it to be 'employment' or an 'employment relationship'; hence Article 2 should be amended, namely in order to offer some degree of protection to children who are service providers and/or self-employed. Also, as discussed above, currently Article 2(2) allows Member States to exclude from the protective scope of the legislation occasional or short-term work involving domestic service in a private household or non-harmful work for a family undertaking. Considering the evidence of the continued existence of grave abuses in these contexts in EU Member States (Milieu 2009b), and the fact that inspecting these areas is difficult, the EU should strongly consider the non-derogable inclusion of these areas within the scope of the YWD. The risk of going against the opinion of some of its Member States could be tempered with using lighter touch regulation for this type of work, thus at least not allowing it to remain outside the scope of EU law altogether. A similar move is favoured in relation to the ILO instruments by Van Bueren, who finds support in the lack of derogations in the CRC provisions (Van Bueren 1995: 266). It is also important to refer to those children performing artistic, sport or other activities allowed by law, but who fall outside the protection of labour legislation due to the civil law nature of the relationship in question. This problem has occurred in Romania, for example, where 'civil contracts for performance of services' have been used to escape labour legislation (Milieu 2009b) and cannot be addressed by the YWD provisions as they stand today. Without calling into question the possibility of children participating in such activities, as they can be beneficial to their physical and mental development, EU law should (through the YWD or another instrument) ensure that children are protected from economic exploitation and by high levels of health and safety even outside the remit of Member States' labour law frameworks (the approach followed by Hungary: Calvo/Rodríguez 2007: 4). More generally, exceptions related to artistic, sport or advertising activities should be rethought and submitted to more precise requirements at EU level beyond the prior authorisation of the Member State's competent authority (Article 4(1) YWD).

Thirdly, the notion of light work could be clarified, perhaps by excluding the possibility of considering whole sectors of activity as 'light work' as, within most sectors (e.g. agriculture), there may be 'light' and 'non-light' activities. Moreover, even when considering an activity to be 'light work', it should be subject to health and safety regulations, as even when carrying out 'light work' children may run risks. Also, an annexe should be added to the directive with a non-exhaustive list of activities constituting 'light work'.[41] The same could be done with regard to the notion of 'dangerous work', as suggested by a Member State (European Commission 2004: point 5). In relation to both these notions, as well as more generally, the YWD could make less use of open-textured words and concepts, following the lead of the ESC (Cullen 2000: 20).

Fourthly, and ideally, the EU would acquire competence in relation to pay and use it with regard to working children. If the EU were able to harmonise (and enforce) an obligation of equal pay between working children and adults, perhaps the situation would drastically change. Indeed, it is worth looking into the 'unappreciated potential' of the principles of fair remuneration and equal pay for equal work: "if children were paid equally to adults would child labour be so widespread?" (Van Bueren 1995: 271).

Fifthly, the categories of children/adolescents/young persons should be replaced by the single category of 'children' – the distinction between legal and illegal work should be made exclusively on the basis of minimum ages and the characteristics of the work. Besides enhancing consistency with the CRC, the current EU agenda on children's rights and other EU law instruments (such as the sexual exploitation and the trafficking Directives), this amendment would also simplify greatly the transposing domestic provisions and avoid or render less excusable regressions in this regard, as has happened in Romania, for example (Milieu 2009b).

Finally, and despite the obstacles that may be raised on grounds of (lack of) competence, the EU should continue to encourage Member States to take a more holistic and CRC-friendly approach, informed by the indivisibility and interdependence of human rights, and consider the relevance of social, economic and educational measures in the enforcement of the applicable legal framework by labour inspectorate authorities and other actors. Knowing that the EU can legislate on health, safety and working conditions through the ordinary procedure (Article 153(2) TFEU), i.e., by engaging both the Parliament and the Council on a quasi-equal standing (Article 294 TFEU), allied with the fact that either the Parliament or the Council can take the initiative of requesting to the Commission to submit proposals (Articles 225 and 241 TFEU), offers some justifiable hope to the possibility of a more children's rights-centred approach being adopted in the field of labour.

---

41 Something the European Economic and Social Committee already suggested: Opinion on the proposal for a Council Decision on the Protection of Young People at Work (92/C 313/19), 23 September 1992, OJ No C 313/92 P 70, 30 November 1992, point 2.4.2.

6. Conclusion

No doubt, any recommendation to strengthen EU law affecting working children will be met by Eurosceptics with arguments relating to competence-creep, excessive costs, negative impact on the economy and detriment to national sovereignty. But that is a criticism that Eurosceptics would direct against almost any action suggested by the EU, so it does not engage with the actual problem and arguments at hand. And one may of course criticise the current legal framework or an even more restrictive one for being overly protective and, consequently, favouring protection to the detriment of children's participation, autonomy and privacy rights (as discussed in section 1). That may well be an attractive criticism, but it is one that forgets that the 'exercise' of those rights is most commonly to the benefit of others (employers and families) and detriment of children themselves, by entrapping them in a likely life-long cycle of low-skilled and low-pay employment. The larger picture entailed by this is the perpetuation of poor social and working standards, race-to-the-bottom-style competition, and a society unprepared to face the economic, environmental and technological challenges posed to us all in the future. Risks of clandestine work or diminishing opportunities of employment or training do not derive from the YWD or any other EU measures related to children. At any rate, none of these risks should be used credibly as an argument to override the principle of protection: rather than relaxing the rules, they should be enhanced and their enforcement secured. This would also send a strong moral message to non-EU countries and promote inside and outside EU borders higher socio-economic standards on a long-term basis.

Bibliography

Allegra, Cécile (2012) Naples – Une enfance au travail. Le Monde, 28 March 2012, Extracts translated by McGovern, Mark (2012) Child labour re-emerges in Naples, Presseurop, 30 March 2012, http://www.presseurop.eu/en/content/article/1722081-child-labour-re-emerges-naples (2015-02-22).

Andor, László (2013) Youth, Jobs and Europe (SPEECH/13/127), Dublin, 15 February 2013, European Commission.

Bond, Abigail (1995) The Young Persons Directive, in: Industrial Law Journal 24, 4, pp. 377-382.

Bond, Abigail (1996) Working for the Family? Child Employment Legislation and the Public/Private Divide, in: Journal of Social Welfare and Family Law, 18, 3, pp. 291-305.

Boyden, Jo (1997) Childhood and the Policy Makers – A Perspective on the Globalization of Childhood, in: James, Allison/Prout, Alan (eds) Constructing and Reconstructing Childhood – Contemporary Issues in the Sociological Study of Childhood, Cambridge, Falmer Press.

Buck, Trevor et al. (2011) International Child Law, London and New York, Routledge.

Calvo, Javier andRodríguez, Ricardo (2007) Council Directive 94/33/EC of 22 June 1994 on the Protection of Young People at Work – Synthesis Report (Studies on the Implementation of Labour Law Directives in the Enlarged European Union). Brussels, Labour Asociados.

Council of Ministers of the European Union (2010) Council conclusions on child labour (3023rd Foreign Affairs Council meeting), Luxembourg, 14 June 2010.

Cullen, Holly (2000) The Collective Complaints Mechanism of the European Social Charter, in: European Law Review 25 Supp (Human Rights Survey), pp. 18-30.

Cullen, Holly (2004) Children's Rights, in: Peers, Steve and Ward, Angela (eds), The European Union Charter of Fundamental Rights, Oxford, and Portland, Oregon, Hart.

European Commission (1994) This Week in Europe, WE/2/94, 20 January 1994.

European Commission (2001) A New Impetus for European Youth. COM(2001) 681 final, Brussels, 21 November 2001.

European Commission (2004) Report from the Commission to the European Parliament, the Council, the European Economic and Social Committee and the Committee of Regions on the Application of Directive 94/33/EC on the Protection of Young People at Work, COM/2004/0105 final.

European Commission (2008) Communication from the Commission to the Council, the European Parliament, the European Economic and Social Committee and the Committee of the Regions – A special place for children in EU external action, COM(2008) 55 final, 5 February 2008.

European Commission (2010) Youth on the Move – An Initiative to Unleash the Potential of Young People to Achieve Smart, Sustainable and Inclusive Growth in the European Union, Luxembourg, Publications Office of the European Union.

European Commission (2011) Communication from the Commission to the European Parliament, the Council, the European Economic and Social Committee and the Committee of the Regions – An EU Agenda for the Rights of the Child, COM(2011) 60 final, 15 February 2011.

European Commission (2012a) Communication from the Commission to the European Parliament, the Council, the European Economic and Social Committee and the Committee of the Regions – Rethinking Education – Investing in Skills for Better Socio-Economic Outcomes, COM(2012) 669 final, Strasbourg, 20 November 2012.

European Commission (2012b) Proposal for a Council Recommendation on Establishing a Youth Guarantee, COM(2012) 729 final, Brussels, 5 December 2012.

Eurydice (2014) Compulsory Education in Europe 2014/15 – Facts and Figures, http://eacea.ec.europa.eu/education/eurydice/documents/facts_and_figures/compulsory_education_EN.pdf (2015-02-22).

Hanson, Karl and Nieuwenhuys, Olga (eds) (2013) Reconceptualizing Children's Rights in International Development: Living rights, social justice, translations, Cambridge, Cambridge University Press.

Hanson, Karl and Vandaele, Arne (2003) Working Children and International Labour Law – A Critical Analysis, in: International Journal of Children's Rights 11, pp. 73-146.

Hartwig, Matthias (2008) The Elimination of Child Labour and the EU, in: Nesi, Giuseppe, Nogler, Luca and Pertile, Marco (eds), Child Labour in a Globalized World – A Legal Analysis of ILO Action, Aldershot, Ashgate.

ILO – International Labour Organization (2003) Investing in Every Child: An Economic Study of the Costs and Benefits of Eliminating Child Labour, Geneva, International Programme on the Elimination of Child Labour (IPEC)/International Labour Office.

ILO – International Labour Organization (2015) Child labour. http://www.ilo.org/global/topics/child-labour/lang--en/index.htm (2015-02-22).

International Labour Office (2009) Operational Indicators of Trafficking in Human Beings – Results from a Delphi Survey implemented by the ILO and the European Commission, Geneva, International Labour Organization.

ITUC (International Trade Union Confederation) (2011) Internationally Recognised Core Labour Standards in the European Union – Report for the WTO General Council Review (Geneva, 6 and 8 May 2011), http://www.ituc-csi.org/IMG/pdf/Final_draft_ICLS_in_the_European_Union_-_6_and_8_July_2011_2_.pdf (2015-02-22).

Jacobs, Antoine (2002) Prohibition of Child Labour and Protection of Young People at Work (Article 32), in: Bercusson, Brian (ed), European Labour Law and the EU Charter of Fundamental Rights, Brussels, European Trade Union Institute (ETUI).

James, Grace (2013) Forgotten Children: work-family reconciliation in the EU, in: Journal of Social Welfare and Family Law 34, 3, pp. 363-379.

Kenner, Jeffrey (2003) EU Employment Law – From Rome to Amsterdam and Beyond, Oxford and Portland, Oregon, Hart.

Larkins, Cath (2011) Can the EU Live Up to the Expectations of its Child Citizens? in: International Journal of Children's Rights 19, 3, pp. 451-476.

McGlynn, Clare (2002) Rights for Children? The Potential Impact of the European Union Charter of Fundamental Rights, in: European Public Law 8, 3, pp. 387-400.

Milieu – Environmental Law & Policy (2009a) Implementation Report for Bulgaria – Directive 1994/33/EC of 22 June 1994 on the Protection of Young People at Work, Brussels, European Commission.

Milieu – Environmental Law & Policy (2009b) Implementation Report for Romania – Directive 1994/33/EC of 22 June 1994 on the Protection of Young People at Work, Brussels, European Commission.

Nadeau, Barbie Latza (2012) Italy has Europe's Highest Percentage of Children in Poverty, Says UNICEF, The Daily Beast, 4 March 2012, http://www.thedailybeast.com/articles/2012/03/04/italy-has-europe-s-highest-percentage-of-children-in-poverty-says-unicef.html (2015-02-22).

Ochaíta, Esperanza, Espinosa, Angeles M.A. and Calvo, Elena (2000) Child Work and Labour in Spain – A First Approach, in: International Journal of Children's Rights 8, 1, pp. 15-35.

Rodríguez, Ricardo et al. (2007) Study on Child Labour and Protection of Young Workers in the European Union – Final Report, Brussels, European Commission – DG Employment, Social Affairs and Equal Opportunities.

Ruxton, Sandy (2005) What about Us? Children's Rights in the European Union – Next Steps, Brussels, Euronet – The European Children's Network.

Sargeant, Malcolm (2010) Young Workers and Age Discrimination, in: International Journal of Comparative Labour Law and Industrial Relations 26, 4, pp. 467-478.

Simms, Melanie (2011) Helping Young Workers during the Crisis – Contributions by Social Partners and Public Authorities (EF/11/29/EN), Dublin, European Foundation for the Improvement of Living and Working Conditions.

Stalford, Helen (2013) Article 32 – Prohibition of child labour and protection of young people at work, in: Peers, Steve et al. (eds): The EU Charter of Fundamental Rights – A Commentary, Oxford, Hart.

Stalford, Helen and Drywood, Eleanor (2011) Using the CRC to Inform EU Law and Policy-making, in: Invernizzi, Antonella and Williams, Jane (eds) The Human Rights of Children – From Visions to Implementation, Farnham, Ashgate.

UNICEF (2009) Progress for Children – A Report Card on Child Protection, Number 8, September 2009.

Van Bueren, Geraldine (1995) The International Law on the Rights of the Child, The Hague, Boston, London, Martinus Nijhoff.

Children's Rights-Based Approaches to EU Development Cooperation: A SWOT-Analysis

Wouter Vandenhole[1]

1. Introduction

With the adoption of the EU Strategic Framework and Action Plan on Human Rights and Democracy in June 2012 (Council of the European Union 2012), finally the European Union has embraced explicitly a human rights-based approach to development (cooperation) as part of its intention to mainstream human rights throughout EU policies, be they internal or external. The Action Plan attached to the Strategic Framework clarifies in Action no. 10 that the rights-based approach to development cooperation is about "integrating human rights principles into EU operational activities for development ... for the synchronisation of human rights and development cooperation activities" (Council of the European Union 2012), both at the headquarters in Brussels and in the field, i.e. at the EU Delegations in third countries.

Within the general ambition to mainstream all human rights in all areas of external policies, the rights of children have been identified as an EU priority – next to many other priorities. In the Action Plan, Action no. 19 unpacks the envisaged outcome of promotion and protection of children's rights into four specific actions for the 2013-2014 period, which will address violence against children, armed conflict and child labour. Actions envisaged include: a targeted campaign on the rights of the child with a specific focus on violence against children; implementation of the Revised Implementation Strategy of the Guidelines on children and armed conflict; input into the World Conference against Child Labour; and the promotion of the establishment of up-to-date hazardous work lists under the ILO Convention No. 182. The concern with child labour is also visible in Action No. 15, in which the promotion of universal ratification and implementation of the four ILO core labour standards is envisaged, among which features the effective abolition of child labour.[2] A fourth issue that is mentioned, in addition to violence

---

1 UNICEF Chair in Children's Rights, Law and Development Research Group, University of Antwerp. The UNICEF Chair in Children's Rights is a joint venture of the University of Antwerp and UNICEF Belgium. UNICEF respects the academic freedom of the chair holder. Opinions expressed by the chair holder do not commit UNICEF.

2 In the text of the Action Plan, reference is made to "the ban on child labour".

against children, armed conflict and child labour, is that of the prevention of early and forced marriages affecting children (Action No. 20). This issue is not mentioned under the children's rights heading, but under that of women's rights.

This is not the first time that the EU pays attention to human rights in its external policies, and more in particular in its development cooperation. However, much of the earlier work focused on human rights conditionality, rather than on the positive contribution the EU can make to a human rights-based approach to development (Hazelzet et al. 2007: 407-409). The same analysis applies to the sub-set of human rights that specifically applies to children, i.e. children's rights. Here too, the emphasis in the past was strongly on conditionality. In addition, EU external action in the area of children's rights has been argued to have fallen in the pitfalls of instrumentalisation, charity and protection (Vandenhole 2011: 478):

> A picture appears in which *needs* rather than *rights* are in fact referred to; protection tends to be over-emphasised to the detriment of acknowledgment of the agency of children; children's rights are instrumentalised for trade and political purposes; and conditionality prevails.

In this chapter, a SWOT-analysis will be made of the prospective children's rights-based approach (CRBA) to EU development cooperation: what are its (potential) internal strengths and weaknesses, and what external opportunities and threats does this process face? Whereas, inevitably, some attention will be paid to the CRBA's substantive orientation and implementation in practice, a particular focus will be on the dimensions of change, i.e. what does it take for an organization like the European Union to adopt a children's rights-based approach, and when can such an approach lead to change on the ground (section 4)? Such a change perspective will interrogate whether the claim that "adopting a child rights-based approach is the most effective way to bring about positive and lasting change for children, their families and communities" (Save the Children 2007: 1) holds true. Before we engage in the SWOT-analysis, a short introduction to the notion of a children's rights-based approach to development, as a specification of a human rights-based approach (HRBA), will be given (section 2), and an overview of key children's rights EU instruments and actors will be provided (section 3).

2. Children's Rights-Based Approaches to Development

Children's Rights-Based Approaches to development are a set of approaches that take a human rights-based approach to development with regard to children. Children's rights are not about any imaginable claim made by children, but about their fundamental rights[3] in order to realize human dignity and social justice.

There is no single definition of a human rights-based approach; I therefore tend to refer to human rights-based approaches to development in the plural (HRBAs). Notwithstanding the variety, some common characteristics can be identified. First of all, HRBA is both about the processes of development (cooperation) and about the outcome, i.e. what is envisaged, the way development as an outcome is conceptualised. Both processes and outcomes should be human rights driven and oriented. In the words of the Office of the High Commissioner for Human Rights, HRBA is a "conceptual framework for the process of human development that is normatively based on international human rights standards and operationally directed to promoting and protecting human rights" (OHCHR 2006: 16). In other words, the outcome of HRBA is human development defined as increased human rights enjoyment, and the process is guided by international human rights standards, and directed to human rights promotion and protection. Central features of most HRBAs can be summarised in the acronym PANEL, i.e. participation, accountability, non-discrimination, empowerment and linkage to human rights.[4]

The United Nations Development Group (UNDG), which unites the 32 UN bodies that deal with development, has defined the mission of HRBA to be to:

> [f]urther the realization of human rights and ensure that human rights standards and principles guide all development cooperation and programming in all sectors and in all phases of the programming process. It focuses on the development of the capacities of 'duty-bearers' to meet their obligations and/or of 'rights-holders' to claim their rights. (UNDG 2010: 23)

This definition draws on the UN Common Understanding that was reached in May 2003 in Stamford, at the second interagency workshop on implementing a human-rights based approach in the context of UN reform.[5] This Common Understanding is built on three pillars:

---

3 These fundamental rights may be legally articulated in, for example, international treaties, the EU Charter of Fundamental Rights or constitutions, or be legally unarticulated but claimed 'from below' (Liebel 2012).

4 Anther acronym to define HRBA, used by the Food and Agricultural Organization, is PANTHER: it adds transparency and the rule of law, and human dignity substitutes linkage to human rights (see http://www.fao.org/righttofood/about-right-to-food/human-right-principles-panther/en/). The United Nations Development Group (UNDG) has come up with six clusters of human rights principles: universality and inalienability; indivisibility; inter-dependence and inter-relatedness; non-discrimination and equality; participation and inclusion; and accountability and the rule of law (UNDG 2010: 24).

5 Report Second Interagency Workshop on Implementing a Human Rights-based Approach in the Context of UN Reform, Stamford, USA, 5-7 May, 2003, http://www.undg.org/archive_docs/2568-2nd_Workshop_on_Human_Rights__Final_Report_-_Main_report.doc.
The Common Understanding was attached to this report (http://www.undg.org/archive_

1. all programmes and policies of UN development co-operation should further the realisation of human rights, i.e. they should make a positive contribution to human rights;
2. all development cooperation and programming, in all sectors and in all phases, needs to be guided by human rights standards and principles;
3. in particular, development cooperation is about capacity development of duty-bearers and rights-holders.

In addition to good programming practices, a HRBA requires that human rights claims and obligations, their respective holders, and the causes of non-realization of human rights are identified; that the capacity of these rights and duty-holders is assessed and developed; that monitoring and evaluation of processes and outcomes are guided by human rights standards and principles; and that programming is informed by the recommendations of the human rights bodies and mechanisms (UNDG 2010: 24).[6]

To what extent, therefore, does a children's rights-based approach (CRBA) differ from HRBA, except for its focus on children and their rights? Does a CRBA have specific characteristics that a HRBA has not? UNICEF's research centre, for example, claimed to have been "the research engine for UNICEF's shift to a rights-based approach over the last decade, measuring the reality for children against the standards required by the Convention" (Innocenti 2001: 1). It thus seems to focus mainly on the outcomes (i.e. the extent to which the required standards have been achieved) and the linkage with human rights norms. UNICEF itself defines its human rights-based approach to programming as follows:

> A human rights-based approach to programming means for UNICEF that the ultimate aim of all UNICEF-supported activities is the realization of the rights of children and women, as laid down in the CRC [Convention on the Rights of the Child] and the CEDAW [Convention on the Elimination of All Forms of Discrimination Against Women]. Human rights and child rights principles guide the organization's work in all sectors – and at each stage of the process. These principles include: universality, non-discrimination, the best interests of the child, the right to survival and development, the indivisibility and interdependence of human rights, accountability and respect for the voice of the child. UNICEF programmes of cooperation support those who have obligations to respect, protect and fulfil rights, by helping them develop their capacities to do so. And UNICEF helps those with rights to develop their capacity to claim their rights. (http://www.unicef.org/policyanalysis/rights/index.html 10.04.2013)

---

docs/3069-Common_understanding_of_a_rights-based_approach.doc). A first workshop on the same topic had been held in 2001 in Princeton.

6 More elaborate accounts of the meaning of HRBA can be found in literature (Sano 2000; Hamm 2001; Gready and Ensor 2005; Darrow and Tomas 2005; Kirkemann, Hansen and Sano 2006).

UNICEF therefore combines some general human rights principles with some general principles as identified by the Committee on the Rights of the Child (albeit in slightly different wording), i.e. the best interests of the child, the right to survival and development, and the voice of the child. The Committee on the Rights of the Child, in its General Comment No. 5 (CRC Committee 2003: 3-5) has identified four general principles: non-discrimination, best interests of the child, the right to life, survival and development, and the right to express one's views. A similar approach can be found with Save the Children, one of the major children's rights NGOs:

> CRP [Child rights programming] puts children at the centre of your programming. It recognises children as rights-holders and helps you engage them as actors in their own development. It recognises governments as the main duty-bearers in fulfilling children's rights, and promotes accountability to their citizens. It will ensure your plans and activities are based on four fundamental principles relating to children's rights: survival and development; non-discrimination; child participation and the best interests of the child. (Save the Children 2007: 1)

This definition coincides with the general HRBA, but emphasizes in particular the four general principles, as defined by the CRC Committee.

Tobin has looked into the conceptual foundations for a children's rights based approach. Somewhat provocatively, he concludes that the four general principles approach is in fact lacking a solid conceptual underpinning (Tobin 2011: 71). He suggests as specific express principles of a CRBA, in addition to the best interests and the right to life, survival and development, two new ones: the principle of due deference and the principle of evolving capacities. The principle of due deference is the "requirement to respect parents and guardians in the exercise of their responsibilities for the care of the child" (Ibid.: 72). Support for this principle can be found in inter alia Articles 3(2), 5, 14(2), 18 and 27 CRC.[7] The principle of evolving capacities, which can be found in Article 5 CRC, refers to the fact that "[a]t different stages in their lives, children require different degrees of protection, provision, prevention and participation" (van Bueren 2007: 37). Van Bueren considers "evolving capacities" as an interpretative principle underpinning children's rights cases in Europe, and seeks an explanation for its omission as a CRC general principle in its symbiotic relationship with the best interests principle (Ibid.: 37).

In sum, there is a large degree of consensus on the focus and key principles of HRBAs: they focus on process and outcome, and revolve around principles of participation, accountability, non-discrimination, empowerment, and linkage with human rights/human dignity. A CRBA is additionally informed by at least two child-specific principles: the best interests of the child and the right to life, survival and development. Whether the EU has incorporated a CRBA in its external policies will be examined in the next section.

---

7 Article-specific commentaries are Kamchedzera 2012; Freeman 2007; Brems 2006; Eide 2006.

3. EU Children's Rights Instruments and Actors[8]

With the envisaged progressive introduction of a HRBA as of 2013, the EU is a latecomer in adopting a rights-based approach in its development cooperation. With regard to children's rights, however, the 2012 Strategic Framework and Plan of Action consolidates rather than initiates EU attention for children (and to some extent also their rights) in its external action. Over the past decade, the EU has moved in its external policies beyond the initial focus on children and armed conflict to adopt a more comprehensive approach (albeit without adopting a CRBA properly speaking). In what follows, we briefly introduce the initiatives taken by the Council, the Commission and the High Representative for Foreign Affairs and Security Policy.

3.1 Council of the European Union

The Council of the European Union adopted *EU Guidelines on Children and Armed Conflict* in December 2003. The guidelines focus on regular monitoring, reporting and assessments as the basis for identifying situations in which EU action is required, and on EU tools for action in relation to third countries – such as political dialogue, *démarches*, multilateral cooperation, crisis management operations and training. The 2007 update did not substantially revise the guidelines, but added some additional EU action, in particular the imposition of targeted measures when renewing EU agreements with third countries (Council 2007a). The EU Council's Working Group on Human Rights (COHOM) is charged with implementation and follow-up. To that effect, an *EU Implementation Strategy on Guidelines for Children and Armed Conflict* was adopted in 2006, and reviewed in 2010 during the Belgian Presidency (COHOM 2010). A *Checklist for the Integration of the Protection of Children affected by Armed Conflict in ESDP Operations* was equally adopted (PMG 2006), and revised in 2008.[9]

In 2007, a set of *EU Guidelines for the Promotion and Protection of the Rights of the Child* was adopted by the Council. The Guidelines deal only with EU *external* policies. They focus mainly on operational tools for EU action in relations with third countries and on general and specific action to strengthen children's rights. Specific action focuses on priority areas, selected by COHOM in principle every two years. The first priority area was that

8 For a substantive, deeper analysis of these documents, see inter alia Vandenhole 2011.

9 The Politico-Military Group (PMG) is a negotiating body within the framework of the European Security and Defence Policy (ESDP).

of "All Forms of Violence against Children" (Council 2007). It presented a two-track approach to violence against children: it stressed the global character of the issue whilst also supporting country-specific action. In order to support the latter, the development of country implementation strategies was undertaken for ten pilot countries. A review process of the Guidelines was initiated in 2012 but does not seem to have been finalized so far.[10] One of the innovations reflected upon during an expert workshop held in Brussels on 16 February 2012 was the creation of info packages.

In May 2008, the Council adopted conclusions on the promotion and protection of children's rights in external action, in order to provide further guidance on specific commitments in relation to the development and humanitarian dimensions (Council 2008a). The need for mainstreaming of children's rights across EU development cooperation tools was stressed, and paying specific attention to "the rights and needs of the child" in programming was called for (Council 2008a: 5, para. 19). The 2010 Council conclusions situated the elimination of child labour within the overall promotion of children's rights, and called for mainstreaming children's rights in poverty reduction strategies (Council 2010).

In June 2012, the Council adopted the EU Strategic Framework and Action Plan on Human Rights and Democracy.[11] The Strategic Framework and Action Plan seek to step up EU efforts to promote human rights across all aspects of external action, including development policy. In the area of development cooperation, a human rights-based approach is embraced. Children's rights are mentioned as one of the EU priorities on human rights. In the Action Plan, under outcome No. 10, "Working towards a rights based approach in development cooperation", one of the actions envisaged is to "[d]evelop a toolbox for working towards a rights based approach to development cooperation, with the aim of integrating human rights principles into EU operational activities for development, covering arrangements both at HQ and in the field for the synchronisation of human rights and development cooperation activities" (Council 2012).[12] Specifically with regard to children's rights, actions are envisaged for the promotion and protection of children's rights with regard to violence against children, children and armed conflict, and child labour. The actions are mainly in the campaigning and policy field, and not so much in development cooperation.

In conclusion, the EU Council has mainly focused on specific themes rather than on children's rights more holistically, with the exception of the

10 See http://ec.europa.eu/justice/fundamental-rights/files/20140916_state_of_play.pdf (16.09. 2014).

11 A new action plan was adopted on 20 July 2015, see http://data.consilium.europa.eu/doc/document/ST-10897-2015-INIT/en/pdf (2015-08-11).

12 The toolbox was finalized in May 2014, see http://register.consilium.europa.eu/doc/srv?l=EN&f=ST%209489%202014%20INIT (2015-08-11).

2007 Guidelines. Whereas there has been an occasional reference to some children's rights principles, the Council has not elaborated a CRBA, but mainly identified instruments and tools for action.

3.2 European Commission

The European Commission for its part took the initiative to incorporate children's rights into all EU internal and external policies in April 2005. A first communication to that end, *Towards an EU Strategy on the Rights of the Child* was adopted in July 2006 (European Commission 2006a). The Communication identified seven objectives for the EU strategy on the rights of the child, most of which were relevant to external action, and one of which was dedicated exclusively to external action: to capitalise on existing activities while addressing urgent needs; to identify priorities for future EU action; to mainstream children's rights in all external policies; to establish efficient coordination and consultation mechanisms; to enhance capacity and expertise on children's rights; to communicate more effectively on children's rights; and to promote children's rights in external relations, with particular attention to the rights of the girl child; children belonging to minorities, children and armed conflict, and violence against children (European Commission 2006a: 7-10). The accompanying Commission staff working document identified political dialogue, trade, and development and humanitarian assistance as instruments, and the recruitment and use of children in armed conflict, child labour and trafficking as thematic priorities (European Commission 2006b: 3). In February 2008, the Commission adopted a Communication dedicated to external policies, entitled *A Special Place for Children in EU External Action*. It is striking to note that there is no reference to children's *rights* in the title of this document. Two staff working papers were attached, one action plan on children's rights in external action and one on children in situations of emergency and crisis (European Commission 2008). This Communication purported to establish a framework for a comprehensive EU approach to children's rights in third countries, and was adopted in preparation for a long-term action plan on children in external action. External action was confined to development strategies. Emphasis was mainly put on complementarity between policy tools and financial instruments.

The *EU Agenda for the Rights of the Child*, adopted in 2011, is mainly geared towards internal action. It now contains one section on children in the EU's external action, but envisaged for a long time only internal action. The EU Agenda singles out four topics: violence against children, child labour, children in armed conflict, and child sex tourism. The document reiterates the use of political dialogue, bilateral and multilateral cooperation (including development programmes) and humanitarian aid (European Commission 2011). The envisaged action focuses on the implementation of the 2007 *Guidelines on the Protection and the Promotion of the Rights of the Child* (which focus on violence against children), and of the 2010 *Revised Implementation Strategy of the EU Guidelines on Children and Armed Conflict.*

Children's rights have been given rather limited attention in development and humanitarian aid policy documents. In the 2005 *European Consensus on Development*, the first ever joint framework of common principles on development cooperation within the EU, a particular commitment was made to strengthening mechanisms to enable children's rights to be mainstreamed (Council et al. 2005: para. 101). Children's rights will thus be promoted in all countries receiving development assistance, and will be systematically incorporated into the development instruments. Priority policy areas identified in the *Consensus on Development* and in the guidelines for implementing this policy included the worst forms of child labour, child trafficking and children in armed conflicts. A common EU vision on humanitarian aid too was agreed upon in the *European Consensus on Humanitarian Aid*, in December 2007. In this Consensus, it is said that in responding to humanitarian need particular vulnerabilities, including those of children, must be taken into account (Council et al. 2007b: para. 39). Neither children nor children rights feature in the 2011 Agenda for Change (European Commission 2011b). Children's rights are mentioned as part of the assessment of fundamental values (Annex 12) of the Budget Support Guidelines, more in particular in step two of the assessment of fundamental values for Good Governance and Development Contracts. Good Governance and Development Contracts offer budget support to countries that agree to respect fundamental values like human rights.

In sum, the Commission cannot be said to have embraced a CRBA in its external action. Whereas documents dedicated to children's rights do contain some elements of a CRBA, these elements are by and large absent in more general development and humanitarian aid documents.

3.3 The High Representative and the European External Action Service (EEAS)

Following the entry into force of the Lisbon Treaty on 1 December 2009, new players have been created in the area of external action. The High Representative of the European Union for Foreign Affairs and Security Policy (hereafter High Representative or HREUFASP), currently Federica Mogherini, is to ensure the consistency and coordination of the European Union's external action. The European External Action Service for its part has to increase coherency and impact of the EU's external action. An EU Special

Representative for Human Rights, Stavros Lambrinidis, took office in September 2012, with a mandate to enhance the effectiveness and visibility of EU human rights policy.

In a joint communication of the Commission and the High Representative on human rights and democracy in EU external action that focuses on mainstreaming human rights and democracy in external action, action was proposed on delivery mechanisms (bottom-up and country tailored), process (a coherent, joined up approach in all external policies) and internal structures. Children's rights were singled out as one of three cross-cutting themes for a targeted EU campaign. The Communication explicitly mentions a human rights-based approach, but does not elaborate on what a CRBA or HRBA means to the EU (European Commission/HREUFASP 2011).

At Headquarters level, the European External Action Service's (EEAS) Directorate on Human Rights and Democracy has some in-house expertise on children's rights. Within the Directorate-General Development and Cooperation –EuropeAid (DEVCO), children's rights can be found in the Human and Society Development Directorate, where there is a unit dealing with governance, democracy, gender and human rights. At country level, human rights focal points in all EU Delegations are envisaged. Delegations have been asked to draw up human rights country strategies that establish country-specific priorities and objectives. Half of them have been reported to include children's rights.[13] Funding opportunities in the field of children's rights, in particular for civil society, are inter alia the European Instrument for Democracy and Human Rights (EIDHR) and the Investing in People programme.[14]

In conclusion, the EEAS undoubtedly pays attention to children's rights as part of its broader human rights agenda. It does not seem to have a clear and explicit vision on a CRBA that is tailored to the EU's mandate and institutional set-up.

---

13 EU Expert Workshop Review of the *EU Guidelines on Promotion and Protection of the Rights of the Child* and Its Implementation, 16 February 2012, Brussels.

14 In the latter, 8.5% of the budget is allocated for 'Protection and participation of children and youth'. "The programme focuses on the global monitoring and policy advocacy for child protection and the rights of children, strengthening child participation, support for pilot country programmes for reintegrating affected children and, finally, promotion of policies to support productive employment and decent work for youth." (http://ec.europa.eu/europeaid/what/children-youth/index_en.htm (09.04.2013).

4. A SWOT-Analysis

Paying lip service to (mainstreaming) children's rights is one thing, the elaboration and implementation of an EU specific CRBA, another. The development and realisation of a CRBA "is not an easy process to embark on – many organisations are still addressing the challenges it involves. It will take time, resources (both human and financial) and commitment, in both the short and long term. You might need to change the way your organisation works, its culture, structures and management. You might also need to change the way you work with children, communities, partners and donors" (Save the Children 2007: 1). A SWOT analysis may help to better anticipate these challenges. A word of caution is nevertheless warranted. This is by and large an *ex ante* analysis of internal strengths and weaknesses, and external opportunities and threats, undertaken at a time when the process of mainstreaming the embryonic policy and implementing it has hardly begun. Whereas the assessment draws as much as possible on experiences gained both outside and within the EU, it remains inevitably speculative to some degree.

In this SWOT-analysis, attention will be paid to the substantive orientation and implementation in practice of a children's rights-based approach to EU development cooperation. A particular focus will be on the dimensions of change, i.e. what does it take for an organization like the European Union to adopt a children's rights-based approach to its development cooperation, and when can such an approach lead to change on the ground. An important preliminary question on social change has to do with the kind of social change that is envisaged. Aberese Ako et al. have distinguished neo-liberal change from progressive change, i.e. "a critical orientation to existing economic and social inequalities, one which entails advocacy for social transformation in the direction of greater equality and basic human rights for all through government redistributive policies." (Abarese Ako et al 2013). For sure, any CRBA is to be concerned with progressive change.

4.1 Internal Strengths

The EU has several strengths internal to the organization, which may help it to succeed in introducing a children's rights-based approach to its development cooperation. First of all, there is generally speaking a high degree of political goodwill for children's rights among external action actors in the EU. That political and institutional commitment is reflected in a growing set of documents and guidance on children's rights in external action, and in particular in development cooperation. Priorities have been decided, and instruments identified. Moreover, with the incorporation of children's rights in the Treaty on European Union and the EU Charter of Fundamental Rights, there is a solid legal basis and even obligation to mainstream children's rights also in external action.

There is also an institutional framework in place to devise and implement the approach. At headquarters, there is the Development and Cooperation Directorate-General – EuropeAid (DEVCO) on the development cooperation side, and the EEAS on the general external action side. On the ground, there are EU Delegations with human rights focal points and human rights country strategies (see further below). These Delegations seem quite open to the idea of children's rights, as illustrated e.g. by the fact that half of these EU delegations identified children's rights themes as a priority in their country human rights strategies. How that will work out in practice is impossible to say, all the more since the EEAS has not been willing to make the country strategies publicly available.

In sum, political will and a degree of institutional buy-in has resulted in a number of policy documents that have made children's rights visible, and that have identified EU tools and instruments. There is an institutional framework in place at headquarters and on the ground. However, there are also a number of important weaknesses.

4.2 Internal Weaknesses

The EU's internal weaknesses with regard to the introduction of a children's rights based approach to its development cooperation are manifold. Substantively, as already argued in section 3, the EU has not yet managed to spell out how it sees its own CRBA, within its unique institutional set-up. How will it ensure that human and children's rights principles are integrated in development cooperation processes and outcomes? Moreover, it tends to single out issues (armed conflict, violence, child labour), instead of taking a comprehensive approach to children's rights.

In addition to these substantive internal weaknesses, there are five more institutional elements. These institutional elements are relevant for understanding why organisational change occurs or fails, i.e. why the EU may manage to elaborate and internalize a CRBA. Scholarship is divided on what factors determine the success of organisational change: some emphasize structural constraints (i.e. constraints based on durable social structures), others individual agency or actors. Actor-centred criteria include leadership; capacity, accountability and role definition (partnering with third countries or confronting them with violations). To me, both dimensions, structure and agency, are important and often seem to operate in tandem.[15] In what follows, I first discuss three more structural weaknesses within the EU, followed by two weaknesses that are more related to agency.

The divide between internal and external policies, i.e. between policies that concern the EU and its Member States internally and those that concern EU action towards so-called third countries, poses challenges of consistency, but also of expertise and capacity to the children's rights mainstreaming exercise. For example, the EU Agenda on the Rights of the Child was for a long time confined to internal policies, for it was drafted by the Commission Directorate-General Justice (DG JUST). Only after considerable pressure from civil society, academia and some States, a section was dedicated to external action. Secondly, the internal-external policy divide is compounded by an institutional divide between Member States, the European Commission, the EEAS, the European Parliament, and the Council of the European Union. Although some bridges have been built – the Human Rights Working Party (COHOM) e.g., created under the EU Human Rights Council, includes representatives of the Member States and of the European Commission, and has now been affiliated to the EEAS – there remains a significant lack of inter-institutional communication, and arguably outright competition. For example, the co-existence of DEVCO and EEAS may cause problems, as every attempt by the EEAS to introduce a children's rights-based approach in development cooperation may be perceived as an intrusion in DEVCO's prerogatives. Or put differently, it could be argued that DEVCO wishes to keep development cooperation independent from foreign policy concerns, and therefore treats EEAS' children's rights mainstreaming attempts with suspicion. Thirdly, there is no track record in external policies of solid past performance in the area of human rights and children's rights. It has been pointed out repeatedly that strong political commitment, as transpires from the adoption of several sets of Guidelines and Agendas, has not been matched with effective implementation on the ground (European Commission/HREUFASP 2011: 4, 6).[16] That gap between formal commitment and practical action in past performance is a weakness that may continue to undermine any new policy initiatives, such as the introduction of a children's rights-based approach to development cooperation.

In addition to these more structural factors, there are also more agency-related weaknesses. Major shortcomings in training and capacity enhancement of staff have been identified, partially in explanation of the gap between commitment and action (EU Expert Workshop 2012). Secondly, another element that also may at least partially explain weak past performance, is the lack of persuasion and leadership. Tobin, drawing on the work of Goodman

15 For a proposal to rather focus on their interaction, through the concept of structuration, see Scott 2008: 48 and 76-79.

16 Also pointed out at an expert workshop on 15.10.2010 in Brussels.

and Jinks, has pointed out the need for persuasion, i.e. the "internationalisation of the values that promote behaviours that are informed by the principles of a rightsbased approach" (Tobin 2011: 84). He sees a strong tension between the reference to universal human rights law or moral standards, and the "policy maker's decision problem which is more likely to be informed by the discourses of risk management and economic utility" (Ibid. 84). That tension may explain a lack of internationalisation, and therefore persuasion, on the part of EU development cooperation actors so far.

This lack of persuasion analysis ties in with the literature on organisational change with regard to the introduction of rights-based approaches, inter alia in UNICEF. That literature has emphasized the importance of leadership and 'true believers'. Whereas international organisations may be able to integrate new approaches, Oestreich points out that outright resistance tends to come from *within* large organisations (Oestreich 2007: 164). In his analysis, "a desire for self-aggrandizement" (Ibid.: 7), the search for increased effectiveness and other bureaucratic imperatives may have some explanatory power, but a group of 'true believers' (Ibid.: 8) and even more strong leadership are the variables with the highest explanatory power (Ibid: 6-10). Agency is important to understand how to overcome *internal* resistance. Oestreich's overall point is that "[t]he persuasiveness of change agents within organizations is a key variable in explaining [inter-governmental organization] change that is not covered by theories that focus on environmental factors and other exogenous forces" (Ibid.: 157). In sum, more true believers in powerful positions across the EU institutions may be needed to really internalize a CRBA.

4.3 External Opportunities

There are at least two external opportunities. First of all, the strengths in theory and practice of HRBA and CRBA as an approach have been established. Secondly, a number of development actors have meanwhile embraced, with varying levels of success, HRBA and CRBA, so that valuable lessons learned can be drawn upon by newcomers like the EU.

In the literature on the added value of HRBA, a number of strengths have been identified. Some have to do with its intrinsic value (normative, ethical), others more with its instrumental or pragmatic value. The intrinsic value added is basically that HRBA is "the right thing to do, morally or legally" (OHCHR 2006: 16). Expanding on this intrinsic value, it has been argued that HRBAs have at least the potential of re-politicising development by addressing the root causes and by raising power issues, calling the state and other actors to account, mobilising the law for development, and re-centring the state in development (Cornwall and Nuami-Musembi 2004: 1416-1418;

Gready 2008: 737-744). The pragmatic value lies in better and more sustainable development outcomes by focusing on the marginalised; by offering a holistic view, additional monitoring tools and instruments for measuring results; by furthering participation, transparency and accountability; and by offering sustainable results and 'greater returns on investment' (OHCHR 2006: 16-18).

Secondly, the growing acceptance and adoption of the approach across governmental-non-governmental and across national-international divides (UNDG, states, non-governmental organizations) is equally providing opportunities for the adoption and implementation of a children's rights based approach by the EU. It allows the EU to benefit from the legitimacy that the approach already enjoys, and to draw on the lessons learned meanwhile by other organisations (for non-governmental organisations, see Gready and Ensor 2005; for UNICEF, see Oestreich 2007 and UNICEF 2012; for UNDP, see Darrow and Arbour 2009). The lessons learned by other large, intergovernmental organisations may be of particular importance. These include inter alia the importance of leadership and true believers; the need to clarify how to link HRBA with results-based management; the need to have internal incentive and accountability mechanisms that are supportive of HRBA; and the need for on-going and solid training of staff (Vandenhole 2011; UNICEF 2012).

The above mainly relates to organisational change processes. There is also an initial evidence base for HRBA's societal impact, although much more research in this area is needed (Gready and Vandenhole 2013). However, it should also be kept in mind that social change is a complex process, and that no linear cause and effect relationship can be assumed in bringing about change, in particular with regard to human rights (Vandenhole 2013). Moreover, the outcomes pursued under an agenda of progressive change challenge the status quo and deeply entrenched inequality. It is therefore unlikely that a major overhaul of these societal relations happen thanks to the adoption of a CRBA by one external actor such as the EU.

4.4 External Threats

HRBAs are a site of contestation: they are imbued with different meaning by different people and organisations. For some, they potentially allow asking the right questions about development processes and outcomes, while for others they have been a device to steer away from discussions on global inequalities and responsibilities (Cornwall and Nuami-Musembi 2004). Tobin has pointed out seven considerations one must be aware of when advocating a CRBA: the contested nature of human and children's rights; the contested content of these rights; the competing nature of rights claims; the marginal status of RBA; the inevitability of political resistance or irrelevance; the potential for disciplinary resistance; and the need to navigate institutional and organisational culture (Tobin 2011: 76-88). Others have listed (in addition to potential) pitfalls on four axes: 1. conceptual, 2. organisational and strategic challenges, 3. political and 4. ideological (Hickey and Mitlin 2009: 210-225).

The on-going debate on the value added of HRBA may pose a threat to a smooth implementation of a children's rights based approach to development cooperation by the EU. Criticism on HRBA revolves around pragmatic and more principled issues. For some, HRBA is too abstract to be amenable to implementation. The persistent failure to produce good, manageable manuals on CRBA may confirm that there is some truth in this criticism. The degree of organisational change brought about by the introduction of HRBA into UN development analysis and programming within United Nations Country Teams may have remained limited (Vandenhole 2013), so one may wonder whether the introduction of a CRBA in EU development policies will be more influential. And all in all, HRBAs may have had a marginal meaning in practice so far (Tobin 2011: 81), which may not encourage the EU to embrace it as a practical, hands-on approach that is likely to yield direct, measurable results.

A second set of issues bears on the capacity of HRBA to bring about fundamental change. Whereas some criticism questions the problem solving capacity of HRBAs, others have challenged its 'progressive' nature, i.e. whether they take "a critical orientation to existing economic and social inequalities, one which entails advocacy for social transformation in the direction of greater equality and basic human rights for all through government redistributive policies" (Aberese Ako et al. 2013: 47). So, will a CRBA help or even force the EU to focus on structural inequality and social justice in its development cooperation? How to deal with charges of imposing Western values or a Western image of the child, based on age limits that are far away from realities in many Southern countries?

Thirdly, it has proved hard for HRBA to gain interdisciplinary legitimacy (Tobin 2011: 85). Oestreich noticed in the organizations that he examined (World Bank, UNICEF and the World Health Organization), that convincing staff with a technical training to accept a normative framework was a challenging task. It may well be that human rights-based change poses specific challenges to leadership, capacity-building and role definition in that it tends to be considered by development actors as imposed from the outside, and to deviate from good development practice – as HRBAs are value- rather than evidence-based and have their legitimizing anchor in law rather than in ownership or effectiveness.

This relates to the gap between human rights and development more generally speaking, as translated in practice in a promotion-protection dichotomy: human rights actors focus on human rights promotion, development actors on human rights protection. This dichotomy ties in with debates on an adversarial versus partner relationship with governments, and has been a continuing challenge for UNICEF, for example (Oestreich 2007: 30, 33, 42, 53 and 56). The corresponding role definition tends to lock up the human rights and development actors in their traditional roles, quite the opposite of what a CRBA seeks to achieve. Whereas this dichotomy between the normative and operational parts of an organisation has mainly been studied within the UN, at headquarters (Darrow and Arbour 2009: 486) and country level (Vandenhole 2013), it also seems a threat to the European Union's children's rights-based approach to development cooperation. Some indication of this dichotomy within the EU can be found in the call for "continuity between political and policy dialogue on human rights issues and development cooperation" (European Commission/HREUFASP 2011: 11). The dichotomy has also been pointed out at the country level, within the EU Delegations, where the operation department is answerable to the European Commission, and the policy department to the EEAS. This has led to lack of coherence, and by and large even an absence of exchange of information between the policy department and projects within EU Delegations at country level.[17]

5. Conclusions

The explicit adoption by the European Union of a human rights-based approach to development cooperation, and the identification in mid-2012 of children's rights as a priority issue in external policies, including development cooperation policies, may offer a unique window of opportunity for solidly mainstreaming children's rights in EU development cooperation. An immediate challenge that arises is that of putting into practice this ambitious agenda in the complex organisational web that the EU represents. Whereas the EU has, at least on paper, some track record of integrating children's rights in its external action, a rights-based approach to development cooperation is altogether new.

This chapter has sought to point out, ex ante and therefore to some extent speculatively, what the strengths and weaknesses are in the EU's internal and external environment. In particular, we have asked what it takes for an organization like the European Union to adopt a children's rights-based approach to development cooperation, and whether such an approach can lead to

17 EU Expert Workshop Review of the *EU Guidelines on Promotion and Protection of the Rights of the Child and Its Implementation*, 16 February 2012, Brussels.

change on the ground. As to the first question, which relates to organisational change, we suggest that experience with introducing a rights-based approach within large intergovernmental organizations allows for inter-institutional learning. Key points include the importance of leadership and true believers; the need to clarify how to link HRBA with results-based management; the need for monitoring and follow-up; the need to have internal incentive and accountability mechanisms that are supportive of HRBA; and the need for on-going and solid training of staff. With regard to social change, the answers currently available are more in the sphere of potential rather than hard empirical evidence. In the end, it may not be reasonable to expect much more: social change is a complex process, and no linear cause and effect relationship can be assumed in bringing about change, in particular with regard to children's rights.

References

Abarese Ako, Matilda et al. (2013) NGOs, Rights-Based Approaches and the Potential for Progressive Development in Local Contexts: Constraints and Challenges in Northern Ghana, in: Journal of Human Rights Practice 5, 1, pp. 46-74.

Brems, Eva (2006) Article 14 – The Right to Freedom of Thought, Conscience and Religion, in: Alen, André et al. (eds) A Commentary on the United Nations Convention on the Rights of the Child, Leiden/Boston, Martinus Nijhoff.

Cornwall, Andrea and Nyamu-Musembi, Celestine (2004) Putting the 'Rights-Based Approach' to Development into Perspective, in: Third World Quarterly 25, 8, pp. 1415-1437.

COHOM (2006) EU Implementation Strategy on Guidelines for Children and Armed Conflict, 8285/1/06, 25 April 2006, Brussels.

COHOM (2010) Revised Implementation Strategy of the EU Guidelines for Children and Armed Conflict, available at: http://eeas.europa.eu/human_rights/child/ac/docs/eu_implementation_strategy_children_armed_conflict_en.pdf (2013-03-28).

Council of the European Union (2003) EU Guidelines on Children and Armed Conflict, available at: http://eeas.europa.eu/human_rights/child/ac/docs/eu_guidelines_children_armed_conflict_en.pdf (2013-03-28).

Council of the European Union et al. (2005) Joint Statement on European Union Development Policy: 'The European Consensus', available at: http://ec.europa.eu/development/body/development_policy_statement/docs/edp_statement_oj_24_02_2006_en.pdf#zoom=125 (2013-03-28).

Council of the European Union (2006) Checklist for the Integration of the Protection of Children affected by Armed Conflict into ESDP Operations, available at: http://register.consilium.europa.eu/doc/srv?l=EN&f=ST%209767%202006%20INIT (2013-03-28).

Council of the European Union (2007a) EU Guidelines for the Promotion and the Protection of the Rights of the Child, available at: http://www.consilium.europa.eu/uedocs/cmsUpload/16031.07.pdf (2013-03-28).

Council of the European Union et al. (2007b) Joint Statement: the European Consensus on Humanitarian Aid, available at: http://eur-lex.europa.eu/legal-content/EN/TXT/PDF/?uri=CELEX:42008X0130(01)&from=EN (2013-03-28).

Council of the European Union (2008) Conclusions on the promotion and protection of the rights of the child in the European Union's external action – the development and humanitarian dimensions, available at: http://www.eu2008.si/en/News_and_Documents/Council_Conclusions/May/0526_GAERC-pravice_otrok.pdf (2013-03-28).

Council of the European Union (2010) Council conclusions on child labour, available at: http://capacity4dev.ec.europa.eu/sites/default/files/file/03/12/2010_-_1254/Council_conclusions_child_labor.pdf (2013-03-28).

Council of the European Union (2012) EU Strategic Framework and Action Plan on Human Rights and Democracy, available at: http://www.mfa.gov.cy/mfa/mfa2006.nsf/All/EC038A42FCA645D3C2257A6F001E620F/$file/EUStrat.FrameworkandActionPlanHR.Democracy11855.12-%2025.6.12.pdf (2013-03-28).

CRC Committee (2003): General Comment No. 5 – General Measures of Implementation of the Convention on the Rights of the Child (Arts. 4, 42 and 44, para. 6), UN Doc. CRC/GC/2003/5 27 November 2003.

Darrow, Mac and Tomas, Amparo (2005) Power, Capture and Conflict: A Call for Human Rights Accountability in Development Cooperation, in: Human Rights Quarterly 27, 2, pp. 471-538.

Darrow, Mac and Arbour, Louise (2009) The Pillar of Glass: Human Rights in the Development Operations of the United Nations, in: The American Journal of International Law, 103: 446-501.

DEVCO (2012) Guidelines nr 1: Budget Support Guidelines – Programming, Design and Management – A modern approach to Budget support, annex 12 assessment of Fundamental Values, availablet at: http://capacity4dev.ec.europa.eu/sites/default/files/file/30/01/2013_-_1429/budget_support_guidelines-part_2_ver_9_online.pdf (2013-3-28).

Eide, Asbjørn (2006) Article 27 – The Right to an Adequate Standard of Living, in: Alen, André et al. (eds) A Commentary on the United Nations Convention on the Rights of the Child, Leiden, Martinus Nijhoff.

European Commission (2006a) Communication: Towards an EU Strategy on the Rights of the Child, available at: http://eur-lex.europa.eu/legal-content/EN/TXT/PDF/?uri=CELEX:52006DC0367&from=EN (2013-3-28).

European Commission (2006b) Staff working document accompanying the Communication from the Commission Towards an EU Strategy on the Rights of the Child, Preliminary inventory of EU actions affecting children's rights, available at: http://eur-lex.europa.eu/legal-content/EN/TXT/HTML/?uri=CELEX:52006SC0889&from=EN (2013-3-28).

European Commission (2008) Communication: A Special Place for Children in EU External Action, available at: https://ec.europa.eu/anti-trafficking/sites/antitrafficking/files/com_2008_55_children_in_external_actions_en_1.pdf (2013-3-28).

European Commission (2011a): An EU Agenda for the Rights of the Child, available at: http://ec.europa.eu/justice/policies/children/docs/com_2011_60_en.pdf (2013-3-28).

European Commission (2011b) Increasing the impact of EU Development Policy: an Agenda for Change, available at: http://eur-lex.europa.eu/legal-content/EN/TXT/PDF/?uri=CELEX%3A52011DC0637&qid=1412922281378&from=EN (2013-3-28).

European Commission/High Representative of the European Union for Foreign Affairs and Security Policy (2011) Human Rights and Democracy at the Heart of EU External Action – Towards a More Effective Approach, available at: http://eur-lex.europa.eu/LexUriServ/LexUriServ.do?uri=COM:2011:0886:FIN:EN:PDF (2013-3-28).

Freeman, Michael (2007) Article 3 – The Best Interests of the Child, in: Alen, André et al. (eds) A Commentary on the United Nations Convention on the Rights of the Child, Leiden, Martinus, Nijhoff.
Gready, Paul (2008) Rights-Based Approaches to Development: What is the Added-Value?, in: Development in Practice 18, 6, pp. 735-747.
Gready, Paul and Ensor, Jonathan (eds) (2005a) Reinventing Development? Translating Rights-based Approaches From Theory into Practice, London/New York, Zed Books.
Gready, Paul and Ensor, Jonathan (2005b) Introduction, in: Gready, Paul and Ensor, Jonathan (eds) Reinventing Development? Translating Rights-based Approaches From Theory into Practice, London/New York, Zed Books.
Hamm, Brigitte (2001) A Human Rights Approach to Development, in: Human Rights Quarterly 23, 4, pp. 1005-1031.
Hazelzet, Hadewych et al. (2007) Conclusions. New Human Rights Duty-Bearers: A Conversation on Policy Implications, in: Salomon, Margot E. et al. (eds) Casting the Net Wider: Human Rights, Development and New Duty-Bearers, Antwerp, Intersentia.
Invernizzi, Antonella and Williams, Jane (eds) (2011) The Human Rights of Children: From Visions to Implementation, Farnham, Ashgate.
Kamchedzera, Garton (2012) Article 5 – The Child's Right to Appropriate Direction and Guidance, in: Alen, André et al. (eds) A Commentary on the United Nations Convention on the Rights of the Child, Leiden, Martinus Nijhoff.
Kirkemann Hansen and Sano, Hans-Otto (2006) The Implications and Value Added of a Rights-Based Approach, in: Andreassen, Bård A. and Marks, Stephen P. (eds) Development as a Human Right: Legal, Political and Economic Dimensions, Cambridge, Harvard University Press.
Liebel, Manfred (2012) Children's Rights from Below: Cross-Cultural Perspectives, Basingstoke, Palgrave Macmillan.
Oestreich, Joel E. (2007) Power and Principle. Human Rights Programming in International Organizations, Washington, Georgetown University Press.
OHCHR (2006) Frequently Asked Questions on a Human-Rights Based Approach to Development Cooperation, New York/Geneva, available at: http://www.ohchr.org/Documents/Publications/FAQen.pdf (2013-04-11).
PMG (2006) Checklist for the Integration of the Protection of Children affected by Armed Conflict in ESDP Operations, available at: http://register.consilium.europa.eu/doc/srv?l=EN&f=ST%209767%202006%20INIT (2013-3-28).
Sano, Hans-Otto (2000) Development and Human Rights: The Necessary, but Partial Integration of Human Rights and Development, in: Human Rights Quarterly 22, 3, pp. 734-752.
Save the Children (2007) Getting it Right for Children. A practitioner's guide to child rights programming, London, Save the Children UK, available at: http://resourcecentre.savethechildren.se/node/2015 (2013-03-28).
Save the Children (2012) Child Rights Governance Analysis Tool, London, Save the Children, available at: http://resourcecentre.savethechildren.se/node/6152 (2013-03-28)
Scott, William R. (2008) Institutions and Organizations: Ideas and Interests, Los Angeles, Sage.
Tobin, John (2011) Understanding a Human Rights Based Approach to Matters Involving Children: Conceptual Foundations and Strategic Considerations, in: Invernizzi, Antonella and Williams, Jane (eds) The Human Rights of Children: From Visions to Implementation, Farnham, Ashgate.
UNICEF Innocenti Research Centre (2001): Annual Review 2000-2001, available at: http://www.unicef-irc.org/publications/pdf/annreve_2001.pdf (2013-03-28).
UNICEF (2012) Global Evaluation of the Application of a Human Rights Based Approach to UNICEF Programming, New York, United Nations Children's Fund, available at: http://

www.unicef.org/policyanalysis/rights/files/UNICEF_HRBAP_Final_Report_Vol_I_11June_copy-edited_translated.pdf (2013-4-11).

Vandenhole, Wouter (2011) Children's Rights in EU External Action: Beyond Charity and Protection, Beyond Instrumentalisation and Conditionality, in: International Journal of Children's Rights 19, 3, pp. 477-500.

Vandenhole, Wouter (2013) Overcoming the Protection Promotion Dichotomy; Human Rights Based Approaches to Development and Organisational Change within the UN at Country Level, in: Gready, Paul and Vandenhole, Wouter (eds) Human Rights and Development in the new Millennium: Towards a Theory of Change, London, Routledge.

Van Bueren, Geraldine (2007) Child Rights in Europe: Convergence and divergence in judicial protection, Strasbourg, Council of Europe Publishing.

Conclusion: How Can the EU Be a Better Children's Rights Actor?

Helen Stalford and Ingi Iusmen

This collection of essays comes at a pivotal point in the evolution of children's rights at EU level: the first comprehensive children's rights strategy, the EU Agenda for the Rights of the Child, has come to an end after a fruitful and far-reaching three years of activity; as we await (with some trepidation) news of the Commission's plans to build on this with a further strategy, the main EU institutions continue to make bold statements attesting to their commitment to endorsing children's rights in a much more overarching manner. There is now an abundance of legal and policy provision targeting children; significant resources have been invested in research, capacity building and data collection on a range of child-related issues; and the EU's relationship with other international polities, particularly when it comes to children's rights activities, is stronger than ever.

In summary, the EU has taken a more central role in the development of children's rights, to an extent that would never have been envisaged 10 years ago. The reach of EU activity has progressed far beyond issues that intersect with internal market or cross-border activities such as free movement, immigration, consumer rights or cross-border family law. It has seeped into issues that would have hitherto been closely guarded by domestic competence, including criminal justice, support for victims, protection against sexual exploitation and de-institutionalisation. The EU has continued to be a strong presence in external activities too, investing important financial and political capital in the global fight against child poverty and social exclusion, exploitative labour, trafficking, forced migration and child soldiering.

This collection has aimed to provide some informed, critical reflections on the EU's achievements in such areas so far and to offer some audacious suggestions as to how EU action in the field of children's rights might be consolidated, developed and sustained into the future. Far from representing the EU as a backwater of children's rights provision, offering modest, tangential contributions to niche aspects of law and policy affecting children, we are lauding and applauding the EU's potential to inspire the international campaign to promote children's rights. The EU has unparalleled legal, political and financial resources at its disposal, and it has already taken important symbolic and rhetorical steps, in a relatively short period of time, on pervasive children's rights issues. But symbolic and rhetorical gestures are one thing; what is less apparent is whether any of these activities are being actively and constructively transmuted where and when it really matters to produce tangible and positive changes to children's lived experiences on the ground.

Beyond decorative provision towards embedding children's rights within the fabric of the EU

Almost all of the chapters in this collection draw attention to the noble intentions of many EU children's rights measures, particularly those enacted in the wake of the EU Agenda for the Rights of the Child, which are now increasingly calibrated to reflect international children's rights norms. The EU child protection initiatives described in the chapter by Lind-Haldorsson and O'Donnell, and the proposed criminal justice initiatives touched upon by Rap in her chapter are a case in point. But there are also a range of EU measures that still fail to fully (or even partially) accommodate the rights of children. Many still do so in a way that is tokenistic and naïve insofar as they pay lip service to notions such as best interests or the right to be heard, but do little to address or even acknowledge some of the more insidious violations of children's rights. The contribution by Savirimuthu, for instance, reveals how the EU's preoccupation with protecting children in the online environment on the one hand, and empowering them to become responsible, digital citizens on the other, fails to address the short and long term effects on children of routine data-profiling undertaken by commercial operators. This, in itself, serves to manipulate children's choices, impede upon the development of their sense of identity and dangerously pervert children's sense of autonomy, all in the name of commercial gain. In the same vein, Drywood's contribution highlights how the EU's regulation of free movement responds first and foremost to the economic demands of commercial operators (in this case the immensely profitable and powerful football industry), whilst glossing over the reality and potential for those provisions to facilitate the exploitative recruitment and, in some cases, reckless dismissal of child players.

All of the chapters highlight, to some degree, that the true test of the EU's effectiveness in advancing children's rights lies not just in the formal fidelity to children's rights principles within the letter of the law, but in their conscientious implementation at the national level, and in the willingness of the EU institutions to hold national authorities to account where implementation is lacking (see particularly the chapters by Ferreira and Lind-Haldorsson and O'Donnell). The contribution by Stalford reveals just how impervious supposedly accessible EU justice mechanisms are to children's rights-related claims at all stages of the legal and policy process, suggesting that even the most child-sensitive approach at EU level will only succeed if it is met by the requisite political will and sensitivity at the national level. Lamont's chapter has also drawn attention to the importance of effective cross-national co-operation between judges and front-line advisors tasked with administering and interpreting EU children's rights measures, with a view to achieving consistency and transparency in their application across different jurisdictions.

The collection has also featured a range of broader perspectives of how the institutional, legal, procedural and cultural landscape of the EU might be adapted to respond more persuasively to the call to embrace children's rights more fully, so that it progresses beyond decorative provision within isolated legal instruments towards a more integral part of the EU legal and policy fabric. A more comprehensive children's rights mainstreaming strategy is posited as an essential starting point in this regard. Schuurman's 'seven steps' model has provided concrete suggestions as to what a child mainstreaming strategy might look like, informed by the views and experiences of EU institutional representatives, existing academic critiques of specific case studies, and good practice models at the national level. Stalford's contribution has drawn attention to the institutional, procedural and ideological blockages that need to be removed at EU level to support such a development. Lamont, Vandenhole, Savirimuthu and Ferreira provide fresh, critical insights into how elements of child mainstreaming might be applied in the discrete areas of cross-border family law, external development co-operation, regulation of the online industry and employment.

What (more) needs to be done to consolidate the EU's role(s) as a child rights actor?

What all contributions to this volume indicate is that over the last decade there has been an emergent EU *presence* in addressing international child rights issues. The EU institutions have adopted legal and policy instruments intended to address violations of child rights either in a direct, targeted fashion, or by integrating more sporadic measures or declarations into policy issues more tangential to children. However, what transpires from the chapters of this book is that there is no unified, well-defined and comprehensive EU role as a *persuasive* child rights actor on the international scene. Indeed, it is not at all apparent that the EU characterises itself as such. On the contrary, the evidence provided in this book suggests that EU's 'actorness' in children's rights varies according to policy sector, division of EU competence and EU internal-external policy spheres, to an extent that the EU is more realistically portrayed as presenting mottled 'responses' to specific children's rights issues. Without doubt certain branches of the EU (such as DG Justice of the Commission) have wholeheartedly embraced the very philosophy of children's rights and sought to firmly embed its principles and methodologies in all new research, legal and policy developments, but this is far from representative of the EU's approach as a whole. Perhaps this is the best we can expect from a polity whose defining *raison d'être* is economic and political growth as opposed to human rights protection, but one cannot help but interpret it as a wasted opportunity.

The raw materials are certainly in place to allow for the EU's actorness in child rights to take shape and acquire the *cohesion, authority, autonomy* and *recognition* (Jupille and Caporaso1998) it has so far lacked. First, the nature and scope of EU intervention in child rights issues is a function of its ever more explicit *legal competence*, as enshrined in the Treaties. The empirical evidence presented in this book clearly demonstrates that the EU has readily adopted measures bearing on children's issues in those legal and policy sectors where it is mandated by the Treaties to do so. It has done so creatively and opportunistically, generating opportunities for intervention on children's rights issues out of seemingly tenuous legal bases (see, for instance, the issue of de-institutionalisation explored in Chapter 6 by Iusmen). Second, the value and legitimacy of the EU in advancing child rights is also determined by how successfully it can incorporate the child rights instruments of other international polities into its own measures. The efforts made to ground EU measures relating to civil and criminal justice in the Council of Europe's Guidelines on Child Friendly Justice provide one concrete example of the value of such cross-pollination (see further the chapters by Rap and Stalford in this collection).

Third, the effectiveness of the EU as a children's rights actor depends not merely on its willingness to adopt specific children's rights issues within a given campaign, but to nurture and sustain them through thoughtful, integrated research, capacity-building, policy and legal initiatives. The EU's significant investment in this regard in the context of child protection highlights just how expeditious its intervention can be in developing more robust child protection laws and procedures across the Member States, to an extent that would simply not have been achievable through Member States acting alone (see the chapter by Lind-Haldorsson and O'Donnell).

The fourth and perhaps more challenging step that the EU has to take if it is to become a compelling children's rights actor relates not simply to how it regards its own role in protecting children's rights, but in how it regards children's rights more fundamentally. Michael Freeman refers to human rights more generally as much more than simply a framework of laws pertaining to different areas of protection; it is essentially a 'way of thinking' (Freeman 2011). This is particularly relevant to our discussion of children's rights. Even the most explicit, binding measures relating to children's rights, to be truly effective in stimulating positive change in children's lives, have to be driven by what Vandenhole in his chapter refers to as 'true believers' in the value of children's rights, both at EU level and at the national level. This is often referred to in human rights discourse as 'norm socialisation' or 'internalisation' (Risse, Ropp and Sikkink 1999; Goodman and Jinks 2004). According to Goodman and Jinks (2004) the socialisation of legal human rights norms is described as a process of '*acculturation*' which entails a 'general process by which actors adopt the beliefs and behavioural patterns of the surrounding culture' (2004: 621), in this case children's rights culture. In the same vein, Risse, Ropp and Sikkink (1999) highlight the importance of 'institutionalisation' and 'habitualisation' as conducive to norm internalisation. This implies a process of not merely acting in a way that is compliant with specified norms, but, more fundamentally, demands that international actors believe in the validity of the norms that shape their behaviour.

Applying these socialisation frameworks to the EU and children's rights implies that the EU institutions would have to appropriate not only the key provisions and principles underpinning the CRC (such as the best interests of the child, child participation etc.), but also the very philosophy underpinning these provisions – that children are equal citizens, deserving at least equal if not special protection to mitigate the effects of their routine disenfranchisement in virtually all spheres of civil, political, economic, social and cultural life. Conceding to a moral and ideological compulsion to uphold children's rights no matter what is how grand, rhetorical declarations of what 'ought' to be done to give effect to children's rights blossom into tangible, sustained change for the better and into an earnest commitment to holding to account those who fail in such commitments.

But achieving this paradigm shift is by no means a quick process, and it is certainly more easily realised in some areas of children's rights than others. It is much easier, for instance, to convince those in authority of the need to embrace children's rights in the context of the highly vulnerable: no one could reasonably argue with the need for a multi-levelled, multi-agency response to the most extreme violations of children's physical, mental, intellectual and social integrity, such as child trafficking, pornography, acute poverty, lack of education, forced labour or abuse. Even the most hardened, detached EU decision-makers would feel compelled to develop supra-national measures in support of national child protection initiatives in this regard. Indeed, Iusmen's account of the EU's response to de-institutionalisation and Lind-Haldorsson and O'Donnell's presentation of the EU's child protection provisions highlight just how effective the EU can be in responding to the plight of our most vulnerable communities of children. It is rather more challenging to disentangle and uphold children's individual rights in the context of immigration and family reunification, for example, in the face of acute political, economic or public security concerns. And it is more challenging again to respond to children's rights concerns which are veiled in presumptions of privilege and opportunity, as the contributions by Drywood and Savirimuthu illustrate.

Learning from children

The paradigm shift required to further legitimise the EU's role as a children's rights actor also lies in convincing those who wield the budgetary, legal and policy-making authority that they might not know how best to tackle such issues instinctively; that the experiences of children and young people themselves need to inform such responses; that alongside top-down implementation of protective measures, children and young people themselves need to be empowered to directly claim and enforce their rights. There is no particular shame in admitting that the EU is woefully ineffective in engaging children directly in shaping and claiming their rights. Even the most established representatives of our children's rights 'industry', whether they be academics, practitioners or civil society representatives, no matter how well intentioned, commonly fail to reflect a genuinely children's rights-based approach to at least some of their campaign, advocacy and support activities. Sometimes it is because of a lack of resources, time pressures or basic lack of training. Other times, it is due to a widespread and toxic complacency that talking the talk of children's rights is good enough, notwithstanding the fact that what we do might have little bearing on children's experiences either in the short or longer term, and notwithstanding the fact that we might never even speak to children in the course of our day-to-day professional activities, purportedly on their behalf.

And yet we have a wealth of knowledge – generated by a proliferate body of empirical research – at our disposal, attesting to the value of involving children and young people more directly in the development of law and policy-making and in the design of services that affect them (Marshall et al. 2015; Daly 2014; Lundy and McEvoy 2012; Cockburn 2010; Tisdall 2008; Cairns 2006; Crimmens and West 2005; Hill et al. 2004). This body of work tells us time and time again that the insights we gain not just from talking directly to children, but from actively listening to them – providing them with direct channels of redress when things go wrong, offering them a platform to tell things as they are from their own perspectives – yields inimitable insights that can stimulate more suitable and effective changes in provision, and enhance children's sense of engagement and confidence in the democratic process.

Of course, children will rarely be equipped to initiate or respond to an invitation to engage in a dialogue with decision-makers – least of all those at the EU level – without the support of adult mediators. This is where civil society can play a crucial role.

Top down and bottom up – the crucial mediating role of civil society[1]

Implementation of the CRC is strongest where there is a powerful and active civil society within the country. This is equally true of the development of children's rights at EU level.

Civil society has thus been at the forefront of the child rights agenda at EU level, and indeed globally, challenging the common understanding of children as objects deserving protection and education, to one of children as subjects and agents of change. Civil society also plays a critical role in holding States to account in implementation of their obligations under the CRC, with the UN Committee reporting process placing considerable importance on the alternative reports and evidence gathered through NGOs and from children themselves.

Nonetheless the extent of children's self-determination and representation remains extremely limited and continues to be mediated by adults. For young people, women, adults with disabilities and many other groups who are oppressed or subordinated, the political slogan "*nothing about us without us*" is broadly embraced within the decision- and policy-making communities. Indeed, self-organisation and self-representation is recognized as critical for the emancipation and realization of human rights. For children, however, the extent of their direct involvement in advocacy continues to be hampered by (mis)perceptions of children's immaturity, irrationality and incompetence, and there are persuasive arguments to suggest that the CRC, in and of itself, has only served to reinforce traditional power imbalances between adults and children (Cordero Arce 2012: 366).

Perhaps because of the absence of effective children's self-representation, civil society in the children's sector has evolved differently from that representing other social groups. Most countries, for example, will have some level of organized civil society involving people with disabilities, older persons or ethnic or religious minority groups as self-advocates. Sometimes a tension exists between civil society organisations that see themselves as di-

1 We are grateful to Jana Hainsworth, Secretary General of Eurochild, for contributing her thoughts to this section.

rectly representing the 'rights-holders' and those representing service providers. These boundaries are gradually blurring, as service providers increasingly adopt a rights-based approach, shed their traditional, paternalistic approach to support and care, and emphasise the empowerment of, and giving a voice to, service users. In the children's sector, similar tensions existed historically between those driving the child rights agenda, and those perceived as primarily concerned with child welfare. Again, these lines are blurring as more and more service providers integrate a *child*-rights approach into their daily work, recognizing children as competent partners and giving them a voice in decisions affecting them. Indeed, service providers active in child welfare and protection are often spear-heading children's self-representation and self-advocacy work[2], as well as developing innovative ways of involving children and young people directly in the design, implementation and evaluation of services.

Three distinct but overlapping issues come to mind when considering the opportunities and, indeed, threats for civil society in seeking to influence EU efforts to protect and promote children's rights: children's rights advocacy; the role of European civil society networks; and the extent of participatory democracy within the European Union. Advocacy can be defined as the act of engaging with and influencing key policies and decision-makers to achieve social transformation and reform. Whilst most non-governmental organisations working with disadvantaged and at risk children, young people and families are primarily concerned with providing care, support and other services, there is growing recognition of the need to complement service delivery with effective advocacy. However, the existence and characteristics of such agencies representing the interests of children and child rights organisations varies considerably across Europe. The oldest, in Finland (Central Union for Child Welfare), was established in 1937 and involves almost 100 NGOs as well as over 30 municipalities. By contrast, several European countries only have an informal coalition of NGOs that come together during the 5-yearly reporting to the CRC with little or no capacity to represent the participating organisations during the intervening period.

This huge disparity (in terms of organisation and resourcing), in turn, makes it particularly difficult to achieve fluid, representative communication between the EU and some domestic regions concerning, on the one hand, the specific children's rights issues that require redress at the European level and, on the other, the opportunities and investment that the EU makes available for the advancement of children's rights. This has been partially overcome by the emergence of strong transnational advocacy networks representing civil society. Keck and Sikkink define transnational advocacy networks as those

2 This is likely to be strengthened now that the 3rd Optional Protocol of the CRC has come into force, allowing for individual complaints from children to be heard by the CRC Committee.

involving 'actors working internationally on an issue who are bound together by shared values, a common discourse, and dense exchanges of information' (Keck and Sikkink 1999: 89). Such networks can pool resources, rally support across countries for issues of common concern, and pursue more coordinated campaigns more forcefully than would otherwise be the case.

One particularly prominent and successful advocacy network representing the rights and well-being of children and young people in an EU context is Eurochild, a relatively young network established in 2004. It has evolved and grown steadily since then, now counting 118 full member organisations and over 30 individual associate members, covering 32 European countries. The network's membership is very diverse and includes national and international NGOs, public and statutory bodies, academic and research organisations and umbrella networks. Its principal role is advocacy, reflected in Goal One of its current strategic plan: 'putting the rights and well-being of children and young people at the heart of policy making at EU, national and sub-national levels'. As an activist transnational NGO, the network acts simultaneously within domestic and EU politics. It is clear that children's lives are most directly influenced by policies and investment of governments at national, or increasingly, at sub-national levels.

However, the real added-value of being part of a transnational network comes from when outside pressure can be applied in support of changes advocated by local civil society. This is referred to as a *boomerang* pattern of influence (Keck and Sikkink 1999: 93). With support from its member organisations, Eurochild (in partnership with other civil society and international organisations) has successfully advocated for greater and more meaningful visibility for children's rights in EU policy, legislation and funding. Three important developments are worth a mention: explicit reference to the promotion of children's rights as an objective of the European Union in the Lisbon Treaty (Article 3(3) TEU); the adoption of the 2011 Communication 'An EU Agenda on the Rights of the Child' (COM/2011/0060 final); and the adoption in February 2013 of the Commission Recommendation 'Investing in Children: Breaking the cycle of disadvantage' as part of the broader Social Investment Package (OJ L 59, 2.3.2013, p. 5-16). And yet, important as they are, in and of themselves, these policy developments will not make a difference to children's lives unless they are used to leverage political progress and investment at national and sub-national levels. This is where Eurochild's work – and that of other similar European advocacy networks – becomes so critical. But international networking is expensive. Eurochild, as is the case with several other civil society networks, receives core funding from the European Commission. In the past, this was through the programme for employment and social solidarity (PROGRESS) and, from January 2014, under the EU programme for Employment and Social Innovation (EaSI). EaSI's primary objective is 'to support Member States efforts in the design and implementation of employment and social reforms at European, national as well as regional and local levels by means of policy coordination, the identification, analysis and sharing of best practices'. A total budget of €500m (over 7 years) is allocated to the part of the programme focused on analysis, mutual learning, grants, social innovation and social policy experimentation. Networks are supported by up to €1m per year.

Such core funding, whilst vital to support a network's activities, should not compromise its independence and autonomy. Democratic governance structures and a strong focus on core values are the primary motivators for membership participation and internal network coherence. The EaSI programme objectives are complementary to Eurochild's members' expectations of sharing information, gaining visibility and widening their sphere of influence, and increasing the political space and attention given to children's rights. So far the demands placed on Eurochild by the European Commission have not compromised the network's self-determination and members' ownership. However the relationship is not unproblematic and if the institutional climate becomes less favourable to children's rights, the network's ability to openly challenge and criticize could be limited due to funding cuts. Indeed, this is where the network's engagement with independent, critical academic scholarship becomes all the more crucial (a point to which we return below).

This leads us into the related discussion as to the place of civil dialogue and participatory democracy in the overall institutional architecture of the European Union. Article 11 TEU expands the European democratic model from purely a representative democracy to a participatory democracy. As stated in the Civil Society Contact Group study on 'Civil Dialogue: Making it Work Better':

> …participatory democracy has the following accepted features: …It extends the concept of citizenship beyond the conventional political sphere; it is based on the principle of policy-makers' permanent accountability between elections; it acknowledges citizens' right to participate in public life through alternative channels, to tackle the shortcomings of representative democracy; it covers some practices of direct democracy, but also emphasizes the role of civil society organisations as important mediators in debates.'(Fazi and Smith 2008: 15)

But can we honestly say that children are part of this vision? Yes, civil society organisations might have developed well-oiled channels of communication with children and young people and be adept at translating these into policy recommendations, but are the channels of communication open at the EU level to enable these recommendations to be communicated? Take, for instance, the 'citizens' initiative', one of the mechanisms specifically highlighted by Article 11 TEU as a tool for achieving participatory democracy. The chapter by Stalford points out just how ineffective this has been as a mechanism for advancing children's rights. The sheer resources (knowledge, administrative assistance, international networks) required to even launch a plausible initiative are simply beyond the reach of most children's rights organisations, such that most instead prefer to invest in alternative forms of lobbying and awareness-raising.

The importance of independent scholarship

It is important not to underestimate the contribution that academic debate makes to the development of children's rights. It is academic scholarship that has stimulated important paradigm shifts in the way that policy-makers, practitioners and civil society address children's rights. The vast literature around children's agency and participation has at least contributed to, if not triggered, a wholesale shift away from exclusively paternalistic, welfare-based assessments of children's interests, and encouraged more direct communication with children as to how their views and experiences might shape decision-making. To accompany this, academics have been at the forefront of developing new, innovative methods to engage directly and meaningfully with children and young people, not just in localised contexts, but on a more ambitious cross-national comparative scale too. This has become increasingly important in responding to the international reach of EU law and policy – finding ways of comparing and contrasting, in qualitative terms, the impact of particular measures on children in a range of different jurisdictional, political, social and socio-economic contexts.

But there are also political reasons why academic engagement in the development of law and policies affecting children is important at all regulatory levels. As stated above, academics are ideally placed to provide objective, critical reflections on the scope and limitations of European intervention. Indeed, it is this very endeavour which defines academic scholarship. The fact that academics are generally funded by and, to a degree, sequestered in the higher educational sector ensures that they can pursue their concerns more freely than their NGO counterparts, without risking biting off the hand that feeds them. They tend to have more resources at their disposal to engage in sustained scrutiny, and are at liberty to test and apply a range of different techniques to promote their campaign, whether that is desk-based erudition or qualitative empirical work involving children and young people.

Of course, some of these strengths are also posited as some of academia's most challenging weaknesses. Academic research can only go so far in advancing children's rights: arguments might look compelling on paper, whilst suffering from distinct deficiency in reality-checking; scholarship on children's rights is all too often advanced within a political vacuum, in blissful (and wilful) ignorance of the profound and perhaps even insurmountable practical implications of implementing some of the recommendations for change that they might advance so passionately.

It is precisely these shortcomings – of a purely academic approach on the one hand, or a campaign driven only by NGO representatives on the other – that supports calls for more sophisticated and meaningful interdisciplinary collaboration. The European Commission should be applauded for investing significant resources in this process. Funding schemes such as DAPHNE, the Fundamental Rights and Citizenship Programme, Safer Internet and more recently Horizon 2020, continue to support a vast range of projects, from large-scale, longitudinal cross-national evaluations, capacity-building initiatives amongst practitioners, to essential educational and rehabilitative work co-ordinated by front-line services at the grass-roots level. The programmes are increasingly proscriptive about the nature of the collaborations they will fund, and about the ultimate goals they wish to achieve and these correspond more explicitly now with the EU's wider legal and policy plans. So, the outputs which the EU hopes to achieve as far as children are concerned (for example, achieving more child friendly justice; achieving better co-ordination between domestic child protection regimes) are becoming increasingly clearly defined. What is less clearly defined, however, is the extent to which these envisaged outputs remain relevant and responsive to children and young people's lived experiences, needs and views.

A final word on achieving legitimacy

Involvement of civil society actors and advocates in policy processes, and the development of civil dialogue and participatory structures, are crucial factors for enhancing the EU's 'input' legitimacy with respect to children's rights issues. This needs to be accompanied by better 'output'-oriented legitimacy, which would reinforce and ascertain the *impact* of EU intervention on the provision and experience of child rights measures on the ground. The input-output sources of legitimisation have been applied particularly with respect to EU processes (Scharpf 1999) and their legitimacy credentials. According to Scharpf, both input legitimacy (qua citizen participation in EU elections and processes, civil society consultation), and output legitimacy (qua effective policy delivery and performance) are important for the EU. This resonates particularly strongly with the different aspects of children's rights mainstreaming explored in a number of the contributions in this collection (Stalford, Schuurman, Lamont, Savirimuthu and Vandenhole). Some have defined this more generally as 'throughput' legitimacy (Schmidt 2013), rather than the input-output legitimacy distinction. By highlighting the quality of governance processes, 'throughput' legitimacy captures what occurs inside the 'black box' of EU governance, and therefore it focuses on the efficacy, accountability, transparency, inclusiveness and openness of EU governance as well as interest consultation and intermediation (Schmidt 2013: 4-5). By being more open to processes of engagement and consultation with civil society actors, and therefore facilitating interest intermediation (Kohler-Koch 2007; Smismans 2003), the Commission in particular can gain public approval for its policies or legitimise its actions in policy sectors which are generally perceived to be within the purview of national authorities.

This is particularly important in those policy sectors where the EU has a more fragile, perhaps even ambiguous legal mandate, such as children's rights. What is needed is not simply the development of new EU legal or policy measures, or bolder statements of intent by the institutions, but rather more accessible and efficient deployment of existing mechanisms. Each of the chapters in this collection provide a critical and, we hope, constructive evaluation of key, often overlooked legal, policy and procedural tweaks that could be made to achieve a more solid foundation for the layers of new children's rights initiatives that will undoubtedly emerge in the course of the next EU children's rights strategy. We have high hopes that the EU can lead the way in progressing beyond robotic, idiomatic references to children's rights in its instruments and public speeches, and harness its enormous legal, political and economic potential to effect meaningful change in children's lives across the world.

References

Cairns, L. (2006) Participation with purpose – the right to be heard, in: Tisdall, K, Davis, J, Hill, M and Prout, A (eds) Children, Young People and Social Inclusion: Participation for What?, Bristol, Policy Press.

Cockburn, T. (2010) Children and Deliberative Democracy, in Percy-Smith and Thomas (eds) A Handbook of Children and Young People's Participation: perspectives from theory and practice, Abingdon, Routledge.

Crimmens, D. and West, A. (2004) Having Their Say: Young people and participation – European experiences, Lyme Regis, Russell House Press.

Cordero Arce, M. (2012) Towards an Emancipatory Discourse of Children's Rights, in: The International Journal of Children's Rights 20, 3, pp. 365-421.

Daly, A. (2014) UN CRC Article 12 – Putting Child Friendly Justice into Practice, paper to the European Progress in Achieving Child Friendly Justice Seminar, Brussels, February 2014.

Fazi, E. and Smith, J. (2006) Civil Dialogue: Making It Work Better, commissioned by the Civil Society Contact Group. Available at: http://act4europe.horus.be/module/FileLib/Civil%20dia logue,%20making%20it%20w ork%20better.pdf.

Freeman, M. (2011) Human Rights: An Interdisciplinary Approach (2nd Edition), Cambridge, Polity Press.
Goodman R and Jinks D (2004) How to Influence States: Socialization and International Human Rights Law, in: Duke Law Journal 54, 3, pp. 621-703.
Hill, M., Davis, J., Prout, A. and Tisdall, K. (2004) Moving the Participation Agenda Forward, in: Children and Society 18, pp. 77-96.
Jupille, J. and Caporaso, J.A. (1998) States, Agency and Rules: The European Union in Global Environmental Politics, in: Rhodes, C. (ed.) The European Union in the World Community, Boulder, CO, Lynne Rienner,
Keck, M. and Sikkink, K. (1999) Transnational advocacy networks in international and regional politics, in: International Social Science Journal 51, 159, pp. 89-101.
Kohler-Koch, B. (2007) The organization of interests and democracy in the European Union, in: Kohler-Koch, B. and Rittberger, |B. (eds) Debating the Democratic Legitimacy of the European Union, Lanham, MD, Rowman& Littlefield.
Lundy, L. and McEvoy, L. (2012) Children's Rights and Research Processes: Assisting children to (in)formed views, in: Childhood 19, 1, pp. 1-16.
Marshall, C., Byrne, B. and Lundy, L. (2015) Face to Face: children and young people's right to participate in public decision-making, in: International Perspectives and Empirical Findings on Child Participation: From Social Exclusion to Child-Inclusive Policies, Oxford, Oxford University Press.
Risse, T., Ropp, S. C. and Sikkink, K. (eds) (1999) The Power of Human Rights: International norms and Domestic Change, Cambridge, Cambridge University Press.
Scharpf, F.W. (1999) Governing in Europe: Effective and Democratic?, Oxford, Oxford University Press.
Schmidt, V. A. (2013) Democracy and Legitimacy in the European Union Revisited: Input, output and 'throughput', in: Political Studies 61, 1, pp. 2-22.
Smismans, S. (2003) European Civil Society: shaped by discourses and institutional interests, in: European Law Journal 9, 4, pp. 482-504.
Smismans, S. (2004) Law, Legitimacy and European Governance: Functional Participation in Social Regulation, Oxford, Oxford University Press.
Tisdall, K. (2008) Is the honeymoon over? Children and young people's participation in public decision-making, in: International Journal of Children's Rights 16, 3, pp. 419-29.

About the Authors

Eleanor Drywood is a Senior Lecturer at the School of Law and Social Justice, University of Liverpool. Her research focuses on applying a children's rights perspective to asylum and immigration law (particularly its regulation at EU level) and sports law. Eleanor has published in leading international journals on EU law and children's rights and acted as an expert on research for the EU Fundamental Rights Agency.

Nuno Ferreira is a Senior Lecturer in Law at the University of Liverpool (UK). He is a member of the Portuguese Bar, worked as a legal consultant at the Legal Affairs and Litigation Department of the Portuguese Securities Market Commission (CMVM), and was a research fellow at the Centre of European Law and Politics at the University of Bremen (ZERP) (Germany). Nuno's main interests lie in the fields of human rights, discrimination law, children's rights, refugee law and European law. He has published on various aspects of children's rights, including the books *Fundamental Rights and Private Law in Europe: The Case of Tort Law and Children* (2011, Routledge) and *The Human Face of the European Union: Are EU Law and Policy Humane Enough?* (edited with Kostakopoulou, 2016, Cambridge University Press).

Ingi Iusmen is a Lecturer in Governance and Policy at the University of Southampton. Her research tackles key questions about the European policy process, especially as it relates to child care issues and the provision of children's rights at EU and national levels. She has published in leading journals such as the *Journal of Common Market Studies*, *International Journal of Law, Policy and the Family,* the *Journal of European Public Policy*, and the *British Journal of Politics and International Relations*. Her latest book, *Children's Rights, Eastern Enlargement and the EU Human Rights Regime* (2014), is published by Manchester University Press.

Ruth Lamont is a Senior Lecturer in Family and Child Law at the University of Manchester (UK), having previously held lectureships at the University of Liverpool and the University of Sheffield. Her research focuses on the effect of legal regulation on international families, particularly in the European Union. Her previous work has focused on the impact of the Brussels II Revised Regulation on gender equality, and the protection of fundamental rights in cross-border family proceedings and following international child abduction. She is currently researching the processes and institutions that support and coordinate proceedings in relation to children subject to care proceedings with an international dimension.

Olivia Lind-Haldorsson is an independent EU advisor and co-founder of the Brussels-based NGO Child Circle, having previously worked for Save the Children EU Office in Brussels. Child Circle promotes European action which strengthens national systems to protect children from violence, abuse, neglect and exploitation. Olivia also works as an independent expert in the field of EU Justice, Home Affairs and External Affairs (www.odonnell-lind.eu). Her previous work has, among other things, focussed on the EU Guidelines on Children and Armed Conflict, the EU Guidelines on Children's rights, the Directive on combatting child sexual abuse, child sexual exploitation and child pornography, and the EU Directive on rights, support and protection of victims of crime.

Rebecca O'Donnell is a lawyer and co-founder of Child Circle, the recently established Brussels based NGO focussing on child protection in EU law and policy (www.childcircle.eu). The work of Child Circle focuses on contributing expertise to regional consultations, connecting practitioners and advocates on EU policy and collaborating on practical projects. She also works as an independent expert with a wide range of stakeholders on strategic advocacy initiatives and regional projects in the field of EU Justice and Home Affairs policies (www.odonnell-lind.eu). From 2007 to 2013, she worked with Save the Children EU Office, where her work focused on EU asylum and migration law and policy. Prior to that, she was a European partner in an international law firm dealing with EU antitrust and regulatory affairs.

Stephanie Rap is an assistant professor at the Child Law Department at Leiden University. She holds master's degrees in Pedagogical sciences and Criminology from Utrecht University. In 2013 she defended her Ph.D. dissertation in juvenile criminal law, titled *The Participation of Juvenile Defendants in the Youth Court*, at Utrecht University. Stephanie has published and presented extensively on juvenile justice, children's rights and child participation. Recently she co-authored *The Effective Youth Court* (with Prof. Ido Weijers, 2014, Eleven International Publishing).

Joseph Savirimuthu is a Senior Lecturer in Law at the University of Liverpool (UK). He has participated in invited panels on technology and privacy in the US and Brussels. Joseph's principal research and teaching interests lie in the social and regulatory challenges posed by new and emerging technologies, with particular focus on privacy, data protection and information security. He is currently engaged in collaborative research with Computer Scientists and Electrical and Electronic Engineers at the University of Liverpool. Joseph's research publications include: *Online Child Safety: Law, Technology and Governance* (2012, Palgrave), 'Singularity', in Holbrook, Britt, and Mitcham (eds): *Ethics, Science, Technology, and Engineering: A Global Re-*

source (2015, 2nd edition, Macmillan Reference USA), 'Singularity and the Art of War: The Geneva Convention on Trial', in Galliot and Lotz (eds.): *Super Soldiers: The Ethical, Legal and Social Implications* (forthcoming, 2015, Ashgate) and *Volume III: Security and Privacy in The Library of Essays on Law and Privacy* (2015, Ashgate).

Mieke Schuurman has been an independent expert in the field of children's rights and EU law since 2009. She has carried out assignments for various international organisations and NGOs, including the Council of Europe, the European Commission, Eurochild, UNICEF, Child Helpline International, Save the Children, the European Foundation for Street Children and the European Economic and Social Committee. She has provided advice, carried out research and given training on children's rights and has a particular expertise in children's participation. She is chair of the Eurochild Group of National Children's Rights Coalitions. Formerly, she was Secretary-General of the European Children's Network (EURONET).

Helen Stalford is Professor of Law at the University of Liverpool and is founding director of the European Children's Rights Unit. She has published extensively on the status and scope of children's rights under EU law including two books: *A Community for Children?: Children, Citizenship and Migration in the European Union* (with Louise Ackers, 2004, Ashgate), and *Children and the European Union: Rights Welfare and Accountability* (2012, Hart). She has worked closely with the Council of Europe, the EU Fundamental Rights Agency and UNICEF to develop children's rights-based approaches to monitoring Member States' compliance with their international children's rights obligations, and to enhancing children's understanding of their legal rights.

Wouter Vandenhole holds the UNICEF Chair in Children's Rights at the University of Antwerp.His research focuses, in particular, on the economic, social and cultural rights of children, and on the relationship between human rights law and development. He is the author of many publications, including: *The Routledge International Handbook of Children's Rights Studies* (with Desmet, Reynaert and Lembrechts (eds.), 2015); 'The Convention of the Rights of the Child in Belgian Case Law' in *Litigating the Rights of the Child: the UN Convention on the rights of the child in domestic and international jurisprudence* (Liefaard and Doek 2014); *National Human Rights Institutions and Economic, Social and Cultural Rights* (with Brems and De Beco, 2013, Intersentia). *Why care? Children's rights and child poverty* (with Vranken and de Boyser, 2010, Intersentia).

Index

Find our journals on

www.budrich-journals.com

- **Single article download**
- **Print + Online**
- **Subscription**
- **Free Content: ToCs, editorials, book reviews, open access content**

Barbara Budrich Publishers
Stauffenbergstr. 7
51379 Leverkusen-Opladen

ph +49 (0)2171.344.594
fx +49 (0)2171.344.693
info@budrich-journals.com